DYNASTY DIVIDED

A volume in the NIU Series in

Slavic, East European, and Eurasian Studies

Edited by Christine D. Worobec

For a list of books in the series, visit our website at cornellpress.cornell.edu.

DYNASTY DIVIDED

A FAMILY HISTORY OF RUSSIAN AND UKRAINIAN NATIONALISM

FABIAN BAUMANN

NORTHERN ILLINOIS UNIVERSITY PRESS

an imprint of

CORNELL UNIVERSITY PRESS

Ithaca and London

Thanks to generous funding from the Swiss National
Science Foundation, the ebook editions of this book
are available as open access volumes through the
Cornell Open initiative.

First published 2023 by Cornell University Press

Library of Congress Cataloging-in-Publication Data

Names: Baumann, Fabian, 1990- author.
Title: Dynasty divided : a family history of Russian and
    Ukrainian nationalism / Fabian Baumann.
Description: Ithaca : Northern Illinois University Press,
    an imprint of Cornell University Press, 2023. | Series:
    NIU series in Slavic, East European, and Eurasian
    studies | Includes bibliographical references and index.
Identifiers: LCCN 2022049845 (print) | LCCN
    2022049846 (ebook) | ISBN 9781501770920
    (hardcover) | ISBN 9781501770937 (paperback) |
    ISBN 9781501770944 (epub) | ISBN
    9781501770951 (pdf)
Subjects: LCSH: Shul'hyn family—Political activity—
    Ukraine. | Shul'hyn family—Political activity—Russia. |
    Nationalism—Ukraine—History—19th century. |
    Nationalism—Russia—History—19th century. |
    Nationalism—Ukraine—History—20th century. |
    Nationalism—Russia—History—20th century.
Classification: LCC DK508.554 .B38 2023 (print) |
    LCC DK508.554 (ebook) | DDC 947.08—dc23/
    eng/20221108
LC record available at https://lccn.loc.gov/2022049845
LC ebook record available at https://lccn.loc.
    gov/2022049846

For my parents

CONTENTS

Acknowledgments   *ix*

Note on Names, Toponyms, and Dates   *xiii*

Introduction   1

1. At the Crossroads: The Search for
   the Little Russian Soul, 1830s–1876   16

2. Niche Nationalism: Kiev's
   Ukrainophiles, 1876–1914   48

3. Patriarchs and Patriots: The Rise of
   Russian Nationalism, 1876–1914   98

4. Triumph and Tragedy: Nationalists
   in War and Revolution, 1914–1920   150

5. Living off the Past: Nationalists
   Write Their Lives in Interwar
   Europe   205

   Conclusion   230

Notes   *237*

Bibliography   *291*

Index   *319*

Acknowledgments

Like all authors, I have incurred many debts in the years leading up to the publication of a longtime project. This book began more than seven years ago at the University of Basel, where Benjamin Schenk was an exemplary adviser: always open to new ideas, always willing to read drafts at short notice, always ready to help me place my research within the historiography. As my co-adviser, Alexei Miller contributed his encyclopedic knowledge of nineteenth-century imperial politics and repeatedly pushed me to sharpen my arguments. Faith Hillis generously hosted two very productive stays at the University of Chicago, in 2018 and 2021–2022, and offered extremely helpful feedback on several drafts of my manuscript. Andreas Kappeler was the first to encourage me to pursue biographical research on nationalism and has been extraordinarily supportive ever since. My work would have been impossible without the support of the Swiss National Science Foundation, which funded my research with a four-year Doc.CH grant as well as a two-year Postdoc.Mobility grant, and also financed the Open Access publication of this book. The Basel Graduate School of History and its coordinators, Roberto Sala and Laura Ritter, provided a welcome institutional frame and office space for my research.

In Basel, I was lucky to work alongside a brilliant and supportive group of graduate students and postdocs, profiting from countless conversations over beer and Turkish meals at Pinar restaurant. Many thanks to Boris Belge (whom I kept asking for detailed feedback down to the level of single sentences), Carla Cordin, Lenka Fehrenbach, Nadine Freiermuth Samardžić, Jörn Happel, Anne Hasselmann, Charlotte Henze, Bianca Hoenig, Alexis Hofmeister, Martin Jeske, Henning Lautenschläger, Sandrine Mayoraz, Sophia Polek, Rhea Rieben, and Alexandra Wedl, as well as Romed Aschwanden, Andreas Gehringer, Sarah Hagmann, and all the members of the Friday writing group.

Colleagues in several countries supported my work with advice on archives and sources, feedback, and constructive criticism. I am grateful to Olena Betlii, Serhiy Bilenky, Anton Chemakin, Heather Coleman, Franziska Davies, Trevor Erlacher, Felix Frey, Iaroslav Hrytsak, Georgiy Kasianov, Michael Khodarkovsky, Anton Kotenko, Fabian Lüscher, Iryna Makedon, Olha Martynyuk, Mariya Melentyeva, Olena Palko, Aleksandr Reznik, Stephan Rindlisbacher, Martin Rohde, Ostap and Viktoriia Sereda, Joshua Teplitsky, Oleksii Tolochko, Gregory Valdespino, Ben van Zee, Alexa von Winning, and Ricarda Vulpius, as well as the participants of workshops in Basel, Munich, Tübingen, Chicago, Regensburg, Halle, Oldenburg, and Kiel.

Three descendants of the Shul'gin/Shul'hyn family kindly provided me with information about their ancestors and photographs from their private collections: Olena Leontovych in Kyiv, Bohdan Pazuniak in Philadelphia, and Olga Matich in Berkeley. Dozens of librarians, archivists, and administrative staff in Ukraine, Russia, Switzerland, Germany, Austria, Slovenia, France, and the United States fulfilled my many requests, found dusty volumes on half-forgotten shelves, and filled out the paperwork that I needed for my research. Among the most resourceful of them were Oleksandra Buz'ko and Nataliia Mykhailova at the Archive of the Archaeological Section of the Academy of Sciences in Kyiv, Dar'ia Moskovskaia at the Gor'kii Institute for World Literature in Moscow, Anne-Marie Dowhaniuk at the Shevchenko Society in Sarcelles, and Agnes Weidkuhn at the Department of History in Basel.

At Cornell University Press I was lucky to have Amy Farranto as my editor. She took an interest in my manuscript from the beginning, expertly steered it through the publication process, and patiently answered my endless questions along the way. Christine Worobec, the series editor, provided very valuable critical comments that helped me to shorten and revise my manuscript. I had two highly knowledgeable and helpful peer reviewers, subsequently revealed to be Theodore Weeks and John-Paul Himka, whose comments guided me as I polished my text before the final submission. Acquisitions assistant Ellen Labbate and assistant managing editor Karen Laun very efficiently took care of all technical issues, Glenn Novak meticulously copyedited my text, and in Leipzig, Silke Dutzmann produced beautiful maps to illustrate the text.

Finally, I want to thank my friends who listened to all my complaints, housed me during archival stays away from home, and, above all, regularly reminded me that there is more to life than nineteenth-century history: David Werner, David Giger, Firmin Kamber, Niggi Furler, Valentin Rohr and Jeannine and Malin Brosi, Matthias Braun, Alba and Numa Stamm, Romano Schneider, Samuel Eglin, Jason and Elias Giger, Lorenz Lauer, Benjamin von Wyl, Florian Gschwend, Anna Rauch, Rafaela Schmid, Michael Hochreutener, Emanuel Ingold, Patrick Illien, William McComish, Tatiana Kulikova and Aleksandr Platonov, Aleksandra Lakovnikova, Mariia Mikhnovets, Alex L. Moran, Patrik Schmidt, Gunnar Take, Birgit Salzburger, Frank Fischer, Joseph Wälzholz, and many others.

I dedicate this book to my parents, Werner Baumann and Elisabeth Ackermann, who not only offered consistent moral support through the years but also read and commented on several early drafts of the text. I also want to thank my grandfather Gilbert Ackermann, my sister Hanna Baumann, my aunt Kathrin Baumann, Matthias Ebner and Kaija Knauer, the late Annie Spuhler, and my cousin Luis Ackermann, whose IT expertise repeatedly came in handy. And finally, I am extremely grateful to Zeynep Tezer, whom I would probably never have met if it were not for this project. Thank you for everything.

With the generous permission of the original publishers, this book incorporates material that has appeared in my articles "Dragged into the Whirlwind: The Shul′gin Family, Kievlianin, and Kiev's Russian Nationalist Movement in 1917," in *Personal Trajectories in Russia's Great War and Revolution, 1914–22: Biographical Itineraries, Individual Experiences, Autobiographical Reflection*, ed. Korine Amacher et al. (Bloomington, IN: Slavica, 2021), 73–92, and "Nationality as Choice of Path: Iakov Shul′gin, Dmitrii Pikhno, and the Russian-Ukrainian Crossroads," *Kritika: Explorations in Russian and Eurasian History* 23, no. 4 (2022), 743–71.

Note on Names, Toponyms, and Dates

I have rendered Cyrillic spellings of Russian and Ukrainian in a simplified version of the Library of Congress system. The question whether to transliterate the names of historical figures from Russian or Ukrainian is complex and often politically charged. The Ukrainophile milieu of the nineteenth century was a bilingual society whose members used both Russian and Ukrainian, depending on context. In order to emphasize that not all Ukrainophiles were primarily Ukrainophones, I reserve Ukrainian names for those individuals whom I know to have spoken Ukrainian well or to have used it regularly in writing. This is why I write Iakov Shul'gin rather than Iakiv Shul'hyn, but spell his wife's name Liubov Shul'hyna. For their eldest son, I use Oleksander instead of Oleksandr; while this spelling is considered odd in contemporary Ukraine, it was preferred by many interwar émigrés, including Oleksander Shul'hyn himself. Where deemed useful, I give both the Ukrainian and Russian version of a name at first mention. In no case is the choice of one or another name form to be read as a definite statement on a person's "national identity."

The same goes for place names. I render them in the language of the state that ruled them before 1914 so as to reflect the period's power relations. Therefore, I write Kiev rather than Kyiv and Lemberg rather than L'viv, Lwów, or L'vov. Exception is made where a commonly used English toponym is available (Moscow, Saint Petersburg, Warsaw), or when speaking about contemporary Ukraine. Dates before 1918 are given in the Julian calendar, which lagged twelve days behind the Gregorian calendar in the nineteenth century and thirteen days behind in the twentieth century. Soviet Russia switched to the Gregorian calendar in early 1918, but the old calendar remained in use among some anti-Soviet forces in Ukraine. Therefore, both dates are provided for 1918 and 1919, only the Gregorian dates thereafter. Unless declared otherwise, all translations into English are my own.

Estate of the Ustymovych Family

Estate of the Pikhno-Shul'gin Family

State border

Regional border

Cartography: S. Dutzmann
Leipzig, 2022
© F. Baumann

0   100   200 km

MAP 1. Ukraine around 1900. Cartography by Silke Dutzmann.

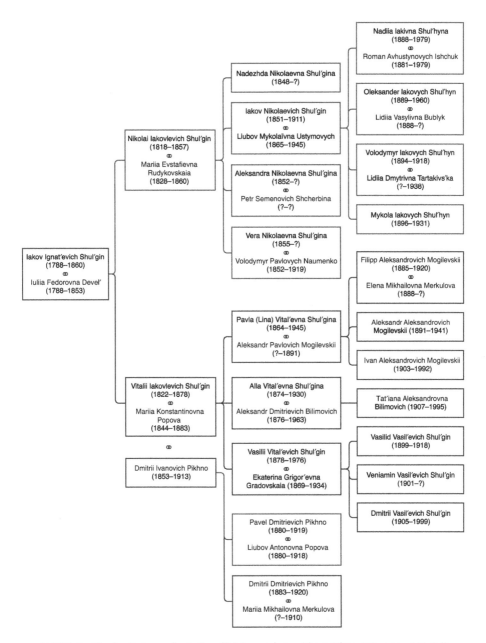

FIGURE 1. The family tree reflects the official genealogy without taking into account Dmitrii Pikhno's illegitimate fatherhood. Pikhno was the biological father of Vasilii Shul'gin (with Mariia Popova) and of Filipp, Aleksandr, and Ivan Mogilevskii (with Lina Shul'gina). All women are listed under their maiden names.

DYNASTY DIVIDED

Introduction

> The Ukrainian question is *an internal quarrel among the Southerners*, some of whom wish to remain Russian, as they have been since time immemorial . . . , while others wish to relinquish the nationality of their forefathers, spitting their father and mother in the eyes. This formulation of the problem becomes absolutely clear in the case of a public quarrel between two Shul'gins, not just men of the same name but *of the same blood, the same family, the same city*.
>
> —Vasilii Shul'gin, 1929

> The family's two branches split up completely. Such cases are not rare in intellectual or aristocratic families among nations awakening to independence.
>
> —Oleksander Shul'hyn, 1935

"Great and terrible" was the year 1918 according to Kiev's most famous novelist, Mikhail Bulgakov.[1] It was particularly terrible for those families who lost a child in the fierce struggle for control of the city. One of the young men who perished in the battles for Kiev was twenty-three-year-old Volodymyr Shul'hyn, a gifted and idealistic student at the university's department of natural sciences. In late January 1918, Shul'hyn joined a hastily formed student detachment to defend the capital of the Ukrainian People's Republic. Shul'hyn's company was sent across the Dnieper river to face the invading Bolshevik regiments. The two forces met near the village of Kruty in Chernigov province, 150 kilometers northeast of Kiev. Vastly outnumbered, the students stood no chance. Dozens were killed, among them Volodymyr Shul'hyn. Back in Kiev, their funeral turned into a patriotic commemoration. Mykhailo Hrushevs'kyi, the leader of the People's Republic, made a speech about the glory of dying for one's fatherland.[2]

Eleven months later, in December 1918, Kiev was again threatened by an attacking army. Now held by the conservative Ukrainian Hetman government, the city nervously awaited the forces of the nationalist leader Symon Petliura, who intended to reestablish the Ukrainian People's Republic. Unable to command a regular army, the Hetman had to rely on retired Russian officers and adolescents such as Vasilid Shul'gin, a nineteen-year-old gymnasium graduate and aspiring poet who volunteered to defend his native city. He and his peers were positioned in the suburb of Petropavlovskaia Borshchagovka when the republican troops arrived. Badly prepared and abandoned by their superiors, the twenty-five young men were all killed. A few days later, Vasilid's mother could only recover her son's dead body.[3]

Although they pronounced it in different ways, Volodymyr and Vasilid shared a last name—and a family history. Both were scions of the Shul'gin/Shul'hyn family, a prominent Kievan dynasty of journalists, scholars, and politicians. Volodymyr was the younger brother of Oleksander Shul'hyn, a Ukrainian nationalist who had just become the first foreign minister of independent Ukraine. Vasilid, their second cousin, was the eldest son of Vasilii Shul'gin, the city's most prominent Russian nationalist politician.[4] Accordingly, Volodymyr thought of himself as a Ukrainian, and Vasilid saw himself as Russian. One of them was killed in battle for the Ukrainian People's Republic, the other died fighting against it. As the former Russian Empire descended into civil war, members of one and the same family parted ways and fought for different imagined communities.

At the time of this writing in May 2022, war is again ravaging Ukraine. On 24 February, Russia's president Vladimir Putin ordered an unprovoked attack on the neighboring state. Since then, tens of thousands of Ukrainian soldiers and civilians have lost their lives. Millions more civilians have fled west within the country and to Central Europe. Yet while Russia's war propagandists claim to liberate Ukraine from a fascist government, they also insist that the victims belong to the same nation as the invaders. Half a year before the invasion, Vladimir Putin himself stated his belief that Russians and Ukrainians are "one people," their countries part of "essentially the same historical and spiritual space," and their ongoing conflict "the result of deliberate efforts by those forces that have always sought to undermine our unity."[5]

Today, Ukraine's elites and the general population are united in their rejection of these claims and of the Russian aggression, irrespective of the language they speak and of the political beliefs they hold. There is a broad consensus in favor of Ukrainian nationhood and independent statehood. However, this outcome was not foreordained. As the case of Volodymyr Shul'hyn and Vasilid Shul'gin reminds us, there was a time when Ukraine's inhabitants diverged in their choice of national affiliation. This was not the result of geopolitics, as Putin would have it, but of heated debates among the local intelligentsia. Over decades, they argued over Ukrainian culture and traditions, over the nature of Ukraine's relationship with Russia and the appropriate degree of autonomy that it should be given within—or outside—the imperial state. In the process, the country's elites became increasingly divided into self-defined Ukrainians and self-defined Russians. Why did people with a similar social and cultural background come to understand themselves as members of two different nations? What role did individuals play in the emergence of nationalist conflicts? And how did the national divide between Russians and Ukrainians become relevant in Kiev's educated society—so relevant that people were ready to die for their vision of the national community?

The family history of the Shul'gins/Shul'hyns offers rich material to answer these questions. Its members engaged in the debates on their region's national belonging over three generations. When the last common ancestors of the family's two branches moved to Kiev in the 1830s, it was not yet a problem to reconcile regional patriotism with loyalty to Russian culture and the empire. However, when conflicts between Ukrainian patriots and Russian imperial loyalists broke out in the mid-nineteenth century, the historian Vitalii Shul'gin took a clear stand for the Russian side. In 1864, he established the newspaper *Kievlianin* as a beacon of Russian loyalism in the region. Vitalii's nephew Iakov Shul'gin (Iakiv Shul'hyn) chose a completely different path. Rejecting his uncle's pro-imperial politics, he followed the lead of his radical university teachers and reinvented himself as a Ukrainian socialist.

This conversion split the family tree into two branches. After four years of Siberian exile, Iakov moved his activism to the domestic sphere. He and his wife Liubov raised their four children to be Ukrainian-speaking patriots and opponents of the tsarist regime. Meanwhile, the young economist Dmitrii Pikhno went the opposite way. Originally from the Ukrainian-speaking countryside, he married Vitalii Shul'gin's widow, took over the family newspaper, and continued the path of imperial loyalism and Russian nationalism. In the early twentieth century, the torch was passed to Iakov's and Dmitrii's children. During the revolutionary period and the ensuing civil war, they fought on different sides to implement their visions of a national society. After the victory of the Bolsheviks, all surviving Shul'gins and Shul'hyns fled to Western

Europe, where they helped constitute the Russian and Ukrainian émigré milieus.

Using the story of the Shul'gin/Shul'hyn family as a narrative frame, this book advances three main arguments. First, it argues that nationalism among nineteenth-century intellectuals was a deliberate choice of path, not a process whereby they "discovered" and politicized their preexisting ethnicity. These men and women first decided to support a political project and only then began their self-fashioning as unambiguous members of their respective imagined communities. Their choices were conditioned by their political worldviews, by social milieus, family ties, or generational dynamics. Nationalists consciously appropriated the image of a stable and unified "national identity" and cultivated those aspects of their personal lives and biographies that suited this narrative. In other words, "national consciousness" preceded national being. Only in the following generation did such choices of path lead to path dependencies. Having grown up in nationalist households, the children of activists often came to understand themselves as members of the same nation that their parents had chosen.

Therefore, the book stresses the importance of private homes and family life as sites of nationalist socialization. In late imperial Russia, families retained their importance as basic economic units and as social networks ready to be instrumentalized for political purposes. Even with mass politics on the rise, the family could function as an organizational nucleus for political movements and an ideological model of a patriarchal nation. The private household provided a safe space to pursue semilegal cultural and political activism. The politics of private life were highly gendered; yet they created opportunities for women, whom the state excluded from bureaucratic and electoral politics. Idealized as "mothers of the nation," nationalist women acquired political agency without participating in the typical feminist struggles for voting rights and legal equality. As home-school teachers, as domestic ideologues free from the constraints of a repressive state, but also as journalists and writers, they played an important role in national movements that has so far left few traces in the historiography.

Finally, the book offers a new interpretation of the relationship between rivaling nationalist projects and the imperial state. Ukrainian and Russian nationalists tried to mobilize the same Orthodox peasant population, which means that they worked with the same ethnographic materials and occasionally pursued similar short-term goals. However, they had very different political ends in mind. Ukrainian nationalists wanted to accommodate the local peasantry's cultural peculiarities by federalizing and democratizing the empire. Meanwhile, the region's imperial loyalists and Russian nationalists sought to use the autocratic state to improve the peasants' socioeconomic standing while assimilating them to Russian culture. Although proponents of both projects continued to look for common ground, their paths increasingly diverged over the long nineteenth century. As the Russian-Ukrainian dichotomy became entrenched in educated society, previously neutral individuals had to choose sides. Thus, different political projects to reconstruct the relationship between the state and its population led to the fracturing of Eastern Europe's elites along nationalist lines. The split within the Shul'gin/Shul'hyn family is a result of this larger process and a powerful metaphor for it.

Ukrainian, Russian, Little Russian

Sandwiched between two powerful neighbors, Ukraine has enjoyed a close and often problematic relationship with both Russia and Poland. Accordingly, Ukrainian nationalism can only be understood in conjunction with its closest rivals: Russian and Polish nationalism. While Ukrainian nationalism vied with Polish nationalism in Austrian Galicia, the competition with Russian nationalism has defined its history in the Russian Empire. The very concepts and practices that make up modern Ukrainian and Russian culture and nationalism only emerged over decades of exchange and conflict.[6]

Three preconditions have defined the historical rivalry between Russian and Ukrainian nationalism: their competition over the same territory and population, the relative similarity of their "national cultures," and the asymmetry of their relationship. First, both camps saw the territories east and west of the Dnieper river as (part of) their ideal historical homeland; both claimed the East Slavic–speaking, Orthodox Christian peasantry of these provinces as their own kin. For Ukrainian nationalists, these peasants were the core of the autonomous Ukrainian nation. For Russian nationalists, by contrast, they were Little Russians, a distinct but integral part of the triune "All-Russian" nation that also included Great Russians and Belorussians. Claiming more than a quarter of the empire's East Slavic population, Ukrainian nationalism appeared to threaten both the state's unity and that of the purported Russian nation.[7]

The emerging competition between two nationalisms led to a shift in ethnic terminology. In the first half of the nineteenth century, "Little Russian" (*maloross, malorus, malorossiianin*) was the most common designation for any Orthodox, East Slavic–speaking inhabitant of the empire's Southwest, as opposed to the "Great Russians" of Russia proper. However, in the middle decades of the century, those who stood for the region's cultural autonomy came to use "Ukraine" for the territory and "Ukrainian" (*ukraïnets'*) as their preferred ethnonym.[8] Conservative supporters of the imperial state rejected this terminology and nicknamed its adherents "Ukrainophiles"—a name that the latter soon adopted for themselves. Meanwhile, "Little Russian," once a neutral term, acquired political connotations. It increasingly became the proud self-designation of (as well as the scoffing appellation for) those who believed that the region's inhabitants were a distinct yet inseparable branch of the All-Russian nation.[9] These conservative self-styled Little Russians provided the cadres for the powerful Russian nationalist movement that emerged in the southwestern provinces after 1905.

Second, rivaling claims to the same peasant population were only possible because, for all their different traditions, Ukrainian and Russian cultures were comparatively similar. Ukrainian dialects were related to those spoken in Central Russia and to the Russian literary language. There was a clear-cut linguistic boundary between Ukrainian and Russian dialects, but the Russian presence in Ukraine had produced mixed idioms in some locations. Assimilation in both directions was relatively easy.[10] In terms of confession, the Russian Empire's Ukrainian and Russian population adhered to the same Eastern Orthodox Church.[11] History, too, offered many commonalities. Both territories had been part of the medieval Rus' state, and, after centuries of Lithuanian and Polish rule, most of Ukraine found itself in the Russian Empire by the late eighteenth century. For Ukrainian nationalists, governed by a state whose dominant culture and language were threateningly similar to the ones they promoted, the main task was thus to demonstrate the distinction between Ukraine and Russia. Precisely this relationship made Russia (i.e., "Muscovy," the empire's Great Russian core) into the constitutive other of the Ukrainian national movement.[12]

The cultural affinities between Russia and Ukraine facilitated the absorption of Ukraine's Orthodox inhabitants into Russian imperial culture.[13] While the Russian state denied them collective national-cultural rights, it did not discriminate against them as individuals. All careers were open to them if they agreed to be treated as Russians.[14] Therefore, many Russian nationalists in Ukraine were not Great Russians from the imperial center but locals loyal to the empire. As exemplified by the Shul′gin/Shul′hyn family, intellectuals' nationality was a conscious choice between various nation-building projects, based on their political preferences. Critics of the imperial state and its centralism turned toward Ukrainophilism; those loyal to the state became involved in Russian nation-building.

Third, the Russian-Ukrainian relationship in the nineteenth century was fundamentally asymmetrical owing to the absence of a Ukrainian state.[15] While earlier studies tended to either conflate Russian nationalism with the imperial state ("official nationalism") or saw the empire as an obstacle to Russian nation-building, recent scholarship has drawn a more nuanced picture of the manifold connections between nationalism and empire.[16] Russia's imperial situation was always on the mind of Russian nationalists. A nonimperial nation was unthinkable to them, although their visions of the exact relations between nation and empire differed. From the perspective of the tsarist administration, Russian nationalism was a tool that could be—and increasingly was—used to legitimate the empire's political system. While Russian nationalists sometimes disagreed with imperial policies, they were much more likely than any other national movement to have the government's ear.

If nineteenth-century Russian nationalism was thus framed by and loyal to an existing state, Ukrainian nationalism was a stateless national movement of the type described by Miroslav Hroch.[17] Whereas Russian nationalism tended to be conservative, monarchist, and often antidemocratic, Ukrainian nationalism was an outlet of oppositional feeling and aligned itself with liberal and socialist currents. Without a state to call their own, Ukrainian nationalists rallied around national culture (language, literature, music, theater), while Russian nationalists, whose national culture was omnipresent, were more preoccupied with questions of state organization or geopolitics. The imperial state repeatedly restricted the use of the Ukrainian language, making it almost impossible to support Ukrainian high culture and the empire at the same time. Thus, repression reinforced the anti-imperial tendency of Ukrainian nationalism.[18]

Aiming to analyze the relations between Russian and Ukrainian nationalism "on the ground," my study is indebted to several predecessors. Alexei Miller was the first to identify local Russian nationalists in Kiev as a third player in the relationship between the empire and Ukrainian nationalism. Miller argues that the state's failure to promote an assimilatory All-Russian nationalism guaranteed the long-term success of Ukrainian nationalism. Thus, his study focuses on the state's actions and intentions rather than individuals' motivation to prefer one nationalist program over the other.[19] Faith Hillis's insightful monograph on the patriotic intelligentsia of Kiev and right-bank Ukraine (i.e., west of the Dnieper river) uncovered their foundational role in modern Russian nationalism and their ambivalent relationship with its Ukrainian counterpart. Hillis posits the existence of a "Little Russian lobby" including both conservative Little Russians and radical Ukrainophiles, which split into rivaling camps only in the late nineteenth century. While this approach is fruitful in examining the common roots of Russian and Ukrainian nationalism, it tends to understate ideological differences that remained hidden behind cautious public utterances.[20] Serhiy Bilenky has discussed the emergence of romantic nationalism in the region as the result of an open-ended triangular debate between Russian, Polish, and Ukrainian intellectuals.[21] By contrast, Johannes Remy's close reading of the classical texts of Ukrainian nationalism stresses the anti-Russian stereotypes and resentments prevalent among midcentury Ukrainian writers.[22]

This book reads the relationship between Ukrainophiles and (Little) Russian nationalists as a process of negotiation, in which various actors repeatedly tested to what extent their ideas were compatible with those of others. Since both nationalist projects targeted the same population, their interests sometimes coincided and made cooperation desirable. However, their ultimate political aims were too different for a lasting alliance, and the two sides repeatedly came to blows. After the Ems Ukaz of 1876, which outlawed almost all forms of high culture in Ukrainian, the Ukrainophiles had to engage in a similar negotiation process with the imperial state. Knowing they were being watched, the Ukrainophiles exploited gray areas in the legislation and gradually extended their scope of action. There were still personal and professional contacts between the Ukrainophile and conservative Little Russian camps, and even occasional cooperation, but overall, their milieus moved ever further apart. When the new semiconstitutional system of the early twentieth century legalized the formation of political organizations, the two sides entered into open struggle.

Nationalist Biographies

Whatever their disagreements, most studies of both Russian and Ukrainian nationalism share a focus on high politics and state policies, on the history of ideas and canonical texts. This narrow definition of political history has excluded many relevant actors from the story—most importantly, almost all women. My study shifts attention from ideas and organizations to milieus and individuals, demonstrating how nationalism as a political ideology and lived practice interacted with biographical paths and personal choices. The biographies of nationalist activists are a rich and largely untapped resource for the study of nationalism. If they take into account the pitfalls of teleology and retrospective interpretation, nationalist biographies can contribute to a better understanding of the ideological differences between various nationalisms, their relationship with other political movements, and their appeal to various socioeconomic groups.[23]

A study of nationalism is not a study of nations. I follow Rogers Brubaker in understanding "nation" not as a category of analysis but as a "category of practice," a "system of social classification, an organizing 'principle of vision and division' of the social world."[24] Rejecting the treatment of national groups as collective individuals acting in their common interests, Brubaker urges researchers to think about how nationalist activists—in his terms, "ethnopolitical entrepreneurs"—try to divide society into clearly delimited groups. His research program leads beyond purely intellectual and political history toward an interest in the everyday practices of national classification, mobilization, and institutionalization.[25] Applying Brubaker's scheme to the Ukrainian-Russian context, one must ask how Ukrainian and Russian nationalists competed for the implementation of their respective ways to divide the social world. To what extent and by what means did the Russian-Ukrainian dividing line, wished for by Ukrainian nationalists and contested by their Russian opponents, become entrenched in the minds of the local population, embodied in social milieus, and ultimately institutionalized by the state?

Inspired by Brubaker's work, historians of the Habsburg monarchy have explored the practices by which populations and institutions came to perceive reality in national categories.[26] They have pointed out that many people were not a priori inclined to embrace national categories and often had to be pressured into doing so. This notion of "national indifference" challenges teleological accounts that show the nationalization of societies as a unidirectional and unstoppable process.[27] The Shul'gins and Shul'hyns, of course, were nationalists and by definition not indifferent to national categories. However, the literature on national indifference serves as a reminder that such activists were a small minority among a rather unresponsive population. Anecdotal evidence suggests that this was also the case with Ukraine's Orthodox peasantry, the target population of both Russian and Ukrainian nationalists. Although these peasants perceived themselves as different from Great Russians (nicknamed *katsapy*, literally "billy goats"), their self-identification as inhabitants of a specific locality was probably stronger than their loyalty to any imagined nation, whether Ukrainian or Russian.[28] Meanwhile, certain members of the Russian Empire's elites consciously resisted nationalist mobilization. In the Southwest, some landowners and intellectuals sympathized with parts of both the Russian and Ukrainian nation-building program and hesitated to break ties with either.[29] It is against this background that we must read the nationalists' fierce ideological battles.

The Shul'gins and Shul'hyns were members of one and the same family who came to understand themselves as members of two different nations. To their contemporaries, such dynamics were familiar. Accounts of individuals consciously choosing a nationality for themselves appear in many recollections of the period. As a Polish memoirist from western Ukraine reminisced years later,

> The sons of Poles sometimes became Ukrainians, the sons of Germans and Frenchmen became Poles. . . . "If a Pole marries a Russian woman," my father used to say, "their children are usually Ukrainians or Lithuanians." . . . In these times, nationality was not an inevitable racial fate but largely a matter of free choice. This choice was not limited to language. . . . Each language carried historical, religious, and societal traditions; each formed an ethos etched by centuries of triumphs, defeats, dreams, and sophistry.[30]

Historians of the period, too, have come to understand the contingent nature of nationality and its conjunction with other social categories such as class, estate, or confession. However, even though recent historiography stresses the central role of "ethnopolitical entrepreneurs" for nationalist mobilization, biographical studies about these activists have hardly explored the element of conscious choice in their lives. More often than not, the biographies of nationalist activists are still written in heroic tone by sympathizers who themselves operate in a national-historical paradigm. Many biographers assume their protagonists' nationality as a given, thus reproducing the inherently nationalist premise that a nationalist by definition defends the interests of a community into which he or she was born. More sophisticated studies acknowledge the voluntarist element in nationalist biographies, but seldom analyze the underlying motivations in depth.[31]

In order to reconstruct the lives and self-understandings of individual nineteenth-century nationalists in all their complexity, my study relies on Rogers Brubaker's and Frederick Cooper's critique of the term "identity." For them, "identity" either presupposes a stability and sameness that fails to account for the complex and malleable nature of the modern self or, in its postmodern variety, becomes so elastic as to lose all analytic sharpness. Brubaker and Cooper propose a series of alternative terms to cover different facets of its meaning: people's self-identification within a category or network, their categorization by external agencies such as the state, their understanding of their self and social location, and, finally, "groupness," that is, a population's perception of belonging, solidarity, and connectedness.[32] My study takes into account several further factors, including loyalty or disloyalty to existing states, the evocation of national others or out-groups, and—in a situation where language carried enormous ideological weight—the languages used in everyday life. Finally, I look at individuals' active participation in social milieus associated with a political worldview: membership in organizations or parties, friendship or neighborhood with other activists, and, most importantly, kinship and family connections.

Nationalists understood the family as an intimate community linking the individual to society at large, an intermediate category through which they reflected their relationship to the nation.[33] This also meant that private life, and above all the role of mothers as educators of the nation's future generation, became politically significant. In the domestic sphere, nationalist women acquired political agency without appearing to undermine traditional gender roles. Recent research has found that the noble family and its domestic space remained crucial sites of political mobilization and intellectual production in the nineteenth-century Russian Empire.[34] In a society that limited political debates in public, the family "served as a vehicle of empire building and also a gateway for ideas and associations that were difficult for the state to control."[35] By shifting attention toward this "intimate theater of history," historians can integrate the experience of women (and, occasionally, children) into political history.[36] This is a particularly important task for historians of nationalism, an ideology that emphasized the parallelism between the purportedly organic communities of the family and the nation.

But why write about the Shul'gin/Shul'hyn family? With one or two exceptions, its members were obscure second-tier figures in late imperial

Kiev. However, their case condenses the shared and divided history of Russian and Ukrainian nationalism in a way that makes them ideal protagonists for a microhistorical investigation.[37] While many components of the family's history were out of the ordinary—the rivalry between the two branches, their peculiar visions of the national community, their scandalous intimate lives—these idiosyncrasies allow for new insights into the process that this study is about: the bifurcation of the Little Russian patriotic intelligentsia into self-defined Russians and Ukrainians. This bifurcation, in turn, was part of a larger historical process, the nationalization of Eastern European elites.

Sources

Source material on the Shul'gin/Shul'hyn family is both overwhelmingly extensive and surprisingly thin. As members of a press dynasty, the Shul'gins and Shul'hyns produced thousands of newspaper and journal articles, spanning many decades and a wide range of political, economic, and historical topics. The most important outlet for their journalism was the newspaper *Kievlianin*, which the family's Russian branch owned for fifty-five years. Three family members—Vitalii Shul'gin, Dmitrii Pikhno, and Vasilii Shul'gin—held the post of editor in chief, and others, both male and female, joined the paper's staff. Particularly in moments of crisis and accelerated change (1905, 1917), *Kievlianin* can almost be read as a political diary of its editors, permitting a day-by-day analysis of how their views evolved.[38] Though less prolific, the Ukrainian branch of the family also published political and scholarly writings in various journals, newspapers, and brochures.

Three family members wrote autobiographical texts. Vasilii Shul'gin in particular was a true graphomaniac. His published and unpublished memoirs fill thousands of pages, replete with anecdotes about relatives' relatives and acquaintances' acquaintances.[39] Ekaterina Shul'gina and Oleksander Shul'hyn, too, wrote autobiographies that describe both their intimate family lives and Kiev's rivaling nationalist milieus.[40] Reliance on memoirs means that the study's protagonists have a voice in the text—for better or for worse. While these texts permit unique insights into their authors' worldviews, they are fraught with retrospective bias and threaten to unduly impose the protagonists' own narratives on the analysis. If read as products of active self-memorialization, however, they can help the historian understand how members of the intelligentsia gradually moved toward an unambiguously national self-identification, a process that they often completed in retrospective by writing their lives.[41]

Most of the family members, however, have left few personal traces, except for the odd letter in an archive in Kyiv or Moscow. Some crucial episodes in the family history remain mysterious, some figures elusive. There is no comprehensive family archive.[42] The remaining records about the Shul'gins and Shul'hyns have been scattered across and beyond the continent by the turmoil of Europe's twentieth century. The surviving correspondence only allows for glimpses into the lives of the Shul'gins and Shul'hyns, while administrative documents and police files expose some of the dilemmas that they faced as they maneuvered between nationalist milieus and the imperial government.

Historiography on the Shul'gin/Shul'hyn family, as could be expected, is split along the national line. Vasilii Shul'gin has been an object of historical research since the 1920s, when the Soviet journalist David Zaslavskii wrote a short study that betrayed both the author's political bias and his fascination with Shul'gin.[43] Over the past few years, Shul'gin has attracted a lively interest among Russian historians as a conservative protagonist in the revolution and civil war.[44] The earliest studies about Oleksander Shul'hyn came out of Ukrainian émigré circles in Western Europe shortly after his death. More recently, he has been the subject of several new studies, which tend to use him as a suitable protagonist for the national-historical narratives that are in great demand in post-Soviet Ukraine.[45] Other family members have only made minor appearances in the historiography.[46]

Diverging Paths

The book's structure is largely chronological. Chapter 1 contextualizes the family history from the 1830s to the 1870s within the emerging debate about "Little Russia" and its relationship to the imperial center. It shows how conservative Little Russian intellectuals, including the historian and newspaper editor Vitalii Shul'gin, engaged initially in a precarious dialogue and subsequently in open conflict with their younger Ukrainophile rivals. The former promoted state intervention to protect the region's peasants from the supposedly pernicious influence of Polish nobles and Jewish traders. The latter similarly idealized the peasants but identified the imperial state as an obstacle to their liberation. In the mid-1870s, this division reached the Shul'gin family itself. Iakov Shul'gin broke with his uncle's worldview, turned toward populism and reconceived himself as a Ukrainian. The chapter explores the interplay of personal, generational, and ideological factors that caused a lasting national rupture both in the family and in the region's Orthodox intelligentsia.

In the years of repression after the 1876 Ems Ukaz, Kiev's Ukrainophiles retreated into two niches: academic work and private life. Chapter 2 foregrounds the self-defined Ukrainian branch of the family within Kiev's tiny Ukrainophile milieu of the 1880s and 1890s to demonstrate how they created their own, oppositional vision of a future Ukrainian society. At the same time, many Ukrainophiles worked for the state and had to compromise with its representatives, leading to a fragile equilibrium in which activists and government officials learned to read each other and exploit gray zones. Consequently, Ukrainophile men faced constant tension between their nationalist commitment and the constraints of imperial society. Less hampered by the state, Ukrainophile women assumed a central role in a movement forced to retreat into domestic spaces, particularly when it came to educating a new generation of nationalist activists. Reflecting on the tensions between a supranational imperial state and a peripheral nationalism, the chapter argues that even repressive structures left a niche for—and to some extent fostered—the emergence of anti-imperial nationalist elites.

Chapter 3 shifts the focus to the conservative Russian branch of the family, examining their attempt to develop a Russian nationalism tailored to the empire's southwestern provinces. Dmitrii Pikhno, the family's patriarch, exemplifies a different choice of nationality: After marrying Vitalii Shul'gin's widow, he chose imperial loyalty and Russian culture over the rural Ukrainian-speaking environment into which he was born. A journalist, economist, and collector of agricultural estates, he developed a program of state-sponsored economic nationalism designed to change rural social hierarchies to the benefit of "Russian"—that is, Orthodox—peasants. After the 1905 revolution, Russian nationalism in the region adapted to the new semiconstitutional system. A literally reactionary ideology that advanced its proposals only in response to external threats and impulses, it began to mobilize the local population for the defense of the nation and the monarchy. The Pikhno-Shul'gin family entered electoral politics in order to transform the empire into a nationalizing state. Juxtaposing the clan's politics and their private lives, I argue that their peculiar model of nationalism was to a large extent inspired by their tightly knit, if unconventional, family circle.

Chapter 4 explores the rapid transformation of nationalist ideologies and political practices after 1914 by tracing the Shul'gin/Shul'hyn family's divided history during the troubled years of war, revolution, and civil war. It weaves back together the two separate narrative threads of the previous chapters: that of the Russian Shul'gins, who had to forge alliances with former opponents, ultimately contributing to the fall of the regime that they set out to defend; and that of the Ukrainian Shul'hyns, who tried to exploit the opportunities offered by the implosion of the empire. Nationalism was not the main cause for the empire's fall in 1917, but in Kiev, Ukrainian and Russian nationalists turned nationhood into the preferred idiom of revolutionary politics. The revolution offered new careers to nationalist activists, whether within the emerging Ukrainian state or in opposition to it. But if nationalists celebrated political successes during the first year of the revolution, they were unable to retain their influence as social radicalism increased and political conflicts turned into civil war. In the course of 1918 and 1919, both the Russian Shul'gins and the Ukrainian Shul'hyns came to realize that they were fighting a losing battle.

In the wake of the civil war, all surviving members of the family ended up exiled in Western and Central Europe. Chapter 5 analyzes how three of them used autobiography to inscribe themselves into national-historical narratives. In writing their own lives, Ukrainian nationalists completed their self-Ukrainization, finally shedding all traces of their past in imperial Russia and positioning themselves as unambiguously Ukrainian politicians. Russian nationalist émigrés, meanwhile, utilized autobiography to realign their account of themselves with the narrative of a Russia ruined by an antinational revolution. Deprived of any real influence, both émigré groups created separate exile milieus and ceased to engage in dialogue with one another. The divergence of their paths was complete.

While a Ukrainian historian singled the Shul'gins/Shul'hyns out as a "nationally divided family" over twenty years ago, all subsequent research has focused on one of the two branches.[47] This study brings them back together to explain why the split in their family came about, how family members came to understand and present themselves as Russians or Ukrainians, and how, ultimately, the Kiev intelligentsia ended up having to choose one or the other nationality.

CHAPTER 1

At the Crossroads

The Search for the Little Russian Soul, 1830s–1876

In 1865, a local journalist in Kiev put the societal cleavages of his home region in a nutshell: "Here, a quarrel between a landowner and a peasant is at the same time a quarrel between a Pole and a Russian."[1] Indeed, in the three provinces of Kiev, Podolia, and Volhynia on the western bank of the Dnieper river—a territory variously known as right-bank Ukraine or the Southwest region—social conflicts were likely to be interpreted in ethnic terms. Yet the identification of the region's peasant population as "Russians" was a deliberate oversimplification. These peasants were Orthodox East Slavs who spoke regional varieties of what was known at the time as the South or Little Russian dialect. Most of them would not begin to identify with national categories before the twentieth century.

If the peasants' Russianness was dubious, the right bank's elites were not Russians by any measure. The nobility consisted of Polish-speaking Catholics, ranging from magnates with huge estates to the numerous petty gentry, the *szlachta*, whose poorest members were barely distinguishable from the peasants. The region's towns were heavily Jewish, and Jews filled most economic functions of the middle classes, working as traders, artisans, estate managers, innkeepers, or moneylenders.[2] On the other side of the Dnieper, in the left-bank provinces of Poltava and Chernigov, the population was more homogeneously Orthodox and East Slavic. The area's formerly Cossack elites had been co-opted into the Russian nobility by the nineteenth century, though many still cherished the memories of earlier Cossack autonomy.[3]

In the early nineteenth century, intellectuals on both banks of the Dnieper began to investigate the region's history and ethnography. Over the years, their scholarly discussions evolved into a politicized conflict between rivaling nation-building projects. While Polish nationalists staked a claim to the Dnieper's right bank, Russian and Ukrainian nationalists saw the entire territory as part of their imagined homelands. Members of the Shul'gin/Shul'hyn family assumed an active role in these debates during the 1860s and 1870s, witnessing, and indeed helping to deepen, the growing rift within the Little Russian (i.e., Orthodox) camp that had once been united in opposition to the Poles.

This chapter charts the earliest known history of the family in the context of the small milieu of local patriots in midcentury Kiev. As the founder of Kiev's first successful daily newspaper, *Kievlianin*, Vitalii Shul'gin brought the family to the forefront of the political struggle over the region. Shul'gin and his associates crafted a political line that tried to balance regional patriotism with loyalty to the empire. However, dissent arose in his own family. Impressed by the intellectual achievements of young academics at the university, Vitalii's nephew Iakov chose to support Ukrainophile populism and ultimately embraced Ukrainian rather than Russian nationhood. In the 1870s, the latent disagreements within Kiev's patriotic intelligentsia came to a head, splitting their milieu into rival camps—and the front line went straight through the Shul'gin family.

Local Patriotism and the Birth of an Intelligentsia Dynasty

The Shul'gin/Shul'hyn family established itself in Kiev around the year 1830. Little is known about the last common ancestors of the family's two branches, a man called Iakov Ignat'evich Shul'gin (in Ukrainian, Iakiv Hnatovych Shul'ha) and his wife, Iuliia Fedorovna Shul'gina. Iakov Shul'gin was born around 1788 in the small town of Nezhin in Chernigov province, northeast of Kiev. A member of the middling imperial bureaucracy, he served in Kaluga in Central Russia before being transferred to Nezhin and subsequently to the growing city of Kiev, where the family settled in the old trading district of Podol on the bank of the Dnieper river. Iakov Shul'gin became inspector of the city's grain storage warehouses and later joined the military provisioning commission.[4]

The Shul'gins apparently had three sons, but only two are known by name. The older one, Nikolai, studied at the Nezhin gymnasium and began to serve in the chancellery of the Kiev governor-general in 1836. The younger son, Vitalii, was born in Kaluga in 1822 and spent his early childhood in his father's hometown of Nezhin. According to family lore, a careless nanny dropped Vitalii on the ground when he was four or five, leaving him with a damaged spine that later developed into a hunchback. Some of Vitalii's acquaintances saw this physical defect as the reason that he became a sickly, but hardworking and bookish, young man. In 1833, Vitalii entered Kiev's First Gymnasium, where he proved to be a very talented student and edited a handwritten journal with his friends. Five years later, he graduated with excellent marks and was ready to matriculate at Kiev's recently founded Imperial Saint Vladimir University, the first in his family to undertake academic studies.[5]

In social terms, the Shul'gins were nobles, but not landed gentry. They belonged to the middle ranks of imperial Russia's service nobility. Iakov Ignat'evich was not born into the noble estate; the church documents from Nezhin variously list his family as merchants or townspeople (*meshchane*).[6] By way of civil service, Iakov acquired the title of collegiate councillor (*kollezhskii sovetnik*) at the sixth level of the imperial Table of Ranks, equivalent to a colonel in the army and at the time sufficiently high to confer hereditary nobility.[7] His wife Iuliia, née Devel', came from the Baltic region, probably from a lesser German gentry family. A family acquaintance later wrote that both had received little formal education, but that Iakov "was distinguished by a practical mind and the morals and habits of an old official," while Iuliia influenced her children through her tender affection and sincere family loyalty.[8] One of their sons would soon join the ranks of the Russian intelligentsia, a social milieu that was largely recruited from the lower nobility in this period.[9]

Iakov Ignat'evich Shul'gin loyally served the Russian Empire his entire life. To what extent he identified with his region of Little Russia (Ukraine) is unclear. According to one source, Iakov was an "indigenous Little Russian who could not speak any other language than Little Russian." According to another he tried to russify himself by adding the Russian ending *-in* to his birth name Shul'ha (a Ukrainian word meaning "left-hander").[10] At any rate, Iakov Shul'gin was one of many enterprising left-bank Little Russians who sought to advance their career in a growing bureaucracy by moving to the region's administrative center, Kiev.[11]

Kiev in the 1830s was still a minor town in the empire's southwestern borderlands, with only thirty thousand permanent inhabitants, not counting thousands of soldiers and religious pilgrims. The city had been ruled by the tsars for over 150 years, but its immediate hinterland, the three provinces of Kiev, Podolia, and Volhynia on the western bank of the Dnieper, had been annexed to the empire only during the partitions of Poland in 1793 and 1795. The court's ideologues had presented this expansion as the completion of the "gathering of Russian lands," the recuperation of a region that had always belonged to Russia. In reality, however, this was a highly diverse territory with a complex socioethnic composition. In the countryside, Polish-Catholic nobles ruled over Orthodox serfs who spoke local Ukrainian idioms. In 1831, some of these nobles joined the Polish uprising against the tsarist government. After crushing the rebellion, the authorities closed Polish educational institutions and opened Russian ones instead. In Kiev, the energetic governor-general Dmitrii Bibikov (in office 1837–1852) embarked on his project of urban beautification and regularization, a project meant to assert imperial sovereignty over the region. Kiev's St. Vladimir University, established in 1834, was to serve a similar purpose as a bastion of imperial loyalty in the borderlands.[12] This was the institution that Vitalii Shul'gin entered as an eager and diligent sixteen-year-old in 1838. After missing out on most of his first year owing to protests by Polish students—as a result of which several Polish professors and most Polish students were dismissed—Vitalii began his studies at the historical-philological faculty in the autumn of 1839.[13]

The faculty's most prominent member was Mikhail Maksimovich (Mykhailo Maksymovych), whom Vitalii Shul'gin would later call "my learned and ever memorable mentor and professor."[14] A botanist by education, Maksimovich began to study and publish Ukrainian folk songs in the 1820s, inspired by the Herderian Romantic belief that folklore was an authentic reflection of a people's "spirit" or "character." From 1843, he took the lead in the new Kiev Archaeographic Commission, a body the authorities established to collect historical documents "proving" the region's primordially Russian character.[15] While he praised the region's central role in East Slavic history, its unique folk culture, and its local dialect, Maksimovich viewed Little Russia as an organic part of an empire united by Orthodoxy and nationality. He did not wish to turn Little Russian culture into a political weapon against the state and dismissed the potential of the Little Russian dialect as a literary language.[16] As such, he was a typical representative of what Miroslav Hroch has called phase A of national movements, characterized by academic interest in the collection of a cultural heritage that is often perceived to be doomed. According to one historian, Maksimovich "simply did not think in nationalistic categories."[17] Nevertheless, he and other contemporary academic folklorists provided later activists with several elements of a discourse that identified Ukrainians (Little Russians) as a nationality distinct from both Great Russians and Poles, with its own language, mentality, and historical continuity through the centuries.[18]

Little is known about Vitalii Shul'gin's university days. Obituaries written decades later portray Vitalii as an extraordinarily hardworking student more interested in reading than merrymaking. Exempted from the compulsory fencing and dancing lessons because of his hunchback, he devoted most of his time to lectures about history, philosophy, and the classics. A few months after graduating at age nineteen, he began to teach history at a gymnasium.[19] In 1845, Vitalii's brother Nikolai got married to Mariia Rudykovskaia, whose father Ostap Rudykovs'kyi (Evstafii Rudykovskii) soon befriended the entire Shul'gin family. A former military doctor and acquaintance of the famous poet Aleksandr Pushkin, Rudykovs'kyi socialized with many university professors, including Maksimovich, and engaged in long discussions with the young Vitalii Shul'gin. All three men shared an interest in Little Russian antiquity, and intimate relations developed between them. Rudykovs'kyi privately dabbled in poetry, writing in both Russian and Ukrainian. His poems show Rudykovs'kyi as an ardent imperial patriot and a lover of local traditions. One of his Russian poems celebrated the state's victory over the Polish uprising of 1831, singing the praises of the "tsar given to the Russians by God." Another one, "The Triumph of Kiev," glorified the city as the cradle of Christianity and Russianness, drawing a direct line from the medieval grand prince Iaroslav to Nicholas I.[20]

Rudykovs'kyi reserved Ukrainian for less solemn, more "popular" or intimate topics. Thus, one Ukrainian poem deplored in half-serious tone that the descendants of Little Russia's warlike Cossacks had turned into lazy drunkards under Muscovite military protection. Rudykovs'kyi also liked to send jocular poems to his relatives and friends. For instance, he mocked Mikhail Maksimovich's obsession with the regional past, asking him why he kept troubling the bones of the ancestors in their graves ("Na shcho ty pradedôv, prababok, turbuesh kôstky v mohylkakh?"). He reminded Iakov Shul'gin that they would have to marry off Vitalii soon and made fun of the latter for writing a book about women's history instead of finding himself a wife.[21] Vitalii, assuming the pose of the unworldly scholar, occasionally answered Rudykovs'kyi's epistles in Latin.[22]

During the 1840s, then, Rudykovs'kyi, Vitalii Shul'gin, and probably his father and brother were connected to a loose milieu of local patriots centered on Mikhail Maksimovich. Like Maksimovich, Rudykovs'kyi saw no contradiction between enthusiasm for the region's history and culture, including the rural Little Russian dialect, political loyalty to the Russian Empire, and the idea of a unitary Russian nation. This symbiosis of local folklore and imperial patriotism that Vitalii Shul'gin experienced in his domestic circle affected his intellectual formation and would assume a political form in his later writings.

The Ukrainophile Challenge

The harmony between region and empire, however, was about to be disturbed. In 1846, an informal circle of patriotic young intellectuals formed around the historian Nikolai (Mykola) Kostomarov, the Brotherhood of Saints Cyril and Method. The Cyrillo-Methodians, among them some members of the Kiev Archaeographic Commission, politicized the interest in Little Russian folk culture by connecting it to pan-Slavism, federalism, democracy, and peasant emancipation from their Polish landlords. Their writings portrayed Ukrainians as an inherently egalitarian nation without a nobility and a key member of the future Slavic federation destined to bring the other Slavs their freedom. Some of them, notably the writer Panteleimon Kulish and the poet Taras Shevchenko, went further in their assertion of Ukrainian difference from Russia and in their condemnation of autocratic rule. Shevchenko's poetry included anti-Russian statements alongside anti-Polish and anti-Jewish stereotypes.[23] Although the state suppressed this attempt at politicization by dissolving the brotherhood, high-standing bureaucrats helped its leaders to conceal their anti-tsarist ideas and punished them only by way of internal exile.[24] It was during this investigation that the Russian authorities first used the term "Ukrainophilism" (*ukrainofil'stvo*), a designation that some of the region's young patriots would soon adopt for themselves.[25]

Vitalii Shul'gin belonged to the same generation as the group's leaders and knew Kulish as a student.[26] However, he was not involved in their activities, and his political opinions at the time are unknown.

Several years later, he dismissed the Cyrillo-Methodians as gifted but uneducated revolutionary youths: "This party's membership was negligibly small and totally irrational in its goals, for it strove to reverse history and resurrect in the nineteenth century a community which even in the sixteenth century stood out due to its savagely poetic but clumsy forms—a life, which, even according to one of the party's activists, 'once was but will not return.' "[27] As late as the 1860s, Vitalii Shul'gin continued to view the region's cultural heritage through the antiquarian lens that had been common twenty years earlier.

The late 1840s and 1850s were a time of successful academic and pedagogical work for Vitalii Shul'gin. In 1849, he received a post as adjunct professor at Kiev University and defended his master's thesis, "The Condition of Women in Russia up to Peter the Great." In his monograph, Shul'gin claimed that women had enjoyed equal rights among the heathen Slavs, but Christianization and Tatar rule had increasingly excluded them from society, before Peter the Great restored their rights. While he described women's role in society in typically gendered terms, associating them with values such as morality, love, modesty, or beauty, Vitalii Shul'gin insisted on the negative effects of their exclusion from society: "By humiliating women, man only showed his own humiliation."[28] Shul'gin's interest in the "woman question" was not merely academic. Since the mid-1840s, he had been teaching at the Institute for Noble Maidens, where he became very popular among the girls for his commitment to their education. At the university, Shul'gin lectured mostly on modern West European history, inspiring his students with liberal interpretations of the Reformation, the French Revolution, and the recent constitutional movements. According to one listener, Shul'gin was considered the university's greatest luminary and most eloquent lecturer. His textbooks received praise for their lively narration and were used in Russian schools for several years.[29] Not yet forty, Vitalii Shul'gin seemed set for a brilliant career in the historical profession.

Probably around the same time, the university gave Vitalii an empty plot of land on the corners of Kuznechnaia and Shuliavskaia (later renamed Karavaevskaia) Streets, near its enormous classicist main building. This part of town, known as Novoe stroenie (New building), was then still near the outskirts but about to become a booming district. Academics were settling nearby, and when Kiev's railway station opened down the hill from the university in 1870, the neighborhood became one of the city's densest and most urban. Over the years, Vitalii built three houses on his plot: two small ones for his relatives, and a larger one on the corner for himself. The same building was to become the editorial office of Vitalii Shul'gin's newspaper.[30]

After a decade of relative calm, the late 1850s saw the reappearance of various oppositional tendencies in the Kiev region. These were the first years of the rule of Alexander II, whose reform promises awakened high hopes among the intelligentsia. Starting in 1859, several Sunday schools for young workers appeared in Kiev with the permission of Nikolai Pirogov, the liberal curator of the school district. In these schools, democratically minded university students experimented with teaching and primers in Ukrainian.[31] In the same year, a group of students at Kiev University donned peasant clothes and traveled the region's countryside in order to become acquainted with the peasantry's way of life and worldview. They also established their own secret school to educate peasant boys in a democratic spirit. Conservative Polish nobles denounced the students to the police, calling them *chłopomani* (Rus./Ukr. *khlopomany*, meaning "peasant lovers") and claiming that they wanted to incite the peasantry to violent rebellion.

The leader of the *khlopomany* was Volodymyr Antonovych, an aspiring historian of democratic opinions inspired by French philosophy. Born Włodzimierz Antonowicz into an impoverished Catholic gentry family, he had become increasingly disgusted with the szlachta's caste-like arrogance, with their contempt for and violent treatment of the Orthodox peasantry, and with their Polish chauvinism—all of which he found to be embodied by his mother.[32] Antonovych and some of his friends, most of whom shared a Polish gentry background, came to identify themselves with the peasants' Little Russian or Ukrainian nationality. In the autumn of 1860, they decided to quit their Polish student fraternity (*gmina*), which engaged in conspiratorial work against the Russian state.[33] Shortly afterward, they joined Sunday school activists from left-bank Ukraine to form a Ukrainophile student association called the Kiev Hromada (commune). Personal ties consolidated this convergence between the right-bank *khlopomany* and the left-bank Ukrainophiles. According to one contemporary, a crucial event was Antonovych's marriage to Varvara Mikhel', whose cousin Pavlo Chubyns'kyi (Pavel Chubinskii) and brother-in-law Oleksandr Kistiakivs'kyi (Aleksandr Kistiakovskii) were leading Sunday school organizers. Rather loosely organized and confidential, the Hromada temporarily gathered over a hundred students.[34]

FIGURE 2. Volodymyr Antonovych (*right*) and Wincenty Wasilewski, ca. 1860. Both are wearing the peasant dress characteristic of the *khlopomany*. IR NBUV, f. II, od. zb. 30447–30456 (dodatok) b, ark. 1.

As the imperial government set out to free Russia's peasantry from serfdom, the ideological center of the renascent Ukrainophile movement shifted to the empire's capital. The former Cyrillo-Methodians Kostomarov, Kulish, and Shevchenko had gathered in Saint Petersburg after returning from their exile. In January 1861, they joined like-minded intellectuals in launching the short-lived periodical *Osnova* (The foundation). Although published in the distant capital and mostly in Russian, *Osnova* became by far the most important organ of the Ukrainophiles. It published several of their seminal ideological texts that advocated Ukraine's distinctive historical fate, federalism, and the development of the local dialect into a full-fledged literary language. *Osnova* provoked the first major discussion about Ukrainophilism in the Russian press, causing some progressive publicists to express their sympathy and alerting others to the dangers of Ukrainian separatism for the All-Russian nation-building project.[35]

The most important of *Osnova*'s articles were Kostomarov's essay "Two Russian Nationalities" and the young Antonovych's contribution "My Confession."[36] Kostomarov's piece became a foundational text of Ukrainian nationalism that defined many of its *topoi* for decades to come. Building on earlier ethnographic and historical work, Kostomarov systematized a series of binary oppositions that purportedly distinguished "South Russians" from Great Russians. In his words, history proved that "the South Russians were characterized by the predominance of individual freedom and the Great Russians by the predominance of community"; a study of folklore showed the South Russians to be spiritual, poetic, inclined toward mutual agreement, tolerant, and close to nature, while the Great Russians were materialistic, submissive, authoritarian, prejudiced, and even felt "a hostility to plants." Kostomarov insisted, however, that the two nationalities were complementary. The South Russians needed the Great Russian capacity for state-building in order to evade subjection by the Poles, whose character was more like their own but whose aristocratism contradicted the South Russians' innate democratism.[37] And yet, his readers could hardly overlook the fact that Kostomarov posited a fundamental difference between the two "Russian" nationalities and that he assigned nearly all the positive characteristics to the Ukrainians.

Volodymyr Antonovych's "Confession," by contrast, was the eloquent expression of the *khlopomany* ethos, the belief that Ukraine's nobles had a duty to the peasantry that they had so long exploited and oppressed. Shedding once and for all his Polish gentry past, Antonovych proudly embraced the epithet of "turncoat" and called upon his fellow nobles to follow his path: "to love the people in whose midst he lived, to become imbued with its interests, to return to the nationality his ancestors once had abandoned, and, as far as possible by unremitting labor and love to compensate the people for the evil done to it."[38] Antonovych's text was testimony to an almost religiously felt national conversion—he did actually convert to Orthodoxy around this time—and a gospel of voluntarily chosen nationality. Having embraced Ukrainian nationality for political reasons, Antonovych explicitly advertised his choice as a model for others. Ten years later, his reasoning and his idealism would inspire a new generation of Ukrainophile activists, among them Vitalii Shul'gin's nephew.

One year after the publication of this text, in the first months of 1863, the Russian Empire's western fringe was shaken by a renewed revolt of the Polish nobility. Led by a central committee in Warsaw, the insurgents engaged the imperial army in guerrilla warfare in the hope of resurrecting the Polish-Lithuanian Commonwealth from the Baltic Sea to the Dnieper. In the spring, the uprising spread to Ukraine, where, however, it resulted in a near-complete failure. Defying the revolutionaries' expectations, the peasants did not join the nobles' revolt, and the imperial authorities managed to restore order within a few weeks.[39] Kiev University had long been the region's main center of Polish agitation, and in 1863, many of its students took up arms against the government.[40] In the wake of the failed insurrection, the government confiscated hundreds of Polish estates in the Southwest, imposed strict quotas for Poles in the region's bureaucracy, replaced thousands of Polish bureaucrats by Russians from the inner provinces, and prohibited the use of the Polish language in all official contexts. From 1865, Poles were no longer allowed to buy land in the provinces of right-bank Ukraine, Belarus, and Lithuania. Meanwhile, the government created favorable conditions for Russians willing to buy confiscated land.[41]

Even though the *khlopomany* and the Hromada had remained neutral during the insurgency, the government also moved against the Ukrainophiles in July 1863. Lobbied by local bureaucrats and by the Moscow journalist Mikhail Katkov, the minister of internal affairs Petr Valuev issued a circular that (provisionally) prohibited the publication of all religious and popular texts in Ukrainian. Stressing the danger of separatism and the Ukrainophiles' alleged collaboration with the Poles, the Valuev Circular declared "that there was not, is not, and cannot be any special Little Russian language, and that their dialect, as used by uneducated folk, is the same Russian language, only corrupted by Polish influence." The Valuev Circular demonstrated that the authorities were ready to tolerate Ukrainophilism as long as it remained the intellectual endeavor of a small elite circle, but strongly objected when it tried to reach out to the peasant masses.[42] Describing Ukrainophilism as the result of a "Polish intrigue," Katkov and Valuev tried to blame the threat of Ukrainian separatism on an external enemy rather than the "Little Russians" themselves—a tendency that would remain typical of Russian reactions to Ukrainophilism.

"Russian, Russian, Russian"

Vitalii Shul'gin was not in the mood for politics in these years. Tragedy struck several times in the historian's family. Vitalii's mother died in 1853, and his brother Nikolai succumbed to tuberculosis in 1857, leaving Vitalii to care for his beloved but sickly sister-in-law Mariia and his ailing nieces and nephew. Mariia also fell ill with tuberculosis and died in December 1860, just two months after Vitalii's father.[43] Within a few years, Vitalii had lost both his parents, his brother, and his sister-in-law. His family circle had shrunk to his brother's four children, whose legal custodian he now became. Weakened by grief and tormented by heavy migraines, he decided to quit university service in 1862.[44]

During the following year, Shul'gin began to recover from the family tragedies. Defying his reputation as an inveterate bachelor, he got married to Mariia Konstantinovna Popova, his former pupil at the Institute for Noble Maidens. In August 1863, he held a highly successful series of public lectures on the French Revolution. At this point, Shul'gin's friends tried to recall him to the university.[45] The problem was that the new University Statute required professors to hold a higher doctoral degree, which Shul'gin had not acquired. In recognition of his long and dedicated service, the university council decided to award him an honorary degree. However, a majority of faculty members prevented Shul'gin's reappointment, officially for formal reasons, although personal disagreements may have played a role.[46]

A new career opportunity soon opened up for Vitalii Shul'gin. The recent Polish uprising had convinced the local administration of the need to strengthen the region's patriotic Russian public sphere. The popularity of Shul'gin's lectures, his political reliability, and his availability recommended him for this task. Governor-General Nikolai Annenkov invited the former professor to edit a new publication that would bring

the imperial administration into closer contact with the region's educated class.[47] "Striving to establish order in the region entrusted to my
administration and to protect in the future its dear Russian nationality
from the illegal and irrational encroachments of Polish propaganda,"
Annenkov reported, "I have found an effective means to achieve this
goal in the foundation of a local newspaper that, introducing the government's ideas to society, will in turn serve as an organ of societal
needs . . . and watch over native Russian interests in the region."[48]

Among the paper's regular contributors were many professors at
Kiev University, as well as the president of the Archaeographic Commission (and former *Osnova* contributor), Mikhail Iuzefovich. Given
the relative weakness of Kiev's Orthodox intelligentsia, the governor-
general awarded a yearly subsidy of 6,000 rubles to the new semiofficial
organ, which was titled *Kievlianin* (The Kievan) in reminiscence of an
earlier publication edited by Mikhail Maksimovich.[49] This subsidy was
far from exceptional in a time when most major newspapers in Russia
were financed by state institutions. In the reform period, a limited public sphere took shape under the auspices of the autocratic state, not in
complete opposition to it.[50] However, when the next governor-general
tried to make *Kievlianin* into an official state publication, Shul'gin
refused, relinquishing his post until he was guaranteed his editorial
independence.[51]

Kiev's new semiofficial organ defined its political line in an announcement published before the first edition. As its motto, Vitalii Shul'gin
chose a quotation from the Slavophile journalist Ivan Aksakov: "This
land is Russian, Russian, Russian!" (Krai etot—russkii, russkii, russkii!).
Deliberately repeating this phrase over and over again, the text went on
to explain that the Southwest of the empire needed an administration
and schools "in the Russian spirit," that its population had repeatedly
proved its loyalty to Russia, and that the region's Poles were "guests"
who had to behave in order to be tolerated. Vitalii also rejected regional
separatism, employing a series of bodily metaphors: "As children of the
Russian earth, flesh of her flesh, bones of her bones, we recognize not
only as illegal, but even as unthinkable, any attempt against the life of
a region cut off from the state's common organism."[52] In the paper's
first issue, Shul'gin repeated his "profession de foi," which *Kievlianin*
would follow for many decades: "The editors . . . see the southwestern
region as Russian from time immemorial, even though it has preserved
its peculiarities that have a right to be recognized."[53] Kiev's wits were
quick to point out that the assertion of a "Russian, Russian, Russian"

land was, for the time being, little more than wishful thinking. A caricature showed Shul'gin surrounded by *khlopomany* in popular attire shouting "You're lying, Muscovite, this is Ukraine!" and by Poles who asserted that the region was a "robbed land."[54]

In its first weeks, Shul'gin made it very clear that *Kievlianin* was directed above all against the Polish nobility of right-bank Ukraine. Historian that he was, the editor turned to the recent past to solve the problems of the present. In a lengthy essay about the region's history over the preceding twenty-five years, he complained bitterly about the humiliations that the enserfed peasants of right-bank Ukraine had suffered at the hands of the Polish nobility. Not long ago, Shul'gin wrote, the Polish nobles "saw the few Russian bureaucrats as barbarians, the Russian peasants as bumpkins and cattle, called Orthodoxy a bumpkin faith, the Russian language a bumpkin language."[55] This vision of the region's rural society, focusing on the exploitative and dehumanizing relations between the szlachta and the Orthodox serfs, was not so different from that of young radicals like Volodymyr Antonovych.

The crucial difference, however, was Vitalii Shul'gin's view of the Russian state. Whereas Ukrainophiles believed that only a future democratized and federalized state could help the peasants in their plight, Vitalii Shul'gin saw the existing autocracy as part of the solution rather than part of the problem. He praised the former governor-general Bibikov, whose heavy-handed rule had fully integrated the Southwest into the empire's legal and administrative structures while improving economic conditions for the peasants.[56] The 1861 emancipation had freed the Orthodox masses, Shul'gin concluded, and the Polish insurrection had awakened educated society from its slumber. It was time for the Russians to shed their "societal lethargy," assume leadership in the region's society, and end the Poles' "national delirium."[57]

Over the following months and years, the specter of "Polish intrigue" loomed large in the pages of *Kievlianin*. The fight against Polish nationalism was not presented as a mere conflict of interest, but as a moral quest to protect the Orthodox population from the national, social, and religious yoke of the Polish nobility. As Mikhail Iuzefovich put it in 1865, "In our struggle against the Polish cause, our opponent is not a material force but a moral force. We do not fight against the Poles but against Polonism—not against a state or a nation but against an idea, which a handful of people represents and wants to force upon us."[58] *Kievlianin* stoked fears of cunning "Jesuit" intriguers capable of using all the region's social elements—the Catholic priesthood, the Jews, and the *khlopomany*—to perpetuate their exploitation of the peasantry. Even if their political activity in Kiev seemed to have subsided, the newspaper repeatedly warned, the Poles retained a disproportionate sway over the countryside and small towns. In order to "depolonize" (*raspoliachit'*) the region, it encouraged Russians to take advantage of the government's favorable land purchasing program and establish a strong Russian landowner class.[59] Such arguments were indicative of a widespread anti-Polish mood in the Russian public sphere after 1863, when the stereotype of the plotting and fanatically Russophobic Pole became a staple of the nationalist press.[60] Since imperial ideology insisted on the essentially Russian nature of the western provinces, it was problematic to demand their Russification. "Depolonization," meanwhile, implied a justified defensive reaction.[61]

Kievlianin's treatment of the Jewish population was more ambivalent. On the one hand, antisemitic tropes abounded in its political editorials and in correspondence from rural regions. Jews were regularly portrayed as agents of the Polish nobility and as exploiters in their own right who precipitated the peasant's ruin through their nefarious work as moneylenders and innkeepers. On the other hand, the solutions *Kievlianin* proposed for the "Jewish question" attested to a rather moderate form of antisemitism. Vitalii Shul'gin advocated the abolition of the Pale of Settlement that limited the area of Jewish residence in the empire—not on humanitarian grounds but because it imposed an undue economic burden on the Orthodox population of the western provinces. If Jews were allowed to live in the large cities and in the Great Russian heartland, Shul'gin believed, they would be absorbed by the Russian nation "like a drop in the sea" and ultimately become "Russian citizens of Mosaic faith." Another journalist advocated Russian-language Jewish schools so as to facilitate assimilation.[62] In short, *Kievlianin*'s authors were confident that legal improvements and Russian education would eventually solve the "Jewish question." However, toward the end of the decade, the paper assumed a more unequivocally antisemitic stance that expressed itself in conspiracy theories and an obsession with the issue of Jewish draft dodging.[63]

The third potential threat to the region's "Russian, Russian, Russian" nature, Ukrainophilism, posed the greatest difficulties for *Kievlianin*. In one of the first issues, Vitalii Shul'gin placed a rather confused commentary on the various forms of *khlopomanstvo*. Some *khlopomany*, he asserted, were cunning agents of Polonization, while others were antinational revolutionaries, and still others were federalist dreamers

В. Я. Шульгинъ.

FIGURE 3. Vitalii Shul'gin, drawing by P. Borel'. *Drevniaia i Novaia Rossiia*, no. 5 (1879): n.p. Courtesy of the Regenstein Library, University of Chicago.

pining for a long-lost past.[64] He also stressed the fundamental difference between the scholarly Ukrainophilism of the 1840s and the radical political "separatism" of recent years, which he saw as the dangerous hobby of bored university students. Yet, in a half-sentence, he grudgingly admitted that some Ukrainophiles were "extraordinary personalities" who had done good pedagogical work in the region.[65]

While he opposed political Ukrainophilism in principle, Shul'gin tried not to alienate the Ukrainophiles completely, perhaps hoping to put them back onto the track of modest regional patriotism. The collaboration of one young Ukrainophile with *Kievlianin* is a telling episode. Mykhailo Drahomanov (Mikhail Dragomanov) had studied history with Vitalii Shul'gin, who recommended him as a candidate for a future professorship. Drahomanov had taught in Kiev's Sunday schools and later at the Temporary Pedagogical School, a private training institution for rural teachers. He planned to write a primer that would lead schoolchildren from readings in their rural Ukrainian dialect toward literary Russian and Church Slavonic texts, a project that ended when conservative bureaucrats became suspicious. Drahomanov saw Ukrainian-language teaching as a means toward popular enlightenment rather than a goal in itself—a viewpoint for which his more nationalistic peers criticized him as a "cosmopolitan."[66] In a series of articles that he contributed to *Kievlianin* in 1865, he timidly praised the educational movement of the early 1860s.[67] According to Drahomanov, Vitalii Shul'gin encouraged him to write about the advantages of reintroducing the "local element"—in Drahomanov's interpretation, the Ukrainian language—into the region's rural schools. Subsequently, however, fearing the governor-general's reaction, Shul'gin told him to publish his texts in the Petersburg press. When Katkov's newspaper *Moskovskiia vedomosti* mentioned one of the articles in the same breath as the recent attempt to assassinate the tsar, Shul'gin advised Drahomanov to drop the topic altogether.[68]

Indeed, *Kievlianin*'s tone toward the Ukrainophiles was noticeably softer for a short while in 1866. Instead of calling them Polish agents or revolutionaries, Vitalii Shul'gin presented *khlopomanstvo* as "the innocent game of university youth," and Ukrainian separatism as a "mirage," invented by Poles in order to deflect attention from their own antigovernment activism. Yet he shied back from praising the Ukrainophiles unequivocally. While the most capable among them opposed separatism, he explained, they had failed to promote the rapprochement between South Russians and Great Russians.[69] Shortly afterward, Iuzefovich and Shul'gin (without naming names) criticized Drahomanov's defense of teaching in Ukrainian—and thus an article that, according to Drahomanov, Shul'gin had himself inspired.[70] When *Sankt-Peterburgskiia vedomosti* asked Shul'gin to state categorically whether he found administrative repressions against Ukrainophilism justified and beneficial, his answer carefully avoided such a statement. Repeating that the Ukrainophile danger was a "mirage," he blamed the Ukrainophiles for helping the Poles create the phantom of separatism, for engaging in actual separatism, and for keeping students from their work.[71] Shul'gin's self-contradictory rambling exposes his dilemma: while afraid of the Ukrainophiles, he still hoped that some of them might become useful to the Russian cause. Later that same year, he gave Volodymyr Antonovych the opportunity to defend himself against criticism in the Polish press and to declare his allegiance to the region's "Russian nationality."[72]

It appears, then, that Vitalii Shul'gin briefly tried to negotiate a minimal (anti-Polish) consensus with the more moderate Ukrainophiles. While severely delimiting the scope of acceptable Ukrainophilism in *Kievlianin*, he occasionally gave them a platform to voice their opinions. Yet Shul'gin's concessions were minute. If an open conflict did not erupt, this was only because the second half of the 1860s was, in Drahomanov's words, "an intermission in the history of Ukrainophilism." Stifled by the Valuev Circular and the exile of several activists, the Ukrainian national movement became almost inactive in Kiev. Several important Ukrainophiles focused on their academic careers: Antonovych, Drahomanov, and Kistiakivs'kyi all received their master's degrees and began to teach at Kiev University.[73] Under such conditions, a tacit understanding with *Kievlianin* seemed possible to some Ukrainophiles on the basis of their shared allegiance to the region's Orthodox peasants. Antonovych later claimed that he had always understood Shul'gin's "moral value" but had compromised with him in order to publicize at least half or three-quarters of his views.[74] It would not take much for the fragile armistice to fall apart in acrimony.

Two Teachers

Honoring his commitment to his deceased brother and sister-in-law, Vitalii Shul'gin saw to it that his nephew and nieces received a good education. Vitalii taught the children at home and even took them on a trip to Germany.[75] He introduced young Iakov to the university students who attended private historical seminars in his home and made use of his rich library collection.[76] One frequent visitor was Mykhailo Drahomanov, who soon became a role model for Iakov. As a gymnasium student, Iakov was taught by several former Sunday school activists, including Drahomanov and Pavlo Zhytets'kyi. These teachers awakened in their students an interest in the regional past by reading to them from the Cossack chronicles of the seventeenth and eighteenth centuries. Drahomanov, teaching "Russian" geography, stressed the difference between Great Russia's industry and Ukraine's grain-producing agriculture. His classes were probably Iakov's first introduction to Ukrainophile ideas and doubtless influenced his decision to become a historian. Alongside three classmates—his cousin Vladimir Shcherbina (Volodymyr Shcherbyna), whose memoirs are the main source on Iakov's youth, and their friends Volodymyr (Vladimir) Naumenko and Ivan Kamanin—Iakov entered Kiev University's historical-philological faculty in 1868.

After a period of stagnation in the 1860s, the faculty was undergoing a revival. Within a few years, several young professors received chairs. When Drahomanov was studying abroad from 1870 to 1873, the gap he left was filled by the former *khlopoman* Volodymyr Antonovych. Antonovych lectured on Russian history, focusing on the region's medieval and early modern past.[77] In his opening lecture, which impressed Iakov and his friends, Antonovych demanded a patriotic yet critical attitude from historians. Whereas Northeast Russia had a history of statehood, he explained, historians of Southwest Russia must describe—and thus become part of—the Little Russian people's struggle for their nationality: "every educated representative of the Russian nationality in the Southwest region must still for a long time continue by peaceful civic activity the struggle that his ancestors began with a weapon in hand."[78] While sticking to the officially acceptable position of struggle against the Polish nobility, Antonovych also stressed the region's particularities as against Muscovy. Outside the classroom, he motivated students to begin independent work with archival sources, encouraged them to excavate a grave field outside the city, and organized them into circles to collect materials for a Ukrainian dictionary.[79]

The years of Iakov Shul'gin's studies were marked by increasing agitation among Kiev students. They organized a student library, a cheap canteen, and an informal mutual savings bank for those who could not afford their studies. Broad self-education became a cherished goal, with lawyers reading about biology and medics delving into sociology or economics. The young Kievans acquainted themselves with the most progressive Russian and European thinkers of their time, including Nikolai Chernyshevskii, Dmitrii Pisarev, John Stuart Mill, Charles Darwin, and Herbert Spencer; the more radically inclined cited Karl Marx, Charles Fourier, and Pierre-Joseph Proudhon. The university lecturer Nikolai Ziber, remembered today as Russia's first Marxist economist, privately taught Marx's *Capital* to student circles. In the early 1870s, Russia's liberal-constitutionalist and revolutionary movements were not yet completely separated, and the student canteen became the scene of heated debates between liberals and radicals. One contemporary later remembered Iakov Shul'gin as the leader of the radical students in these debates.[80] At a student assembly in 1875, he read out an article from Petr Lavrov's socialist journal *Vpered!*, causing an exchange of insults with a liberal law student who ended up giving Iakov a thrashing. A student tribunal vindicated Iakov's behavior, but the gendarmes warned him that they would arrest him if he turned up at another assembly.[81]

Ukrainophile ideas became popular among some students around 1872 or 1873. At this time, Iakov Shul'gin participated in a mixed-gender Ukrainian circle that met in private homes for discussions and drinking bouts.[82] Few Kiev students combined radicalism and Ukrainophilism like Iakov did, however. Mykhailo Drahomanov later remembered his exasperation about the antagonism between Ukrainophile and radical circles that he found in Kiev upon his return in 1873: "I would answer them that they were just poor radicals, for a radical who does not recognize Ukrainianism in Ukraine is only an intellectually incomplete radical, just as a Ukrainophile who has not thought enough to become radical is only a poor Ukrainophile."[83]

The emergence of Ukrainophile student circles followed the reawakening of the city's older Ukrainophile milieu after years of stagnation. The membership of the Kiev Hromada increased; its most active members during these years included university lecturers (Antonovych, Drahomanov, Ziber), gymnasium teachers (Zhytets'kyi, Fedir Vovk, Vil'iam Berenshtam, Iurii Tvitkovs'kyi), the playwright Mykhailo Staryts'kyi, and the energetic writer Pavlo Chubyns'kyi.[84] Exiled to northern Russia for his Ukrainophile activism, Chubyns'kyi had acquired the reputation of a gifted ethnographer. In 1869, the Imperial Russian Geographic Society chose him to lead an extended expedition across right-bank Ukraine—a venture meant to prove that this was ethnographically Russian, not Polish territory.[85] For the next year and a half, Chubyns'kyi traveled across and beyond the region, collecting ethnographic material and statistics with the help of Hromada members and sympathizers. In 1872, he combined forces with Governor-General Aleksandr Dondukov-Korsakov and with several conservative public figures (including Vitalii Shul'gin) to get permission for the opening of a local branch of the Imperial Geographical Society.

The Kiev branch of the Geographical Society (KGS) opened in February 1873, offering a legal channel for several of the activities that the Hromada had so far conducted clandestinely: the publication of

Ukrainian popular songs and fairy tales, the preparation of material for a Ukrainian dictionary, and the distribution of popular literature in Ukrainian. More than half of the society's founding members belonged to the Hromada, others sympathized with it, and only a few were outsiders, among them Vitalii Shul'gin, Mikhail Iuzefovich, and the university's rector Nikolai Bunge.[86] The role of these conservatives in the society has been subject to debates. While some accounts present Shul'gin and Iuzefovich as the true initiators of the branch's foundation (which seems to have been their own view), other sources claim that the Ukrainophiles only invited them in order to profit from their solid reputation.[87]

Between 1869 and 1873, Vitalii Shul'gin's *Kievlianin* championed the Ukrainophiles' cultural endeavors as evidence of an increasingly active Russian society in the region. The paper regularly reported on the progress of Chubyns'kyi's expedition, encouraging readers to support his patriotic yet scholarly and neutral effort.[88] One journalist hailed the Ukrainophile composer and Hromada member Mykola Lysenko as a serious musical ethnographer and a talented representative of the "Russian national school."[89] *Kievlianin* also praised the newly opened Geographical Society branch, and in turn, Chubyns'kyi catered to imperial patriots by calling the region "the cradle of the Russian nation."[90] Once more, imperial patriots and Ukrainophiles put their differences aside, but these could easily resurface.

A telling event took place in September 1871, as the city's entire (Orthodox) intelligentsia gathered to celebrate the fifty-year anniversary of Mikhail Maksimovich's literary work. Such diverse figures as Vitalii Shul'gin, Mikhail Iuzefovich, Nikolai Bunge, and Volodymyr Antonovych delivered speeches honoring the leader of Kiev's nonpolitical Ukrainophiles of the 1840s. Even as they appeared to speak for the same cause, a latent disagreement between Shul'gin and Antonovych was discernible in their speeches. While Antonovych asked Maksimovich's blessing for a new generation of scholars following his path, Shul'gin complained that this young generation failed to honor their predecessors, creating new idols instead.[91] However, if Shul'gin was right that Antonovych and his peers worked toward a different long-term goal than had Maksimovich, there could be no doubt that they were now at the forefront of scholarship in the region.

Indeed, Ukrainophilism became attractive to Kiev's youth in the early 1870s precisely because its proponents formed the university's and the city's most vibrant intellectual community. Drahomanov, Antonovych,

Chubyns'kyi, Ziber, and the lawyer Kistiakivs'kyi impressed the students with their academic work, initiated them into scholarly methods, and thus acquired authority in political questions, too.[92] Iakov Shul'gin's mentors were Drahomanov and Antonovych. While the former influenced his increasingly radical views on social and educational questions, the latter impressed him with his meticulous yet politically committed historical research. Inspired by his teachers and by Lev Tolstoi's pedagogical ideas, Iakov cofounded a private school at the Shatov brickyard in the working-class suburb of Demievka. He even planned to use his substantial inheritance of 15,000 rubles to organize Ukrainian-language popular schools.[93]

The few extant sources suggest that Iakov Shul'gin's worldview was formed by impulses that also radicalized youths elsewhere in the empire. A high moral standard frustrated by the continuing injustice of Russian society; acquaintance with "progressive" political and scientific literature through student reading circles; an avid reception of the illegal socialist press published abroad; first contacts with "the people" during attempts to teach factory workers—all these often figure in the (auto-)biographies of those whom a recent study calls the "Seventies generation."[94] In provincial Kiev with its small intelligentsia, the university was particularly significant in shaping the ideas of youth. Like his teachers Drahomanov and Antonovych, Iakov Shul'gin came to view the national and social question as deeply interconnected. His wish to improve the peasantry's situation likely sparked his dedication to Ukrainian national culture. At any rate, his growing sympathies for Ukrainophilism did not reflect a desire to express his inborn "ethnicity" or "native culture" more freely. For, having grown up among Kiev's Russian-speaking intelligentsia, Iakov hardly knew any Ukrainian. He would learn to speak the language only as an adult, from Galician émigrés in Vienna.[95]

Iakov's nonnative command of Ukrainian was far from exceptional for a Ukrainophile of this period. His mentor Antonovych, born into the Polish gentry, learned Ukrainian as his fifth language after Polish, French, Russian, and Latin. Drahomanov descended from Ukrainian Cossacks and learned the language growing up in the countryside and reading Ukrainian literature as a teenager.[96] Yet he, too, felt most comfortable using Russian and continued to publish in both languages even in exile. Antonovych and Drahomanov conducted their correspondence in Russian throughout the 1870s and 1880s, while their wives often wrote to each other in Ukrainian.[97] Iakov's friend Volodymyr

Naumenko came from a family of Ukrainian Cossack origin, but—except for his father's Ukrainian anecdotes and proverbs—only Russian was spoken in his childhood home. A gifted linguist, Naumenko would become the Hromada's main expert in the Ukrainian language, but only after studying it at the university. Among the Hromada members, Ziber was half Swiss, Berenshtam was a Jewish convert to Lutheranism, Aleksandr Rusov was Russian, and his wife Sofiia Rusova (née Lindfors) came from a Russian-speaking family with French and Swedish roots.[98] Even Ivan Franko, the son of a rural Galician blacksmith, tried his hand at Polish prose, wrote German letters, and flirted with Russophile circles during his youth. Only under the influence of Drahomanov's socialism did he embrace the Ukrainian project to become the best-known Ukrainian writer of his generation.[99] Their political views, not their ethnic background, united the Ukrainophiles. In Kiev, the Russian language remained their preferred means of communication, a tendency that was increased by repression against Ukrainian literature. A popular epigram of the late 1870s mocked the Ukrainophiles' custom of resorting to Russian whenever they had to discuss complex matters:

Sobiralis' malorossy	Gathered were the Little Russians,
V tesno splochennom kruzhke	Meeting in their tight-knit throng
Obsuzhdali vse voprosy	They debated all the questions
Na rossiiskom iazyke.	Speaking in the Russian tongue.[100]

Kiev's Ukrainophiles of the 1870s were not radical nationalists intent on breaking all cultural and political ties with Russia. Most of them were employed by the tsarist state. As Drahomanov wrote in 1872, "The cause of Ukrainian education in Russia is tightly connected with the progress of the entire state and the development of that new, free Russia, of which democratic Ukrainophilism was and is only one aspect."[101] For Drahomanov, Ukrainophilism only made sense within a broad All-Russian progressive movement. Ukraine needed Russian literature and the Russian language in order to profit from the most progressive European artistic and scholarly trends. Ukrainian-language literature, he argued, could not cover all intellectual needs and should be written about and for the simple people. In political terms, Drahomanov envisaged Ukraine as an autonomous part of a future federalized Russia or even of a pan-Slavic federation, but this part of his program was rather vague.[102] This was hardly the credo of a staunch anti-Russian nationalist, and yet it would be enough to provoke angry reactions from the conservative sector of Kiev's intelligentsia.

Unlike Drahomanov, Kiev's other Ukrainophiles did not write detailed programs for future action. While most of them were committed to building a Ukrainian high culture, they did not find it realistic or desirable to replace Russian in all sectors of public life. However, they saw Ukraine's traditions as profoundly different from those of Russia and believed that the region needed different educational and political solutions. This brought them into conflict with pro-imperial conservatives and with the centralizing state. In all likelihood, this disagreement between a commitment to local specificity and a centralist approach, as well as different attitudes toward the autocracy, also fueled arguments within the Shul'gin family between the young radical Iakov and his conservative uncle Vitalii.

Uncles and Nephews

By 1874, Kiev's Ukrainophiles were successfully using for their own purposes several institutions unintentionally provided by the government: Kiev University, the Kiev branch of the Imperial Geographical Society, and the ethnographic expeditions organized by the latter.[103] As their popularity among the students grew and their standing in Kiev's academic institutions improved, they began to propagandize their Ukrainophile views more boldly. In the autumn of 1874, Drahomanov and other Hromada members became editors of the local newspaper *Kievskii telegraf*, thus acquiring their own press organ to compete with Vitalii Shul'gin's *Kievlianin*. At about the same time, *Kievlianin* launched an attack against Ukrainophilism in general and against the KGS and Drahomanov in particular.

Kievlianin attacked on various fronts, but the thrust of its accusations was always the same: that the Ukrainophiles were promoting Ukrainian separatism under the "neutral flag" of science.[104] Translations of Russian literature into Ukrainian were repeatedly targeted. Already in February, the paper criticized the text of an opera by the Hromada members Staryts'kyi and Lysenko for "forcing a common literary quality onto a language where every bell tower has its own idiom."[105] A few months later, *Kievlianin* reviewed a Ukrainian translation of *Taras Bul'ba* by Nikolai Gogol' (Mykola Hohol'), in which the words

"Russian, Russian land, Russian person" had been translated as "Ukrainian, Ukraine, Cossack." "You are playing with fire," wrote a furious Vitalii Shul'gin, insinuating that, as in the 1860s, the state might punish the Ukrainophiles.[106] *Kievlianin* also lambasted Drahomanov's views on the usefulness of local dialects in education, claiming that the Little Russian dialect was dying out and inhibited the acquisition of Russian literacy.[107]

Another point of disagreement concerned the census conducted by the KGS in Kiev in early 1874. *Kievlianin* objected to the design of language categories in the census: in addition to "Great Russian," "Little Russian," and "Belorussian," the demographers had included "Common Russian" (i.e., the literary standard language) as a fourth option. *Kievlianin* suspected a deliberate attempt to split up and minimize the number of Russian speakers in Kiev. The KGS denied the charge, and an exchange of rather sophistic arguments ensued. Despite some good scholarly work, Vitalii Shul'gin wrote, the KGS had become hermetically closed like a Catholic order and spent much of its energy trying to force the Little Russian dialect upon a Russian-speaking population.[108] *Kievskii telegraf*, in turn, accused *Kievlianin* of impeding the population's enlightenment and conjuring up the phantom of anti-Russian agitation, inspired by the same anti-peasant and anti-Ukrainophile prejudice that had motivated the Polish nobility back in the 1860s.[109]

The ideological feud between Vitalii Shul'gin and Mykhailo Drahomanov took a personal turn after a failed attempt at reconciliation. In August, a *Kievlianin* correspondent claimed that Drahomanov had denied the connection between Great Russian and Little Russian folk epos (*byliny* and *dumy*) at a recent congress.[110] Drahomanov reacted with an angry open letter to *Kievlianin*, complaining that his views had been intentionally misrepresented in order to politicize a scholarly disagreement. Instead of printing the letter, Shul'gin offered peace to his former student. Tired of this "matter of which everybody is sick," he sent Drahomanov a private letter, assuring him that he still respected him and would prefer not to continue the polemic. At this point, Drahomanov added insult to injury. Not only did he insist that his letter be published (which Shul'gin did, adding snide comments), but he also printed Shul'gin's private note in *Kievskii telegraf*. A deeply offended Shul'gin declared an end to their friendship: "Where is your moral instinct, Mr. Dragomanov? . . . We regret that you have chosen such a . . . path."[111]

As the polemic between *Kievlianin* and *Kievskii telegraf* continued into 1875 and spread to the Moscow and Petersburg press, it was too late for mediation. Vitalii Shul'gin wrote that he had read and understood Dra-homanov's pseudonymous programmatic articles in the Galician press "despite all cunning obfuscation"—implying that, notwithstanding all his statements of Ukrainian-Russian solidarity, Drahomanov was re-ally a political separatist.[112] In spring, Iuzefovich angrily denounced the Ukrainophile danger at a dinner in honor of Governor-General Dondukov-Korsakov. Instead of acting against the KGS, Dondukov even prevented the publication of a polemical article that Iuzefovich had written for *Kievlianin*, hoping to avoid publicity for the Ukraino-philes.[113] In July, Platon Antonovich, the curator of the Kiev educational district, recommended that the Ministry of Popular Enlightenment re-move Drahomanov from Kiev University. Two weeks later, however, he vouched for the political reliability of his (unrelated) namesake Volody-myr Antonovych, referring to the recommendations of none other than Antonovych's direct superior, the anti-Ukrainophile denunciator Iuze-fovich.[114] Around the same time, Drahomanov, Chubyns'kyi, and the other Ukrainophiles (including Iakov Shul'gin, who had written very little) left *Kievskii telegraf*.[115]

When the attempt to act through the local administrative organs failed, Iuzefovich sent a denunciation to the central police in Saint Pe-tersburg. In August 1875, Tsar Alexander established a Special Council on Ukrainophilism, for which Iuzefovich composed a lengthy memo-randum. Listing all the supposedly separatist activities of the KGS and Kiev's Ukrainophiles, this memorandum served as the basis of new re-pressions.[116] In April 1876, Iuzefovich drafted a resolution for action against "Ukrainophile propaganda," which, after substantial correc-tions, the tsar signed on 18 May during a stay in the German spa town of Ems. Reinforcing and sharpening the provisions of the 1863 Valuev Circular, the Ems Ukaz prohibited the publication of all texts in the "Little Russian dialect," except for fine literature and historical or eth-nographic documents, which, however, had to be published in Russian orthography. It also prohibited stage performances in Ukrainian and the publication of Ukrainian-language song lyrics. Furthermore, the edict stipulated that the southwestern schools be purged of Ukrain-ophile teachers, that the KGS be closed, that *Kievskii telegraf* be shut down, and that Drahomanov and Chubyns'kyi be immediately exiled from the region.[117]

By this time, Drahomanov was no longer in Kiev. After rejecting several offers to leave the university voluntarily, he was fired in September 1875 and soon departed for Vienna. Iakov Shul'gin, too, traveled abroad in the autumn of 1875. Realizing that he would not be employed by one of the increasingly conservative gymnasia, he embarked on an extended study trip to Austria, Germany, Switzerland, and France.[118] Historians have noted that Drahomanov and Chubyns'kyi, the most prominent victims of the KGS affair, were ironically among the most pro-Russian of Kiev's Ukrainophiles.[119] The extremely cautious Volodymyr Antonovych enjoyed the trust of the local authorities, though some officials suspected that he was in fact more nationalist and less conciliatory toward the state than Drahomanov and Chubyns'kyi. Vitalii Shul'gin apparently shared this opinion, commenting in private that the authorities had "missed the horse and hit the cart" (*ne po koniu, tak po ogloble*).[120] Vitalii Shul'gin himself had become extremely unpopular among Kiev's Ukrainophiles, who blamed "the hunchback" (*gorbun*) and Iuzefovich for the repressions.[121] Isolated from the city's progressive intelligentsia, Vitalii Shul'gin died from a heavy cold on Christmas day 1878, leaving behind his wife, his daughters Lina (Pavla) and Alla, and his one-year-old son Vasilii.

The division within the Kiev intelligentsia can be analyzed on several intersecting levels. Most obviously, this was a conflict between emerging national movements, between those who wanted to promote an autonomous Ukrainian culture and those who saw it merely as a local variant of an overarching Russian culture. Drahomanov, Chubyns'kyi, Antonovych, and other Ukrainophiles tried to create a nationally tinged science, to provide Ukraine with such "compulsory" elements of national culture as ethnographic studies, dictionaries, and a fully developed literary language. *Kievlianin* fought against Ukrainian-language schools and against the creation of a Ukrainian high culture because Vitalii Shul'gin saw cultural particularism as a preliminary stage of political separatism. Instead, he and his allies wanted to stick to traditional Little Russian patriotism, where local ethnographic specificities could be celebrated but political aspirations had to be subordinated to Russian state interest and directed exclusively against the Poles.[122] As Mikhail Iuzefovich put it in his memorandum to the Special Council, "The Little Russians have never put their homeland [*rodiny*] above their fatherland [*otechestva*], and if some educated people expressed their love for it with sympathy for its tribal element—its customs, melodies, poetic work, historical traditions and similar local traits—this was a natural feeling just like the love for one's domestic hearth."[123] In Miroslav Hroch's terminology, Shul'gin and Iuzefovich had sympathies for the "antiquarian" phase A of the Ukrainian national movement, but could not tolerate its passage to the politicized phase B.

At the same time, this was a struggle over the relationship between local society and the imperial state. The KGS activists were not only nationalists but also proponents of social change and democratization through popular education. In their view, the Ukrainian peasantry needed to be intellectually and politically mobilized through bottom-up activism. While they saw the autocratic state as an occasionally useful tool for their educational purposes, their long-term goal was to democratize and federalize it so as to serve the needs of the peasant masses. For Vitalii Shul′gin, by contrast, the autocratic state was the ideal instrument to improve the situation of the peasants, whom it had freed from serfdom. He concurred with most bureaucrats that the state had to control elementary education so as to assimilate the peasants directly into the empire's Russian majority culture. Neither side tried to achieve a total independence of "civil society" from the state. Both parties consisted of local activists, and both enlisted the help of imperial authorities: Iuzefovich appealed to the gendarmes, whereas Governor-General Dondukov-Korsakov repeatedly tried to protect the Ukrainophiles. Certain bureaucrats were ready to use the Ukrainophiles' intellectual potential for educational purposes while containing their political aspirations.[124]

The conflict took place in the same year as the "Going to the People," which reached its apogee in the summer of 1874. Thousands of students left Russia's cities to preach revolutionary populist (*narodnik*) ideas among peasants.[125] In Kiev, increasing numbers of students adhered to the various strands of populism, and the city was affected by the first wave of arrests of *narodniki* in 1874.[126] During his trip abroad, Drahomanov had been in contact with Petr Lavrov, one of the main populist ideologues. Antonovych had long shared Lavrov's views about the intelligentsia's debt to the people. Iuzefovich's memorandum alluded to these ideological affinities by claiming that the Ukrainophiles' democratic agitation among the peasants might reawaken "the old violent instincts of the population" and result in armed uprisings akin to those of the Haidamaks, Ukrainian bandits of the eighteenth century.[127] Overall, however, although the rising tide of revolutionary agitation certainly helped to alert the authorities to all kinds of oppositional behavior, the threat of socialist revolution was not the main argument used against the Ukrainophiles. Indeed, a broader convergence between Ukrainophiles and socialists only happened in the second half of the decade.

Finally, there was a generational dimension to the dispute. Iuzefovich and Shul′gin resented the rejection of their authority and expertise

by the younger men. They must have expected more respect from
Shul'gin's former student Drahomanov and from Antonovych, Iuzefovich's subordinate at the Archaeographic Commission. According to
one Ukrainophile, Vitalii Shul'gin had hoped to become president of
the KGS and felt affronted when the younger activists relegated him to
a minor role.[128] Drahomanov slighted Shul'gin by criticizing *Kievlianin*
in the Petersburg press and by refusing reconciliation; disparaging remarks about Iuzefovich's advanced age may also have been involved.[129]
What is more, Vitalii Shul'gin had always seen political Ukrainophilism
as a result of immaturity and youthful enthusiasm. The leaders of the
"young generation" were no longer in their first youth: Antonovych was
forty in 1874, Chubyns'kyi was thirty-five, and Drahomanov thirty-
two. It is thus symptomatic that Vitalii Shul'gin repeatedly referred to
Ukrainophile activities as "the mischief of adult children" and called
his opponents "little-big people," "not worthy of enmity or anger but
only of laughter."[130] However, as popular gymnasium and university
teachers, the "adult children" attracted many of the brightest young
students to their side. Vitalii Shul'gin must have been extremely an-
noyed that these younger men were drawing the even younger ones (including his own nephew) away from the cause he had so long defended.

Within the intellectual genealogy of Kiev's patriotic intelligentsia,
Vitalii Shul'gin and the Ukrainophiles had a common ancestor in
Mikhail Maksimovich and his nonpolitical, ethnographic Ukrainophilism. However, they developed Maksimovich's heritage into very different directions. While Shul'gin used it to bolster claims of the region's
historical Russianness, the KGS activists followed in the footsteps of
Nikolai Kostomarov, who had turned Maksimovich's ethnographism
into a modern nationalism.[131] In this sense, Antonovych, Drahomanov,
and Chubyn'skyi may be seen as Vitalii Shul'gin's metaphorical "nephews." Vitalii's "father" Maksimovich was their intellectual "grandfather," but they did not stem directly from Vitalii's line.[132] It is only
fitting that Iakov Shul'gin, Vitalii's biological nephew, came to follow
their path.

The definitive split between Vitalii and Iakov must have happened at
some point during the KGS conflict. Isolated pieces of information and
offhand remarks in letters, diaries, and memoirs present the following
picture: Iakov, who was already a radical and Ukrainophile by 1874, decided at some point to break off contact with his uncle out of loyalty to
his political mentor Drahomanov. On 28 March 1875, Iakov became a
member of the KGS; he was accepted at the same session during which

Vitalii Shul'gin and Iuzefovich, in accordance with their own wishes, were excluded from the society.[133] Iakov's sister Vera also sympathized with Ukrainophilism. In 1874, she married Iakov's friend Volodymyr Naumenko, who was already getting involved with the Kiev Hromada; she soon lost contact with Vitalii and his family.[134] In the spring of 1876, Oleksandr Kistiakivs'kyi noted in his diary that "his brother's children, including his young nephew, a candidate of the philological faculty, are ardent opponents of Shul'gin as a public figure."[135]

Some private disagreement may have played a role in the split as well. Over fifteen years later, Iakov wrote in a letter that "thanks to his [Vitalii's] wife, who ended up brutally humiliating him, my relationship with him seemed to end externally, but internally it always remained strong, and my uncle himself acknowledged this in the last days of his life."[136] Here Iakov was referring to his aunt's adultery with the student Dmitrii Pikhno; however, this letter was written in a context in which Iakov had a strong incentive to downplay political reasons for the conflict. At any rate, several sources confirm that Iakov Shul'gin continued to be grateful to his uncle for his good education and to hold him in high regard long after his death in 1878. As an elderly man, he regretted having broken with Vitalii.[137]

However, the split within the Shul'gin family was definitive. Two separate branches emerged that hardly ever met anymore. Iakov Shul'gin was to remain a Ukrainophile for the rest of his life. The promulgation of the Ems Ukaz became a decisive event for his cohort of Ukrainophiles. By severely restricting the range of legal Ukrainophile activities, the edict defined the parameters of the Ukrainophile milieu that was about to emerge on the margins of Kiev's educated society. Its leaders became masters of circumspection, uniquely skilled at negotiating with the authorities and exploiting gray zones. Iakov's children grew up within this milieu and were taught its values. Yet, if there were "nephews," there were also "sons." At *Kievlianin*, Vitalii Shul'gin's intellectual heritage continued to take effect. The banner of Little Russian unity with Russia was upheld first by his former protégé, the young economist Pikhno, and later by Vasilii Shul'gin, a man who was known as (but was not) Vitalii's biological son.[138]

The ideological rift within the Shul'gin family, and the conflict between conservative Little Russians and Ukrainophiles at large, pitted two different national-political projects against each other. Although they both took inspiration from early nineteenth-century regional patriotism, one was meant to strengthen the imperial state, while the other was populist and potentially subversive. Both targeted the same population of Orthodox peasants, and both were interested in the same ethnographic materials and folklore, which meant that their interests occasionally coincided. Over the years, representatives of both projects engaged in a negotiation process over potential commonalities and conflicts.[139] In these debates, the conservative Little Russians usually prevailed, for their positions made it easier to get the state to intervene on their behalf—but the government did not quite adopt their nationalist positions.

Vitalii Shul'gin's career serves as an excellent example of a Little Russian patriotism that remained fully compatible with imperial loyalism and All-Russian nationalism. A disciple of Mikhail Maksimovich's antiquarian regionalism, Shul'gin shared intellectual roots with the most influential Ukrainophiles of his time. However, unlike them, he believed that the centralized state and the Little Russian peasants could only benefit from each other. The state had the means to institutionalize the region's Russianness, and in turn, it would be rewarded with a prosperous and loyal Russian population. Shul'gin managed to secure state funding to propagate his political project, which was directed above all against the Polish-Catholic elites of right-bank Ukraine. The region's Jewish population, for Shul'gin's *Kievlianin*, was a secondary opponent. The same goes for the Ukrainophiles: Shul'gin had personal connections with many of them and only broke with them definitely when he had lost all hope of turning them back onto the All-Russian path.

The diverging development of ethnographic regionalism into a Ukrainian nationalist project was but one instance of a process that took place all over Central and Eastern Europe in the middle decades of the nineteenth century. In the western borderlands of the Romanov Empire, Finnish, Lithuanian, Latvian, and Estonian nationalists began to connect their enthusiasm for local traditions with demands for peasant-oriented social reform as well as increased cultural and, later, political autonomy.[140] However, as has been convincingly argued in the case of the Habsburg monarchy, most nationalists of this period did not aim to destroy the imperial state. Rather, they worked for a redistribution of resources and cultural privileges within the empire.[141] This also applies to the nineteenth-century Ukrainophiles and, indeed, to most nationalist movements in the Russian Empire—with the notable exception of the Polish nationalists, many of whom never gave up the hope of reestablishing a Polish state.[142] The early protagonists of

Ukrainian nationalism were federalists who participated in all-imperial debates and continued to think within an imperial framework. Nikolai Kostomarov was one of Russia's most prominent historians, Mykhailo Drahomanov championed a progressive movement including both Russians and Ukrainians, and Volodymyr Antonovych made a successful career in the imperial academic institutions. If the state, lobbied by Russian nationalists, nevertheless repeatedly moved against Ukrainian nationalism, this was because the latter represented a direct challenge to the project of a tripartite All-Russian nation.

Younger activists such as Iakov Shul'gin, too, were involved both in a specifically Ukrainian movement and in larger all-imperial debates about socialism and the peasant question. Iakov's biographical path shows that Ukrainian nationalist mobilization in the nineteenth century was not a case of people "becoming conscious" of their preexisting ethnicity (culture, language) and then politicizing it. On the contrary, Iakov chose a political project, populist socialism, and then worked to become a good member of the corresponding national community by learning Ukrainian and studying the region's history. His path toward nationalism was very much that of an urban intellectual trying to approach the peasantry. Nationalism, then, was not the natural political expression of a collective cultural identity. Rather, nationalists consciously chose and crafted their "national identity" to conform to their political goals.

CHAPTER 2

Niche Nationalism

Kiev's Ukrainophiles, 1876–1914

In 1893, Eduard Sedlaczek, the Austrian consul in Kiev, sent a report to the foreign minister in Vienna. Describing Kiev's Ukrainophiles, he singled out their cautiousness and secrecy: "The art of hiding their innermost thoughts and feelings is highly developed and almost innate in the Little Russians. . . . In public life the Little Russians never reveal their national ideals; in the struggle for existence, they strive to attain any available post, behaving correctly in office but remaining true to their national ideals." Among his acquaintances, Sedlaczek continued, were many bureaucrats and teachers "whose behavior in office is considered praiseworthy but who reveal a less than government-friendly disposition in their intimate circle."[1] The Austrian consul was a good observer. Indeed, the repressive political climate under the Ems Ukaz had forced Ukrainophilism out of the public sphere. In order to avoid state repression and succeed professionally, Kiev's Ukrainophiles had to retreat into societal niches and compromise with the authorities.

With regard to the history of the Ukrainian movement in the Russian Empire, the decades between 1876 and 1905 have attracted little scholarly attention. According to the generally accepted narrative, Ukrainian nationalism all but died out in the empire after the restrictions imposed by the Ems Ukaz. The movement's center shifted to

Austrian Galicia, where Ukrainian political parties were formed and achieved their first political successes. Galician Drahomanovite circles and, later, Social Democratic groups, further developed the ideology of Ukrainian nationalism, while the few remaining Ukrainophiles in the Russian Empire dedicated themselves to nonpolitical cultural activism. Only in the last years of this period did a younger generation of activists reintroduce political goals to the movement.[2]

While this account is not incorrect, it fails to explain how Kiev's Ukrainophiles adapted to the repressive conditions and why a seemingly nonpolitical milieu ultimately created a new political dynamic. Ukrainophiles' personal and private lives, the subject of this chapter, provide some of the answers. Private life and academic research provided safe spaces for the expression of Ukrainophile views.[3] In the Russian Empire, these two niches assured the survival of Ukrainian nationalism during the 1880s and 1890s and prepared the ground for its blossoming in the early twentieth century.

Several aspects of Iakov Shul'gin's biography after 1876 are emblematic of the Ukrainophile experience in this period. These include his contacts with Russia's radical opposition, his encounter with state repression, and the constant conflict between biographical constraints and idealistic aspirations as he sought to forge a pedagogical career within a state that contradicted his principles. As a Ukrainophile historian, Iakov Shul'gin contributed to an intellectual tradition that constantly had to maneuver between the expectations of nationalist readers and the demands of state censorship. The main arena of Iakov's activism, however, was his private and family life. Kiev's fin-de-siècle Ukrainophile milieu constituted itself in private households, with women playing leading roles as organizers, educators, and domestic ideologues. Iakov and his wife Liubov tried to educate their children in a Ukrainian patriotic spirit, following a model of nationally framed domesticity. This "patriotic education" was formative for a new generation of nationalists—and yet, even this younger generation did not break all ties with Russian imperial society.

Radical Populism, Ukrainophilism, and the State

The sketchy evidence on Iakov Shul'gin's travels in Western Europe suggests that he completed his path toward social radicalism and Ukrainian nationalism during this time. In the winter of 1875–1876, he heard lectures on political economy and history in Vienna. In the

Austrian capital, Iakov befriended a few members of the Galician student organization Sich. Among them, far away from Ukraine, he first
began to speak Ukrainian. Via Munich and Straßburg, Iakov arrived
in Switzerland in the summer of 1876.[4] Meanwhile, Mykhailo Drahomanov also traveled to Geneva, where he planned to publish the radical Ukrainian-language periodical *Hromada*, a venture to which Iakov
Shul'gin contributed 12,000 rubles from his inheritance.

During this early Genevan period, Drahomanov established close
contacts with the Russian socialist emigration, and it is likely that Iakov, who stayed in Drahomanov's flat, also befriended the members
of Geneva's radical émigré colony.[5] In a letter from this period, he described the Jews of Ukraine as exploitative proponents of capitalism
in the region; even Jewish proletarians supposedly lived at the expense
of the Orthodox peasants and could therefore not become revolutionaries.[6] Thus, Iakov's socialism at the time still contained elements of
the economically grounded antisemitism propagated by his uncle—but
with an anticapitalist turn. In March 1877, he was arrested in Paris
during a talk given by Victor Hugo. Wrongly accused of having beaten a
police officer, he was sentenced to a month of imprisonment.[7] After his
release, Iakov Shul'gin returned to Geneva, and later in the same year he
traveled back to the Russian Empire.

Since his departure almost two years earlier, the political mood in
Kiev had changed dramatically. Local society was agitated by the Russo-
Turkish War in the Balkans and by several processes against socialist
agitators, many of whom had been active in Ukraine. The Ukrainophile
Hromada circle was shaken by nasty personal quarrels as well as by disagreements of principle, as some younger radicals accused the group of
wasting its forces on useless cultural and educational work instead of
political propaganda. Although some members sympathized with the
radicals, the majority of the Hromada decided to continue focusing on
the study and "enlightenment" of the people.[8]

Iakov Shul'gin, who had joined the Hromada, may well have been
disenchanted with the apolitical course of the Kiev Ukrainophiles. After his return, he began to travel to Odessa regularly and ultimately
settled there. Both Odessa and Kiev were hotbeds of revolutionary
agitation in this period, but Odessa's Ukrainophiles were more inclined to cooperate with the socialist *narodniki*. In the recently founded
Odessa Hromada, the influence of Drahomanov's journal reigned supreme; its leader Leonid Smolens'kyi insisted that the group's main
task was to serve the interests of the peasant population.[9] In Odessa,

Iakov met with revolutionaries such as Volodymyr Mal'ovanyi and Vladimir Debogorii-Mokrievich. He also befriended Andrei Zheliabov, who would be involved in the assassination of the tsar in 1881.[10] Zheliabov hoped at the time that "slowly but surely the two revolutionary currents, the common Russian and the Ukrainian, were merging: not only federation, but unity was near." However, many Hromada members wanted precisely a loose, "federal" connection with the Russian radicals. As the latter increasingly tried to incite peasant uprisings and resorted to political terrorism, most Ukrainophiles no longer found cooperation desirable.[11]

Yet the temporary convergence between Ukrainophiles and radical populists in the late 1870s was no coincidence. The two movements overlapped on several levels. First, there was an ideological affinity between Ukrainophilism and Russian populism. Both disliked the autocratic state and the feudal vestiges in the rural order; both saw the peasantry as the nucleus of a more just and vital society; both idealized the peasants but believed in the need to educate and mobilize them.[12] It would be wrong, however, to see Ukrainophilism as nothing more than a variety of Russian populism transplanted to Ukrainian soil. Ukraine had its own, indigenous populist tradition that stemmed from the Cyrillo-Methodians and the *khlopomany*, drew upon specifically local (Cossack) symbolism and imagery, and sometimes predated analogous developments in Central Russia.[13] Kiev's *khlopomany* had begun to travel the countryside in the late 1850s, long before the first Russian attempts at "Going to the People." And Volodymyr Antonovych's "Confession" of 1862 anticipated the idea of the elite's moral debt to the peasant masses that Petr Lavrov popularized in his "Historical Letters" of 1870. It is no wonder, then, that some Ukrainophiles saw the possibility of an alliance when radical populism spread through Ukraine in the mid-1870s.

Second, Ukrainophiles and *narodniki* drew on a common tradition of political practice. Most members of both movements were intellectually socialized in student reading circles, where they familiarized themselves with progressive fictional, scholarly, or political literature that was excluded from official curricula.[14] As self-education transformed into political activism, these circles became more secretive. One high-ranking gendarme later remarked that Kiev with its large student and worker population and with its hilly, irregular topography was a particularly fertile ground for the creation of secret meeting-places and underground organizations.[15] Both the Hromada and the *narodniki* preferred to meet conspiratorially at private homes, such as the apartment of the Ukrainophile teacher Fedir Vovk or the radical "Kiev commune" in the home of Ekaterina Breshkovskaia, where followers of Lavrov and Mikhail Bakunin engaged in theoretical debates and practical preparations for revolutionary action.[16] The 1874 "Going to the People" revealed further similarities of practice. Like the *khlopomany* fifteen years earlier, the populists donned peasant garb and tried to blend in with the rural population. When the *narodniki* went into the Ukrainian countryside to propagate socialist teachings, they often found that the ground had already been prepared by local Ukrainophiles who worked in the village schools and distributed Ukrainian-language brochures.[17]

Third, there were personal connections between the two movements, intermediaries who rubbed shoulders with both Ukrainian circles and revolutionary underground groups. For a brief period in 1878 and 1879, Iakov Shul'gin fulfilled such a function. Several sources mention him as an emissary between the older, moderate Ukrainophiles and the younger, more revolutionary students.[18] However, the exact scope of his activities is impossible to determine, for the main source of information is police reports of dubious reliability. These reports were based on the denunciations of captured activists, who often hid parts of their knowledge or tried to incriminate as many people as possible. It was extremely difficult for police officers to distinguish actual revolutionary organizations from loose circles or one-off meetings of like-minded people. As a result, they tended to treat all kinds of interaction between suspect individuals as punishable membership in a secret society.[19]

In July 1879, Iakov Shul'gin was arrested in Odessa and exiled by administrative order to Eniseisk in Central Siberia. The reasons given for his arrest were characteristically murky: A document dated November 1879 states that Shul'gin "was in regular contact with the Koval'skii circle, attended meetings at Vitten's and Afanas'eva's, belonged to the revolutionary party, was in contact with members of the Odessa party of the dissatisfied, and corresponded with Kiev revolutionaries." The police also noted his arrest in Paris and rather bizarrely accused him and a friend of traveling to Zhmerinka and drawing attention "with peculiarities of their dress, wearing disgracefully broad-brimmed hats."[20] According to the agents, "Shul'gin was a Ukrainophile and subsequently became a socialist, too, without ceasing to be a Ukrainophile." Some documents in the file suggest that Iakov and others wanted to establish a secret Ukrainophile printing press. In 1880, long after Iakov had arrived in Siberia, dozens of pounds of movable type were found in Zhmerinka and Bendery, two towns close to the Romanian border. The man who had smuggled them across the border testified that they belonged to Iakov Shul'gin, who had planned to publish a Ukraino-phile newspaper.[21] While the police treated this as further proof of Ia-kov's political unreliability, they never referred to the interdiction of Ukrainian-language publications in the Ems Ukaz.

Iakov's arrest and exile must be seen in the context of the massive an-tisocialist campaign that the Russian state began in April 1879 after an unsuccessful attempt on the life of Tsar Alexander II. Distinguished gen-erals were installed as temporary governor-generals in Saint Petersburg, Kharkov, and Odessa; arrests and executions of revolutionaries began immediately. The repression was particularly heavy in Odessa, where every single newspaper office was searched.[22] The Odessa governor-general Eduard von Totleben had eight revolutionaries executed, eighty-eight sent to Siberia, and another forty-one exiled elsewhere.[23] A letter Totleben sent to his colleague in Kiev proves that the main reason for his repressions against Ukrainophiles was fear that their circles might become a recruitment pool for revolutionary socialists:

> The Ukrainophile party has a significant influence on the social movement in Russia. As any party hostile to the government, it is a fertile soil for revolutionary ferment, and, what is most im-portant, perhaps more than any other party it supplies adherents of social doctrine, which is already clear from the fact that so-cialism has manifested itself particularly fiercely in Kiev. . . . The Ukrainophile party in the South includes many teachers, and al-ready from the gymnasium benches they fill the children's heads with social ideas by means of their commentaries on Shevchenko, their tales of free Cossack times, their exaggerated worship of the simple people, their hatred of the authorities etc. Many socialists understand that Ukrainophiles may become excellent "*narodniki*," since the Ukrainophiles, due to their principles—worship of the Little Russian nationality and the autonomy of Ukraine—develop the desire to study the language, everyday life, and customs of the Little Russian people as thoroughly as possible.[24]

If Drahomanov's dismissal in 1875 had been motivated primarily by fear of separatism, the reasons for Iakov Shul'gin's arrest four years later were altogether different. The revolutionary terror campaign against leading government figures concerned the authorities more than manifestations of an independent Ukrainian culture, which it had practically outlawed anyway.

"I Am by No Means a Ukrainophile"

Like most political exiles, Iakov Shul'gin relied on his family's support.[25] His sister Vera and her husband Volodymyr Naumenko sent him money until he began to teach the children of a local official.[26] Through the Naumenkos' efforts, Iakov's case reached the highest echelon of the tsarist administration. They persuaded Nikolai Bunge, the former rector of Kiev University and now Russia's minister of finance, to help the nephew of his late friend Vitalii Shul'gin. The minister asked Viacheslav von Plehve, the head of the Police Department, to reassess the case of this "hotheaded and passionate young man" who "got into the company of people who led him astray." Despite Bunge's intervention, Iakov's situation even deteriorated, as he was imprisoned under accusation of complicity in a fellow exile's escape. His second sister Aleksandra traveled to Saint Petersburg, where she pleaded for Iakov with the vice-minister of the interior, arguing that her brother would not survive another Siberian winter.[27]

When a medical report confirmed the need for Iakov to return to his "native" southern climate, the Police Department allowed him to leave in March 1883, half a year before the end of his sentence.[28] After his arrival in Kiev in October, his hardships were far from over. The Siberian climate had severely damaged his health, and during the following years he repeatedly had to take expensive cures to treat various ailments.[29] His main problem, however, was how to get a job—having given his inheritance to Drahomanov, he was in dire need of money. Since he saw his vocation in teaching history, Iakov would spend the following years trying to get employed by a state whose political form he rejected in principle.

A short article that Iakov published in a Galician journal elucidates this career choice. Ukraine's university students, Iakov wrote, were divided into three groups. The first group were careerists without interest in Ukraine who studied in order to qualify for lucrative government posts. The second, smaller group were politicized students who joined the All-Russian radical movement instead of studying. Since they were no resource for the Russian state, these people usually ended up being sent to Siberia for hard labor. In Iakov's opinion, the only useful group were those students who concentrated on studying Ukraine. However, they were a small minority because the secondary schools were "factories for the production of so-called 'All-Russians.'"[30] After his exile, then, Iakov Shul'gin concluded that it was useless to waste his forces fighting against the state. Instead, he decided to try to improve the educational system from within.

However, the door to state employment was closed soon after Iakov's arrival in Kiev. In September 1884, Colonel Vasilii Novitskii, the head of the Kiev provincial gendarme department, filed a report that classified Iakov as "unreliable" (*neblagonadezhnyi*). Once more, the accusation was based on rumors and on association with other revolutionaries.[31] Nevertheless, Novitskii's report carried enough weight to prevent Iakov from getting employed as a secondary school teacher. In 1888, Iakov wrote to the Kiev school district, begging the curator to give him a chance to "be useful during a pedagogical career." The charges against him, Iakov claimed, were all wrong. He had only been faintly acquainted with some university students who later became revolutionaries, and he had been abroad in the year when he was said to have made an incendiary speech in Kiev.[32] However, all protestations did not help Iakov's cause. Denied state employment, he taught private lessons and continued his historical studies.

Yet money remained scarce, and even more so after the birth of his first two children. In 1892, Iakov once again appealed to Nikolai Bunge, who was now chairman of the ministers' committee. "In the name of your long-standing friendship with my late uncle," he asked Bunge to find him a teaching position. Once more, Bunge failed, owing to the resistance of the local authorities.[33] However, he did procure Iakov a post as bank controller at the new state bank in the provincial city of Elisavetgrad, three hundred kilometers south of Kiev, a well-paid job that solved Iakov's financial troubles. In December 1893, Iakov took up his new post. He served his new employer accurately, even though he lacked all interest in financial matters. In 1899, suspecting the bank's director of enriching himself during the construction of a new bank building, Iakov quit his service and returned to Kiev with his family.[34]

Iakov Shul'gin was now almost fifty years old, and his clandestine activities had taken place twenty years earlier, but their specter continued to haunt him. In 1900, he assumed a modest position in the railway administration. The next year, he began to teach literature at a private gymnasium. However, Iakov's old nemesis intervened once more: gendarme director Novitskii reported to the Kiev governor that "with regard to Iakov Nikolaevich Shul'gin's previous criminal political activity, it would be undesirable to admit him to pedagogical service."[35] In a desperate attempt to save his modest teaching career, Iakov traveled to Saint Petersburg and filed a letter to the minister of the interior. Presenting himself as a loyal state servant, Iakov insisted "that I am by no means a Ukrainophile, of which, as rumor has it, they accuse me."[36] Of course, this was a calculated self-denial to curry favor with the authorities.

This strategy was at last successful. In January 1902, General-Major Novitskii filed another report on Iakov Shul'gin, which completely reversed his earlier position. He had known Shul'gin, "who sinned in his youth by belonging to the Dragomanovites" for twenty-three years, Novitskii wrote: "The above-named Shul'gin is now a frail person oppressed by poverty, pitiable, of a sickly character, but in essence Shul'gin is a wonderful person, impeccably honest, and his misfortune consisted in his sickly, excitable character and his straightforwardness, of which others knew to make use." A victim of the "unrest of minds" during the 1870s, Novitskii continued, Iakov Shul'gin had not thought about politics for twenty years. He recommended admitting him into the pedagogical service, for Iakov "now, in his personal conversations with me, appears as a completely new-born man who fully repents the sins against the state committed in his youth."[37]

What may have caused Novitskii's sudden change of mind? According to Oleksander Shul'hyn, Iakov was told to go meet the gendarme, who was also in Petersburg. Novitskii gave him an unexpectedly warm welcome and told him that none other than Dmitrii Pikhno had vouched for him—the very Pikhno who had been one of the causes for Iakov's rupture with Vitalii Shul'gin in the 1870s, who now managed Vitalii's monarchist paper *Kievlianin*, and whose face Iakov had allegedly once slapped in public in a fit of rage. If we are to believe Oleksander Shul'hyn, Iakov was grateful to his old opponent and paid Pikhno a visit, which Pikhno returned. After this episode there was no further contact between the two.[38] The story cannot be corroborated by any further evidence, but it is fairly plausible in light of the two men's common past and Pikhno's influential position in Kiev's pro-imperial circles.

The Russian state treated Iakov Shul'gin quite harshly, given that the accusations against him were based on hearsay. This treatment was due to his links with revolutionary circles rather than his Ukrainophile convictions. Throughout the period, politically cautious Ukrainophiles such as Volodymyr Antonovych or Volodymyr Naumenko were allowed to teach at the city's university and schools, even though the police

FIGURE 4. Iakov Shul'gin in his later years. *Zapysky Naukovoho Tovarystva im. Shevchenka* 107 (1912): n.p. Courtesy of the University of Illinois Library, Urbana-Champaign.

knew about their dissident views. Meanwhile, the authorities did not encourage Iakov Shul'gin to reverse his national choice and become a Russian loyalist. Rather, he repeatedly had to tout his potential to become useful to the state. Having challenged the patriarchal authority of both his family and the empire, he was forced to appeal to the patronage of powerful relatives and acquaintances—and they, in turn, had to give family loyalty priority over official procedure and political concerns.[39] In general, the degree of micromanagement by these high-ranking bureaucrats is striking. Even though Iakov Shul'gin was a very minor figure among the Russian Empire's suspicious subjects, Finance Minister Bunge and two future ministers of the interior (Viacheslav von Plehve and Ivan Durnovo) were repeatedly involved in his case. When it came to decisions, however, they relied on the local authorities, above all the Kiev gendarme Novitskii.

After his long-delayed admission to pedagogical service, Iakov Shul'gin's relationship with the Russian state was unremarkable. In the following year, he transferred to the First State Gymnasium, where he taught Russian language and literature for the rest of his life.[40] He never again drew the police's attention, but he was not allowed to teach his favorite subject, history, which was considered politically sensitive. During his ten years at the gymnasium, he taught, among others, two subsequently famous Russian writers, Mikhail Bulgakov and Konstantin Paustovskii, the latter of whom mentioned Shul'gin rather dismissively in his memoirs.[41] Iakov Shul'gin died from pneumonia in 1911, at age sixty. Allegedly, more than a thousand people followed his coffin during the funeral procession, among them many students who brought wreaths in the blue and yellow colors of the Ukrainian national movement.[42] The famous Ukrainian historian Mykhailo Hrushevs'kyi honored the deceased in a speech. Hrushevs'kyi praised Iakov as "one of the most characteristic protagonists of Ukrainian life in the 1870s, a distinguished Ukrainian historian, and a man to be remembered for his idealistic disposition and the purity of his character."[43] Hrushevs'kyi's appreciation for this humble and unfortunate schoolteacher points to their shared roots in Kiev's Ukrainophile academic milieu.

Academic Ukrainophilism

The years after 1880 exacerbated the divide within the Russian Empire's Ukrainian movement. Some activists, inspired by the exile Drahomanov, wanted the movement to be openly political and radical.[44] The majority, however, believed that this was not the time for political action; rather, cultural and scholarly work for the nation was needed. Most of Kiev's remaining Ukrainophiles in the heavily reduced Hromada—now known as the Old Hromada—dedicated themselves to teaching and to the study of the region's history and culture, always wary of overstepping the boundaries of the law. In academic discourse, Ukrainophile views could still be expressed, albeit discreetly. Iakov Shul′gin's decision to focus on lawful activism within the state was thus in line with a broader tendency among Kiev's Ukrainophiles.

In moving from political confrontation to cultural gradualism, the Ukrainophiles followed the example of Polish intellectuals. After the crushing defeat of the Polish uprising in 1863, moderate and conservative Polish circles—the so-called Warsaw Positivists and the *Stańczycy* in Cracow—had concluded that insurrections against the ruling empires were counterproductive to the national cause. Instead, they began to concentrate on "organic work" (*praca organiczna*): legal activities aimed at raising the cultural and economic level of the Polish masses. Working within the imperial societies, they focused on popular education, social reform, economic innovation, and historical scholarship, hoping for the gradual improvement of the Poles' political position.[45] Another contemporary parallel was the former Russian populists around the journal *Russkoe bogatstvo*, who in the reactionary 1880s embraced the idea of "small deeds."[46]

Under the prohibitions of the Ems Ukaz, the Ukrainophiles had very limited means to broaden the appeal of their cultural-political project. One of the older Ukrainophiles, Oleksandr Kistiakivs′kyi, insisted that in order to reach out, Ukrainophilism must become a practical, localist endeavor "free of Drahomanovite passions": "The landlord and house owner, industrialist and artisan, merchant and innkeeper, priest and scholar, pedagogue and schoolteacher, tenant and farmer—each and every one must be a conscious Ukrainophile." This, Kistiakivs′kyi believed, would only happen if the Ukrainophiles did not question "the indivisibility of Little Russia and Great Russia."[47] Not all Ukrainophiles were quite as conciliatory as Kistiakivs′kyi, but the moderates prevailed at least with respect to tactics. In 1886, the disagreements between Drahomanov and the Old Hromada erupted into an open conflict. The Hromada had been supporting Drahomanov financially in Geneva, using the funds donated by Iakov Shul′gin. Drahomanov had used the money to issue five volumes of his thick journal *Hromada* between 1878 and 1882. Now, however, the Hromada's members expressed their dissatisfaction with the product of his work, claiming that the dissemination of political pamphlets abroad was ineffective at best and harmful at worst. Rather, they wrote to Drahomanov, the Ukrainophiles should adhere to moderate stances in order not to alienate "those who may not have fully accepted these ideas yet" and who "may still be useful in many of our endeavors."[48]

More than anyone else, it was Drahomanov's old associate Volodymyr Antonovych who stood for this definitive turn toward "culturalism" (*kul'turnytstvo*). A famously cautious character, Antonovych had always adeptly maneuvered the thin line between acceptable local patriotism and subversive Ukrainian nationalism. During the anti-Ukrainophile purge of 1875, Antonovych remained unscathed, not least because the curator of the Kiev school district, his namesake Platon Antonovich, assured the police that Antonovych gave "no cause at all for accusations of political unreliability."[49] He successfully continued his academic career after the Ems Ukaz and was even elected dean of the historical-philological faculty in 1880. In the words of his brother-in-law Kistiakivs'kyi, Antonovych was "a great tactician, a diplomat, and a cagey man" who knew how to hide his radical views from his superiors.[50] Under the restrictive conditions of the Ems Ukaz, Antonovych's capacity to deal with the authorities and to express his ideas cautiously made him the ideal leader for Kiev's small group of Ukrainophiles.

The most pressing problem of the time was the creation of a local press organ sympathetic to Ukrainophile ideas. In the forced absence of a political press, a Russian-language academic journal became the leading Ukrainophile medium.[51] In 1881, several academics, including Antonovych, the historian Aleksandr Lazarevskii, the priest and journalist Petr Lebedintsev, and his brother, the historian Feofan Lebedintsev, decided to establish the historical journal *Kievskaia starina* (Kievan antiquity) and submitted a program proposal to the General Directorate for Press Matters.[52] Feofan Lebedintsev was chosen as the journal's editor. As a middle-aged church historian and brother of a high-ranking priest, he must have seemed like an acceptable, politically reliable figure to the censors.[53] In a similar spirit, the program stressed the journal's intention to research an explicitly Russian antiquity, the "inner, spiritual life" of the "South Russian people." Yet the program also stated that "all this—from the mouths of the Dnieper to the shores of the Bug and Neman, to the headwaters of the San and the foot of the Carpathians—has a common history with Kiev, and all of its past appears to us in one indivisible image of Kievan antiquity."[54] By stressing the cross-border historical and geographical unity of this "South Russian" space, the authors betrayed their Ukrainophile sympathies to those who wanted to see them.

The tension between most authors' Ukrainophile views and the need to accommodate strict censorship guidelines was thus inherent in the project from the very beginning. Among the journal's contributors were Ukrainophiles of the older generation like Nikolai Kostomarov, Antonovych, and the exile Drahomanov (under pseudonym), as well as younger historians of Antonovych's school, such as Iakov Shul'gin. The source publications and studies in *Kievskaia starina* focused on recent centuries, from the time of Polish domination to the early nineteenth century. In line with Antonovych's personal views, the journal showed particular interest in the resistance of the "South Russian" population against Polish rule and Catholicism. Its articles about the Cossacks of the sixteenth and seventeenth centuries and about the poet Taras Shevchenko helped to turn Shevchenko and Cossackdom into two central myths of Ukrainian nationalism.[55]

By using terms like "South Russian," "Little Russian," or "South-western Rus'" instead of the politically contaminated "Ukrainian," the contributors to *Kievskaia starina* let readers decide for themselves whether they wanted to see the region's history as part of a larger Russian history or to focus on its local specificity. Not all the journal's contributors were Ukrainophiles, and even some state officials saw the publication as a useful instrument to advance the study of the region's *Russian* past.[56] When Feofan Lebedintsev died in 1887, *Kievskaia starina* drew closer to the Old Hromada, whose members increasingly shared the editorial responsibilities. In 1893, Iakov Shul'gin's brother-in-law Volodymyr Naumenko became the new editor, keeping this post for the next fourteen years.[57]

For Kiev's academic Ukrainophiles, the writing of history was a practice in the service of nation-building. In the age of nationalism, historians tended to see scholarly objectivity as fully compatible with national commitment.[58] As Volodymyr Antonovych wrote in an obituary for his senior colleague Kostomarov, "A true historian knows that history is national self-awareness and that the more light, truth, and scholarship a people receives, the higher, the more moral, and the mightier it becomes. Spiritual forces are not developed from fantastic tendentious images, but from a sober and, above all, truthful understanding of one's past."[59] Thus, Antonovych saw history writing as an almost metaphysical collective process that could help a nation reach spiritual maturity. While he did not state this openly, the population he hoped to assist in this process was doubtless that of Ukraine—although he may still have conceptualized it in connection with an overarching All-Russian nation. For Antonovych, the main adversary was always the Poles, whose aristocratic culture he disdained since his youth.

The works of Kiev's Ukrainophile historians immensely advanced the idea of a coherent Ukrainian territory with a common past. Besides proclaiming the historical-geographical unity of right-bank Ukraine, the journal also began to include articles about the Dnieper's left bank. Antonovych encouraged his students to write historical monographs about several regions in the southwest and northwest of the Russian Empire. About a dozen of these regional studies were published in the 1880s and 1890s.[60] In the following years, Antonovych's students, sometimes grouped as the Kiev "documentary school" of historiography, became a dominant force in the region's academic life. By 1905, several of them taught at universities in Ukraine.[61]

Antonovych's own work fulfilled another central tenet of nationalist historiography: the construction of the nation's historical continuity.[62] In the very first issue of *Kievskaia starina*, Antonovych took on the Moscow historian Mikhail Pogodin, according to whom Kiev had been founded by Great Russians who migrated northeast after the Tatar invasions, while their former territory was resettled by Little Russians from the Carpathians.[63] Antonovych tried to refute Pogodin's hypothesis by looking at Kiev's Lithuanian period from the conquest by Grand Duke Algirdas (Ol'gerd) in 1362 to the Polish-Lithuanian unification in 1569. Following the lead of earlier Little Russian scholars, he argued that Kiev was continuously settled by Little Russians and remained a strong cultural center that soon turned the Lithuanian Grand Duchy into an Orthodox, linguistically "Russian" state. He presented the city's Lithuanian rulers as sympathizers of the Orthodox Church and the "Russian" population who opposed the Polish-Catholic influence promoted by the ruling branch of the dynasty. In later periods, Antonovych claimed, this task of defending Orthodoxy and nationality had passed on to the free peasants who settled the steppe and became known as Cossacks. "This estate was soon predestined to defend the national rights of Kievan Rus' . . . and win the struggle that the privileged estates of the country had lost before."[64] Thus, a favorable interpretation of the Lithuanian period enabled Antonovych to close the gap between two nationally connoted epochs, medieval Kievan Rus' and the Cossack period.

After the works of Antonovych and other *Kievskaia starina* contributors, only two more steps were needed to complete the construction of a
Ukrainian historical master narrative: the declaration that Ukraine had
a history completely separate from Muscovy's, and a synthesis of the
nation's past—ideally in Ukrainian.[65] Antonovych, who was an archival
worker of an analytic bent rather than a synthesizer, left these tasks to
one of his students, Mykhailo Hrushevs'kyi. The twenty-eight-year-old
Hrushevs'kyi was appointed professor at Lemberg University in Galicia in 1894, a position in which he was allowed to lecture in Ukrainian.[66] Hrushevs'kyi published the first volume of his monumental
Ukrainian-language *History of Ukraine-Rus'* in 1898. His book referred
to "Ukrainian lands" even in the earliest periods, making it quite clear
that the "Rus'ian" state (*Rus'ka derzhava*) was not to be identified with
Russia. Hrushevs'kyi stated this view most succinctly in his 1904 article on "The Traditional Scheme of 'Russian' History and the Problem
of a Rational Organization of the History of the Eastern Slavs." Here
Hrushevs'kyi claimed that Kievan Rus' was created by the Ukrainian
nationality, whereas the later Vladimir-Suzdal' principality was the first
expression of Great Russian statehood. With this article, the Ukrainian
national paradigm took shape as a completely separate historiographical tradition, even though Hrushevs'kyi developed it in constant dialogue with his Russian colleagues.[67]

If various publications in *Kievskaia starina* helped prepare the ground
for this paradigm shift, the politically modest organ of Kiev's Ukrainophiles also contributed to the struggle for a Ukrainian-language press.
Constantly wrestling with censorship, its editor Naumenko increasingly undermined the prohibition of Ukrainian-language publications.
"Legal" bits of Ukrainian text (in Russian orthography), such as folk
songs or dialogues in fiction, appeared in the journal from the beginning. By addressing petitions to the authorities and traveling to Saint
Petersburg every year, Naumenko gradually managed to ease the rules.
In 1897, he was granted the right to publish fiction in Ukrainian, and
in the following year the authorities abolished the rule that Ukrainian
texts had to be judged by a censor in the capital rather than the local
censor. Apparently, the latter initiative was even supported by Kiev's
governor-general Mikhail Dragomirov, who was in friendly relations
with Volodymyr Antonovych and other Ukrainophiles.[68]

Naumenko's obstinate lobbying led to a negotiation process with
the censorship authorities. His cautious approach and good working
relationship with some government officials permitted modest but

significant improvements for the Ukrainophile cause in Kiev. The authorities, too, knew how to play the game. At one point, the Odessa censor was unsure whether to permit the publication of a collection of Ukrainian children's stories. When several administrative organs dodged a definitive ruling, the curator of the Kiev school district left the decision to none other than the notorious Ukrainophile Naumenko. This left Naumenko in an awkward situation: the volume did not contain anything explicitly forbidden, but by recommending it for publication, he would have assumed responsibility for its contents. The manuscript remained caught in administrative limbo.[69]

Openly political debates only entered the pages of *Kievskaia starina* in the late 1890s, after almost twenty years of political quietism. In January 1899, Naumenko engaged in a polemic against the Kievan Slavist Timofei Florinskii, who had criticized the Ukrainian literary language that was increasingly entering the official and scholarly sphere in Austrian Galicia.[70] Responding in *Kievlianin*, Florinskii accused the Galician Ukrainophiles of hiding under their scholarship a "fanatical hatred for Russia, the Russian language, and Russian education."[71] Naumenko took to the defense of Galician attempts to create a Ukrainian high culture. While confirming that he saw Great Russians, Little Russians, and Belorussians as "three branches of one tree," he claimed that even Russophile writers from Galicia were incapable of writing in decent Russian. In his eyes, this alone proved the need for a Ukrainian literary language.[72] However, Naumenko limited his arguments to the "Austro-Russians" of Galicia and Bukovina. Clearly, he did not judge the time ripe to demand the introduction of literary Ukrainian into Russia's schools.

Naumenko's cautious policy achieved its most remarkable success during the revolutionary turmoil of 1904–1905, when Kiev and Petersburg Ukrainophiles persuaded the Imperial Academy of Sciences to release a memorandum in favor of lifting the restrictions against the Ukrainian language. Naumenko headed one of two delegations to Prime Minister Sergei Witte, who raised the issue in the committee of ministers. The committee then commissioned reports from the Academy of Sciences, as well as two universities and the Kiev governor-general. All four reports recommended the immediate abolition of the restrictions of the Ems Ukaz.[73] The memorandum of the prestigious Academy of Sciences, written with the support of Petersburg Ukrainophiles, unequivocally declared that a separate Little Russian literary language was justified both on historical-philological and practical grounds. It stressed that the repressions against the language had been the result of "various coincidences and a one-sided assessment of the social movements of the 1860s and 1870s."[74] The memorandum did not have any practical effect because the Ems Ukaz was simply superseded by the "Provisional Regulations on Censorship" of December 1905. However, its symbolic value was significant, and it continued to be cited in debates over the Ukrainian language in the following years.[75]

While he worked tirelessly for the Ukrainophile cause, Naumenko privately had a pessimistic view of the movement. In a letter written in 1900, he bitterly deplored the lack of talented Ukrainian writers: "Everybody thinks he too can be a writer just because he speaks Ukrainian."[76] As he sarcastically told a friend, he even suspected that the movement depended on the state's repression to hide its own insignificance: "For twenty years I have been saying that we only have some strength because the authorities forbid us everything, and a true debacle would happen if they suddenly told us to write whatever we want—we would lose all our dignity."[77]

Naumenko's frustration is understandable. His cause was advancing at a very slow pace, and the reach of *Kievskaia starina* remained minuscule. During the twenty-five years of its existence, it never had more than eight hundred subscribers and always remained in deficit.[78] Until 1905, the Ukrainian movement in the Russian Empire relied on a small group of intellectuals. Some of these activists, however, were extraordinarily dedicated. The continuation of *Kievskaia starina* was only possible thanks to the generous donations of the sugar manufacturer Vasyl' Symyrenko, the landowner Ievhen Chykalenko, and the journal's editors themselves. Most contributors wrote for free.[79] Given such difficult conditions, the journal's impact on Ukrainian nationalism in the empire was remarkable. It kindled interest in the region's past and cultural specificity among readers all over Ukraine, including the future historian Hrushevs'kyi, who discovered his passion for history by reading *Kievskaia starina* as a teenager.[80]

Walking a Fine Line

Iakov Shul'gin's historical works throw into relief how cautiously Ukrainophile academics had to communicate their project of constructing the nation's past. The research he conducted during the 1880s belongs in the context of the Ukrainophile populist historiography promoted by his teacher Antonovych. Iakov studied the Koliivshchyna, a large peasant uprising that had shaken the Kiev region in 1768, twenty-five years before the second partition of Poland that incorporated right-bank Ukraine into the Russian Empire. After the Cossack wars of the seventeenth century, Poland had restored its rule over most of right-bank Ukraine. As the central authority of the Polish state continuously withered away, rich landowners imposed an oppressive serfdom on the peasantry. At the same time, Polish society increased the religious pressure on the population, incorporating Orthodox monasteries and eparchies into the Uniate (Greek Catholic) Church. This combination of economic grievances and ethno-religious tensions repeatedly unleashed peasant violence against the Polish-Catholic gentry, Catholic and Uniate priests, and Jewish estate managers. In 1768, such a wave of violence coincided with an insurrection of Polish nobles against the king, leading to a civil war–like situation. In the Kiev and Bratslav palatinates, bands of free-roaming peasants and Cossacks, known as Haidamaks, killed several thousand landlords, clergy, and Jews. Finally, the Polish state subdued the Haidamak uprising with the help of the Russian army, resulting in court-martials and executions that were no less brutal than the Haidamaks' violence.[81]

Iakov's choice of this research topic was not accidental. His teacher Antonovych had previously published a short monograph on the Haidamak uprisings of the eighteenth century, describing them as a popular reaction against the arrogance of the Polish nobility, aggravated by criminal and anarchic elements who profited from the state's weakness.[82] Furthermore, the 1768 rebellion held a particular place in the national mythology of the Ukrainian movement due to the 1841 Romantic poem *The Haidamaks*, in which Taras Shevchenko had depicted the events in all their brutality and yet presented them as an exploit of national feeling.[83] Iakov Shul'gin based his analysis of the events on one primary source, the so-called Kodnia book, a collection of documents on a Polish court-martial, which was then part of Volodymyr Antonovych's private collection. In 1890, Iakov's "Sketch of the Koliivshchyna" was serialized in *Kievskaia starina*.[84]

Iakov Shul'gin's account was influenced both by Antonovych's scholarly analysis and by Shevchenko's poetic vision. Around 1700, he wrote, Cossackdom had disappeared on the right bank of the Dnieper "without completing its task of freeing itself and South Russian society from the oppression of Polonism and Church union. . . . But the life of the South Russian people, even in the districts afflicted by war, did not end definitely in this time of ruin." Precisely the Haidamaks of the peasant uprisings succeeded the Cossacks as "defenders of Russian nationality and Orthodoxy."[85] Defying the traditional (Polish) reading of the peasant rebels as bloodthirsty savages, Iakov set out to prove that theirs was a consistent movement with a firm organization and clear ethno-religious goals. By portraying the uprising as an expression of Orthodox and East Slavic identity, he tried to fill yet another gap in the Ukrainophile historical narrative. What his teacher Antonovych had achieved for the Lithuanian period, Iakov Shul′gin sought to do with respect to a time when Polish culture and politics had seemed paramount in right-bank Ukraine. Mykhailo Hrushevs′kyi would end up weaving such reinterpretations into an unambiguously Ukrainian narrative. Iakov Shul′gin's contribution, like that of Volodymyr Antonovych, was still ambivalent in national terms.

Iakov stressed that the uprising's leaders tried to occupy crucial points in the Kiev palatinate in order to take control and impose their own vision of society. The insurgency's goals, in his view, included the "eradication of the Church union, the nobility and the Jewry." He juxtaposed the judgments of the Polish court-martial with local folk songs to prove the popularity and the idealization of the Haidamak leaders among the popular masses. Iakov even praised one of them, Semen Nezhyvyi, for his "humane" attitude toward the common people: "Poles and Jews had a tough time with him, but he did not offend anyone else."[86]

Remaining true to his populist views, the historian did not overemphasize the role of the Koliivshchyna's leaders. Rather, he saw the peasants of the Kiev and Bratslav regions as the uprising's true protagonists: "The strength and intensity of the movement was doubtless caused by the sheer number of participants, by the identical views of a great mass of people." While he acknowledged and described in detail the extreme brutality of the insurgents' actions, Iakov stressed that only a minority of the Haidamaks were mere criminals. The violence, he wrote, could largely be blamed on the previous oppression by nobility and clergy, reflecting "the absolute inadequacy of the [social] order in the region." Accusing Polish memoirists and historians of denying the uprising's idealistic side and representing the Orthodox peasants as merciless brutes, Iakov occasionally tended toward the opposite extreme. Thus, he wrote that in a certain village, "the Poles had to pay with their lives for the yoke that they had imposed on society."[87]

If the study had clear populist undertones, there was little in it to which an imperial bureaucrat could have objected in a national sense.

Indeed, its anti-Polish thrust seemed rather praiseworthy. Where Iakov implicitly criticized the Russian government, he did so because it saved the teetering Polish state instead of standing by its religious and national brethren, the Orthodox peasants. His criticism of the Polish state and nobility was much harsher, not only for leaving the peasants in miserable economic conditions and imposing a foreign confession, but also for the cruel retributions after the suppression of the uprising.[88]

Clearly, Iakov Shul'gin saw the socioethnic and religious gap between the Ukrainian peasants and their Polish-Catholic lords as more decisive than their difference from Great Russians. The interdependence of the social and national questions, so characteristic of his generation's thinking, favored a view of Polish rather than Russian culture as the historical main antagonist of the Ukrainian people. Fittingly, the only negative reaction to the study came from a Polish historian. Tadeusz Korzon, one of the Warsaw Positivists, placed a highly critical review in a Galician historical journal, accusing Iakov of shamelessly glorifying peasant violence. He even insinuated that Iakov might hope to see "his favorite scenes from the seventeenth and eighteenth century repeated in the nineteenth."[89] The pronounced anti-Polonism of Iakov Shul'gin's study goes to show the continuities between the views of the midcentury Little Russian milieu and those of the Ukrainophiles in the 1880s. Just like his uncle in the 1860s, Iakov defended the historical role of the region's Orthodox peasants against the viewpoint of the Polish szlachta.

Iakov Shul'gin's account of the Koliivshchyna was much more ambiguous regarding Russian-Ukrainian relations. Depending on the reader's point of view, it could be read either as a confirmation of the region's historical Russianness or as a covert statement of Ukrainian difference. Iakov called the peasants "South Russians" or even just "Russians." By this time, virtually all Ukrainophiles preferred the self-designation "Ukrainian" to "Little Russian" or "South Russian" but replaced the former term by the latter in texts meant to reach a public beyond narrow Ukrainophile circles—a practice that has been aptly described as a kind of "double-speak."[90] Iakov Shul'gin only used "Ukraine" as a regional designation for the historical Kiev and Bratslav palatinates.[91] In this respect, his study was superficially compatible with the Little Russian historical narratives promoted by *Kievlianin*. Readers with Ukrainophile sympathies, however, would have known about the limitations of censorship and may well have read the study as a statement of the continuity and particularity of "South Russian" society as opposed not only to Polish, but also to Great Russian culture—as visible, for instance, in the Ukrainian-language dialogues that were included in the text. Thus, the study exemplifies the Aesopian discourse of Kiev's Ukrainophiles under the Ems Ukaz. If a text was to pass the preliminary censorship, it needed at least to permit an interpretation favorable to the official view of Russian-Ukrainian relations.[92]

There is some evidence that Iakov Shul'gin was aware of his text's ambiguity and perhaps even intended it to be read differently by different audiences. Writing to the minister of the interior in 1901, Iakov cited his work as proof that he was politically reliable: "My book 'Sketch of the Koliivshchyna . . .' includes *only legal opinions* on this period."[93] On the other hand, the book was translated into Ukrainian by the poet Mykola Voronyi and published in Galicia as part of the "Ruthenian Historical Library," a series established by Antonovych for a Ukrainophile audience. In his foreword, Mykhailo Hrushevs'kyi described the Koliivshchyna as one of several popular movements in "Ukraine-Rus'" during the seventeenth and eighteenth centuries, thus already beginning to incorporate Iakov's analysis into his national framework of Ukrainian history.[94]

A second historical work Iakov Shul'gin wrote in the 1880s shows just how narrow the scope of acceptable opinion was for Ukrainophile historiography. In his survey article about the gradual integration of left-bank Ukraine into the Russian Empire after 1654, Iakov took a more openly critical stance toward Russia. Ukraine, he wrote, joined the Muscovite state with four goals in mind: separation from Poland, autonomy in all internal matters, liberty from serfdom, and the maintenance of the region's traditional church organization. In Iakov's opinion, the Russian state's policies of the period, from the narrowing of the Hetmanate's borders and the increasing administrative centralization to its unwillingness to protect the peasants from the landowners' encroachments, "did not correspond to the Ukrainians' wishes." He singled out tsars Peter I, Anne, and Catherine II for their particularly heavy centralism and their attempts to "bring the Ukrainians closer to the Great Russians" by giving Ukrainian land to Great Russians, introducing Great Russian bureaucrats, and promoting marriages between the Muscovite and Ukrainian nobilities.[95]

While this account did not deny the official historiographical view of 1654 as the "reunification" of Ukraine with coreligious Muscovy, it presented the empire as incapable of serving Ukraine's needs. The Ukrainian people were here conceived in typically nationalist fashion as a collective individual with common interests and aspirations. Even though Iakov characterized the relationship between Ukraine and Muscovy as a misunderstanding rather than open enmity, it is obvious why this article could not be published in the Russian Empire. Even Lebedintsev's *Kievskaia starina* found its content too problematic.[96] It appeared over ten years later, translated into Ukrainian and under a pseudonym, in the *Annals of the Shevchenko Society*, a journal published in Lemberg by Hrushevs'kyi for a Ukrainophile and nationalist public.[97] While Iakov Shul'gin's work on the Koliivshchyna passed state censorship easily, a text on conflicts of interest between Russia and Ukraine did not even make it through the self-censorship of the Kiev Ukrainophiles. The difference in tone between these two texts, then, marks the fine line between what was and what was not permissible to write about the region's history under the restrictions of the Ems Ukaz.

Mothers, Children, and the Nationalization of Private Life

Under the repressive political conditions of the 1880s and 1890s, most activities of Kiev's Ukrainophiles moved into the private sphere. Activists' private households were the only environment where Kiev's Ukrainophiles could discuss freely and try to develop a Ukrainian high culture. Under a regime that repressed attempts to deprovincialize Ukrainian culture, even modest cultural work acquired a subversive, political quality.[98] Kiev's police knew about the persistence of Ukrainophile circles but hardly acted against them as long as they remained hidden and refrained from openly political propaganda. A tightly knit Ukrainophile milieu came into being in the years around 1900, consisting of a handful of seasoned activists and their families—among them Iakov Shul'gin, his wife Liubov, and their four children. The family's domestic life became the main ground of their national activism.

The lacking publicity of the Ukrainophiles in this period confronts the historian with a source problem. The absence of programmatic publications makes it difficult to assess political points of view. The constant personal contact and the indispensable secrecy mean that very few letters are available. Most information comes from activists' memoirs, often written much later and probably biased by hindsight. There is little reason to doubt, however, that many of Kiev's Ukrainophile activists were more radical in their (semi-)private circles than when speaking in spaces accessible to the authorities.

By the time Iakov Shul'gin left Kiev for Elisavetgrad in 1894, he had become a family man. While his professional career was a long series of failures, he found more fulfillment in private life. In 1887, four years after his return from exile, he got married to Liubov Ustymovych, a landowner's daughter from Poltava province whom he had met in the editorial offices of *Kievskaia starina*. In the following years, the couple had four children: Nadiia, Oleksander, Volodymyr, and Mykola—or, as official registers would list them by their Russian names: Nadezhda, Aleksandr, Vladimir, and Nikolai.[99] Liubov's father Nikolai Ustimovich was a nobleman of Cossack stock who, to the dismay of his relatives, had married a former serf girl called Iefrosyniia. A man of liberal views, Ustimovich had a history of unconventional pro-peasant activism.[100] His daughter Liubov shared her father's sympathies for Ukraine's peasants and the desire to educate them. Already at age seventeen, having just finished boarding school in Moscow, she had attracted the attention of the imperial police by frequenting the local school in her father's village.[101] After her studies at the Women's Higher Courses in Kiev, she had returned to her family estate, where, inspired by Tolstoian ideas of pedagogical reform, she had organized a school for peasant children.[102]

Liubov Shul'hyna-Ustymovych's rural background meant that her children, too, got to know Ukrainian peasant society from a young age. When the children were small, the family lived in Elisavetgrad and Kiev only during the winter months. They spent six months a year at the grandparents' estate of Sokhvyne (Rus. Sof'ino) in Poltava province, about 230 kilometers southeast of Kiev. Formerly a part of the autonomous Cossack Hetmanate, the region was considered to be a Ukrainian heartland and was the birthplace of many Ukrainophiles, including Drahomanov. Oleksander Shul'hyn's memoirs evoke the beauty of the Ukrainian steppe landscape, the greenery of his grandmother's gardens, and the children's good relationship with the local peasants, whose fundamental difference from the Jewish and Great Russian traders (in language, looks, and character) he claims to have recognized even as a small boy. Although Shul'hyn stresses the family's "democratic" character, there remained a clear dividing line between the Shul'hyn-Ustymovyches and the peasants. Grandmother Iefrosyniia is described as an able administrator who wanted to help the peasants improve their economic standing. Yet even though herself born a serf, she believed in a foreordained difference between lords and peasants. The village's peasants, in turn, resented the landlords' wealth and had little respect for intellectual work. Oleksander Shul'hyn recalled that he occasionally helped the peasants in their fieldwork, but also that they addressed him as *panych* ("young lord") and mocked his physical weakness.[103] Like many urban populists before them, the Shul'hyns failed to overcome the class barrier separating them from their purported co-nationals.

In contrast to Kiev, the village was a largely Ukrainian-speaking environment. Growing up in the countryside with a peasant mother, Liubov Shul'hyna had learned the Ukrainian language—or more precisely, Poltava's rural dialect—from childhood. Her Ukrainian fluency played a crucial role in the Shul'hyns' self-fashioning as a family of "patriotic spirit."[104] Writing his memoirs several decades later, Oleksander Shul'hyn claimed that in his childhood home "the Ukrainian language always dominated. . . . During all our lives, neither I, nor my sister, nor my brothers ever said to our mother or father a single word in Russian."[105] Yet Iakov's Ukrainian was never very good and was sprinkled with Galician expressions that sounded foreign to Kievans. He was always keenly aware of his "bad language."[106] Until the end of his life, he preferred Russian in both conversation and correspondence, although he spoke Ukrainian with some friends and occasionally wrote Ukrainian letters. Liubov, on the other hand, taught her children the "real Poltavan pronunciation," even though their speech was influenced by the Russian they read in books and later spoke at school. In the public sphere, the appearance of a Ukrainian-speaking intelligentsia family confused some observers: Oleksander's memoirs mention how Russian-speaking women in Elisavetgrad were astonished to see his mother, this "strange lady who wears Little Russian dress, holds her children by the hand and speaks to them in Little Russian." Meanwhile, Ukrainophiles such as the playwright Ivan Karpenko-Karyi were impressed when they heard the children speak Ukrainian.[107]

Within the national movement, the Ukrainian language fulfilled three functions. First, it was the preferred medium to communicate the Ukrainian project. In practice, however, Ukrainophiles in the Russian Empire usually wrote, and often spoke, in Russian. Second, the institutionalization of the Ukrainian language was one of the movement's central goals. After 1876, activists fought for the legalization of Ukrainian publications; after 1905, for Ukrainian-language schools and law courts. At the same time, discussions about the further standardization and functionalization of the language continued. Third, there was an important symbolic dimension to the use of Ukrainian. As long as majority society considered "Little Russian" a mere peasant dialect, speaking the language in urban intelligentsia surroundings identified one as a Ukrainophile. It signaled to both sympathizers and opponents that Ukrainian could become a fitting medium for all spheres of life. Thus, the repressions of 1876 were counterproductive insofar as they strengthened activists' identification with the Ukrainian language. The case of the nineteenth-century Ukrainian intelligentsia exemplifies Eric Hobsbawm's dictum that "languages become more conscious exercises in social engineering in proportion as their symbolic significance prevails over their actual use."[108]

The Shul'hyns' daily use of the language had such a high symbolic value because Ukrainian prevailed in very few intelligentsia households in fin-de-siècle Kiev. The memoirist Ievhen Chykalenko only names a handful of Ukrainian-speaking families, including those of the historian Antonovych, the composer Mykola Lysenko, and his cousin and brother-in-law, the playwright Mykhailo Staryts'kyi. Drahomanov's sister, the poetess Olena Pchilka (Ol'ha Kosach), was a prolific writer in Ukrainian, as was her daughter Lesia Ukraïnka (Larysa Kosach), while her husband Petro Kosach spoke a "Belorussian-Muscovite-Little Russian jargon."[109] Chykalenko's own family was fully Ukrainian-speaking, and so was that of Drahomanov's widow Liudmyla, who returned to Kiev with her two children after her husband's death in 1895.[110]

In order to pass on Ukrainophile and populist views to the children, Liubov Shul'hyna home-schooled them up to the age of about fourteen.[111] This allowed her to teach some subjects in Ukrainian and add some specifically Ukrainian content to the official curriculum. As Olena Pchilka, another Ukrainophile woman who home-schooled her children, remembered years later, "It then seemed to me that [Russian] school would at once ruin my attempts to educate the children in Ukrainian. This was an unfounded fear, for I later saw that if the children are well instructed in the Ukrainian language, school does not ruin that language."[112] Iakov Shul'gin was less involved in the children's education. He taught occasional geography lessons and told stories about the Cossacks, thus passing on the central historical myth of Ukrainian nationalism. In addition, the family hired external tutors as well as French and German housemaids, so that the children would learn foreign languages.

The most important discipline of the Ukrainophile "national education" was literature. Liubov read Shevchenko's poems to her children from a very early age; allegedly, Volodymyr was able to recite from *The Haidamaks* at age five. Alongside the Bible and a Russian translation of Homer's works, Liubov also acquainted her children with Leonid

FIGURE 5. Liubov Shul'hyna with her children Oleksander and Nadiia, 1897. Ishchuk-Pazuniak private collection, courtesy of Olena Leontovych.

Hlibov's Ukrainian fables and the works of Ivan Kotliarevs'kyi, the "founding father" of modern Ukrainian-language literature. However, it was the Russian-language works of Nikolai Gogol' that made the strongest impression on young Oleksander. The depiction of Cossack society in *Taras Bul'ba* awakened his fascination with the national past. The Shul'hyns also saw performances by the highly popular traveling Ukrainian theater troupes, whose Cossack-themed historical plays fueled Oleksander's imagination.[113] Later, when he was a teenager, his favorite reading matter was fairly conventional for boys of his generation in the Russian Empire: Russian novelists like Ivan Turgenev, Sergei Aksakov, Aleksei Tolstoi; popular foreign writers such as Charles Dickens, Walter Scott, and Jules Verne.[114] No popular Ukrainian youth literature could develop under the strict rules of censorship. During the 1890s, additions to the Ems Ukaz explicitly prohibited all translations from Russian into Ukrainian and the publication of children's literature.[115] Writing his memoirs at the end of his life, Oleksander Shul'hyn was convinced that Liubov's home tuition was the main factor that made him and his siblings embrace a national worldview: "At least from a national point of view, mother's system had a great positive effect; it strengthened our Ukrainian essence, and neither the gymnasium, nor the university, nor later our enthusiasm for great revolutionary or socialist ideas could destroy our almost natural national consciousness and devotion to Ukraine."[116]

Oleksander's emphasis on his mother's ideological influence was not accidental. The idea of mothers as transmitters of cultural traditions and the "mother tongue" is a central topos in European nationalist discourse. Whereas school education is usually seen as part of the "masculine" public sphere, the primary, "emotional" transmission of the national language and mind-set within the domestic sphere is usually depicted as an inherently "feminine" task.[117] In the minds of Kiev's nineteenth-century Ukrainophiles, mothers occupied a pivotal position as conveyors of national modes of thought under repressive conditions. Since the Ukrainian language was practically confined to the domestic sphere by law, Ukrainophiles insisted on their wives' duty to teach their children Ukrainian—which not all of them could do. Thus, Ievhen Chykalenko complained that "the children of the majority of the Ukrainian intelligentsia could not speak Ukrainian because their mothers either could not or did not want to speak it, and the family language depends more on the mother than on the father."[118] In his private lectures on anthropology, Volodymyr Antonovych even claimed that marriages between Ukrainians and Russians were doomed to failure and that such mixed families would always become hostile to Ukrainian culture.[119] Given the prevalence of such ideas in the milieu, it is possible that Iakov Shul'gin intentionally chose a Ukrainian-speaking wife to share his political project, and it becomes clear why Oleksander Shul'hyn singled out the fact that his mother, as he put it in a telling tautology, "knew her own language so well."[120]

The gendered use of language among Kiev's Ukrainophiles was linked to men's and women's different relationship with the state. In some families, the fathers spoke Ukrainian only with their Ukrainophile friends, using Russian both at work and at home. Most activists of this generation served in state institutions as teachers, university lecturers, or civil servants, and many of them refrained from speaking Ukrainian at home in order not to awaken their superiors' suspicions.[121] Ukrainophile women, by contrast, could not seek state employment and rarely pursued professional careers at all. Therefore, female activists were not bound to lead the "double life" of such men as Iakov Shul'gin, who had to please the authorities while at work and only expressed oppositional views in their intimate circles.

Yet it is difficult to separate empirical evidence for mothers' role as transmitters of values and beliefs from patriarchal and nationalist discourse that connects mothers to the sphere of national traditions, the home, the soil. Accounts of activists' private lives are always informed by gender stereotypes, whereby women are "represented as the atavistic and authentic 'body' of national tradition," while men are shown as a "progressive agent of national modernity."[122] In the case of the Shul'hyns, the opposition between Liubov's rural origins and Iakov's urban background reinforced such associations. Thus, Oleksander Shul'hyn wrote that his father lacked "the natural nationalist element coming from the earth, the fields, the common people," while his peasant grandmother brought into the family "the energy hidden in the deep roots of the people." His entire account of his childhood makes use of the gendered dichotomy between his intellectual father's "theoretical nationalism" and his practical-minded mother's "atavistic understanding of the people."[123] At the same time, the juxtaposition of an energetic, active mother and a sickly, passive father also inverts gender stereotypes.[124]

And there is a case to be made that nationalist women gained political agency precisely because their ideology defined the domestic sphere as exclusively feminine. It has been argued that the nationalist dichotomy between the (feminine) home and the (masculine) outer world was closely linked to the distinction between the spiritual and material worlds. Nationalists saw the home as a sanctuary for a pure, uncompromised national culture as opposed to the cosmopolitan, modernizing outside world.[125]

However, since nationalism was supposed to engulf the totality of social life, the seemingly nonpolitical private sphere—and above all, the education of the nation's future generation—became a highly political matter. Thus, the private household at once limited women's political agency and enabled it.[126] This dynamic was even more pronounced among Kiev's Ukrainophiles. Women of Liubov Shul'hyna's generation were excluded from public politics. Most of them did not overstep the boundaries of the gender roles defined by Russian majority society. However, since Ukrainophilism was driven into the private households, women were able to occupy a central place in the Ukrainophile milieu. Unlike women in the Russian radical underground, Ukrainophile women did not need to renounce their feminine roles within the family in order to be activists. Rather, the government's restrictions against Ukrainian nationalism turned domestic life into a political arena and politicized their motherhood.[127]

The Ukrainophile Household

Meetings in a domestic setting structured the life of Kiev's Ukrainophile community. Over many years, the clandestine Old Hromada, the circle of Kiev's veteran Ukrainophiles, gathered in a private household every Saturday to collect material for a Ukrainian-Russian dictionary. Some Ukrainophile women participated in the dictionary work, while others sat in the adjacent room embroidering *vyshyvanky*, the traditional shirts of the Ukrainian peasantry.[128] Volodymyr Antonovych gave secret lectures at private apartments, talks that were doubtless more radical than his official lectures at the university.[129] In the 1890s, Antonovych and the writer Oleksandr Konys'kyi hosted salons for political debate, while the "literary families" of the Staryts'kyis, Lysenkos, and Kosachs staged literary evenings and musical matinees, which sometimes served as cover for political discussions. Around 1900, Ievhen Chykalenko began to gather about twenty or thirty of his Ukrainophile friends at his home every Monday night, treating them to theater performances or meetings with Galician guests. A newly formed Women's Hromada, including Liubov Shul'hyna, also met at the Chykalenkos' house. When the secret "General Ukrainian Organization" was founded in 1897 to unite Ukrainophiles throughout the Russian Empire, it held all meetings in the homes of its members under cover of birthday parties or cultural events.[130] The journal *Kievskaia starina*, too, was a product of these Ukrainophile households. Throughout the 1890s, the editorial board met at Volodymyr Naumenko's private flat to discuss upcoming editions; these meetings "usually ended with a dinner and . . . were of a familial character."[131]

Forced to retreat into private spaces, Kiev's Ukrainophiles consciously cultivated the image of domesticity and idealized the harmony of their family lives.[132] As a purportedly "natural" community, the family could easily be interpreted as the nucleus of the equally "organic" community of the nation at large. Therefore, the nationalization of private lives was never directed at the family only, but also meant to make an impression on visitors. Arguably, the display of idyllic domesticity was as central to the Ukrainophiles' meetings as the exhibition of national culture.[133] Besides the conspicuous use of Ukrainian as the intimate family language, this demonstration of nationally colored family harmony often included the dressing of women and children in *vyshyvanky*.[134] A letter by a newly arrived student that the police intercepted in 1892 evoked an image of domestic harmony encouraging nationalist sympathies: "There are many Ukrainian families here, where the Ukrainophile students and nonstudents often meet, where the lively, free, and affectionate speech flows, where everyone feels close to each other and bound to each other by a common cause. Under the influence of these native elements I too have developed my weak forces; I have begun to write a lot and hope to print my works in Galician journals. . . . In a word, I am stepping onto native soil—the soil of Ukraine."[135] Another contemporary, the politician Mykola Galagan, also wrote about the lasting impression that the acquaintance with an educated Ukrainophone family, the Drahomanovs, made on him as a young man. Having grown up in the Russian-speaking environment of Kiev's schools and public life, Galagan recalled that he "profoundly felt the need to be surrounded by the family life of a Ukrainian intelligentsia family."[136] According to her son's memoirs, Liubov Shul'hyna was fully aware of this effect that nationally marked domestic culture could have on potential sympathizers of Ukrainophilism and, as a "born propagandist," frequently invited university and gymnasium students to their home.[137]

Thus, the households of Ukrainophile families served as spaces of assembly, exchange, recruitment, and mutual affirmation. They were the setting in which the tightly connected milieu of Kiev's Ukrainophiles constituted itself since the 1880s, and even more so in the years around 1900. This milieu consisted mainly of the older generation of activists and their families, a close-knit group held together by numerous personal, intellectual, and professional ties. Most of these people had known each other for decades and regularly met at clandestine and public events. Liubov's and Iakov's family was integrated into this milieu by means of old friendships, kinship, marriage, and neighborhood. To give but a few examples: The Hromada's unofficial head Naumenko was married to Iakov's sister Vera. The milieu's intellectual leader, Antonovych, was both Iakov's and Naumenko's former teacher; Iakov held him in very high regard, and his son later wrote that "a true cult of this extraordinary man prevailed in our family." The composer Lysenko was a good friend of both parents. Liubov was the godmother of his youngest son, and the Shul'hyns often went to his concerts or had tea with his family. Other close friends of the family included the teacher and literary historian Pavlo Zhytets'kyi (Nadiia's godfather), the Ukrainian-speaking Kosach and Chykalenko families, the Hromada member Ielisei Trehubov, and Iakov's cousin and boyhood friend Vladimir Shcherbina.[138]

Such close ties between families prevailed in Kiev's entire Ukrainophile milieu, and marriages between activists' children were quite common. This situation did not escape the Ukrainophiles' opponents. In 1908, *Kievlianin* wrote that "all the 'Ukrainian intelligentsia' consists only of a few families, and so it is not surprising that in the Ukrainophile camp a lot is done in a familial and domestic way."[139] This also meant that personal animosities occasionally harmed political solidarity. Thus, Volodymyr Antonovych's temporary break with the Hromada in the late 1880s was not caused by strategic disagreements (as in Drahomanov's case) but by other activists' disapproval of his domestic situation: he had separated from his wife and lived with another woman.[140] The initiator of the General Ukrainian Organization, Oleksandr Konys'kyi, was on bad terms with Volodymyr Naumenko, which at first impeded the new group's cooperation with the Hromada.[141] Overall, however, regular meetings and manifold connections with likeminded people strengthened these intellectuals' self-identification as Ukrainians and their political loyalty to the national movement. Kiev's Ukrainophiles created a tightly connected space of communication, where the Ukrainian language served both as a medium (though not as the only one) and as a uniting symbol.

This space of communication had a very concrete territorial dimension. In the years around 1900, most of Kiev's Ukrainophiles lived in the Novoe stroenie neighborhood. Many of them had their apartments on Mariinsko-Blagoveshchenskaia Street (now vulytsia Saksahans'koho) between the university's main building and the train station. Among them were Liubov and Iakov Shul′gin, who moved to 44 Mariinsko-Blagoveshchenskaia in the early 1900s.[142] Just across from them lived Iakov's sister Vera and her husband Naumenko, while somewhat farther down the street were the Kosach, Staryts′kyi and Lysenko family homes. Konys′kyi and Chykalenko also had houses on the same street. The nickname "Ukrainian street" was truly deserved.[143] Antonovych lived one block farther down, and his former student Hrushevs′kyi would buy a house on a perpendicular street when moving back to Kiev in 1908.

Besides private homes, the area also hosted the city's first Ukrainophile institutions. In 1899, *Kievskaia starina* opened a bookshop on

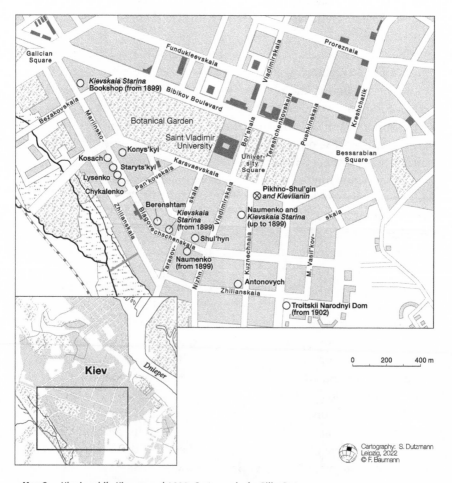

MAP 2. Ukrainophile Kiev around 1900. Cartography by Silke Dutzmann.

Bezakovskaia Street to sell Ukrainian literature, including prohibited Galician editions. As a police agent reported to his superiors, its employees tried to "speak and correspond exclusively in Little Russian."[144] When the Kiev Literacy Society, a cultural organization headed by Naumenko, built a new building (funded by the Jewish millionaire Lazar' Brodskii) in 1901–1902, it also chose the same neighborhood. Even though the society's board included Ukrainophile, Russophile, and Jewish members, the Troitskii narodnyi dom (People's house) became a meeting point for Kiev's Ukrainophiles: *Kievskaia starina* moved into the building, as did, in 1907, the Ukrainian educational association Prosvita and the first permanent Ukrainian theater, where both the performances and the daily business were conducted in Ukrainian.[145] Meanwhile, the editorial office of Dmitrii Pikhno's *Kievlianin* and his private home were still in Vitalii Shul'gin's house, only one block away from his Ukrainophile relatives. Yet both Oleksander Shul'hyn and his second cousin Vasilii Shul'gin later claimed never to have met in person.[146] By the beginning of the twentieth century, the separation between Kiev's Ukrainophile and conservative milieus was sufficient for relatives to ignore each other even though they lived in each other's immediate vicinity.

The retreat into private spaces did not mean that the Ukrainophiles completely escaped the state's attention. The city's police agents were fully aware that most activists of the 1870s were still in Kiev and had not changed their opinions. In 1886, when Ukrainophilism was hardly noticeable in Kiev's public life, the city's police organs compiled a list of Ukrainophile activists that contained over fifty names, including well-known men like Antonovych or Naumenko, but also dozens of students, both male and female.[147] In 1893, Mykola Lysenko complained that it was hard for the Kievans to receive the Galician Ukrainian press, "for every patriot's name is known to all and our mail goes directly to the censorship!"[148] In 1899, the police reported that even though Volodymyr Naumenko had "now moderated his criminal activity, knowing that it is known to [gendarme] General Novitskii, he remains a man of antigovernment tendency, as he used to be."[149] Two years later, another report stated that "Naumenko's political unreliability has de facto not manifested itself in anything to the present day."[150] Throughout his activist career of over four decades, Naumenko was never subject to repression. The state was prepared to tolerate the cultural work of the Old Hromada as long as it remained in its niches. Ukrainophiles were not persecuted for their opinions alone, and the Hromada's cautious practice of accepting new members only by a unanimous vote made it difficult to prove that the activists ever went beyond the limit of acceptable commitment. As the police quotation ("knowing that it is known to General Novitskii") shows, both the police and the Ukrainophiles understood that they were observing each other, and this made it possible for the Ukrainophiles to exploit legal gray zones.

Nor was Kiev's Ukrainophile milieu a completely closed community. State-employed male members like Iakov Shul'gin must have been in regular contact, and probably in friendly relations, with non-Ukrainophile colleagues. Iakov's children got to know their conservative relatives during stays in the countryside. Whereas the Ukrainophile and the Russian monarchist milieus of Kiev led fairly separate existences by 1900, no such division was in place in rural Poltava province. Liubov's sister Marusia had married the wealthy landowner Konstantin Leontovich, a conservative monarchist whose estate was managed more aristocratically than Sokhvyne.[151] Liubov's brother Nikolai Ustimovich (Mykola Ustymovych) was also a wealthy monarchist landowner in Poltava province. Ustimovich idealized the Cossack period, owned three hundred horses, and liked to wear Cossack costumes. His was a form of Ukrainophilism that combined a nostalgic appreciation of local history and tradition with political loyalty to the ruling dynasty, more akin to early nineteenth-century Romanticism than to the modern cultural nationalism practiced in his sister's family. For several years, the Shul'hyns had no contact with their conservative relative, but they always let the children visit him.[152]

Of course, the memoirs of nationalist activists display a particular interest in practices and networks that can be read as part of the national movement's history. There is little space in such texts for mundane everyday situations, in which Kiev's Ukrainophiles probably behaved in much the same way as their non-Ukrainophile contemporaries. The same goes for police sources, which emphasize potentially subversive practices. But even nationalist activists could not interpret their entire lives in ethnic or national terms.[153] In a largely Russian-speaking city, the Ukrainophiles' daily interactions in public must have taken place predominantly in Russian. They went shopping in the same shops as their fellow Kievans, saw exhibitions at the city's museums, and attended performances in the city's successful Russian-language theater. In all likelihood, they also went to church alongside other Orthodox Kievans.[154] When they entered the state gymnasium, the Ukrainophiles' children experienced a quintessential institution for the reproduction of the empire's urban elites. The Russian language dominated both in the classroom and the schoolyard of the *gimnaziia*. The teachers wore uniforms and taught a state-approved curriculum.

The situation of the Ukrainophiles in fin-de-siècle Kiev was thus opposite to that of nationalists in nineteenth-century Bohemia. In Prague, according to Gary Cohen, "sharp Czech-German distinctions developed first in public affairs and apparently only later in the private sphere of life." By the turn of the century, Czech and German nationalists had created nationally segregated parties, associations, schools, and businesses. They were even organizing boycotts of each other's institutions. Meanwhile, informal contacts continued in private households, intellectual circles, and everyday professional interactions.[155] In Kiev, where a public Ukrainophile associational life was impossible under the Ems Ukaz, it was the other way round: Ukrainian nationalists mingled with Russian-speaking majority society in their city's public life but remained among themselves in their private spaces.

A New Generation?

The first years of the twentieth century brought momentous change both to the Russian Empire at large and to the Ukrainian national movement. After the defeat in the Russo-Japanese War, the revolutionary events of 1905 shook the autocracy and brought about a semi-constitutional political system. The Fundamental Laws of April 1906 granted civil liberties and created a parliament, the State Duma, even though the tsar retained the right to veto laws and dissolve the Duma anytime. Russian semiconstitutionalism did away with the restrictions of the Ems Ukaz and made it possible to develop a Ukranian nationalist associational life in public. Following the Galician example, Prosvita (Enlightenment) societies were established in all the larger cities of Russian Ukraine to promote Ukrainian-language education and national culture. The Prosvitas set up village reading rooms, published pamphlets, and organized Ukrainian-language entertainment for the peasant population. In Kiev, Mykola Lysenko initiated a popular Ukrainian Club, which staged lectures, literary evenings, choir concerts, and theater shows.

The years 1905–1906 also saw the political reorganization of Ukrainian nationalism. On the left side of the spectrum, the illegal Revolutionary Ukrainian Party (RUP), founded by radical students in 1900, adopted a Marxist program and renamed itself the Ukrainian Social

Democratic Workers' Party (USDRP). Ievhen Chykalenko and other moderate Ukrainian federalists tried to establish a party of their own. After long discussions, the Ukrainian Democratic-Radical Party (UDRP) came into being, but it continued to be plagued by internal disagreements and personal rivalries. Some older Ukrainophiles, among them Volodymyr Naumenko, soon left the UDRP. Instead, they joined the Kiev branch of the Russian liberal party, the Constitutional Democrats (Kadets), in which some local actors saw Ukrainian education as an instrument of liberal transformation. In 1908, the Society of Ukrainian Progressives (Tovarystvo ukraïnskykh postupovtsiv, TUP) was founded to replace the inert UDRP. A nonparty but illegal organization, the TUP was meant to unite Ukrainian activists all over the empire on the basis of federalist and autonomist positions.[156]

In the first Duma elections of March 1906, some UDRP members gained seats by means of an electoral alliance with the Kadets. After their arrival in Saint Petersburg, they organized a caucus of Ukrainian delegates that met with surprisingly high interest among the nonparty peasant deputies. About forty delegates joined the caucus, which attempted to bring the demand for Ukrainian federal autonomy onto the Duma floor but did not succeed because the government soon dissolved the parliament. After the election of a second, socialist-dominated Duma in January 1907, peasant delegates from Ukraine formed a Ukrainian Labor Group. Again, the Duma was dissolved before the Ukrainian delegates achieved anything practical.[157] In the Third State Duma (1907–1912), the majority of deputies from the southwestern provinces joined the Russian nationalist and right-wing monarchist caucuses, leaving even less space for Ukrainian demands. Thus, Duma politics garnered empire-wide publicity for Ukrainian national matters but did not affect the legal situation.

The loosening of censorship was perhaps the most drastic change of these years. For the first time since the 1870s, the "Ukrainian question" could be debated in public, in an openly political manner, and in Ukrainian. A legal Ukrainian-language press emerged, the most important product of which was the Kiev daily *Hromads'ka dumka* (Public thought), largely funded by Ievhen Chykalenko and relaunched as *Rada* (The council) after the authorities closed it down in August 1906. Despite *Rada*'s importance to the Ukrainian movement, not least because its journalists experimented with the creation of a Ukrainian journalistic language, it was never very popular with the public in Kiev or elsewhere. Its publisher Chykalenko was soon disillusioned with the project. As he noted in 1909, there was "no reader for such a newspaper." The cities, Chykalenko complained, lacked a significant Ukrainian-speaking intelligentsia, whereas the rural population was "either completely illiterate or crippled by Russian school."[158]

Faced with the sudden freedom of the press, the Ukrainian nationalists struggled with the insufficient standardization of their language. If peasants encountered a Ukrainian newspaper, they expected it to be written in their village's dialect and complained about each unknown word. They also knew that the authorities might consider reading Ukrainian papers a subversive act.[159] Thus, most Ukrainian publications that emerged after 1905 were very short-lived. *Kievskaia starina*, too, was remade into a Ukrainian-language journal titled *Ukraïna* in 1907. However, the journal ceased publication after just one year, for, as its editor Naumenko explained, "the basic reason to publish such a journal as the only representative of the Ukrainian movement, which *Kievskaia starina* was for twenty-five years, is now gone."[160] With the new freedoms after 1905, cautious cultural activism was no longer needed as a substitute for political action.

Accordingly, the initiative within the movement passed from Naumenko's age cohort to younger activists. To be sure, Naumenko himself continued to be involved in public affairs: he served as vice-director of the newly founded Ukrainian Scientific Society in Kiev, published in various liberal newspapers, and worked as the director of his own private gymnasium.[161] Others, however, were increasingly weakened by illness and old age, and the older generation of Kiev's (male) Ukrainophiles was heavily decimated during these years: Oleksandr Konys'kyi had already died in 1900, and Mykhailo Staryts'kyi in 1904. Volodymyr Antonovych died in 1908, Petro Kosach in 1909, Iakov Shul'gin in 1911, and Mykola Lysenko in 1912.

In Kiev's emerging Ukrainophile public life, the most visible figures besides the evergreen Naumenko were those of the "middle generation" born in the 1860s. Ievhen Chykalenko was influential as the publisher of *Rada* and often hosted the meetings of the Society of Ukrainian Progressives. The combative writer Borys Hrinchenko took over the editing of the Hromada dictionary from Naumenko and published it under his own name in the years 1907–1909.[162] The historian Mykhailo Hrushevs'kyi moved back from Lemberg to Kiev and became very active in the city's press and the Ukrainian Scientific Society. In political terms, these men were fairly moderate, although they were less inclined to cooperate with the Russian liberals than Naumenko and some of his peers. Among the prominent literary voices of this age group were two daughters of older Kiev Ukrainophiles, Liudmyla Staryts'ka-Cherniakhivs'ka and Lesia Ukraïnka (Larysa Kosach). The emergence of a Ukrainian press also offered opportunities for yet younger people to make a name for themselves. Men in their twenties such as Symon Petliura (born 1879), Dmytro Doroshenko (born 1882), or the politically radical novelist Volodymyr Vynnychenko (born 1880)—many of them politicized in the ranks of the Revolutionary Ukrainian Party around 1900—established a reputation as writers. These three, and many others who made their debut in this period, would occupy center stage in the revolutionary events of 1917 and the following years.

It is thus understandable that some historians link the repoliticization of the Ukrainian question in the early twentieth century directly to the appearance on the scene of a new age cohort of activists. Olga Andriewsky speaks of the "Generation of 1917": "those men and women who were born between 1875 and 1885, became politically active around the turn of the century and came to support . . . the idea of political autonomy and statehood."[163] As student numbers in the Russian Empire rose, she argues, the Ukrainian national movement gained an entire generation of young activists whose experience with student protests prepared them to act decisively on behalf of Ukrainian nationalism. The Shul'hyn children were at the younger end of this age cohort. Born in 1888 and 1889, Nadiia Shul'hyna and Oleksander Shul'hyn only finished school in 1907 and 1908, respectively. Still, in contemporary Ukrainian historiography Oleksander Shul'hyn has been described as "a representative of the new generation of the Ukrainian elite—the nationally conscious Ukrainian intelligentsia which did not oppose itself to the people but saw itself as part of it and clearly declared its national rights."[164]

Nationalist authors tend to assume that the kind of education the Shul'hyn children received automatically produced young people with a solidly national identity. Thus, one memoirist wrote of his contemporaries: "The few lucky ones among Ukrainian children who were born in the families of nationally conscious parents can perhaps not quite appreciate what great luck they had in their lives that they did not need to search their national consciousness over zigzag roads and complicated paths."[165] This assumption is also implicit in Oleksander Shul'hyn's memoirs: that his patriotic education made him and his siblings into culturally unambiguous Ukrainians and consolidated their "national consciousness," preparing them ideally for a career as nationalist activists. As he put it in a speech shortly before his death, "I did not need the great effort that somebody from a nationally indifferent milieu had to make in order to attain Ukrainian positions. It was almost impossible not to follow my father, it would have been strange if my mother's patriotism had not made an impact on my life and work." The telos of this narrative, again, is the "national revolution" of 1917, when the young generation was supposedly ready for action.[166]

Of course, the idea is not implausible. Growing up in a Ukrainian-speaking environment, the Shul'hyn children must have understood from an early age that their family was different from Kiev's and Elisavetgrad's Russian-speaking majority society. All four of them later considered themselves Ukrainian nationalists and actively participated in Ukrainian cultural and political ventures. Similar observations have been made with regard to other national movements. Thus, the rising political self-confidence of Czech nationalists in the 1880s has been attributed to the fact that many among the younger generation had received their entire education in Czech and, unlike their parents, saw their Czech nationality as self-evident.[167]

One should be wary, however, of reading the history of the Ukrainian national movement as a linear sequence of increasingly nationalistic generations. Some Ukrainian activists at the time were anything but convinced that ever-rising nationalization would be the natural course of their movement. In 1909, Ievhen Chykalenko had doubts about the national self-definition of his son Levko, a close friend of Oleksander Shul'hyn's. Levko and his sisters, Chykalenko complained, were "not very intensely Ukrainian" and had many friends who did not care about the Ukrainian project. "In general, people born into the Ukrainian movement are less intense than those who have made their way into it themselves."[168] Half a year later, Chykalenko reached conclusions that seemed to negate all possibilities of a successful education in a national spirit:

It is a misfortune with these children! They are only brakes for a public activist. In any case, I am certain that our children will only be our material, but not our spiritual heirs. I am currently negotiating with Karpenko-Karyi's children about the publication of his first volumes and have come to the conclusion that a man of ideas should not get married and, heaven forbid, have children. Procreation should be imposed on the "plebs," from which all Ukrainian activists have sprung, while nothing useful for the

Ukrainian movement has come from the children of our activists. I know the children of Antonovych, Zhytets'kyi, Naumenko, Komar [Mykhailo Komarov], Smolens'kyi, Lysenko, Karpenko-Karyi and so on and so forth. They are either completely indifferent to what their fathers lived by, or even hostile to it.[169]

Chykalenko was being somewhat unjust to the younger generation. Several of the "children" he mentioned were actually active in Ukrainian nationalist circles or joined the movement later. Others, such as Naumenko's two sons, remained indifferent. The Ukrainophiles' "national education" only brought the expected fruit in some cases. Like their parents in the 1870s, some of the children refused to take an older generation's priorities for granted.

One reason for this lack of national "intensity" was the very unequal standing of Russian and Ukrainian culture in late imperial Kiev. Russianness was an "unmarked" cultural feature: it was a property of a majority among the educated population, and therefore manifestations of Russian culture were not necessarily perceived as *Russian*. Many Kievans saw Russian-language culture simply as culture per se or as expression of a cosmopolitan worldview. Even such a dedicated Ukrainian nationalist as the writer Volodymyr Vynnychenko admitted that praise from Russian literary circles almost tempted him to start writing in Russian instead of Ukrainian, which would have allowed him to reach a much larger audience and earn a decent living.[170] By contrast, Ukrainianness was "marked" in the sense that it was always visible as such and carried political connotations. Ukrainian-language culture may have appeared parochial and narrow to some children of the Ukrainophiles. Faced with a choice between career opportunities on the imperial scene and possible hardships in a minuscule nationalist movement, some of them doubtless considered the possibility of full assimilation to Russian culture.

What is more, Ukrainophile ideas faced powerful ideological competition among Kiev's youth in the early 1900s. If the Ukrainophiles of the 1870s and 1880s had formed their political worldview in constant exchange with Russian populism, those who came of age around 1905 found themselves confronted with the enormous appeal of Marxist socialism. By the early twentieth century, the influence of Marxist ideas was pervasive in oppositional circles of university and gymnasium students. All politically interested youths read and commented on Marx. Initiated to politics in the national-revolutionary RUP, many younger Ukrainian activists (e.g., Dmytro Antonovych, Volodymyr Vyn-nychenko, Symon Petliura, Mykola Porsh) were torn between Marxism and nationalism for years.[171]

These activists tended to champion radical views both in the national and social question, dismissing the older generation's Ukrainophilism as an outdated form of nationalism without political consequences. Since the 1890s, many younger Ukrainian nationalists rejected even the term "Ukrainophile," which they associated with political passiv-ity, insisting that they were simply Ukrainians.[172] Members of the RUP attacked their predecessors for compromising with the imperial state that they hated. Switching back and forth between nationalist and so-cialist arguments, the young radicals would deliberately offend their "fathers" in their proclamations—in Dmytro Antonovych's case, this included his literal father, whom he liked to refer to as "Professor An-tonovych." At the same time, however, they continued to visit the older Ukrainophiles' houses, retained friendly relations, and regularly sought their advice.[173]

Oleksander Shul'hyn, too, came into contact with Marxism at an early age. He first read Marx in a gymnasium reading circle and was impressed by "the simplicity and clarity" of the concepts explained in the *Communist Manifesto*.[174] During the revolutionary upheaval of 1905, sixteen-year-old Oleksander was an enthusiastic Marxist, attended clandestine Social Democratic meetings, and admired the revolution-ary writer Vynnychenko. When the gymnasium students organized protests during this year, they were mostly interested in social issues. Oleksander Shul'hyn claims to have put forward a resolution that de-manded teaching in Ukrainian, arousing the anger and mockery of a conservative teacher. However, he also recalls his schoolmates' indiffer-ence toward the Ukrainian national movement: "The boys had simply not arrived at this question, at the time one could live in Kiev without knowing about it."[175] Like Oleksander, his sister Nadiia was also infatu-ated with Marxism in her youth. In 1908, her father Iakov wrote to her landlord, his old friend Fedir Vovk, "You criticize her for her inclina-tion toward the Social Democrats. It seems to me that she nevertheless remains a true Ukrainian. . . . That the Ukrainian Social Democrats' plans are not good, obscure: this matter requires lengthy debates which my daughter has not heard."[176]

Like Iakov Shul'gin, many Ukrainophiles saw Marxism as a tem-porary deviation from nationalist commitment. In a similar vein, Oleksander Shul'hyn would later claim that his Marxist phase did not last much longer than a year. Allegedly, he was soon disappointed by the obscure language of Marx's *Capital*, by its determinism, and by the "pseudo-internationalism" of most Social Democrats. Reflecting in the 1930s on his youth, Shul'hyn described Marxism, cosmopolitanism, and Russian high culture as a "seductive influence" that he and his siblings had to withstand: "Only the family and its traditions could give us the strength to resist it and to remain loyal to the patriotic Ukrainian idea."[177] This is, of course, an ideologically colored retrospective interpretation of his own biography, in which developments leading away from the nationalist bildungsroman are presented as mere episodes to be corrected in due time. While it is certainly possible that Oleksander's Marxist enthusiasm was short-lived, it is important to note that he could well have developed in a different political direction. After all, socialism belonged to his parents' political heritage as much as nationalism.

Young Ukrainians in the Capital

In the years after 1905, Saint Petersburg once more became an important center of the Ukrainian national movement. The capital's universities attracted many students from Ukraine, including Nadiia and Oleksander Shul'hyn. Nadiia left her native Kiev in 1907 to study mathematics at the Bestuzhev Courses, Russia's most durable academic institution for women, where most courses were taught by professors from the university.[178] One year later, Oleksander chose Saint Petersburg University because of its liberal reputation. At first, he enrolled at the law faculty but immediately changed his mind and began his studies at the faculty of natural sciences. After two years, he switched to history and studied with the then-famous liberal historian Nikolai Kareev.[179] While Nadiia's four years in Petersburg are almost completely undocumented, the scarce evidence about Oleksander's nine-year stay suggests that he was torn between his nationalist convictions and his academic aspirations. While he was active in Ukrainian circles, his burgeoning career moved him away from Kiev. As Oleksander wrote during a visit to his hometown, he found both Kiev's academic institutions and social climate underwhelming: "As if all human thoughts and wishes had frozen."[180]

Oleksander nonetheless retained strong connections to Ukraine, not least thanks to his initiation into "national science."[181] During his first years in the imperial capital, he studied ethnography and anthropology with his father's friend Fedir Vovk. A chemist by education, Vovk had been one of the most revolutionary-minded Ukrainian activists in Kiev before he was forced to flee the country in 1879. After studying anthropology and ethnography in Paris, he returned to Russia in 1905 and began to teach at Saint Petersburg University, pioneering new Western methods of anatomic measurement (osteometry).[182] According to Vovk's pet theory, Ukrainians and Great Russians constituted fundamentally different types in terms of physical anthropology. While Ukrainians were supposedly tall, brachycephalic ("short-headed"), dark-haired, and dark-eyed, the neighboring Great Russians, Belorussians, and Poles tended to be shorter and light-haired with longer skulls. Vovk and his students tried to substantiate this hypothesis by conducting body measurements in villages all over Ukraine. Vovk stressed that his findings were devoid of political significance "because race and nation are by no means the same thing."[183] Nevertheless, the reception of his work suggests that Ukrainian nationalists understood it precisely as an argument to bolster national claims.[184]

Evidently enthusiastic about the new, "scientific" possibility to prove Ukraine's distinctness, Oleksander Shul'hyn and his childhood friend Levko Chykalenko organized their own expedition to Kherson province in the summer of 1910. Traveling across the South Ukrainian steppe, they sought out ancient Cossack settlements, where they expected to find authentic ethnographic artifacts and anthropologically pure Ukrainian bodies to confirm their teacher's theory. Their failure to produce unambiguous measurements may have contributed to Oleksander's decision to concentrate on history rather than anthropology.[185] Outside the classroom, Oleksander joined the Ukrainian study circle at Saint Petersburg University, where he showed particular zeal in reading and promoting the writings of Mykhailo Drahomanov. After 1905, the formerly clandestine Ukrainian study circles existed legally at the city's universities, serving as a platform for both scholarly lectures and, unofficially, political debates. Before the outbreak of the war, Petersburg counted about twenty such circles with allegedly over three hundred members.[186]

Like the Ukrainian movement in general, Petersburg's Ukrainian scene was torn by generational conflict in these years. A few harsh attacks on the Ukrainophiles' "culturalism" and "ethnographism" appeared in the Petersburg journal *Ukraïns'kyi student* and other periodicals. However, their political and ideological significance should not be overestimated. According to Oleksander Lotots'kyi, one of the capital's older Ukrainian nationalists, many such disagreements arose in reaction to radical (nationalist or socialist) agitation outside the Ukrainian student circles. In order to prove their own radical credentials, some of the student leaders would join the outsiders' attacks on the political passivity of the older generation. Lotots'kyi further claimed that the idea of an independent Ukrainian state became popular among Petersburg's Ukrainian youth in this period.[187] Given subsequent developments, however, there is reason to doubt this assertion. If some may have dreamed of an independent state, few can have seen it as a concrete prospect before 1914. As one former student of the Bestuzhev Courses later wrote, "At that time we were in favor of a federation with Russia. The idea of Ukraine's independence, which was thrown into our ranks around the beginning of the [First World] war, seemed attractive and dazzling but unrealistic, both due to the insufficient preparation of the Ukrainian masses and due to Russia's military might."[188]

In order to find new recruits, Ukrainian students entered the universities' *zemliachestva*, fraternities that united students from the same region. As leaders of the Kiev fraternity, Oleksander Shul'hyn and Levko Chykalenko tried, without success, to unite it with other groups from Ukraine. The *zemliachestvo* was not a nationally defined organization, and the memoirs of the historian Nikolai Antsiferov, a fellow Kievan and Oleksander's friend at the time, shed doubt on Oleksander's retrospective self-description as an unambiguously nationalized Ukrainian. Antsiferov contrasts Oleksander with Levko Chykalenko, "a true son of Ukraine": "Sashko [Oleksander] was a Ukrainian, but one of Russian orientation who spoke his native language poorly. 'You'd rather speak Russian,' the true Ukrainian Levko would say mockingly when listening to his native tongue with a grimace. Shul'hyn was a terribly enthusiastic character, but inside him there was a certain cold which moderated his passions and led him onto the path of moderacy in all matters. Russian culture was dear to him (Russian science, Russian art)."[189]

Antsiferov's assessment of Oleksander's language skills may be overly harsh, but there is more evidence to corroborate his account. During his Petersburg years, Oleksander fell in love with the medical student Lidiia (Lilia) Bublyk, a friend of his sister's and the daughter of a Kievan liberal with Ukrainophile sympathies. Oleksander and Lilia got married in 1912. While involved in political circles, she was hardly a committed Ukrainian nationalist. According to one source, the newly married couple spoke Russian when no "witnesses" were around.[190] The anecdote confirms the highly performative and symbolic character of

FIGURE 6.   Oleksander Shul'hyn as a university student, ca. 1908. TsGIA SPb, f. 14, op. 3, d. 52119, l. 15.

the Ukrainian language among nationalists. Even in Saint Petersburg, Oleksander spoke it demonstratively in order to bolster his nationalist credentials. However, he must have spoken Russian in most of his daily interactions. Nor was his narrow circle of friends limited to fellow

Ukrainians. Among Oleksander's closest friends was a former school-
mate from Kiev, Boris Tolpygo, who even considered himself a Russian
patriot.[191] Oleksander also engaged in non-Ukrainian politics, such as
the student demonstrations following Lev Tolstoi's death. In a letter
home, he described with outrage how the protesters were dispersed
with violence as they faced the troops of the "evil government beast."[192]

Overall, the sources suggest that Oleksander Shul'hyn was not exclusively attached to Ukrainian culture and dedicated to Ukraine's political
independence. He certainly saw himself as a member of the Ukrainian
national movement, opposed the autocratic government, advocated a
federalization of the Russian Empire, and liked to use the Ukrainian
language conspicuously in public. Like him, many other students of
his generation were self-confidently Ukrainian in their self-perception
and their cultural practices. A good knowledge of Ukrainian and its use
in conversation and correspondence was certainly more common than
twenty years earlier. In political terms, however, most young Ukrainian
nationalists did not advocate solutions to the "Ukrainian question"
radically different from those of their parents' generation.

Membership in Ukrainian circles and associations did not preclude
the possibility of a career in the empire's (academic) institutions. Nor
could Ukrainian nationalists refuse involvement in these institutions
if they wanted to achieve any professional success beyond the narrow
Ukrainian milieu. In this situation, young nationalists often chose
practical considerations over idealism. For Oleksander Shul'hyn, his
father's sad story doubtless served as a cautionary tale against open
opposition to the state. After finishing his course of studies, he began preparations to attain a professorship. During much of the First
World War, Shul'hyn worked on his dissertation about the beginnings
of capitalism in France, even though he had doubts about his academic
prospects.[193] "I am thinking about pedagogical work," he informed his
mentor Vovk at the beginning of 1915. "To tell the truth I have hardly
dreamt about this, especially given the current order in the gymnasia.
But what can you do."[194] These are hardly the words of a national revolutionary waiting for his chance to take up arms against the empire.

Russia's Ukrainian national movement as a whole, too, remained
fairly modest both in terms of its forces and in terms of its program.
A mixture of state repression and popular indifference limited it to
fairly small intelligentsia circles.[195] As Ievhen Chykalenko pessimisti-
cally noted in his diary in 1910, "We have few conscious people, at any
rate no more than two thousand souls, and they are less disciplined

than other nations were at the time of their rebirth."[196] In the very last years before the war, Kiev saw Ukrainian shows of force on a few occasions, as hundreds of people gathered for the funeral of the composer Lysenko in 1912, the funeral of the poet Lesia Ukraïnka in 1913, and a demonstration on occasion of the Shevchenko centenary in 1914.[197] However, these events attest more to the appeal of Ukrainian high culture than to the popularity of nationalist political demands. The demand for an independent Ukrainian state had been voiced both in Austrian Galicia and in the Russian Empire since the late 1890s.[198] Still, very few activists in Russia considered it realistic or desirable. As in the preceding generation, most Ukrainian nationalists in the Russian Empire were federalists who favored an institutional and cultural connection between Russia and Ukraine.[199] While the age cohort of the Shul'hyn children had gained political self-confidence thanks to their nationally colored education, their experience with student politics, and their growing number, few of them were hostile to all things Russian from the beginning.

After the promulgation of the Ems Ukaz in 1876, Ukrainophile activists were confined to private and semiprivate niches, forced to exploit gray zones and negotiate with the state for every minor concession. The story of the Shul'hyn-Ustymovych family exemplifies the difficulties that these committed men and women faced as they tried to walk the fine line between their political convictions and the strict rules of tsarist society. Both in their writings and their associational life, they had to find ways to make Ukrainophilism acceptable to the watchful authorities. However, Iakov Shul'gin's interactions with the tsarist police show that one should not overestimate the government's fear of Ukrainian nationalism. The severe repressions against him had more to do with his radical socialist connections than with his Ukrainophile leanings. Politically cautious Ukrainophiles remained practically unbothered.

How successful was the policy inaugurated by the Ems Ukaz from the Russian Empire's point of view? Did it manage to prevent political separatism? Yes and no. The restriction of Ukrainophile activities to the private and academic spheres meant that nearly all Ukrainophiles, many of whom were educated in the humanities, depended on the imperial state to make a living. It was thus unthinkable for them to shed all their attachments to official society and Russian-language culture. The Ems Ukaz forced the Ukrainophiles to adopt a gradualist policy and engage in a constant process of negotiation with the state. To people like Volodymyr Naumenko, this cautiousness became second nature. Most Ukrainophiles of this generation were moderate, academic types who continued to conceive of the "Ukrainian question" as an issue to be solved within the framework of a future constitutional, ideally federalized Russian Empire. This would become obvious in 1917, when Naumenko and other men of his age were overwhelmed, indeed shocked by the Ukrainian nationalists' rapid progress.

For several decades up to the first years of the twentieth century, the restrictions of the Ems Ukaz succeeded in keeping the Ukrainophile milieu small, moderate, and largely culturalist. However, this seemingly apolitical milieu already contained the seeds of the repoliticization of the Ukrainian question. Making use of their domestic spaces, Ukrainophile activists, above all the milieu's women, promoted an autonomous Ukrainian high culture whose mere existence was a political challenge to the regime. While the Ems Ukaz prevented the movement's open politicization, it paradoxically politicized cultural work.[200] Furthermore, in the long term, the repressions against the Ukrainian language arguably made the language issue particularly emotional for the national movement. The Ukrainian language became much more than the Ukrainophiles' idealized (if not always practically preferred) medium of communication; it was simultaneously a powerful symbol and the object of the movement's central political demands. It is not surprising that Ukrainian nationalists became increasingly unwilling to imagine Ukraine as a bilingual nation—something that had still seemed obvious for many of their midcentury predecessors.

Those who grew up in Kiev's Ukrainophile and increasingly Ukrainophone milieu would be more capable of imagining a Ukraine no longer linked to Russian culture and the imperial space. Their "native proficiency" in the Ukrainian language and in a nationally defined Ukrainian culture enabled them to reimagine themselves as unambiguously national intellectuals. However, the decisive break with the older gradualist attitude was a political choice that only happened when the Ukrainian nationalists were faced with a power vacuum after the monarchy's implosion in 1917. The case of Oleksander Shul'hyn's early career suggests that imperial Russian society had not completely lost its integrative force before 1914.[201] At the time it was still imaginable for Ukrainian nationalism to develop as an autonomist movement within a constitutional Russian Empire. This would change with the Russian defeats in the World War, the ever-growing hostility of Russian society against Ukrainian nationalism, the power vacuum of 1917, and the unexpected geopolitical opportunities that followed. It was these momentous experiences that radicalized the political outlook of many younger activists and that, retrospectively, make Oleksander Shul'hyn and his peers appear as a generation of thoroughly nationalized and nationalist politicians.[202]

CHAPTER 3

Patriarchs and Patriots

The Rise of Russian Nationalism, 1876–1914

The last decades of the nineteenth century were a period of almost unchallenged Russian imperial dominance in Kiev and the surrounding provinces. Polish nationalism was incapacitated as a political force by the anti-Polish measures that the government had implemented in the region after the failed uprising of 1863. Ukrainian nationalism was reined in by the Ems Ukaz and retreated into its domestic and academic niches. Socialist movements, so present in the region during the 1870s, lost most of their activists to forced exile or emigration. During the conservative reign of Tsar Alexander III (1881–1894), the administrative and cultural integration of Ukraine and its elites into the Russian Empire made headway. When new challenges to the imperial regime appeared around the turn of the century, Kiev saw the emergence of a vigorous Russian nationalist movement willing to defend Russian culture, Orthodoxy, and the autocratic state.

At the forefront of the struggle for the Russian nationality in Kiev was *Kievlianin*, the newspaper that Vitalii Shul'gin had established in 1864. After Shul'gin's death in 1878, the direction of the paper passed to Dmitrii Ivanovich Pikhno, a man of astonishing social mobility and political acumen who would retain this position for more than three decades. Pikhno assumed Vitalii Shul'gin's place both at the newspaper and in family life. In his capable hands, *Kievlianin* remained the city's most important news outlet until the revolution of 1905, and the dominant conservative press organ thereafter. While other newspapers came and went, *Kievlianin* remained true to its conservative and monarchist stance, gradually adapting to the changing conditions for Russian right-wing politics. After 1905, members of the Pikhno-Shul'gin family built a powerful political machine, securing considerable influence in Russia's new semiconstitutional regime. Meanwhile, their intimate life was unconventional and sometimes outright scandalous. While advocating legitimist politics, they regularly flouted the period's moral and marital conventions.

The nexus between politics, business, and private life offers a fresh perspective on Kiev's Russian nationalists. Dmitrii Pikhno's professional successes and failures were inseparable from his national-political choices and his family network. His specific brand of agrarian nationalism was rooted both in his academic work as an economist and in his practical experience as a buyer and owner of several estates in right-bank Ukraine. During the political watershed of 1904–1905, Pikhno and his associates radicalized their vision of the Russian nation in reaction to several external threats. As the Russo-Japanese War and the following revolutionary agitation plunged the empire into a deep crisis, *Kievlianin* launched a powerful counterattack and became the vanguard of a nationalist movement that found fertile soil in an ethnically diverse region. After 1905, Pikhno and his son Vasilii Shul'gin transferred their nationalizing project from Ukraine to the grand political stage of Saint Petersburg. In doing so, the Pikhno-Shul'gins used family connections as a political vehicle—to the point of turning politics into a family business.

"A Cultured Man"

The reconstruction of Dmitrii Pikhno's biography is no easy task. Although one of the empire's most important provincial newspaper editors, Pikhno never wrote his memoirs. Only about a dozen of his letters survive, and other people's writings contain only snippets of information about this extraordinary man. Born in 1853 near Chigirin, some 250 kilometers southeast of Kiev, Pikhno came from a humble social background. His father, a member of the modest townspeople (*meshchane*) estate, worked as an estate manager for the wealthy Iakhnenko and Symyrenko families. Later he bought himself a homestead (*khutor*) with a mill, earning his living as a miller.[1] Growing up in a rural milieu, young Dmitrii likely spoke a Ukrainian dialect rather than standard Russian. According to his daughter-in-law, Pikhno spoke Russian "not with a 'Ukrainian' accent but with Southern word stress" even as an adult. One of his obituarists also stressed his fluency in the "Little Russian dialect."[2] Unlike most Ukrainophiles of his generation, Pikhno was a native speaker of the region's rural idiom.

Dmitrii Pikhno came to Kiev in 1862, entering gymnasium at age nine. Depending on the source, he was brought there at the instigation of an older brother or of a relative living in Kiev. One memoirist even claims that he was one of the peasant boys selected for a free education in the Ukrainophile Hromada's secret elementary school. During his school years, Pikhno's tuition fee was waved, and he was granted free board at a dormitory for underprivileged students. Soon he began to finance his education by teaching private lessons to younger students. After his graduation, young Dmitrii enrolled at Kiev University in 1870.[3]

It is unclear to what extent Pikhno was involved in the political unrest that gripped the university during the 1870s. According to his collaborator and obituarist Aleksandr Bilimovich, Pikhno headed a circle of law students, but one that focused exclusively on scholarly studies in civil and criminal law. Oleksander Shul'hyn, by contrast, claimed that Pikhno attended Mykhailo Drahomanov's socialist Ukrainophile circle as a young student and later "betrayed" his comrades; as a punishment Iakov Shul'gin allegedly slapped Pikhno's face in public. There is no conclusive proof for this version, but the student Pikhno did work at the Shatov elementary school in Demievka, where Iakov Shul'gin was also teaching. A photograph from the early 1870s shows the organizers of the Demievka school, with a very young Dmitrii Pikhno seated on the left side and a still beardless Iakov Shul'gin standing on the right.[4] According to one memoirist of Kiev university life, the two already differed ideologically: "The leader of the liberals was the law student P–no (later a professor); the radicals, by a strange coincidence, were headed by the philology student Sh–n."[5] Pikhno would later acknowledge his relationship with Iakov by vouching for him with the authorities.

If Pikhno eventually embraced a moderate brand of liberalism instead of socialism or Ukrainophilism, this can be ascribed to the influence of his teachers. Like Iakov Shul'gin, Pikhno found two mentors at the university. One of them was Nikolai Bunge, the renowned liberal economist, university rector, and later Russia's minister of finances. Bunge recognized the young man's talents, procured him a stipend to

FIGURE 7. The organizers of the Demievka school, 1870s. Dmitrii Pikhno is seated at left; Iakov Shul'gin stands at right. *Kievlianin*, 6 September 1913, n.p. Courtesy of the Ukrainian National Library in Kyiv.

prepare for a professorship, and exerted a decisive influence on Pikhno's worldview.[6] Twenty years later, Pikhno would remember that "in those days, when young minds were drawn to the reformist plans of dreamers who wanted to renew and delight humanity, our teacher's merciless logic destroyed these seductive constructions, and they fell to our feet like children's broken toys."[7]

The brand of liberalism that Bunge passed on to Pikhno was in the tradition of the reformist bureaucrats of the 1860s. "Dedicated to transforming the state without shaking the fundamental principle of autocracy," these Russian liberals valued private property as the basis of social order but did not deny the state's prerogatives in strategic economic branches. By reforming the autocracy, they hoped to make it more efficient as a manager of the country and restore peace and order.[8] Bunge's protection at faculty and university council meetings helped Pikhno defend his master's dissertation as a lawyer and to become a lecturer in political economy at the age of only twenty-four years. Bunge even threatened to leave the university if the skeptics, among them the Ukrainophile lawyer Kistiakivs'kyi, would not approve his protégé's appointment.[9] Kistiakivs'kyi had already developed an antipathy for Pikhno, whom he perceived as a careerist looking for sinecures. "The milk on his lips has not dried yet," he noted in his diary, "but this greenhorn already smells of practicality, party spirit, and sarcasm."[10]

Pikhno's second mentor was Vitalii Shul'gin, the historian and editor of *Kievlianin*. In 1876, Pikhno began to write for the paper on economic topics. More importantly, he got into close relations with Shul'gin's family, especially his wife Mariia. Already in February 1876, Volodymyr Naumenko wrote to Iakov Shul'gin that Pikhno had "made himself adjutant to Shul'gin, and above all to Mariia Konstantinovna, he goes to the theater with them, rides around in a carriage with Mariia Konstantinovna, works for *Kievlianin* . . . ; in a word: 'a cultured man.'"[11] Ironic though his comment was, Naumenko was right: Pikhno was becoming a "cultured man," a member of the intelligentsia, which in his case equaled gradual assimilation to imperial Russian culture. When Mariia Shul'gina gave birth to her third child, Vasilii, on New Year's Day 1878, it must have been clear to the family that the father was not the frail Vitalii Shul'gin, but Dmitrii Pikhno. According to family lore, Mariia Shul'gina threw herself into a pond in desperation, but her husband forgave her and accepted the child as his own.[12]

When Vitalii Shul'gin died a year later, his widow became the publisher of *Kievlianin*, and the paper was quick to announce Pikhno as its new editor—a position gained through personal connections rather than journalistic merit. However, Pikhno, who promised to stand by the paper's political principles, soon proved a worthy successor to Vitalii Shul'gin.[13] In January 1880, he got married to Mariia Shul'gina, who soon gave birth to two more—legitimate—sons. Newspaper editor, university lecturer, family man: the miller's son had come a long way from his homestead near Chigirin. "Before getting his degree, he has begun to teach," grumbled Oleksandr Kistiakivs'kyi. "Before finishing his studies, he has entered the newspaper business. He is superficial. . . . No principles, except for the principle of snooping and swimming with the current. Selling everything for profit. At twenty-seven, he has attained a prosperity which honest people attain toward the end of their lives, if at all."[14]

Over the 1880s, *Kievlianin* continued to defend the Russianness of the empire's Southwest against the threats supposedly posed by Polish landowners and Jewish traders. The Ukrainian movement, extremely cautious and secretive during these years, remained a minor foe mentioned only on special occasions. Still, Pikhno's private anti-Ukrainophile views were beyond doubt. In a typical mixture of be-littlement and fearmongering, Pikhno was certain that Ukrainophilism ("khokhlomania," as he called it) "was and remains to this day the cause of a minuscule circle," but also warned that its leaders planned to form "an independent federation consisting of the western region, the Little Russian provinces, and Galicia."[15] And three years later, he remained suspicious: "This issue is currently on hiatus, but there is no doubt that it will resurface on the first suitable occasion; and even at pres-ent there is no guarantee that invisible but busy preparation work is not going on somewhere."[16] When a popular Ukrainian theater troupe visited Kiev in 1882, *Kievlianin* launched a series of articles mocking the actors as "amateurs" and their enthusiastic audience as "ignorant" or "mentally ill."[17] Pikhno, however, opposed the prohibition of musical performances and plays in the "Little Russian" language. Instead of re-pression, he championed counterpropaganda. In 1882, he co-initiated the foundation of the Kiev Literacy Society, an educational association meant to counteract Ukrainophile and Polish school activism by pro-moting Russian literacy.[18]

Under the economist Pikhno, *Kievlianin* turned its attention to eco-nomic questions. In the early 1880s, Pikhno began a lengthy controversy on railway tariffs against Sergei Witte, who was at that time director of the Southwestern Railways. In a time when private railway companies were undercutting each other's prices to the point of ruin, the ques-tion was politically significant. While Witte wanted to prevent excesses through a schedule of shipping rates, Pikhno preferred state ownership of the track network and a fixed tariff determined by the state.[19] For all their differences, both men shared a commitment to state-supported economic modernization, agreeing with many contemporaries that railways were of strategical importance to the empire as a means of ter-ritorial integration, stabilization, and possibly expansion.[20]

In 1885, Pikhno got the opportunity to work inside the state appara-tus. Nikolai Bunge, now finance minister in the tsar's cabinet, offered him a position on the railway council in Saint Petersburg. During his two years serving the ministry, Pikhno became involved in the conflict between his protector Bunge, then considered a very liberal minister, and the archconservative and highly powerful ober-procurator of the Holy Synod, Konstantin Pobedonostsev. When Pobedonostsev emerged victorious and Bunge was demoted to a largely ceremonial post, Pikhno returned to Kiev in 1887. This new turn in his career was again linked to his private situation. After the death of his wife Mariia in 1883, Pikhno

FIGURE 8.   Mariia Shul'gina-Pikhno, in a picture published after her death in 1883. The deceased is portrayed as the matriarch of the *Kievlianin* family enterprise, with Kiev's iconic Saint Andrew's Church in the background. *Khudozhestvenno-literaturnyi al'manakh "Kievlianka."* Kiev: Tipo-Litografiia I. N. Kushnereva, 1884, n.p. Courtesy of the Ukrainian National Library in Kyiv.

had entered a relationship with her eldest daughter Lina (Pavla), who was then eighteen years old. A marriage to his deceased wife's daughter was prohibited by church law, and therefore the couple lived together unmarried.[21] According to Sergei Witte, Pobedonostsev used Pikhno's illegitimate relationship to remove one of Bunge's liberal allies in the ministry.[22]

The family's intimate situation remained tense after Pikhno's return. Lina had to take care of an entire host of children and teenagers: her sister Alla and half-brother Vasilii, Pikhno's sons Pavel and Dmitrii, and her own illegitimate child with Pikhno, Filipp, who was born in 1885. Over the years, Pikhno and Lina Shul'gina had two more sons, Aleksandr and Ivan. During Lina's second pregnancy, Pikhno arranged a fictional marriage with his acquaintance Aleksandr Mogilevskii, who was apparently promised a monthly pension for giving his name to Pikhno's and Lina's children.[23] Mogilevskii died in the following year, and Lina wrote to her friend, "Even though it is very bad to be happy about a person's death, I still feel greatly relieved."[24] Yet Lina Mogilevskaia would never be fully accepted in Kiev's higher society and could not appear as Pikhno's wife in public. Nor was the following generation's love life unproblematic. Vasilii Shul'gin, Pikhno's eldest son, began a relationship with Ekaterina Gradovskaia, an actress nine years his senior and also his first cousin. They got married after Vasilii came of age in 1899. Since this union, too, violated the rules of the Orthodox Church, their wedding had to take place in Odessa, under concealment of the couple's cousinship.[25]

Pikhno's unconventional private life did not prevent his social advancement. The *Kievlianin* editor became one of Kiev's most influential public figures during the decade following his return. He became a full professor at Kiev University and turned *Kievlianin* into one of the most-read provincial newspapers in the Russian Empire, a serious publication with a focus on economics and foreign policy. Despite the paper's pro-government line, the liberal intelligentsia valued its earnest tone, independent positions, and detailed treatment of local news.[26] The editorial office on the corner of Kuznechnaia and Karavaevskaia Streets, and the family home next to it, became a meeting place for "visiting dignitaries and civil servants from Saint Petersburg, local higher administrators, churchmen, professors and public figures, local landowners and men of commerce" who came to ask Pikhno for advice or discuss politics.[27] In 1896, Pikhno cooperated with the Jewish millionaire Lazar' Brodskii to establish the Kiev Bacteriological Institute; two years later, he was involved in the foundation of the Polytechnical Institute. He was also a member of the City Duma for some time.[28] The events of 1904–1906 catapulted Pikhno into the highest echelons of imperial politics in Saint Petersburg. By the time of his death in 1913, he was a respected member of the State Council and had been promoted to privy councillor, the third-highest civil position in the Table of Ranks.

Against the background of Iakov Shul'gin's biography, Pikhno's trajectory shows that great social mobility was possible in the Russian Empire, given the necessary mixture of talent, luck, and suitable political views. Iakov Shul'gin, a nobleman born into an educated family, lost his secure social position, his freedom, and his health because he chose to support socialist and Ukrainophile causes. Pikhno, by contrast, was born into a poor and uneducated family and rose to wealth and influence during the reactionary reign of Alexander III. This was only possible thanks to his powerful patrons and his decision to support the governing system. Having chosen the political side of the autocratic state, Pikhno also embraced Russian nationality. Although he knew to take advantage of the state, it would be wrong to classify him as a cynical opportunist. If his opinions often dovetailed with the government's policies, this need not mean that they were not sincerely held. On the contrary, Pikhno was deeply convinced that only an autocracy could govern Russia and improve the lot of the peasant masses.

Economic Nationalism in Theory and Practice

An economist by profession, Dmitrii Pikhno grounded his politics on an economic analysis of society. Building on Vitalii Shul'gin's ideas, Pikhno saw the Russification of the regional economy—or, to put it the other way around, the economic strengthening of the "Russian" population—as the most urgent task for Russian nationalism in the Southwest. Unlike Shul'gin, Pikhno attempted to put his program into practice by buying up estates in the empire's western borderlands. Rooted in classical liberalism, Pikhno rejected both Marxist economics and the Moscow economic school inspired by *narodnik* socialism. In his seminars at the university, he passionately tried to dissuade his students from the increasingly popular Marxist analysis of society.[29] However, he agreed with the German Historical School that different locations followed different economic paths—and in the case of the underdeveloped Russian Empire, this meant that some state intervention was indispensable to stimulate the economy. Like his teacher Bunge,

Pikhno was thus an eclectic scholar who was more interested in the practical applicability of his analyses than in the creation of a systematic theory.[30]

Pikhno never wrote a comprehensive scholarly treatise on the Russification of the economy. However, his colleague and close friend Evgenii Kartavtsov published a study, "The Russification of Landownership in the Southwestern Region," in 1877. Kartavtsov's views were very similar to Pikhno's later ideas and likely exerted an influence on their formation. Kartavtsov analyzed the government's land policy in right-bank Ukraine since 1863, concluding that the restrictions on Polish land purchases, the confiscation of rebels' estates, and the promotion of Russian land acquisition had only brought meager results. Only when half the estates belonged to Russian nobles would the region be "sufficiently russified." Kartavtsov proposed the introduction of rural self-administration (*zemstvos*) in the Southwest to strengthen Russian landowners' influence, improve the peasants' material situation, and create a stratum of loyal Polish nobles.[31] Pikhno would adopt and develop this plan many years later.

Even without the introduction of zemstvos, Russian landownership in right-bank Ukraine made slow but steady progress. By 1896, Russian (i.e., Orthodox) landowners owned 51 percent of private estates in the provinces of Kiev, Podolia, and Volhynia, having acquired about twenty-six thousand square kilometers of land from Poles since 1866. Rising land prices boosted the wealth of both Russian and Polish estate owners, and the rapidly growing sugar industry provided a new source of income for nobles and non-nobles alike.[32] The region's economic growth transformed Kiev into one of the largest and most modern cities in the Russian Empire. A census in 1874 had yielded no more than 127,000 inhabitants, and in the early 1880s, Kiev still resembled a provincial town. The city lacked modern transportation and hygiene facilities, and herds of pigs roamed its many unpaved streets. In the following years, the population exploded, and by 1897, Kiev boasted 248,000 inhabitants, making it the empire's seventh-largest city. By 1914 the population doubled again, to reach over half a million.[33] The sugar industry of the surrounding provinces gave rise to a cosmopolitan capitalist elite, consisting of Polish and Great Russian aristocrats, as well as socially mobile Jewish and Little Russian (Ukrainian) entrepreneurs. Using its influence in the City Duma, this emerging bourgeoisie provided the city with modern infrastructure (electricity, railway connections, the empire's first electric tramway) while securing its own financial interests.

The booming economy attracted mass labor immigration. Jewish artisans and Ukrainian-speaking peasants flocking to the factories from their *shtethlekh* and villages turned Kiev into an increasingly diverse city, although both these populations tended to assimilate into the Russian language and culture over time.[34]

During the 1880s and 1890s, *Kievlianin* denounced the region's emerging capitalist elite. Sugar production, the newspaper charged, allowed a few individuals to accumulate immense wealth while exploiting the Orthodox peasant masses. Stressing the high percentage of Poles and Jews among the "sugar barons," *Kievlianin* once more framed the region's economic inequalities as an ethnic antagonism and portrayed the Jewish population as a nefarious "kulak nation" whose economic power ought to be curbed.[35] When Orthodox workers ransacked the homes and shops of Kiev's Jewish traders and artisans after the assassination of Alexander II in 1881, *Kievlianin* had little sympathy, arguing that the pogrom was a result of Jewish exploitation and demonstrated the impossibility of Jewish assimilation.[36] Yet the paper was not unequivocally antisemitic. During the 1890s, several articles demanded the gradual abolition of the Jewish Pale of Settlement, criticized antisemitic police chicanery, and advocated assimilation.[37] In 1903, an editorial denounced the Kishinev pogrom, defending the region's Jews as "an enterprising and energetic class of traders and industrialists" as well as "hardworking, frugal, and sober artisans."[38] In this period, Pikhno's antisemitism only targeted the Jewish elites within the region's ethnically marked socioeconomic order, and what he called the "Jewish stranglehold" (*evreiskoe zasil'e*) over the Russian peasantry.

In a 1901 speech, Pikhno outlined the empire's and the Southwest's recent economic successes: fixed railway tariffs had improved transport conditions, the gold standard had stabilized the ruble and made credit affordable, and the mitigation of industrial protectionism had strengthened agriculture. Incidentally, these were policies that Pikhno had advocated for years. Now, Pikhno said, estate owners and smallholders had to cooperate for the sake of the region's agricultural economy. He denied that there was a fundamental conflict between large estates and peasant farms. Rather, the estates were drivers of technical progress that perfectly complemented the peasant farms, those strongholds of tradition and providers of high-quality mass labor. What really counted for Pikhno was "the beneficial law of symbiosis, peaceful coexistence, i.e. the law of mutual aid, support, and defense."[39] It was the old nationalist dream of cooperation and unity across estates and classes, of a harmonious rural society whose close connection to the soil would form the basis of a healthy nation.

However, Pikhno was far from idealizing traditional rural society. Himself a former country lad, he dismissed both the conservative Slavophile utopia of an idyllic village community (*obshchina*) and the Tolstoian or *narodnik* glorification of peasant simplicity and honesty. Modernity and urban culture would penetrate the Russian village no matter what, he wrote; therefore it was better to let the state introduce them than to wait for their spontaneous arrival "with all the distortions of a tavern riffraff perspective." Rather than rely on the archaic and harmful village community, the state ought to turn the peasants into individual landowners, make them full citizens, and subject them to the same laws and courts as the rest of the population. Lower taxes, better credit, and the development of a small-scale processing industry in the villages would create a stratum of prosperous and politically loyal smallholders.[40]

The insistence on state-driven modernity, the rule of law, and a "Western" capitalist development was typical of Pikhno's thought but rather uncommon among Russian conservatives, most of whom combined an agrarian worldview with an antisemitically grounded distrust of industry, finance, and the gold standard.[41] While Pikhno did not address the national question explicitly, the region's social stratification assured that his proposals would exclusively benefit the "Russian," Orthodox population. As he phrased it a few years later,

> The privileges and protection of some nationalities and the oppression of others during a long period have created stark inequalities in the distribution of incomes, the accumulation of wealth and education, and finally, in the level of culture and welfare. . . . Western Rus' has alien upper classes and Russian lower classes: Polish large landownership, Jewish industry and trade, and Russian small landownership. . . . We must give the Russian population the possibility to improve its lot, we must stretch out a helping hand and offer it a guiding star to happiness.[42]

Like Vitalii Shul'gin, then, Pikhno saw the imperial Russian state as an instrument to improve the peasantry's situation, as part of the solution rather than part of the problem.

Pikhno also promoted economic Russification in practice. As soon as he began to earn money in the newspaper business, he invested it in land in right-bank Ukraine. *Kievlianin* was economically successful during these years. It began to appear daily in 1879, and by 1882, Mariia Shul'gina-Pikhno could afford to refuse the newspaper's government subsidy.[43] In 1887, Pikhno bought his first estate, Agatovka, near the village of Babin-Tomakhovo in the Rovno district of Volhynia, about 250 kilometers west of Kiev. The purchase was facilitated by a mortgage from the Nobles' Land Bank, an institution meant to support the land-ownership of nobles, specifically excluding Poles.[44] When Pikhno's sons grew up, he bought land for them, too: the small estate Kurgany near Agatovka for Vasilii Shul'gin and his wife Ekaterina in 1905; Kashovka, also in Volhynia, for Pavel Pikhno; and Zalivanshchina in Podolia for Dmitrii Pikhno (jr.). The seller of Kurgany was a Pole, one Count Kra-sicki, and it is likely that Pikhno bought his other estates from Polish nobles, too.[45] "Dmitrii Ivanovich's greed for land was purely peasant-like," wrote his daughter-in-law Ekaterina Shul'gina. "What is more, Dmitrii Ivanovich saw the acquisition of estates as a matter of Rus-sian nationalism and of the establishment of Russian culture, as a re-placement of Polish by Russian landownership, and as economic and cultural-educational assistance to the peasants."[46]

Once a landowner, Pikhno implemented his program for the socio-ethnic transformation of the countryside on a local scale. Following the example of his father, he built a water mill at Babin-Tomakhovo, and later three more mills on the family's estates. Shortly before his death in 1913, Pikhno began the construction of a sugar factory at Babin-Tomakhovo that later employed about two hundred workers. For Pikhno, these investments were more than a means to increase the family's wealth. By developing rural industry and accumulating capital, he offered the local peasants a possibility to earn money with-out depending on "alien" Polish employers or Jewish moneylenders.[47] Pikhno saw himself as a socially aware patron with a responsibility for his workers. He voluntarily paid pensions to former employees of *Kievlianin*, invited the paper's typesetters to his estate for summer vacations, and paid "insurance" to peasants whose huts had burned down.[48] He was also dedicated to rural education, patronizing an agri-cultural college in Kiev province (on the estate of his younger brother Vasilii) and several village schools in Volhynia. His son and daughter-in-law financed the construction of a school at the Kurgany estate and paid part of the teachers' salaries.[49] Unlike the old Polish nobility, the Pikhno-Shul'gins viewed themselves and the peasants as members of one common nation, which implied certain commitments on the land-owners' side.

Pikhno's attempt to russify the entire production process on his estates failed. The socioethnic composition of Volhynian rural society was
such that national exclusivism could not be implemented consistently.
Pikhno's attempts to buy grain and sell flour himself, without the in-
termediary of Jewish traders, resulted in immediate financial losses.
Jewish flour traders (*peremol'shchiki*) had low prices and good business
contacts; even the worst antisemites cooperated with them. Unable to
exclude all Jewish middlemen, Pikhno decided to work with petty traders, providing his own capital from the mill. These traders ostensibly
held Pikhno in high regard, and he was said to enjoy bargaining with
them.[50] Vasilii Shul'gin later went so far as to describe life on his own
estate as a perfect model of interethnic cooperation:

> My coachman Andrei was a Pole; but he never meddled with poli-
> tics. . . . In general we did not mix the two crafts. We were national-
> ists in politics but cosmopolitans in everyday life. My wife's maid
> Lena was a Polish girl but they got along very well. The mill's man-
> ager was a Pole. The engineer was Czech, the hop grower as well.
> This Internationale worked in great harmony. The estate manager
> was a Pole; the head mechanic and the machine operators were
> Russians; the accountants Russians, the fisherman a Russian, the
> mill workers Russians, and the farmhands, too; the flour traders
> were Jews. And all lived in agreement—there were no politics in
> Kurgany.[51]

While this statement certainly exaggerates the harmony of the lost idyll,
it nevertheless shows that the family, for all its nationalism, did not en-
visage a nationally purged rural society. Their goal was to change the
socioethnic hierarchies, not to drive out all non-Russians. That said,
the Pikhno-Shul'gin family did remain separate from the region's Polish landowners. As Pikhno's de facto wife Lina wrote from Volhynia in
1890, "We are surrounded by Poles, people whose interests are foreign
to us, and neither do we seek their acquaintance, nor they ours."[52]

The vision of a harmonious rural society blinded the eyes of these
nationalists to the social cleavage between themselves and the peasants.
Just as Oleksander Shul'hyn's memoirs idealize the countryside of Poltava province and its peasants, Ekaterina Shul'gina and Vasilii Shul'gin
romanticize rural Volhynia in their own reminiscences. Particularly
Vasilii Shul'gin's unpublished memoirs "Flour" and "Honey," written
in a Soviet prison in the early 1950s, abound with romantic descriptions of Volhynia's fields and forests, of country life and the coarse but

goodhearted peasants. He and his wife generally portray them as peaceful and hardworking but in need of the landlord's guiding hand. Thus, Vasilii Shul'gin relates a strike of the mill's peasant workers, which he claims to have solved easily by hiring strike-breakers from the neighboring village and negotiating a small wage raise.[53] Despite such episodes, the Pikhno-Shul'gins continued to believe in a harmonious coexistence between estate owners and smallholding peasants, both before and after these dreams were crushed in the violence of the revolution and civil war.[54] Writing in the 1920s, Ekaterina Shul'gina's asserted that her three sons Vasilid, Veniamin (Lialia), and Dmitrii "terribly loved Kurgany, where they essentially grew up as 'young squires' of the feudal days or as *panychy*, as they say in these parts, loved and spoiled by the 'domestics.'" However, Shul'gina adds, the servants' devotion was much more valuable than that of serfs "because these were free and freely hired people."[55]

Unsurprisingly, the Shul'gins' memoirs portray the Volhynian peasants as Russians, as a breed of simple country folk descended directly from the peasants of medieval Rus'.[56] Given that local peasants were hired as servants and wet nurses, Ukrainian dialects must have been constantly present in the Shul'gin-Pikhno household. Dmitrii Pikhno likely spoke to them in his own native dialect, too. Still, Ekaterina Shul'gina was convinced that these peasants saw themselves as Russians: "I have lived in the village for many years and not once have I heard even one peasant yearning for the 'native language' [*ridnia mova*, i.e., Ukrainian]. Generally, I have not observed any signs of separatism. The word 'Ukraine' was simply unknown to them."[57] While this might well be true, it probably testifies to the peasants' national indifference rather than their conscious Russianness. Vasilii Shul'gin admitted as much when he wrote that Evdokha, the cook at Agatovka, probably would not have known either one of the words "Little Russian" and "Ukrainian."[58] When the semiconstitutional system brought electoral politics to the Volhynian countryside after 1905, the peasants' national and political allegiances would remain unclear and fleeting.

Landownership and engagement with the agricultural economy were at the core of Dmitrii Pikhno's nationalism. While their Ukrainophile relatives felt somewhat embarrassed by their gentry connection, the Pikhno-Shul'gins fully embraced the life of estate owners. Yet they, too, imagined themselves as close to the common people, as generous (if somewhat patronizing) benefactors of the peasants, whom they saw as the Russian element in the Southwest's social order. Like their cousins, the Pikhno-Shul'gins were genuinely dedicated to improving these peasants' economic standing; unlike them, they did not fundamentally question the existing order. After 1905, Pikhno and his son Vasilii Shul'gin would try to initiate political reforms meant to strengthen the region's Orthodox smallholders and to hand local government to the loyal Russian population. However, Pikhno's politically motivated dedication to his estates remained a marginal phenomenon. While the years around 1900 saw a growth of gentry entrepreneurship, technical innovation, and commercialized agriculture in the Southwest, the majority of the new Russian gentry farmers were absentee landlords with little interest in social reform. Many of them leased their estates to Polish or Jewish tenants. The region's economy grew rapidly, but the state and most landowners lacked Pikhno's commitment to the project of an economically strong nation carried by the solidarity of all social classes.[59]

"Under Siege"

The Russo-Japanese War of 1904 and the wave of revolutionary protest that shook Russia in 1905 had a profound impact on Dmitrii Pikhno's political views. Faced with external and internal threats to the tsarist state, his sense of national antagonism grew, and his politics shifted toward antireform, autocratic conservatism. According to Sergei Witte, Pikhno had still advocated a gradual limitation of the autocracy at the turn of the century. "Later, when our so-called revolution broke out in 1905, Pikhno immediately jumped rightward like a madman and . . . began to preach the most reactionary views in *Kievlianin*."[60] From the beginning of Russian-Japanese tensions, Pikhno had argued against the government's strategy of railway-driven expansion in the Far East, fearing huge financial losses.[61] When fighting began in early 1904, however, *Kievlianin* took an uncritically patriotic stance, presenting the war as a legitimate defense against a perfidious attack. The Kiev psychiatrist and pioneer of "scientific" racism Ivan Sikorskii wrote of a "great biological event" in which Russia would fulfill its historical mission of civilizing the racially inferior Asians by "pouring their healthy juices into the flesh and blood, the nerves and soul of the Mongolian tribes."[62]

As the war uncovered the inferiority of the Russian navy to the Japanese, the paper continued to support the military unconditionally. Pikhno insisted on the need for victory even after the crushing defeat in the battle of Tsushima in May 1905, and was dissatisfied with the rather favorable peace that Witte, the new chairman of the ministers' committee, negotiated in August.[63] With regard to internal political developments, Pikhno kept a measured tone throughout 1904. He condemned revolutionary agitation in no uncertain terms but also advocated a cautious inclusion of society in matters of government. He welcomed the abolition of some anti-Jewish restrictions and criticized other conservatives for equating Jews and revolutionaries. In reality, he repeated, most of Russia's Jews were useful and patriotic citizens.[64]

Over the following months, exasperation about the hopeless war combined with other social and political grievances to spread the revolutionary upheaval over the entire empire. Factory workers staged massive strikes in all major cities. Thousands of students refused to continue their studies. Groups of peasants attacked and pillaged noble estates. Sailors mutinied in Odessa. Jewish activists called for equal rights, and Polish nobles began to talk about territorial autonomy. Liberal lawyers, engineers, and zemstvo members demanded the immediate introduction of elected representative institutions. The state's local organs were incapable of keeping up order, condemned to passivity and occasional violent repression that only further fueled the population's anger.[65]

Under the impression of this loss of control, Pikhno began to single out particular groups of people as enemies of the Russian state and of "sensible conservative society." At the root of the upheaval, according to Pikhno, were the university students, Russia's "nonlearning youth," as he liked to call them, demanding a temporary closure of universities and secondary schools.[66] Next came the liberal intelligentsia, the lawyers, medics, engineers, and teachers, who according to Pikhno should have despised radicalism because of their societal responsibility. Instead, he complained, they used their authority to instigate the trusting and gullible masses against the existing order. Even worse were the socialists of all parties, who were motivated by the immoral doctrines of foreign Marxism and whose propaganda had fatally undermined the war effort against Japan.[67] Finally, the agriculturalist Pikhno expressed a peculiar dislike for the urban proletariat, the "depraved urban mob, which is everywhere like a filthy and murky scum." In his eyes, the protests in the cities included as many beggars and alcoholics as actual factory workers.[68] By contrast, he remained convinced that the bulk of the peasantry were conservative monarchists and that occasional rural riots were the result of outside agitation.

Pikhno rarely failed to mention that non-Russians (*inorodtsy*) made up a disproportionately high share of all these revolutionary groups. In particular, his paper voiced ever sharper antisemitic resentments. While continuing to assert the innocence of the Jewish masses, Pikhno began to blame antisemitic riots on the "provocation" of Jewish revolutionaries, whom he accused of spreading pogrom rumors in order to form armed self-defense units. Jewish society, he explained, must restrain its revolutionary youth. Pikhno was less concerned with Polish autonomy, which he no longer saw as a major threat to the Russian Empire. After all, it mainly concerned the Polish Kingdom now that the Poles' social position in the western borderlands had been weakened.[69] Meanwhile, the danger of Ukrainian nationalism hardly figured at all in *Kievlianin* during 1905—even the Latvian national movement was accorded more attention.[70] Indeed, Ukrainian nationalism was rather marginal to the year's events, at least in Kiev. The Revolutionary Ukrainian Party was active on the region's sugar beet plantations, and some Ukrainian Social Democrats agitated among Kiev's workers. Demands for Ukrainian autonomy or even independence were voiced at university meetings. Most strikes and demonstrations, however, were driven by economic and social grievances.[71]

The winter and spring had seen strikes in several Kiev factories, but over the summer of 1905, revolutionary agitation seemed to be on the wane. In August, the minister of the interior Aleksandr Bulygin presented his draft for a constitution, which would have introduced a consultative parliament elected on a narrow, property-based franchise. Pikhno's *Kievlianin* welcomed the Bulygin proposal as a sufficient concession and a cautious step toward reform within the limits of the autocracy. Most opposition groups, meanwhile, found the proposal less than satisfactory. In early October, Moscow's railway workers initiated a new wave of protests that soon evolved into an empire-wide general strike. Pressured by his advisers, above all Sergei Witte, Tsar Nicholas II issued a manifesto on 17 October, promising civil liberties and a State Duma with legislative powers elected by all classes of the population.[72] The popular reaction was enthusiastic. On the following day, a huge crowd gathered in front of Kiev's City Duma to celebrate the new "constitution." Social Democratic agitators made revolutionary speeches while protesters ripped the imperial insignia from the building, tore down national flags, and damaged several portraits of tsars. After a few hours, an infantry unit dispersed the crowd by opening fire, and in the evening an antisemitic riot broke out in the city. Right-wing observers later blamed the destruction of tsarist symbols exclusively on Jewish revolutionaries and claimed that the protesters had shot at the soldiers first.[73]

On 19 October, conservative workers organized a "patriotic demonstration." Thousands of Kievans marched from the Duma building to the university, singing the imperial anthem. Carrying flags, an icon, a cross, and portraits of the tsar, the protesters arrived outside the editorial offices of *Kievlianin*. There, they were met by the paper's typesetters and by Pikhno, who asked them to end the fighting and restore order in the city.[74] After the demonstration, however, many participants joined the ongoing pogrom of Kiev's Jewish population, which went on for three days. Three hundred people were injured, at least twenty-seven killed, and eighteen hundred Jewish shops and homes ransacked.[75] Historian Natan Meir describes both the demonstration and the subsequent pogrom as shows of force by the city's right-wing monarchists, a symbolic reconquest from a purported Jewish revolutionary danger.[76]

Unlike the city's liberationist press, *Kievlianin* refused to see a connection between the "peaceful patriotic manifestation" and the "horrible day of elemental destruction." The presence of young Jews among the revolutionary "madmen," Pikhno declared, had insulted the patriotism of the city's Russian population: "The Russian nation is dark and poor ... but its belief in God is sacred, its earthly lodestar is the Russian tsar, it profoundly loves its fatherland. Do not touch its sanctuaries and respect its national feeling." Despite his antisemitic accusations, Pikhno called on the population to stop the violence against their Jewish fellow citizens.[77] His central concern was to restore order, and a pogrom was clearly not what was needed to get there. By belittling the violence, blaming the victims, and expressing regret about the "darkness" of the masses, he reproduced the traditional conservative reaction to anti-Jewish pogroms.[78] But his old resentment against the Jews' economic "stranglehold" now combined with the image of the seditious Jewish revolutionary. As he privately wrote to Sergei Witte, he feared that the Jews might assume a dominant political position, further alienating the region's peasants from the state: "The Jewish question is that terrible question over which Russia might lose the Little Russians. . . . The pogroms are a pure trifle compared to what will happen if the *khokhol* says that the *moskal* has given or sold him to the Yids."[79]

Kievlianin was Kiev's only paper—and one of very few in the empire—to appear in these days, even though protesters tried to close it down several times. According to Vasilii Shul'gin, this was only possible thanks to military protection and the loyalty of the typesetters to their patron.[80] During the following weeks, Pikhno almost filled the paper alone, allegedly working seventeen to eighteen hours a day. He feverishly wrote against the revolutionaries and against the October Manifesto, advocating heavy government repression instead.[81] The introduction even of a limited democracy, for Pikhno, contradicted the monarchist convictions of the peasants and the army; it handed over power to the uneducated masses, who were not even interested in voting. His opposition to a broad electoral franchise mirrored his paternalistic conception of the agrarian economy. In his eyes, only an autocrat could govern such a huge and diverse state as Russia. As a proud Russian citizen and *khokhol*, he declared, he would not let "a gang of robbing railwaymen and strikers, Jews and socialists" dictate the law.[82] Pikhno sharply criticized his old acquaintance, Prime Minister Witte, for kindling the revolution instead of putting it down. He sent him several telegrams urging repressive measures but declined an invitation to discuss matters in Saint Petersburg.[83]

Pikhno's staunch resistance to the revolution made a him well-known political figure in Kiev and beyond, turning *Kievlianin* into a rallying point for pro-government opinion in the entire region. The identification of the paper with the autocracy was so widespread that protesters tore it out of newsstands in symbolic defiance.[84] After the October days, Pikhno began to print daily selections from readers' correspondence. Many of these letters were signed by dozens of people and simply thanked Pikhno for writing the truth about the revolutionaries, for defending the "Russian spirit" and the "truly Russian people." Other letters were directed against the "lies" of the oppositional press; many readers specifically defended themselves or others against accusations of having participated in pogroms.[85] The newspaper editors made a point of mentioning the social status and profession of all their correspondents in order to demonstrate the diversity of the growing patriotic movement. Letter writers often spoke as conservative representatives of a particular professional group: railway workers condemning railway strikes, students criticizing radical student activism, telegraph officials lambasting protests in their administration. There was even a "repenting Social Democrat" who claimed to have been saved from the "bad ideas of mediocre people" by reading a few issues of *Kievlianin*.[86]

The editors were particularly keen on printing letters from peasants, whom Pikhno kept presenting as a bulwark of conservatism. Usually written "in a half-literate way," these letters accused the opposition of insulting Russia, religion, and the tsar. A group of peasants from Berdichev characteristically presented the revolution as the work of educated and non-Russian populations: "Red Hundreds, stop it! You have

sufficiently satiated yourselves with dead bodies and streams of peaceful citizens' blood. . . . Students, lawyers, engineers, Polacks and Yids,
back off. . . . Hooray to the Tsar-Father, hooray to the Heir Apparent
and all the Imperial House!" A peasant called Red'ka proposed a series
of measures to reinstate order, from the improvement of the rural administration and the enforcement of Prussian discipline in the army to
the expulsion of all Jews to Africa, "where they can establish their own
tsardom and roam with red flags." Many letters, the editors claimed,
were so antisemitic that Pikhno decided not to print them. *Kievlianin*'s
correspondents also included many women, whose letters differed little
from those of male readers. Ol'ga Reitlinger, an officer's wife, called on
the "well-meaning majority" to fight the "enemies of the Russian land,"
while the village teacher Kulomina wanted to send peasant representatives to Saint Petersburg so that the tsar could calm them in person.
A fifteen-year-old peasant boy called Okhrim Chepurnyi contributed a
clumsy patriotic poem in a mixture of Russian and Ukrainian.[87]

Thus, in the absence of popular associations, *Kievlianin* became a forum for newly politicized conservatives across Ukraine. In turn, Pikhno
and his associates found the letters to confirm the popularity of their
own opinions. In a kind of feedback loop, readers echoed the views that
Pikhno stated in his articles, which Pikhno understood as confirmation
that the majority shared his conservative views. The letters cemented
his vision of Kiev as an antirevolutionary citadel that acknowledged
its Russianness precisely because of its borderland position—an image
that *Kievlianin* would continuously project over the following decade.[88]
The editor's turn to the right in 1905 was the direct result of the impression that his most cherished values—the monarchy, Russianness,
private property, law and order—were under attack from all sides. When
Russia's liberals joined a broad liberationist movement for mass democracy, representative institutions, and equal rights for non-Russians
that even questioned the legitimacy of private landownership, Pikhno
abandoned his former liberal views. These views belonged to an earlier
stage of Russian liberalism, one that had been fully compatible with an
autocratic state. Now, the autocracy needed to be defended. As Pikhno
put it shortly after the events, in February 1906, "The staff of *Kievlianin*
endured a heavy siege both in a literal and in a figurative sense. Not for
one minute did it lower the old Russian banner in ancient Kiev in the
face of red flags, in the face of the attacking revolutionary psychosis."[89]

The metaphor of the siege is crucial to understand the formation,
in 1905-1906, of a powerful Russian monarchist and nationalist

movement. Thus far, Russian nationalism had been a dormant political force, more often implicitly assumed than explicitly uttered. In the face of powerful adversity, it began to organize. The conservative sympathizers of the autocracy had long hesitated to form political associations, for they contradicted both the law that they idolized and their ideology, according to which the empire did not need popular representation. But as the government was forced to grant freedom of association to its liberal and socialist challengers, conservative monarchists, too, made use of the new organizational possibilities. For the autocracy's defenders, the fact that the tsar and the state had come "under siege" justified the adoption of political practices that threatened to undermine this very autocracy. A reality that they perceived as catastrophic prompted them to act.[90]

Right-Wing Mobilization in the Face of Adversity

In the course of 1905, several right-wing organizations were formed in Moscow and Saint Petersburg. The journalist Vladimir Gringmut pioneered conservative party politics with his Russian Monarchist Party, which advocated views similar to Pikhno's. The Russian Assembly, an upper-class cultural club formed in 1901, turned to politics and convened the first congress of monarchist associations. Slavophile aristocrats formed the Union of Russian Men, which embraced a traditionalist, religious nationalism. Most importantly, the medic Aleksandr Dubrovin founded the Union of the Russian People, whose brochures successfully targeted shopkeepers, clerks, artisans, workers, and peasants. By 1907, the Union of the Russian People had over a thousand branches all over Russia. It was particularly successful in rural Volhynia, where its most fervent leaders were the Orthodox monks of the Pochaev monastery. While different in social makeup and political strategies, all those groups shared a commitment to the autocracy, a hatred of both liberals and socialists, and a strongly antisemitic rhetoric. Some of them dreamed of an idealized Muscovite past, others looked back to the heavy-handed rule of Alexander III, but most Russian monarchists were too busy defending the existing order against the perceived onslaught of enemies to come up with concrete visions of the future.[91]

If the political practices of Russian nationalism underwent a profound transformation after 1905, its ideology continued earlier trends. It is sometimes argued that this period saw the rise of an ethnic conception of the Russian nation, as opposed to the earlier dynastic or state-oriented view of Russianness.[92] Some among the period's conservatives doubtless moved toward a more ethnically exclusive nationalism, with certain (rather isolated) voices sounding openly racist notes.[93] However, as seen above, nineteenth-century Russian nationalist discourse in the western provinces had already included a sentiment of deeply seated ethnic antagonism between "Russians," Jews, and Poles. What is more, post-1905 developments should not distract from the fact that the entire nationalist and monarchist political spectrum remained not only loyal to, but almost obsessed with, the existing state, its autocratic dynasty, and its imperial strength.[94] It is thus understandable that the labels "conservative," "monarchist," "rightist," "nationalist," and "truly Russian"—as well as, polemically, "Black Hundredist" (*chernosotennyi*)—were often applied interchangeably during the first few years of the new semiconstitutional order. Politicians' simultaneous membership in various organizations and the constantly transforming parliamentary caucuses further blurred the boundaries. A more or less clear-cut distinction between hard-right reactionary monarchists and more constructive nationalists emerged only after 1908, and only the First World War saw cracks appear in the right-wing camp's unconditional solidarity with the autocracy.

The sudden crystallization in 1905 of a vague patriotic feeling into a full-blown nationalist movement illustrates a crucial historical difference between Russian and Ukrainian nationalism. In a Russian state with a Russian majority culture, many people saw their Russianness as self-evident and perceived Russian culture as culture *per se*, not as specifically national. Only when Russian statehood came under attack did people begin to rally around unambiguously national symbols. By contrast, Ukrainian nationalism, deprived of political organizations, centered on a series of nationally "marked" cultural symbols: from spoken language via literature, theater, and music to material objects. The declamation of a poem by Shevchenko, the wearing of an embroidered shirt, or a Ukrainian-language conversation among urban intellectuals carried great symbolic value and were understood as demonstrations of Ukrainophile views. In a predominantly Russian urban society, Russian-language culture was "unmarked" in a national sense, lacking such political implications.[95]

Thus, Russian nationalism was "state-framed," while Ukrainian nationalism was a "counterstate" nationalism built around a "national culture" that was imagined as a homogeneous set of symbols, values, and practices.[96] Therefore, Russian nationalism was reactionary in a most literal sense, mobilizing support in reaction to rival nationalisms and other threats to the state. It flourished in situations when there was a visible and purportedly powerful "other," such as after the Polish insurrection of 1863 or in 1905. In the empire's multiethnic Southwest, such a national "other" was permanently present, making it easier to perceive Russian culture as nationally marked. This explains why Russian nationalism remained so strong in the region over the following decade, while it soon lost its dynamism in Central Russia. If Russian nationalism proved successful in Ukraine, this was because the region's socioethnic structure lent itself well to a nationalist framing.

The centrality of adversity to the mobilization of Russian nationalist feeling is very evident in the biographies of two younger members of the Pikhno-Shul'gin family: Dmitrii Pikhno's (inofficial) son Vasilii Shul'gin and daughter-in-law Ekaterina Shul'gina. For them, as for many educated Russians of their generation, 1905 was a "moment of truth" that challenged their fundamental assumptions and shaped their worldview for decades to come.[97] Reading Vasilii Shul'gin's many volumes of memoirs, one is struck by the fact that he never gives an account of a "national education" comparable to Oleksander Shul'hyn's. Surrounded by Russian-language culture throughout his childhood, he appears to have perceived being Russian as a matter of course. While the Shul'hyn children were encouraged to learn Shevchenko's verse by heart, young Vasilii preferred Jules Verne or Arthur Conan Doyle to the Russian classics—but, of course, he read them in a Russian translation.[98] "Although I had been brought up in a political family," Shul'gin later wrote, "I had no interest whatsoever in politics."[99]

According to his own account, Shul'gin began to sympathize with conservative politics at university. During the student strike of 1899, protesters—allegedly mostly Jews—closed down the lecture halls to stop the professors from lecturing. Shul'gin later wrote that this was the moment when he first felt the despotism of revolutionaries and began to defend the existing order against them. This early experience likely had a personal component, for Dmitrii Pikhno was among the professors most harshly attacked by the protesters in 1899.[100] However, Shul'gin remained an unpolitical man for all practical purposes. He and his wife spent much of the years 1903 to 1905 in rural Volhynia, managing the family's estates. Vasilii Shul'gin had literary ambitions and began to write a historical novel in the style of Henryk Sienkiewicz, depicting sixteenth-century Volhynia from a Russian point of view.[101]

The upheaval of 1905 changed Shul'gin's priorities. On 18 October, he was on military duty as a reserve officer and led a small detachment instructed to quell the ongoing pogrom. In a barely fictionalized account of this day, his alter ego watches in horror as a revolutionary crowd celebrates the announcement of the October Manifesto. Like many Russian nationalists, Shul'gin blamed the state's weaknesses— the military defeats in the Far East, the widespread dissatisfaction, the violence—on the Jewish population: "The Yids are cheering, so Russia is in danger. . . . They were also cheering at the time of Mukden, Tsushima . . ."[102] According to Shul'gin, Jewish revolutionaries desecrated national and monarchical symbols, tearing the imperial crown off the Duma's balcony, destroying portraits of the tsars, and ripping apart Russian tricolor flags in order to wave the red stripe as a socialist banner. These examples and even the choice of words—the "mad" (*bezumnye*) Jews and their "defiant" (*vyzyvaiushchee*) behavior—are strikingly similar to the accounts in *Kievlianin*, suggesting that the family formed a common, resentment-laden narrative about these fateful days as they unfolded. By his own account, Shul'gin did everything in his power to calm the mob in Kiev's Demievka suburb. For all his antisemitism, he felt that the pogromists had to be kept under control: "I understood

FIGURE 9. Vasilii Shul'gin and Ekaterina Shul'gina, early twentieth century. GARF, f. R-5974, op. 2, d. 4, l. 19.

their feelings . . . but I abhorred their actions."[103] Antirevolutionary fury and fear of the unleashed mob would soon draw Vasilii Shul'gin into electoral politics.

Perhaps even more instructive than Vasilii's case is the experience of his wife Ekaterina Shul'gina. Unlike her husband, Ekaterina had not grown up in a conservative household. Her father Grigorii Gradovskii was a liberal journalist who had started his career in *Kievlianin* and later became known as a defender of press freedom and Jewish rights. Ekaterina was raised in a literary-artistic milieu in Saint Petersburg and began an acting career before her marriage. By her own account, she adhered to an aesthetic, apolitical liberalism; she occasionally trans-lated literary texts for *Kievlianin* but found the paper's politics boring and overly pro-government. Only at the age of thirty-five, during the Russo-Japanese War, did Shul'gina embrace the Russian nationalism promoted by her father-in-law. As she later recalled, her conversion was caused by the Japanese attack on Russian battleships in January 1904: "I began to feel very distinctly that I was at war with Japan . . . ; not the government, not the army, but *I, I* was at war with her, *I* hated and de-spised her because I loved . . . Russia!"[104]

Shul'gina's memoirs make it very clear that precisely the political adversity experienced by the Russian state and monarchy triggered her patriotic outburst. "As long as nobody touched her [Russia], I did not love her, but since they started to attack her and hit her time and again, I did." If the external threat of war had caused her to identify with the state, the ensuing revolution sparked her affection for the tsar: "As long as nobody touched him I was completely indifferent to him, even ironic, and now I loved him and was outraged by all that happened. I hated the 'revolution' with the same hatred I felt for Japan, I hated and despised it." Yet for all her insistence on the passionate emotion at the bottom of her monarchism, Shul'gina insisted that she and her family "loved the tsar not as a person—whom we did not know—but as a symbol of Russia."[105] Her newfound patriotic feelings went along with the delib-erate choice of a conservative political program. Of course, Shul'gina's self-assessment is retrospective, and her description of 1905 is colored by the knowledge about 1917. But the narrative of her conservative political awakening during the revolution is plausible: only when the Russian state came "under siege" did she feel that she had a stake in the empire's welfare.

Even as the revolutionary tide began to ebb away in 1906, the rise of constitutional politics further antagonized Russia's conservatives.

Defying Dmitrii Pikhno's expectation of a monarchist majority among the peasants, the elections of March and April 1906 brought an overwhelming victory for the opposition. Since the socialist parties boycotted the election, the liberal Constitutional Democrats (Kadets) gained about 180 of the 499 seats, while a hundred nonparty peasant deputies formed the left-wing Labor Group (Trudoviks), and seventy non-Russians joined the autonomist caucus. In Kiev, the Kadets allied with Jewish and Polish elites as well as moderate Ukrainophiles, campaigning for Jewish equal rights, Polish and Ukrainian cultural liberties, and regional autonomy.[106] The Kadet coalition swept the first round of elections in March, gaining sixty-nine of eighty elector posts. Dmitrii Pikhno was also an elector but refused to stand for a Duma seat.[107] The candidate who won the second round for the Kadet coalition, Baron Fedor Shteingel', was a politically inexperienced Baltic German who sympathized with cultural Ukrainophilism. When the Duma opened its first session in April 1906, Pikhno began to place a daily commentary in *Kievlianin*. Discussing the parliament's oppositional ("revolutionary," "criminal," "anarchist") declarations with a mixture of indignation and sarcasm, he advocated its dissolution as the only means to restore order.[108] The government fulfilled Pikhno's wish. On 9 July, Tsar Nicholas dissolved the Duma and announced new elections to be held early in 1907.

Light from the West

By the time of the elections to the second State Duma, Russian monarchist nationalism had become a force to reckon with in the southwestern provinces. In Kiev alone, several thousand people had joined the various right-wing organizations. In preparation for the new elections, all these groups formed a coalition and ran a vigorous campaign.[109] Although Pikhno still preferred the "bureaucratic or service-aristocratic regime" of the past to all constitutional experiments, he and Vasilii Shul'gin began to use *Kievlianin* as a basis to build political careers. At first reluctantly, but with increasing commitment and conviction, they transformed their economic nationalizing agenda into an electoral project. Before the first round of elections in January 1907, Pikhno urged his readers to vote for the antiliberal monarchist bloc, which won two more electors than the Kadets and radicals. In the second round in February, the right-wing candidate, Bishop Platon of Chigirin, narrowly defeated the Kadet and Hromada member Ivan Luchitskii. Kiev, with its religious institutions and relatively weak modern industry, was Russia's first major city to send a right-winger to Saint Petersburg.[110]

Pikhno's son Vasilii Shul'gin concentrated his efforts on Volhynia, the province west of Kiev where his estate was located. In Volhynia, the first Duma elections had yielded mostly nonparty peasant deputies, alongside two Russian and three Polish landowners.[111] In a province without elected zemstvo self-administration or stable party organizations, where most Orthodox landlords were recent arrivals or absentees, mobilizing the conservative electorate was a difficult task. But for somebody who claimed to dislike politics, Vasilii Shul'gin proved to be a gifted political organizer. Having thoroughly studied the complex electoral law, Shul'gin and another landowner set about organizing a monarchist majority. The elections were held on a relatively broad male franchise, but they were indirect, with votes weighted according to land property. Every district's electors were to be chosen by an assembly of peasant delegates from the local communes and by an assembly of landowners. In the last step, these electors would vote for Volhynia's Duma deputies in Zhitomir, the provincial capital. Shul'gin found out that in his Ostrog district, small landowners could "pool" their land and outvote the Polish nobles by allying with the Russian estate owners. Most of these small landowners were rural priests (representing their parishes), somewhat wealthier peasants, or Czech settlers. In order to mobilize voters for the district assembly in Ostrog, Shul'gin rode around the district on his horse, telegraphed absentees, and sent postcards imploring village priests to motivate their flock for the elections. Ultimately, he got the small landowners to choose sixty representatives, who, alongside twenty rich Russian landowners, defeated the Polish slate and gained all elector posts.

On 6 February 1907, the provincial election day in Zhitomir, Shul'gin successfully lobbied the Russian nobles to turn down an estate-based coalition with Polish landowners and Jewish townspeople. Instead, together with Archimandrite Vitalii of Pochaev, a cleric and local leader of the Union of the Russian People, he negotiated a coalition of Orthodox landlords, peasants, and priests, complemented by the Czechs. Thus, the assembly elected eight Orthodox peasants, three Orthodox noble landowners (including Shul'gin himself), one Orthodox priest, and one Czech settler.[112] All the Volhynian peasant deputies were members of the Union of the Russian People and registered as right-wingers, even though most of them later joined the Duma's nonparty group.[113] Not a single Pole was elected this time, nor was a Jew. As Vasilii Shul'gin later commented, "I broke the class agreement with the Poles. . . . Unexpectedly and unintentionally, I found myself leading those whose national feelings prevailed over their class consciousness."[114]

By redefining the electorate in national terms, Vasilii Shul'gin transmitted his father's long-term project—a rural society ordered by ethnicity rather than social estate—from the economic to the political realm. However, historian Olha Martynyuk has shown that the right-wing victory in Volhynia was not simply the result of the grassroots mobilization described in Shul'gin's memoirs. Reports of the Volhynian governor credit Archimandrite Vitalii with securing a monarchist majority among the peasant electors and prove the local authorities' involvement in the selection of reliable peasants. The monarchist triumph was an outcome favored and promoted by the province's state authorities.[115] This kind of intervention was in line with the general policy of the new prime minister Petr Stolypin.[116]

Despite the right-wing victories in Volhynia and the city of Kiev, the second State Duma turned out even more radical than the first. Even the neighboring right-bank provinces of Kiev and Podolia sent predominantly socialist peasants. The assembly was dominated by various socialist parties (Trudoviks, Social Democrats, Socialist Revolutionaries) and Kadets; the right-wing monarchist caucus could only claim 20 of the 518 deputies. Many of the peasants from the Southwest joined the Ukrainian Labor Group, and the demand for Ukrainian-language education was voiced. It is hardly surprising that Vasilii Shul'gin refused to participate constructively in a parliament that kept making radical demands for land reform and political liberalization. Instead of addressing the topics under discussion, Shul'gin's speeches passionately denounced the "cowardly" and "cruel" revolutionaries. His vitriolic sarcasm soon earned him a name as one of the Duma's most ardent defenders of the autocracy. In one of his first speeches, Shul'gin presented a mock resolution from the "newly formed parliamentary caucus of Social-Capitalists," demanding the socialization and redistribution of all capital, as well as talents, knowledge, capacities, and intelligence. Exemplifying Shul'gin's rejection of representative democracy, this parody of political programs and parliamentary conventions provoked "whistling and shouts of indignation." The left-wing deputies were even more furious when Shul'gin asked whether one of them might not be carrying a bomb in his pocket—a deliberate provocation that got him banned from the hall.[117]

Meanwhile, Pikhno's *Kievlianin* kept calling for the dissolution of the "revolutionary meetings in the Tauride Palace" and criticized Stolypin's patience with the "Social-Bandits and Social-Expropriators."[118] Vasilii Shul'gin and his fellow right-wing deputies were so keen to see the parliament disbanded that they raised the issue at an audience with Tsar Nicholas in the Imperial Palace.[119] When the tsar and Stolypin finally did dissolve the Duma on 3 June 1907, *Kievlianin* triumphally titled its commentary "Russia for the Russians," announcing the end of the rule by "foreign elements" and "street riffraff": "Return into the nothingness where you used to be until recently! We, the Russian lords of the Russian land, did not know you and did not call you, we do not want you and your kind to decide the fate of our state; . . . We will dictate you the laws and you will fulfill the commands of our state power."[120]

By this time, Dmitrii Pikhno, too, had been called to Saint Petersburg. Defying Pikhno's distaste for representative institutions, Nicholas II personally named him to the State Council in March 1907. "Under the current conditions I consider it essential to appoint strong and Russian people to the State Council," the tsar declared in his handwritten order. "My first such candidate is Prof. Pikhno, the editor of *Kievlianin*. Notify him about this and inform him about my hope that he will continue his useful publication after his nomination for the State Council." A dedicated monarchist, Pikhno could not refuse the sovereign's will; nor was he probably indifferent to the yearly stipend of 10,000 rubles that he was granted.[121] The State Council had just been refashioned into the parliament's upper chamber, with half the deputies elected (by the zemstvos, the noble assemblies, and the church, among others) and the other half nominated by the tsar. In a body composed almost exclusively of hereditary nobles, most of them with long careers in the bureaucracy, Pikhno was one of only two appointed members born into the lowly estate of townspeople.[122] Following Pikhno's appointment, rumors circulated that he might soon be named minister of education or even replace Prime Minister Stolypin in a more conservative cabinet.[123] A liberal newspaper published a caricature that showed the *Kievlianin* editor heading a cabinet of well-known reactionaries. In reality, Pikhno was about to become Stolypin's ally.

Pikhno's and Shul'gin's gradual conversion to Stolypin's politics began with the dissolution of the Second Duma. The new electoral law passed by the tsar and Stolypin on 3 June 1907 favored more conservative forces, namely landowners and wealthy urban elites, at the expense of peasants, industrial workers, and non-Russians.[124] Under this law,

Министерство Пихно.

1. Премьеръ. 2. Министръ внутр. дѣлъ (Грингмутъ). 3. М. иностр. дѣлъ (Крушеванъ). 4. М. провокаціи. 5. М. финансовъ (Гурко.)
6. М. торговли и промышленности (Лидваль).

FIGURE 10. "The Pikhno Ministry." Caricature by K. Dulin (Vladimir Kadulin), from *Kievskaia mysl'*, pictorial supplement no. 16 (1907): 127. Caption: "1. The Prime Minister [Pikhno]. 2. The Minister of the Interior (Gringmut). 3. The Minister of Foreign Affairs (Krushevan). 4. The Minister of Provocation. 5. The Minister of Finance (Gurko). 6. The Minister of Trade and Industry (Lidval')." Courtesy of the Ukrainian National Library in Kyiv.

the Volhynian Duma elections yielded an exclusively right-wing delegation: five peasants, three priests, three landowners (including Shul'gin),
a teacher, and a medic.[125] The city of Kiev elected the former right-wing
mayor Vasilii Protsenko alongside the Kadet Luchitskii. Overall, the
government acquired a comfortable majority in the assembly, with over
150 moderately conservative Octobrists and almost as many members
of the various right-wing caucuses: Rightists, Moderate Rightists, and
the National Group.

This new situation made it possible for the likes of Pikhno and
Shul'gin to scale down their aggressive rhetoric and move toward more
constructive positions. In the autumn of 1906, Stolypin had initiated
his land reform, which aimed to create a class of rural smallholders by
encouraging peasants to leave their commune and turn their allocated
land strips into private property. Pikhno, who had long advocated rural
smallholdings as the basis of a healthy nation, could not but be pleased
by this policy, even though he disliked the preservation of some estate-
based restrictions on peasants' economic rights.[126] Vasilii Shul'gin, too,
was impressed by the premier's forceful style of politics and gradually
became a serious participant in the democratic practices of Russian
semiconstitutionalism. The British journalist Bernard Pares later singled Shul'gin out as a politician who learned politics in the "school of
the Duma."[127] Unlike extreme right-wingers like Nikolai Markov and
Vladimir Purishkevich, Shul'gin no longer limited his participation in
the Duma to provocation and blockade.[128]

The years 1908–1910 saw a reshuffling of the political forces in the
right-wing and monarchist spectrum. The Kievans played a decisive
role by establishing the Kiev Club of Russian Nationalists in the spring
of 1908. Its president was Anatolii Savenko, a native of Poltava province, former student of Pikhno's, and columnist for *Kievlianin*. The activities of the Kiev Club mirrored those of Mykola Lysenko's successful
Ukrainian Club: it operated a reading room with conservative newspapers, welcomed religious pilgrims from Galicia, hosted meetings with
right-wing Duma deputies and lectures—mostly by Savenko—on topics
ranging from Russia's foreign policy to recent archaeological discover-
ies, from the "Jewish question" to the life of Russians in America. The
club's fairly diverse membership was dominated by urban house owners and railway administrators besides merchants, civil servants, and
rural landlords. Besides Pikhno and Shul'gin, its prominent members
included the rich landowner Count Aleksei Bobrinskii, the Kiev censor
Sergei Shchegolev, the anti-Ukrainian philologist Timofei Florinskii,

and the psychiatrist Ivan Sikorskii. There were also several dozen female members, including Ekaterina Shul'gina, but only few played an active role. At the height of its success in 1913, the Kiev Club had over seven hundred members and stood at the center of an increasingly vigorous Russian nationalist milieu, whose main press organ was still Pikhno's *Kievlianin*.[129]

Alongside the Duma's National Group and Moderate Rightist caucus, as well as two Petersburg organizations, the Kiev Club served as an organizational nucleus around which a new party of Russian nationalists was formed in January 1910. The Nationalist Party, officially called the All-Russian National Union, was dominated by western landowners and pledged to be loyal to both the autocracy and the new representative institutions. Its program included the defense of the empire's unity and of private property, opposition to equal rights for Jews, and economic support for private peasant landowners. Around this time, Stolypin's working relationship with the Octobrists deteriorated, offering the Nationalists an opportunity to work closely with the prime minister.[130] In short, the new party provided an ideal vehicle for the ideas of Vasilii Shul'gin, who had become disillusioned with the extreme right's divisive style of politics. Shul'gin soon joined the new caucus and party and became one of its most eloquent spokesmen. As a leader of the "government party," Shul'gin had direct access to the prime minister, who occasionally invited him and other Nationalist politicians to late-night meetings in his office.[131]

During the Third Duma, the most important piece of legislation for Pikhno and Shul'gin, as well as the Nationalist Party in general, was Stolypin's bill to introduce elective zemstvos in the western provinces of the empire.[132] Pikhno may even be credited with starting the debate. At the State Council meeting of 8 May 1909, he criticized the way in which the empire's western provinces elected their state councillors. Elsewhere, the provincial zemstvos chose the State Council deputies, but in the western provinces, where no such institutions existed, a noble assembly held a vote. Since these assemblies were dominated by the Polish nobility, all nine elected deputies from the western provinces were Polish aristocrats. Under the historical conditions of "western Russia," Pikhno explained, these people could not possibly represent the region's majority. He therefore introduced a proposal to establish national curiae for the elections that would grant six seats to Russians while leaving three to the Poles. Accused of heating up national passions, Pikhno replied that, by contrast, the separation of local politics into Russian and Polish spheres would improve their relations according to the principle "to each his own."[133]

Premier Stolypin gladly took up the impulse and announced his willingness to get to the root of the problem by establishing new zemstvos in the western provinces according to national principles—an idea first brought up in the 1860s.[134] Encouraged by Stolypin's words, Vasilii Shul'gin published a pamphlet to promote zemstvos elected by Polish and Russian national curiae. Shul'gin wanted to determine the number of seats per curia according to landholdings rather than population size; otherwise the law would risk creating an "overly democratic" zemstvo dominated by peasants. Like Pikhno, Shul'gin argued that the complete separation of Polish and Russian political spheres would alleviate national conflict during election campaigns.[135] Father and son shared an apartment in Saint Petersburg and clearly concerted their efforts during the western zemstvo debate.

The bill that Stolypin presented in 1910 even surpassed Shul'gin's expectations. It was tailored to guarantee the supremacy of Russian landlords in the new organs of local self-administration for Kiev, Volhynia, Podolia, Minsk, Mogilev, and Vitebsk provinces. In each province, Russians and Poles would get a fixed number of zemstvo deputies, to be determined by the arithmetic mean of their population and land property percentages in every district. A Russian and a Polish curia would elect their respective deputies. A number of seats were reserved for Orthodox priests, the share of communal peasants was limited, and Jews were excluded. The chairmen had to be Russians.[136] During the debate on the Duma floor, Vasilii Shul'gin ardently defended Stolypin's project as an opportunity to overcome the Polish domination in western Rus'. "National feeling, nationalism cannot bear the power of one tribe over another," Shul'gin declared, extolling the zemstvo as a powerful tool "to create a Russian middle class and a Russian upper class, developed, educated, and cultured."[137]

The project, however, met with much resistance from the Kadets and Poles, as well as some Octobrists and right-wingers. While the Nationalist Party and the Kiev Club enthusiastically supported the bill, the parliament continually chipped away at it. Ultimately the Duma passed the project's crucial points, including the national curiae. But when it entered the upper house, Stolypin's archconservative opponents began an intrigue against his plan. Pikhno adjured his colleagues to use this opportunity to settle the Polish question once and for all and secure a precarious borderland for the Russian nation.[138]

Ignoring his arguments, the State Council defeated the national curiae in the final vote. When the Kiev Club sent Stolypin a telegram
of support, he replied by assuring them of his belief "that the light
of the Russian national idea that has begun to glow in the West of
Russia will not go out but will soon enlighten all of Russia."[139] This
was Stolypin's tribute to the Little Russian messianism that *Kievlianin*
had long promoted. Pressured by the nationalists, the prime minister bypassed the parliament and implemented the western zemstvo
bill by emergency decree in April 1911. Stolypin's decision triggered
a political crisis that further alienated him from both constitutional-
ists and conservatives and prepared the way for his downfall.[140] Five
months later, having lost the tsar's favor, Stolypin was assassinated at
a theater in Kiev.

The western zemstvo bill epitomizes the agrarian nationalism of
the Pikhno-Shul'gin family like no other project. Relying on a section
of the rural population defined by property and ethnicity, it aimed
to put local activism to good use without touching the state's autocratic foundations. For the social upstart Pikhno, property rather than
inherited nobility was the main guarantee of political reliability. At
the same time, the law established the national categorization of the
electorate (on which Shul'gin had relied since 1906), thus substantiat-
ing the claim to right-bank Ukraine as a truly Russian territory with
a loyal population. In the short run, the bill appeared to achieve its
goal. In the first western zemstvo election of summer 1911, nationalist
and right-wing candidates won a landslide victory, helped by the boy-
cott of many Poles. However, most of the new delegates turned out to
be less enthusiastic about zemstvo work than envisioned.[141] By 1912,
the Volhynian authorities suspected the region's zemstvo administration of using zemstvo funds for Ukrainophile propaganda among the
peasants.[142]

Vasilii Shul'gin himself was elected to both the Ostrog district
zemstvo and the Volhynian provincial zemstvo. He also defended his
Duma seat in the 1912 elections, even though he still claimed to "feel
an unsurmountable aversion" against his "quasi-legislative activity."[143]
A heated campaign also brought seats to his Kiev Club companions
Anatolii Savenko in Kiev province and Vsevolod Demchenko in the city.
The club's canvassing, as well as the government's protection and financial subsidies, secured the Nationalists and right-wingers a near-
complete triumph in right-bank Ukraine. They won all the Duma seats
except for one.[144]

The Anti-Ukrainian Reaction

After the 1907 Stolypin coup, the threat of Ukrainian nationalism made a comeback on the pages of *Kievlianin*. For decades, the Ukrainophiles' lack of public presence had made it unnecessary to criticize them much, except for occasional philological or literary debates.[145] When the Ukrainian movement raised its voice in the relatively free semiconstitutional public sphere, however, the reaction from Kiev's Russian nationalists followed almost immediately. In 1908, the freshly founded Kiev Club issued a resolution against a proposed Duma bill to introduce Ukrainian-language teaching to the region's elementary schools. The resolution dissuaded the Octobrists from supporting the bill, so that it was buried without debate. Anatolii Savenko began to fill his *Kievlianin* column almost obsessively with polemics against the Ukrainophiles, alerting his readers time and again that they had moved from "ethnographic" goals to political separatism. His main target was the historian Mykhailo Hrushevs'kyi, whom he identified as the leading separatist. Other right-wing journalists followed Savenko's lead, and in the spring of 1910, the anti-Ukrainian lobby achieved another success: the Kiev Prosvita, a Ukrainian association for popular education, was closed down following Stolypin's order to dissolve "alien" (*inorodcheskie*) organizations. *Kievlianin* was satisfied but immediately demanded the closure of the "much more harmful" Ukrainian Scientific Society as well.[146]

The anti-Ukrainian arguments were hardly new. The mockery of the "artificial" literary language, the historical and philological demonstrations of unbreakable unity between Great and Little Russians, the accusations of serving Polish intrigues or promoting cultural barbarism had all been heard and debated since the mid-nineteenth century. Among the few innovative rhetorical devices were the denunciation as "Mazepists" (derived from the eighteenth-century Cossack Hetman Ivan Mazepa, who had sought an alliance with the Swedish king against Russia) and the allegation of conspiring with Austria, an idea directly linked to the Russian-Austrian diplomatic tensions since the annexation of Bosnia in 1908.[147]

The pivotal difference from the preceding decades, however, was the urgency that Kiev's Russian nationalists now ascribed to the Ukrainian problem. According to a 1911 Kiev Club resolution, "the Mazepist movement is the most threatening and dangerous of all the movements directed against the unity and wholeness of the Russian Empire, for this movement strives to destroy the very foundation of Russia's wholeness and greatness: the unity of the Russian nation."[148] Anatolii Savenko, reminding his readers that Russians would cease to be a majority in the empire without the Little Russians, branded the "Mazepists" as Russia's "main enemy." And Vasilii Shul'gin fumed, "We are fighting the traitors of Russia. . . . They bring our beloved land sorrow. They bring it slavery, they bring it Austro-Yiddish bondage, they poison it with hatred toward everything inherited and ancient, they are worse than the Tatars, worse than the Polovtsians."[149]

From the autumn of 1911, the Kiev nationalists stepped up their efforts to spotlight the Ukrainian issue in the imperial public sphere. The Kiev Club devoted an entire series of historical, political, and anthropological lectures and brochures to the denunciation of alleged Ukrainian separatism. Savenko spoke on the topic in Moscow and Saint Petersburg to "wake up" the Great Russians. The censor Shchegolev published a six-hundred-page anti-Ukrainian diatribe, pedantically listing hundreds of incidents where "separatist" opinions were voiced in schools, universities, or the press.[150] Perhaps with his own path to assimilation in mind, Pikhno brought up the Ukrainian issue in a State Council debate on elementary schools. To a paragraph permitting instruction in local languages during the first two years, Pikhno added a clause that exempted the Little Russian and Belorussian population. His proposal passed the vote.[151] Savenko even wrote letters to highly placed government officials in the capital, desperately warning of the Ukrainian danger that they, in his eyes, dangerously underestimated.[152]

The police, too, took note of Savenko's denunciations, although they assessed his claims of a separatist conspiracy skeptically.[153] While the government acted against some Prosvita sections, police reports stated that most Prosvita members were politically loyal "sentimental lovers of the Little Russian language and customs." By 1914, however, the gendarmes also used the term "Mazepist" that Savenko had popularized. The Kiev, Poltava, and Kharkov provincial police organs now agreed that the fears about separatism "are very well-founded and deserve most serious attention."[154] To some extent, then, the campaign was successful. In a new blow to the Ukrainian movement, the authorities closed down the popular Ukrainian Club in Kiev in October 1912, only to see it immediately reopened under the name Rodyna (Family).[155]

But perhaps more important was the growing distrust of the Ukrainian movement among Russian liberals, a distrust nourished by the

accusations of Russian nationalists from Kiev who presented themselves as local insiders. This skepticism was best expressed by Petr
Struve, a former Marxist turned Kadet who had recently embraced a
liberal form of nationalism. Echoing views often uttered in *Kievlianin*,
Struve pointed to the threat of a national bifurcation that might endan-
ger Russia's geopolitical position by depriving her of access to the Black
Sea. Ukrainian intellectuals, he wrote, should content themselves with
a provincial version of Russian culture, suitable only for "those quiet
and profound coves of popular life where the mostly rural way of life is
concealed from the all-unifying and all-shaking civilization of railways,
factories, demonstrations, entertainments and cinematographs."[156]

Struve's article deepened the rift between the Ukrainian movement
and Russian society. Even though his views were fairly moderate, they
made a strong impression coming from a liberal. Especially younger
Ukrainian nationalists suspected that Struve had only said aloud what
most Russian liberals secretly believed (while officially supporting
Ukrainian cultural demands). They took his statement as proof that
the Ukrainians could not trust the Russian opposition in the struggle
against government centralism.[157] Ironically, *Kievlianin*'s constant accusations of separatism may thus have indirectly contributed to the
strengthening of openly anti-Russian tendencies among Ukrainian nationalists. The prophecy turned out to be self-fulfilling.

Almost all anti-Ukrainian statements of this period displayed a tension between two contradictory claims: that Ukrainian nationalism
was without support in the region's population and that it posed a
huge threat of dividing the nation by turning the region's Russians into
aliens. This paradoxical attitude was perhaps best summarized in the
Kiev Club's charter, which stated that "the Ukrainophile movement is a
phenomenon that is as harmful as it is groundless."[158] It stems from the
dilemma that Russian nationalists faced with respect to Ukraine. They
had to acknowledge the region's cultural specificities in order not to
make Russian nationalism appear like a foreign ideology imposed from
above. Yet they also needed to downplay these specificities to warrant
the unity of an All-Russian nation.

Like their nineteenth-century predecessors, Kiev's Russian nationalists had to balance regional patriotism and imperial nationalism.
Anatolii Savenko always stressed his own Little-Russianness while de-
nouncing the Ukrainians: "I am myself a pure-blooded Little Russian
and adore my homeland, its wonderful nature, customs, language,

tradition, history, as I love the lazy and good-natured *khokhly*. But with all the force of my soul I hate Ukrainophilism, a treacherous and base movement." On the Duma tribune, Vasilii Shul'gin even praised such Ukrainophile heroes as Shevchenko, Antonovych, and Lysenko, only to add that they formed a pedestal for the greatest Little Russian artist, Nikolai Gogol', who had transcended regional egoism.[159] The veneration of Gogol' was no coincidence. While steeped in Ukrainian traditions, his work was written in Russian and widely seen as a celebration of imperial patriotism.[160] Electoral competition sharpened the rivalry between Russian and Ukrainian nationalism. Unlike the Social Democrats or Jewish and Polish parties, the Ukrainian movement targeted the same electorate that Russian nationalists hoped to mobilize: the Orthodox peasants and urban intelligentsia. Whereas Ukrainian nationalists saw these people as yet unconscious Ukrainians that must be protected from assimilation, Russian nationalists understood them as Little Russians endangered by separatist propaganda.[161]

This situation also defined the political trajectory of Dmitrii Pikhno and Vasilii Shul'gin. Working in both chambers of the parliament, they lobbied the government to classify its populations by ethnicity, to tie citizenship to nationality, and, ultimately, to increase the political influence of the Russian, Orthodox population. At the same time, they had to defend the Russianness of their target electorate against the pretensions of Ukrainian nationalism. At first extremely critical of Russia's new parliamentarianism—after all, a product of the loathed revolution—the Pikhno-Shul'gins came to see it as a useful tool to mobilize the population and implement their program. In doing so, they inadvertently moved away from a defense of unfettered autocracy toward national-democratic positions. Their associate Savenko praised the Nationalist Party as "representatives of a healthy democratism" working "to awaken the national forces in the Russian people and to unify them for broad societal activity and initiative."[162] In 1913, disgusted with the reactionary post-Stolypin government, he even wrote to his wife that he no longer feared revolution: "it—even it—is a lot more patriotic than our abominable government, than all this rotten bureaucracy, which is completely indifferent toward Russia."[163] Even if Pikhno and Shul'gin did not go quite as far, the *Kievlianin* group had moved out of the reactionary monarchist camp into the constitutionalist wing of Russian nationalism. This development caused tensions that would greatly damage Kiev's Russian nationalists immediately before the outbreak of the First World War.

Secrets and Solidarity

Even as he rose to prominence in Petersburg politics, Dmitrii Pikhno kept things in the family. By 1907, his house on the corner of Kuznechnaia and Karavaevskaia Streets was the headquarters of a successful political enterprise, home to two members of the legislative organs and to one of the empire's most-read provincial newspapers. At the same time, the family's intimate life remained unconventional, even outright scandalous. Yet, rather than destroy the family's unity, the scandals and gossip strengthened its cohesion, helping the Pikhno-Shul'gins work together in the everyday business of nationalist politics. Their family loyalty became intertwined with political loyalty to the tsarist state and the Russian nation.

The family's tradition of domestic scandals, begun by Pikhno's relationships with Mariia Shul'gina and subsequently her daughter Lina, continued in the next generation. Pikhno's eldest son Vasilii Shul'gin breached church law by marrying his first cousin Ekaterina. In 1903, Vasilii's younger brother Dmitrii got married to one Mariia Merkulova, who soon turned out to be prone to "scandalous" behavior. In 1905, she began an affair with her husband's brother Vasilii; five years later she took her life after several suicide attempts. The third brother, Pavel, fell in love with a married woman, Liubov' Tkachenko (née Popova), moved in with her, got her a divorce, and married her.[164] Liubov' later became the secretary of her brother-in-law Vasilii Shul'gin. Having divorced Pavel, she, too, began a passionate love affair with Vasilii. For several years, they spent the winters together in Saint Petersburg, while Ekaterina Shul'gina and the children remained in Kiev. Over the summer, Vasilii Shul'gin stayed in Kurgany with his family.[165] The sources also hint at homosexuality. Vasilii's half sister Alla lived with her "best friend" Sofiia Rudanovskaia for many years. When she got married to Pikhno's former student Aleksandr Bilimovich, Sofiia experienced this as a tragic end to their friendship—a friendship that Lina Mogilevskaia thought would better never have begun. And after Dmitrii Pikhno's death, Lina herself closely befriended a female doctor.[166]

The family's prominence in Kiev makes it almost certain that they were a regular object of gossip. Yet the very nature of gossip, its somewhat unsavory character and oral transmission, makes it hard to pin down historically. Still, a few instances can be found in the sources, scattered over several decades. After Vitalii Shul'gin's death, a rather mean poem mocking him and his family circulated in Kiev's intelligentsia.

Titled "V. Ia. Shul'gin's Message from the Afterworld to M. V. Iuzefov-ich," it pretended to be Shul'gin's report about his arrival in hell:

Ty tam ne zhdi sebe nagrady,	Do not expect rewards down there,
Zasni skoree vechnym snem:	Sleep rather the eternal sleep.
Vot ia: trudilsia blaga radi	Take me: I worked for our welfare
A vkusit plod zhena s Pikhnom.	My wife, Pikhno, the fruits may reap.
. . . .	. . . .
A esli mozhno—zakhvati-ka	And if you can, then fetch me rather
Lakeia-bludnika—Pikhna.	That lecherous lackey called Pikhno.
I soberetsia nasha klika	And our cabal again will gather
I vozlikuet satana.	And Satan will rejoice and crow.[167]

Remarks in Oleksandr Kistiakivs'kyi's diary from the 1880s and in Sergei Witte's memoirs written around 1910 show that Pikhno's relationship with Lina Shul'gina was common knowledge in the city. According to Witte, "rumor has it that [Vasilii] Shul'gin is Pikhno's son."[168] In 1920, a Warsaw newspaper referred to Vasilii as the "ill-bred offspring of the incestuous house of Shul'gin-Pikhno, about which all Kiev knows."[169] The prominent newspaper dynasty could not hide its amorous escapades, and Kiev's gossips took a keen interest in them.

And yet, the Shul'gin-Pikhnos had to make concessions to the period's morality. Particularly Pikhno's de facto wife Lina Mogilevskaia lived in an uneasy tension between societal family and gender norms and the open secret of her irregular situation. While pregnant with her second son, Lina complained to her friend about the "very cumbersome" birth preparations: "Moving around hotels and other people's houses for some months, then the necessity to hide the child away during the first time: all of this is not a very joyful prospect." People would ultimately accept her second child, she added, but giving birth at home was impossible. "Instead I must embark on faraway travels and come up with various farcical stories which of course no one will believe but which are somehow indispensable."[170] When she gave birth to her third son, Lina hid on her country estate, Agatovka, commenting laconically that "in the autumn, I think, this news will cease to be news, and people will no longer make an overly surprised face upon seeing Vania [Ivan]."[171] Even though Kiev society perfectly understood Lina's relationship with Pikhno, she was painfully aware of the need to keep up appearances.

While the Pikhno-Shul′gins halfheartedly concealed their intimate relations from the public, they addressed them openly within their circle. Lina Mogilevskaia's letters to her confidante, the writer Mariia Krestovskaia, are peppered with details about the various "extraordinary romances." Lina saw the propensity to scandal as the family's

FIGURE 11. Dmitrii Pikhno, portrayed in a domestic setting. *Kievlianin*, 6 September 1913, n.p. Courtesy of the Ukrainian National Library in Kyiv.

FIGURE 12. Lina Mogilevskaia. Olga Matich private collection.

outstanding characteristic: "We cannot have a decent marriage in a traditional setting. . . . There is infallibly a little scandal and a need for
extraordinary secrecy."[172] Writing about Britain in the same period, historian Deborah Cohen explains that a family's secrets were often seen
as a safeguard for its privacy: "Skeletons, the Victorians recognized,
were inevitable and as a sign of family unity, even laudable."[173] Lina
Mogilevskaia made a similar link between the family's cohesion and

the "skeletons" in its closet. "We are still living quietly in our tightly closed circle into which fresh faces hardly manage to penetrate," she wrote in 1900, "but since there are many of us, it is always crowded and busy in our living room."[174] However, this solidarity and self-sufficiency seduced the family's women to "fall in love with the men of their own house, disregarding both age and kinship, and this results in wild, bizarre love affairs. From the outside they seem simply depraved, but God in Heaven knows how virtuous they are." Thus, Lina distinguished between social norms, according to which the family's love life was a reason for shame, and her own moral standards, by which it was not. Lina and Ekaterina Shul'gina liked to speak of "the House of Usher," cultivating their own myth as morally dubious and possibly doomed bohemians.[175] Faced with a certain ostracism in the city's better society, the Pikhno-Shul'gins embraced their unconventional intimate life as part of who they were.

However, the scandals also produced friction within the family circle. Vasilii Shul'gin's 1905 affair with his sister-in-law Mariia was an ordeal for the entire family, leaving his wife heartbroken, his father disappointed, and Vasilii himself rather confused. The otherwise stoic Lina was furious. "You can imagine what a horrible state our family is in," she wrote to her friend. "Apparently the end of our entire house has come."[176] However, Lina was wrong. The family overcame this conflict and continued to hold together in solidarity. Faced with intimate adversity, the Pikhno-Shul'gins applied their combined strength to a new field, politics. Seen in this light, Ekaterina and Vasilii Shul'gin's turn to politics in 1905 was also a flight from their private troubles. The common purpose they found in patriotism—"the basis of our closeness" in Vasilii Shul'gin's words—salvaged their marriage for many years. "From this period," Ekaterina Shul'gina remembered, "politics forcefully entered our lives and in many ways moved our private life to the background."[177] Domestic scandals enhanced family solidarity among the Pikhno-Shul'gins, and politics were a common ground, a higher purpose that helped them overcome occasional disagreements. Thus, the family's unconventional intimate life is directly linked to the emergence of their nationalist family enterprise.

Politics as a Family Business

As newspaper publishers and politicians, the Pikhno-Shul'gins were "ethnopolitical entrepreneurs" in the most literal sense. In Rogers

Brubaker's poignant formulation, they lived "'off' as well as 'for' ethnicity."[178] Their political project was very much a family business, involving most adult family members and in-laws. Especially after 1905, Dmitrii Pikhno relied on the cooperation of both male and female relatives in writing, editing, and publishing *Kievlianin*. Vasilii Shul'gin entered the paper's pages with literary texts before beginning to write on politics, too. His sister Alla translated French and German texts for the literary section, while her husband Aleksandr Bilimovich wrote on economic topics. Pikhno's younger sons Pavel Pikhno and Filipp Mogilevskii contributed pseudonymous poems and feuilletons as "Paul Viola" and "Efem," respectively. Konstantin Smakovskii, the official editor since 1910, was married to the corrector, Ekaterina Shul'gina's sister Sofiia. Ekaterina, too, began to write political articles, signing as "Aleksei Ezhov" and hiding her real identity even from Pikhno. Later the family was informed, but the pseudonym was kept secret from the public. The choice of a male pen name was not accidental. Readers had complained when she had used a female pseudonym, finding it inappropriate for a woman to write about politics.[179]

Perhaps the most important person at *Kievlianin* was, however, Lina Mogilevskaia. Never an author herself, she had managed the accounts and the paper's literary section since her youth. After 1907, she assumed the direction of the entire newspaper whenever Pikhno and Shul'gin were in Saint Petersburg, and the extant letters between her and Pikhno prove that Lina had a say in the paper's editorial line. On several occasions, it fell to her to mediate between the cautious Pikhno and the more hotheaded younger staff (Savenko, Bilimovich, Vasilii Shul'gin). Pikhno trusted Lina, but during one of his absences he also chided her for defining the newspaper's policies without consulting him. As Lina once wrote to him with a mixture of irony and pride, "In such heated times as these, it is not easy to be the editor of a solid political newspaper."[180] Well-read and thoughtful, Lina came to be seen as the "soul" of *Kievlianin*, the woman who held the entire business together in the background.

In Petersburg, Dmitrii Pikhno and Vasilii Shul'gin shared an apartment, sometimes along with Vasilii's wife Ekaterina and half-brother Filipp, then a student. This capital office of the political family business must have resounded with permanent political debates.[181] Even in Petersburg, Pikhno and Shul'gin preferred to work with fellow Kievans. Their most important accomplice was Anatolii Savenko, the Kiev Club president and deputy in the Fourth Duma. A great organizer but a famously difficult person, Savenko provided a crucial link between the Kiev nationalists and Petersburg officialdom. He repeatedly angered Pikhno with his impetuous behavior and fell out with the *Kievlianin* family, only to be readmitted into their circle after some time.[182] Other close collaborators included the Kievan Duma members Sergei Bogdanov and Vsevolod Demchenko.

Pikhno liked to manage things in a "do-it-yourself way" (*po-kustarnomu*), relying on his patriarchal authority and on relatives' loyalty. He was an honorary member of the Kiev Club and officially headed the Kiev branch of the Union of the Russian People, but was not very active in either organization. Skeptical of modern party politics, he preferred personal channels of influence.[183] Unlike the younger generation, Pikhno was wary of tying his newspaper's fate to the Nationalist Party: "*Kievlianin* must not be a narrow party organ, which is what not only Savenko, but unfortunately also Vasia [Vasilii Shul'gin] are trying to make of it."[184]

Paradoxically, Pikhno's patriarchal ways enhanced the political agency of women inside the family circle, whom he trusted more than men outside it. As in their love life, the Pikhno-Shul'gins were open-minded to unconventional arrangements, placing great responsibilities on women, who otherwise at most fulfilled auxiliary functions in right-wing politics. Like most nationalist women, Lina Mogilevskaia and Ekaterina Shul'gina based their worldview on the same patriotic values as their male counterparts, showing little interest in feminism. Women's emancipation or female suffrage was neither the goal of their personal actions nor part of their political program.[185] And yet they began to transcend traditional gender roles in their newspaper work.

Despite its remarkable electoral and political successes, the Pikhno-Shul'gin "family enterprise" remained aloof from the period's major political milieus. The Shul'gins were separated from the liberal intelligentsia by their conservative monarchism, and from most right-wingers by their dislike of Slavophile utopianism as well as their bohemian lifestyle and disregard for marital conventions.[186] Their unconventional private life taught them a certain political flexibility that allowed them to jettison outdated ideological premises, and that did not always sit well with other conservatives. The same in-betweenness applies socially. The Shul'gins lacked the inherited status and habitus of the old landed aristocracy, but they were too wealthy and too "agrarian" for urban intellectual circles. It is thus no coincidence that the *Kievlianin* family spent the entire constitutional period looking for a stable political affiliation.

During the first years of the Duma, Vasilii Shul'gin hobnobbed with extreme reactionary monarchists. However, this far-right connection soon turned out to be less than ideal. There was nothing that Pikhno and Shul'gin feared more than chaos in the streets, and they could not approve of the incendiary speeches by leaders like Aleksandr Dubrovin, whose followers (the "Black Hundreds") regularly initiated antisemitic riots.

While Vasilii Shul'gin shared his father's dislike of spontaneous bottom-up activism, he was a more iconoclastic character and went a good deal further in embracing modern mass politics. The rise of the Nationalist Party offered him an opportunity to engage constructively with the semiconstitutional framework. As a landowner from the western provinces, Shul'gin belonged to the new party's dominant social group and personally shared its economic goals.[187] The party became an even more attractive vehicle for the family's ambitions when it entered a working relationship with Prime Minister Stolypin, whose agrarian policy dovetailed perfectly with Pikhno's views. Stolypin epitomized Vasilii Shul'gin's ideal of energetic authoritarian leadership and would remain his political idol for decades to come.[188] Here seemed to be a chance to combine economic modernization with the preservation of a patriarchal state and a degree of political participation for the elites.

However, Stolypin's vision of a nation framed by a modernizing state and united by landownership clashed with Nicholas II's dream of a direct, almost mystical communion between tsar and people.[189] While Pikhno and his family sympathized with Stolypin's program, they remained devoted to an unfettered autocracy. Their case demonstrates that traditional conceptions of (ultimately God-given) monarchical authority were only partially compatible with a modern nationalism that wanted political legitimacy to emanate from the people. This problem is inherent to Russian nationalism in the imperial period and related to what Dominic Lieven has termed a "key dilemma" of modern empires: nationalism offered a unique possibility to rally the population behind the imperial state, but it also had the potential to undermine that very authority, particularly in multiethnic borderlands.[190]

Pikhno's attempt to overcome this dilemma was closely linked to his intimate life. A dedicated family man, he was aware of the connections and parallels between family life and politics. "One can live without many things," he wrote in March 1905, "but one cannot live without the family, just as one cannot live without air. A social class that has destroyed the family soon chokes and dies."[191] For him, the revolutionary upheaval of 1905 was not least a crisis of parental authority. "Fathers and mothers," he wrote, "have turned out to be moral bankrupts vis-à-vis their children because they have not given them . . . positive ideas, moral ideals and a feeling of duty that they could oppose to false ideas and ideals."[192] While this article was about the student protests, Pikhno was clearly speaking about his own family, too. This was the period when the family's domestic peace was endangered by the love affair between Vasilii Shul'gin and his sister-in-law Mariia. On the very same day he wrote his article, Pikhno also penned a private letter deploring the situation of his sons Vasilii and Dmitrii, whom, in strikingly familiar (but reversed) terms, he described as "my bankrupts."[193]

Thus, Pikhno's perception of political dissolution paralleled his fear of losing his authority in his own family. Against both, Pikhno recommended an unswerving legitimism and paternal authoritarianism:

> The general principles of social life are unchangeable. A sense of lawfulness and duty; respect for religion and morality; the family and family authority and the resulting caring and well-meaning but commanding relationship of the older generations toward the young; the right of property and the resulting authority and commanding power of the master over the servants and workers; respect for the individual and for civil liberty—such are the cornerstones of social life for all cultured nations and in all political forms of public life.[194]

Faced with his dubious position as an upstart in a society still largely based on birthright, as well as his illegitimate fatherhood and marriage, Pikhno became the apostle of legitimate authority. In the words of Anne McClintock, the family offered nationalists a "'natural' figure for sanctioning social *hierarchy* within a putative organic *unity* of interests."[195] And it is tempting to think that Pikhno imagined the ideal Russian state to be managed like a large-scale version of his family enterprise: based on the people's unquestioned loyalty to an authoritative but benevolent patriarch who would cautiously apply economic reforms beneficial to all (Russian) social groups. In a nationalist movement that mostly reacted to external challenges, Pikhno tried to develop a positive, progress-oriented program. His conservative utopia was not simply backward-looking, but mixed patriarchal and nationalist values with a practical commitment to modernization. In late imperial Russia's polarized politics, such a program did not find enough adherents to make a lasting impact.

After Stolypin's death in the autumn of 1911, his Nationalist-Octobrist coalition began to crumble. Meanwhile, the Shul'gin-Pikhnos found themselves increasingly isolated during the so-called Beilis affair. This antisemitic show trial started in March 1911, when the dead body of a boy named Andrei Iushchinskii was found in the Kiev suburb of Luk'ianovka. Far-right activists soon claimed that Iushchinskii was the victim of a ritual murder by Jews plotting to bake matzo with Christian blood. Under right-wing pressure, the prosecutor Georgii Chaplinskii, a Kiev Club member, pursued the ritual murder theory, ignoring all evidence pointing to a criminal gang around one Vera Cheberiak. Another club member, the psychiatrist Sikorskii, penned a medical report describing the murder as a case of "racial revenge." In July, the judicial authorities arrested Mendel Beilis, the Jewish manager of the brick factory near which Iushchinskii had been found. Subsequently, a ritual murder trial against Beilis was fabricated, and Chaplinskii dismissed investigators who followed the more promising Cheberiak lead.[196]

A team of prominent liberal lawyers, both Jewish and gentile, assumed Beilis's defense and publicized the case all over Russia and abroad. In May 1912, Dmitrii Pikhno published the results of a private investigation by a former police detective who accused Cheberiak's gang and hinted at irregularities in the prosecution. Many of his fellow Nationalists were furious. Even Anatolii Savenko insinuated in a Petersburg paper that Pikhno had been bought with Jewish credits for the sugar factory he was about to build.[197] Tensions in the Nationalist and right-wing camp were mounting. Still, the various groups managed to barter an agreement for the Fourth Duma elections in autumn 1912, which they swept.[198]

As the Beilis affair drew to its much-disputed conclusion, the *Kievlianin* family suffered a heavy loss: Dmitrii Pikhno died of a heart attack in July 1913, at age sixty. Even the liberal press paid tribute to "almost the only 'intelligent reactionary' in our black camp."[199] The death of Pikhno, who was enormously respected in the right-wing camp, opened the way for intensified attacks on his successor, Vasilii Shul'gin. Like his father, Shul'gin condemned the methods used in the Beilis case: "One need not be a lawyer," he wrote, "one only needs some common sense, to understand that the Beilis indictment is mere prattle which any slightly capable defense lawyer could easily take apart. And one involuntarily feels embarrassed for the Kiev prosecution and for all of Russian justice."[200] Although the authorities immediately confiscated this issue, the article caused an enormous stir among Kiev's right.

Readers sent *Kievlianin* angry letters and canceled their subscriptions. One furious reader abused Shul'gin as "Judas-traitor" and "Mr. Yiddish hireling" who had "sold Christian blood."[201] When the jury, largely composed of peasants, narrowly acquitted Beilis, Shul'gin triumphed. "These gray citizens of the Kievan earth," he wrote in *Kievlianin*, had defended "the purity of Russian justice and the honor of the Russian name before the whole world."[202]

However, Kiev's once successful right-wing coalition was disunited as never before, with *Kievlianin*'s moderate constitutionalist faction pitted against violently antisemitic extremists. A caricature in a far-right paper depicted Shul'gin as a monkey dancing to the tunes played by his Jewish masters. At a Kiev Club meeting, members shouted each other down. Some of them launched a new daily that breathed fire and brimstone against *Kievlianin*. Vasilii Shul'gin quit the Kiev Club and almost challenged Savenko to a duel. In January 1914, a local court convicted him to three months of prison for alleged disinformation about the Beilis trial, but he never had to serve the sentence because war broke out.[203]

Even though many observers were bewildered by Pikhno's and Shul'gin's stance in the Beilis affair, it was perfectly in character. Fearing popular unrest and disorder, both wanted a modern and regular, if authoritarian, state apparatus instead of one that satisfied the "medieval" passions of the dark masses. As trained lawyers, they cherished the rule of law and insisted on proper legal procedure, lest the imperial state be compromised. They thought of themselves as rational antisemites who fought in the economic and political arena, and they usually condemned pogroms. Shul'gin may have been concerned by the incarceration of an obviously innocent man, but he indignantly rejected accusations of sudden philosemitism: "We Russians must not adopt purely Jewish methods in our struggle against Jewry." Russian morality, he believed, "must be immeasurably higher than the ethics of this people, whose laws allow it all perfidies and infamies if they are directed against aliens."[204] Another article declared the need for a "healthy and reasonable antisemitism" to counter the "Yiddification" of the "Aryan" Russians.[205] Despite this rare instance of racialist rhetoric in *Kievlianin*, Shul'gin's priority was always the strength of the Russian state. Even antisemitism had to serve it to be appropriate.[206]

As soon as the Beilis affair was over, the Nationalist Party experienced discord between the supporters of an alliance with the Octobrists and those who preferred cooperation with the anticonstitutionalist far right.[207] On the eve of the First World War, the Nationalists threatened to fall apart. The new prime minister Vladimir Kokovtsov was not inclined to cooperate with a party whose chauvinism he found counterproductive. The Duma and State Council engaged in obstructionism, creating the impression of a complete political blockade.[208] With Dmitrii Pikhno dead, many of the city's right-wingers hostile, and competing local newspapers on the rise, the *Kievlianin* family enterprise, too, had reached an impasse.[209]

Dmitrii Pikhno's biography can be read as the antithesis of Iakov Shul'gin's. Shul'gin, a Russian-speaking urban nobleman, reimagined himself as a Ukrainian populist. Pikhno, born into the provincial Ukrainian-speaking lower middle classes, became a Russian nationalist and an advocate of legitimate authority in politics and private life. He, too, made a political choice—that of throwing his lot in with the imperial state—before he fashioned an unambiguously national identity for himself. Once more, consciousness preceded being. In the southwestern provinces, embracing the empire meant embracing Russianness, and Pikhno assimilated into Russian elite culture as he rose through the ranks of imperial society. Like the Ukrainophiles, Pikhno cared deeply about improving the peasantry's lot, but unlike them, he saw the Russian state as a suitable instrument for this task. The state, he hoped, would realize his program of agricultural modernization and create ethnically marked private property.

The year 1905 was a watershed for Russian nationalism. The attack on the autocratic state and on Russian centralism by radical liberals, socialists, and various national movements activated the state's supporters. The emergence of a semiconstitutional political system forced the monarchists to organize, abandoning their traditional rejection of party politics. While committed to the autocracy, they modernized their political practices, which brought some of them closer to national-democratic positions—although few wholeheartedly embraced electoral mass politics. The Pikhno-Shul'gins, too, participated in the emerging parliamentary sphere, at first reluctantly, but later with increasing success and enthusiasm. Making use of family ties, they developed a formidable political and media business that enabled them to carry their nationalist cause onto the highest levels of Petersburg politics.

Of course, the Pikhno-Shul'gins' brand of politics was rather idiosyncratic. Their combination of staunch monarchism and economically grounded nationalism with hierarchical family solidarity and disregard for conventions was hardly the norm among Russian conservatives. However, their case sheds light on broader political issues. Thus, Dmitii Pikhno's rightward shift in 1905 exemplifies how economic liberalism could take an illiberal turn when political mass mobilization threatened private property. The Pikhno-Shul'gins also illustrate the family's value as a nucleus for political organization in a time when party organizations were still unstable, especially in the right-wing spectrum. The family was a locus of political socialization and mobilization, in particular for women, who paradoxically gained political agency within its patriarchal structures. And finally, the family served as a societal model that might transcend the apparent contradictions between modern nationalism and traditional autocracy.

For that was ultimately the goal of Dmitrii Pikhno's political project: to use nationalism so as to create a community of interest between the autocratic state and its Russian (read: Orthodox East Slav) masses. Rather than equal electoral participation, the state was to provide its peasants with access to landownership. In return, it would receive a loyal majority population, which could no longer be seduced by socialism or Ukrainian nationalism. Pikhno's vision, which had much in common with Petr Stolypin's, celebrated a few successes but never gained the full approval of the tsarist state. Its bureaucracy and the tsar himself did not embrace the populist, democratic components of nationalism, perhaps recognizing their potential to undermine the fragile balance of power between the empire and its peripheral non-Russian elites. Given this political dead end, it becomes clear why Vasilii Shul'gin readily shifted to the left during the First World War, when a broad alliance of patriotic but reform-oriented forces suddenly appeared possible. Ironically, the national crisis of war and revolution offered Shul'gin and his family an opportunity to reinvent themselves politically—an opportunity, however, that would end in disaster.

CHAPTER 4

Triumph and Tragedy

Nationalists in War and Revolution, 1914–1920

Russia's entry into the First World War
spelled catastrophe for the empire and its autocratic government. As
the war triggered a domestic revolution and, ultimately, a series of connected civil wars, imperial Russia's territories entered a "continuum
of crisis," during which politics became increasingly dependent on the
use of military force.[1] The imperial state disintegrated both socially
and geographically, only to be reassembled by an unlikely contender for
power, the far-left Bolshevik party. Far from being peripheral, Ukraine
was one of the central theaters of these events. Its territories witnessed
the battles of the eastern front, the political struggle between various
national and social movements in 1917, German occupation in 1918,
and the desperate fighting between White, Bolshevik, and Ukrainian
armies during the postimperial civil wars.[2] The city of Kiev experienced
twelve regime changes between 1917 and 1920.[3]

As part of the local elites, several members of the Shul'gin and
Shul'hyn families became deeply involved in the struggle for control
over Ukraine and its capital. Trying to shape revolutionary events, they
continued to use prerevolutionary networks and family connections.
However, they had to adapt both their political practices and their ideological positions to the unprecedented conditions of social upheaval,
militarization, and mass involvement in politics. Thanks to their

flexible tactics, they temporarily managed to steer Kiev's revolutionary politics in a national direction.

Thus, the first years of war and revolution were ripe with opportunity for both Russian and Ukrainian nationalists. On the Russian side, old alliances and enmities crumbled after 1914. The initial enthusiasm for the war resulted in a realignment of patriotic forces, which ultimately turned against the government and led such staunch nationalists and loyalists as the Shul'gins into the opposition's camp. Kiev's Ukrainian nationalists profited from the power vacuum after the fall of tsarism in 1917 to establish autonomous institutions. Among the city's most energetic Ukrainian activists was Oleksander Shul'hyn, who put his patriotic education to good use and rose through the ranks of the emerging Ukrainian state. Meanwhile, Ekaterina and Vasilii Shul'gin launched an extraordinary campaign to unite and defend "Russian Kiev" against Ukrainian and socialist parties.

Throughout the ensuing civil war, Vasilii Shul'gin continued to toil for the "White cause" of a united and indivisible Russia. While the escalation of military hostilities jeopardized his former position, Shul'gin retained his influence among Russian nationalists until the Bolshevik victory forced him and his family to emigrate. The Shul'gins shared this fate with Oleksander Shul'hyn, whose futile attempt to secure international recognition for the disintegrating Ukrainian state also forced him into exile. Both branches of the Shul'gin/Shul'hyn family experienced triumphal moments during the revolutionary years but ultimately suffered tragic defeats.

Shifting Alliances

On 19 July (1 August) 1914, Germany declared war on the Russian Empire, whose general mobilization on the previous day had signaled that it would stand by its Serbian ally.[4] *Kievlianin* reacted to the outbreak of the war like most Russian newspapers: by calling for unity and patriotism, blaming Austro-German imperialism, and declaring Russia's purely defensive war aims. An editorial accused the Germans of plans to conquer the Kingdom of Poland and the Southwest region. Like the medieval Teutonic knights, the warlike Germans were attacking the peaceful Slavs, and as in the battle of Grunwald in 1410, the Slavs would beat them. Aware of the need to secure Polish support in the war, a traditionally anti-Polish newspaper did not hesitate to appropriate a Polish national myth.[5] Three days later, it praised two patriotic demonstrations in Kiev, a Russian and a mostly Jewish one. "Yesterday, these people were still each other's fierce enemies," the author declared, but now "the feuding people have understood that they, who used to oppose each other in all matters, are allies in one thing: their common God is not evil and blood but peace and justice."[6]

Kievlianin's message was clear: all prewar differences, whether political or ethnic, had to be forgotten in order to beat the external enemy in a "holy war between civilization and barbarism." No wonder that Vasilii Shul'gin enthused about the declarations of loyalty at the ceremonial State Duma meeting of 27 July, delivered by "representatives of the tribes and dialects sheltered by the broad wings of the double-headed eagle." Besides Russia's Germans, Balts, Muslims, and Jews, he particularly praised the Polish deputies for choosing the side of their Slavic "brothers by blood" in the upcoming conflict.[7] The slogan of "internal peace" (*vnutrennii mir*) was proclaimed by all Russian papers from the liberal to the moderate right spectrum and defined *Kievlianin*'s political line during the war.[8]

Nationally framed conflicts between Russians and the empire's other populations, formerly a main topic in the paper, were almost completely suspended in its reporting during 1914 and 1915. The eastern front ran through territories with Polish population. Therefore, *Kievlianin* encouraged the Poles to help Russia's war effort in a spirit of "common Slavic nationalism," vaguely promising Poland's "resurrection" within the empire.[9] However, as soon as some politician made concrete demands for Polish autonomy, *Kievlianin* declared that the issue would have to await victory in the war. According to Anatolii Savenko, Polish autonomy within Russia was desirable in the economic and cultural spheres, but not regarding government, courts, and bureaucracy.[10] Despite all conciliatory rhetoric, the Russian nationalists made few concrete concessions to the Poles.

The "Mazepist danger," so prominent in *Kievlianin* before the war, hardly figured anymore at all. The editors proclaimed that the war had led to the "self-liquidation of the 'Ukrainian question'" by proving the loyalty of the Little Russian population and thus the fact that the Ukrainian movement was an irrelevant political sect.[11] Similarly, the "Jewish question" simply disappeared from the pages for several months. By the summer of 1915, a mildly antisemitic tone crept back into a few articles, but even then it was combined with rather benevolent policies. Thus, one article proposed the abolishment of the Pale of Settlement to free the Southwest from the burden of its large Jewish population.[12] Neither did *Kievlianin* join the campaign against "enemy aliens" that identified Russia's ethnic Germans with the external enemy and pushed for their expropriation or deportation.[13] While many conservative papers propagated "internal peace," *Kievlianin* differed from others by enforcing it more or less consistently.

This editorial line was counterbalanced by increasingly shrill invective against the external enemy, the Central Powers. *Kievlianin* began to include a daily page "For the Russian Army" with motivational patriotic texts, heroic front reports, and, above all, denunciations of the enemy's cruelty. While Austria-Hungary and the Ottoman Empire were presented as fragile states on the verge of collapse, Germany appeared as the main enemy. The topos of German atrocities on the battlefield gave rise to an image of German "barbarians" who violated international law, bullied smaller states, and terrorized the peaceful civilian population of occupied territories. The German emperor Wilhelm II was presented as a bloodthirsty butcher who enjoyed committing war crimes as much as shooting thousands of deer.[14] Among *Kievlianin's* most aggressive propagandists was Ekaterina Shul′gina, who began to perceive Germany as a dark, Satanic power; she even sacked her children's Baltic governess because she could no longer bear hearing German in the house. In one of her articles, Shul′gina wrote that the war had unmasked the seemingly civilized Germans as beasts. Comparing them to the Japanese, whom she retrospectively found a "noble, respectable opponent," Shul′gina described the Germans as a "scum nation" with whom one could not negotiate.[15]

During the Great War, then, short-term changes of alliance could overrule long-standing sympathies and rivalries in the nationalist imagination. "War nationalism" accelerated not only political mobilization, but also the creation and suspension of ethnically framed enemies.[16] Shul′gina's memoirs confirm that she directly substituted one constitutive other with a new one. While she began to hate Germany, she decided to stop writing anti-Jewish articles and suddenly felt enthusiasm when the commander-in-chief, Grand Duke Nikolai Nikolaevich, promised autonomy to the Poles.[17] The same flexibility is apparent in *Kievlianin's* furious reaction to Bulgaria's gradual rapprochement with Germany and Austria. Traditionally considered Russia's Orthodox "brother nation," Bulgaria was immediately declared a national enemy when its government was drawn into the orbit of the Central Powers. Using a racialized language he probably borrowed from his fellow Kiev Club member Sikorskii, Anatolii Savenko abused the Bulgarians as "freaks" and "cripples" among the Slavs, whose disloyalty stemmed from their non-Slavic, "Mongolian" ancestry.[18]

Vasilii Shul'gin was barely involved in *Kievlianin*'s efforts at war propaganda. According to his memoirs, he was pleased by the patriotic upsurge in July 1914 but did not share the enthusiasm of his Duma colleagues, foreseeing the destruction that the war would bring. Moreover, he felt useless as a journalist in Kiev. Now that all newspapers took a patriotic stance, *Kievlianin* had lost its former purpose as a lone defender of the autocracy. As a Duma member, Shul'gin could have been exempted from military service, but he decided to fight at the front, asking to be transferred from the sappers to the 166th Rovno Infantry Regiment. He chose this regiment so as to fight alongside the brothers of his lover Liubov' Popova, although he later claimed that he had felt the need to "share the manly fate" of his Volhynian peasants. In September, Ensign Shul'gin reached his regiment near Przemyśl, in occupied Austrian Galicia. Leading a small detachment of soldiers, Shul'gin was wounded by a bullet that hit his arm and shoulder after only two hours in the field. On the following day, his commander sent him back to the rear.[19]

The family's women, too, felt the urge to join the war effort. Ekaterina Shul'gina and her sister-in-law Alla Bilimovich regularly attended to wounded soldiers in a Kiev military hospital. For Shul'gina, this experience was "if not a Going to the People, then at least a real approaching the people [*podkhozhdenie k narodu*]." For the first time, she felt that she was encountering "the people" as an equal. The family's favorite myth of a national community beyond all social barriers was reinvigorated by the image of a united "nation in arms." Medical service gave women an active role in this wartime nation, especially in cities like Kiev, where up to three thousand wounded soldiers from the front arrived per day.[20] In one of her feuilletons of the period, Ekaterina Shul'gina waxed poetic about the wounded soldiers who gracefully bore their lot: "These people may be neither very educated nor well-read—but they are definitely *well-bred* in the best sense of the word."[21] Like other upperclass women in military hospitals, Shul'gina idealized the simple but goodhearted peasant soldiers and their ability to suffer. Texts written by such nurses combine genuine admiration for soldiers' fatalism and courage with a "maternalistic" view of the rank-and-file as "children" in need of guidance. While these women saw the war as an opportunity to serve the nation on a par with men of all estates and classes, their accounts betray the persistence of deep social cleavages within imperial Russian society.[22]

Having recovered from his own wounds, Vasilii Shulgin also became engaged in medical aid. In late 1914, he returned to the front with the Southwestern Regional Zemstvo Organization (IuZOZO). IuZOZO was the foundation of Shul'gin's party colleague Petr Balashev. Part of the "parastatal complex" that tried to compensate for the state's short-comings during the war, it relied on the recently established western zemstvos, which were supposedly less dominated by left-wing doctors and statisticians than other zemstvos.[23] Throughout the first half of 1915, Shul'gin commanded a mobile infirmary that included a Polish doctor, a Jewish aide-de-camp, his half-brother Filipp Mogilevskii, and his lover Liubov' Popova. Stationed directly behind the front line, they evacuated wounded soldiers from the fighting scene and transported them to the rear. It was in this capacity that Shul'gin witnessed the Russian army's disastrous retreat. While the Russians had advanced far into enemy territory during the first months of the war, the tables were turned in the spring and summer of 1915. A series of catastrophic de-feats forced the imperial armies to retreat from occupied Galicia and the Russian Empire's own Polish provinces. By September 1915, the front had moved into Volhynia, so that Ekaterina Shul'gina evacuated the servants of the Kurgany estate to Podolia, while the sugar factory's machines were disassembled and brought eastward. By this point, Vasi-lii Shul'gin was no longer at the front. Upon learning that a new ses-sion of the State Duma was to be convened, he had left his unit for Petrograd (as Saint Petersburg had been renamed in an act of symbolic de-Germanization).

The state's weakness laid bare by the retreat caused a realignment of political forces in the Duma. Several members of Vasilii Shul'gin's Nationalist caucus were outraged by what they perceived as the govern-ment's criminal neglect of armaments and supplies for the retreating army. When the session began, it emerged that there was enough com-mon ground for cooperation between the Duma's critical but patriotic caucuses. The liberal Kadets were positively surprised by Nationalist de-mands for more Duma involvement in government; the Nationalists, in turn, praised the Kadets' newfound patriotism. The Kadet-Nationalist rapprochement caused a split among the Duma's Russian National-ists. Led by Vladimir Bobrinskii, Anatolii Savenko, and Vsevolod Dem-chenko, about thirty deputies left the caucus in mid-August. They formed a new "Progressive Nationalist" group to cooperate with the liberals, while the rest of the caucus preferred an alliance with the hard right. Vasilii Shul'gin, who missed the deliberations because of an illness and was unhappy about the split, nevertheless became the "progressive" caucus's vice president and turned *Kievlianin* into its press organ.[24]

The split in the Nationalist caucus opened the path for a formal agreement of the Duma's moderate opposition. After several weeks of negotiation, six Duma caucuses (Kadets, Progressists, Left Octobrists, Zemstvo Octobrists, Center, Progressive Nationalists) announced the formation of the Progressive Bloc in August 1915. Its program included long-standing liberal demands such as equal rights for peasants, renewal of labor union activity, an amnesty for political prisoners, and the introduction of local (volost') zemstvos. The Kadets temporarily disavowed their demand for a ministerial cabinet responsible to the Duma. Instead, the bloc's program asked for the creation of a "ministry of public confidence" with competent ministers who would strengthen the war effort in cooperation with the Duma.[25]

If this concession was difficult for the Kadets, the Progressive Nationalists had to compromise on the "national questions." The bloc's demand for the immediate creation of an autonomous Poland was no longer particularly controversial, but the Nationalists negotiated hard to weaken the demand to revoke laws against Polish land acquisitions in the borderlands. The program also contained a point on the "reestablishment of the Little Russian press," which had been prohibited in 1914.[26] The question of equal rights for Jews was by far the most contested issue. While it had been a central point of the Kadet program for years, the bloc's right wing found the abolition of legal constraints either untimely or undesirable. The compromise formula of "entry onto the path" (*vstuplenie na put'*) of abolishing the restrictive laws left almost everyone dissatisfied. The Jewish press was disappointed by the lukewarm commitment, while the hard right charged that the bloc's conservative members had abandoned their ideals.[27]

Vasilii Shul'gin and his associate Savenko saw the formation of the Progressive Bloc as the direct continuation of their "internal peace" policy. Savenko insisted that the Kadets had swallowed at least as many bitter pills as his own group. Indeed, the shift in the Kadets' attitude toward the government was more momentous than the Nationalist concessions on national issues. The liberals had embraced an unconditionally defencist stance and were ready to accept an autocratic government, as long as it would be staffed with competent and cooperative ministers. In order to keep up the war effort, Shul'gin insisted, it was now up to the government to close ranks with the Progressive Bloc.[28]

However, on 3 September 1915, Tsar Nicholas and his prime minister Ivan Goremykin announced the closure of the Duma session until further notice.[29]

Decline and Fall of the Russian Empire

When they joined the Progressive Bloc, Shul'gin and his associates had genuinely hoped to work alongside the government. By ending the Duma session and dismissing several liberal ministers, the tsar declared his hostility even to a constructive and patriotic opposition. In uncharacteristically harsh terms, *Kievlianin* commented that the government had shouldered a "terrible responsibility" by removing the only force truly dedicated to the army's needs. Savenko and Shul'gin were particularly angry about the Duma's far right, whom they blamed for the prorogation of the session. The so-called black bloc became a target of constant attacks in *Kievlianin*, variously accused of serving a reactionary regime, of defending their own aristocratic privilege, or even of secretly hoping for German victory.[30] "How pleasant would it be if the stupid rightists were as smart as the Kadets," Vasilii Shul'gin complained in private.[31] As during the Japanese war, the nationalists' wrath turned from external to internal enemies. This time, however, they were allied with the liberals and began to perceive the autocracy itself as an obstacle to victory. The policy of "internal peace," at first meant to support the government, turned against it.

While the Duma was not in session, Shul'gin, who had come to see himself as a spokesman for the army, set to work in the Special Council on Defense. This committee united representatives of the War Ministry, the Duma, societal organizations, and industry, and was one of several organs founded over the summer of 1915 to rally patriotic forces behind the war effort. Shul'gin and his colleagues tried hard to improve the production and transportation of the army's ammunition supplies. Shul'gin saw the Special Councils as an instrument for monarchists to strengthen the authority of competent ministers and counteract the damage done by the tsar without having to undermine his prestige.[32] By October 1915, the imperial army managed to stall the Austro-German advance, and in the renewed Duma session of spring 1916, the Progressive Bloc worked relatively successfully on municipal reform, cooperatives, and peasant legislation. However, the "national questions" remained a potential bone of contention within the fragile liberal-conservative coalition.[33]

Vasilii Shul'gin understood the dilemmas that the bloc's program posed for Russian nationalism. In the months following its formation, he published several articles to clarify his stance toward his camp's traditional opponents. The first of them concerned the "Ukrainian question." It was a reaction to an article by Mykhailo Hrushevs'kyi, where the leader of the Ukrainian movement had declared that he and his followers wanted to achieve their goals by developing the Russian Empire's constitutional structures, not by allying with Austria. Shul'gin welcomed this declaration of loyalty, although he once more critiqued the poverty of the Ukrainians' language and literature. As long as they did not engage in state treason, he concluded, Hrushevs'kyi and his peers should be free to compete against Russian and Polish culture: "If the 'Ukrainians' absolutely want to create their own culture, there is not much to be done—let them try. We cannot wish them success without violating our conscience, but we believe that the government would act wisely if it granted them full liberty to do their ungrateful business."[34] In short, Shul'gin advocated a liberal practice toward a movement he perceived as a minor threat in the face of the external enemy.

Shul'gin's statement on the "Jewish question" followed in March 1916. Russia's Jewish population, he wrote, was not monolithic: some Jews were heroes in the army, others were traitors, most were somewhere in between. While he admitted the destructive effects of Jewish inequality, he insisted that the problem was based in "the factual difference of tribes." In order to equalize Russian-Jewish relations, both nations would have to work on their weaknesses: the Russians on their apathy and "weakness of will," the Jews on their lack of ethics and "unscrupulousness of means." Shul'gin's wife Ekaterina held similar views, distinguishing between individual Jews, many of whom had achieved great things, and "Jewry," which she characterized in stereotypically antisemitic terms as a rootless nation, a "principle deeply inimical, opposed, hateful to Christianity." Like her husband, she insisted that fundamental differences stood in the way of all reforms: "If one fights against Jewry, Jews who deserve pity and mercy will suffer. If one stops fighting against Jews, Jewry will begin to triumph."[35]

Finally, Vasilii Shul'gin reformulated his views on the "Polish question." Rejecting an independent Polish state as geopolitically too unstable, he suggested that Poland become an autonomous territorial unit within the Russian Empire after the war. Foreign affairs, military matters, the budget, customs, currency, post, telegraph, and citizenship would remain the domain of the imperial government, while "all the remaining issues" would be dealt with by an elected Polish parliament and a government named by the tsar. Advocating for a Poland "within its ethnographic borders," Shul'gin disingenuously pretended that the Poles would accept whatever the Russian state defined as ethnographically Polish territory.[36] Obviously, Shul'gin's Polish program was a purely theoretical exercise. In 1916, with the Polish core provinces under German occupation, the Russian government was in no position to impose reforms on territories it no longer controlled.

It is clear, then, that the Great War did not revolutionize Russian nationalists' attitude toward their traditional "others." A moderately liberal view of the Ukrainian movement was possible because its leaders declared their loyalty and seemed unable to mobilize the masses. Jewish activists also supported the war effort, and the Shul'gins were ready to reward their attitude with vague promises of legal change; yet they still perceived the Jews as fundamentally different and dangerous. Finally, owing to socioeconomic change over the previous decades, the Poles no longer seemed threatening in the empire's Southwest, which allowed Vasilii Shul'gin to treat Poland soberly as an issue of geopolitical considerations. Even though his concessions were modest and hypothetical, Shul'gin doubtless believed sincerely that his new course could help stabilize the wartime empire.

In the second half of 1916, both liberals and nationalists increasingly identified a new threat to the Russian war effort: the upper echelons of the empire's bureaucracy. Back in 1905, Dmitrii Pikhno had staunchly defended the "bureaucratic regime," but by now, his successors found reactionary ministers and court intrigues to be an obstacle in the way of efficient wartime administration. In the Duma, the Progressive Bloc harshly attacked the government of the new prime minister Boris Stürmer—widely perceived as a nonentity—for its diplomatic blunders and corruption scandals. Vasilii Shul'gin and the Kadet leader Pavel Miliukov drafted a declaration demanding Stürmer's resignation. On 1 November 1916, Miliukov climbed the Duma's rostrum to insinuate that Stürmer and his allies were guilty of either "stupidity or treason," if not both.[37] Two days later, it fell to Vasilii Shul'gin to second Miliukov's attack. Whether the accusations were true or not, he explained, the horror of the Stürmer government was that everyone believed them to be possible. For Shul'gin, there remained only one solution: "To fight this regime until it goes away."[38] In Ekaterina Shul'gina's words, this speech marked her husband's "transition to the opposition."[39] Yet, perhaps misled by the mood among his fellow politicians, Shul'gin remained convinced that the Duma would be able to prevent anarchy. As late as mid-December, he asked those who worried that it might instead kindle the flames of popular dissatisfaction, "Is it not obvious that Russia is disgusted by the idea of a revolution? . . . Do they really doubt that the entire societal movement has only one aim: to heal the government from its illnesses?"[40]

Despite Stürmer's dismissal, the new year brought no significant improvement in the relations between Duma and cabinet. The Duma's session was postponed, and ruling circles discussed its definitive dissolution. Meanwhile, the workers of Petrograd, suffering under food shortages, launched a new wave of strikes. The police reacted by stepping up repression against socialist parties. This, in turn, caused discord in the opposition, as some liberals advocated a revolutionary alliance with the workers or a palace coup.[41] Vasilii Shul'gin kept calling for calm and unity, as well as more involvement of the Duma, which he saw as the true expression of society's patriotism.[42] Some of his articles must have contained much harsher attacks on the government. The censors regularly cut out paragraphs, and the monarchist paper appeared with the white gaps otherwise characteristic of the left-wing press.[43] In private, Shul'gin expressed his despair openly. On 15 February 1917, he bitterly complained to Grand Duke Nikolai Mikhailovich, a critical uncle of the tsar, about the incompetence of Russia's ruling class and intelligentsia: "For us, as people educated in a monarchist spirit, it is unbearable to think that they cast aside the warnings of the monarchy's friends and will surrender to the fist of the street, once this fist gathers enough courage and force."[44]

Eight days later, the February revolution broke out on the streets of Petrograd. On 23 February, the city's working-class women staged a rally for bread and peace, setting off a new, more radical wave of protest. The leaders of the Progressive Bloc found themselves in a dilemma between the revolutionary pressure from the street and the imperial court's intention to dissolve the Duma yet again. On 27 February, a "private meeting" of Duma deputies gathered in the Tauride Palace and formed a provisional committee under the leadership of Duma president Mikhail Rodzianko. The committee included most of the Progressive Bloc's leaders such as Miliukov and Shul'gin, but also two socialists, the Trudovik Aleksandr Kerenskii and the Menshevik Nikolai Chkheidze. A few hours later, the last bureaucratic cabinet simply ceased to exist, and the Duma's provisional committee proclaimed itself the acting government.[45] Vasilii Shul'gin had definitely ended up in the ranks of the revolution.

Over the following days, as the parliamentarians tried to establish power over all branches of government, it became increasingly clear that Tsar Nicholas could not remain on the throne. On 2 March, the committee decided to dispatch a delegation to the tsar, whose railway car had been stranded in Pskov, in order to wrest an abdication manifesto from him. Vasilii Shul'gin volunteered to go alongside the Octobrist Aleksandr Guchkov. When Shul'gin and Guchkov arrived in Pskov on the same evening, it was no longer necessary to convince the autocrat. Persuaded by his general staff, Nicholas II had already decided to abdicate and name the liberal aristocrat Georgii L'vov prime minister. The Duma's two delegates could only acquiesce in Nicholas's demand to be succeeded by his brother, Grand Duke Mikhail, rather than his underage son, even though this wish contradicted the law. Meanwhile, in Petrograd, L'vov and Miliukov formed a Provisional Government consisting largely of the Duma committee's members but excluding Rodzianko and Shul'gin. When Shul'gin and Guchkov returned to Petrograd the next morning, they were called to a meeting with the designated emperor Mikhail. Like everyone else present, except for Miliukov and Guchkov, Shul'gin advised Mikhail not to accept the throne, arguing that he would have too little support. After thinking it over for half an hour, Mikhail renounced the throne.[46]

Although Vasilii Shul'gin's role in the dynasty's abdication was by no means decisive, it carries symbolic weight. The war had shattered political certainties, including the unconditional monarchism of the Nationalists. Incapable of making concessions to the patriotic elites, Nicholas II and his entourage had managed to alienate even such staunch monarchists as Shul'gin. By February 1917, all but the most reactionary politicians saw the weak tsar as an obstacle rather than an asset in the war. This disillusion with the autocracy was reinforced by the impression that republican France and parliamentary Britain were waging war more successfully than Russia.[47] Committed to "internal peace," the likes of Shul'gin were now ready to exclude the court and the high bureaucracy from the nation. Justifying his involvement in the abdication, Shul'gin later wrote that he had hoped to save the monarchy by sacrificing the monarch and had wanted the tsar to abdicate in the presence of monarchists. He also stressed his revulsion at the sight of the crowds entering the Tauride Palace during demonstrations.[48] However, this account obscures another aspect of Shul'gin's reaction: relief that the bureaucratic regime was gone, and cautious optimism concerning the new government. After the declaration of the Provisional Government, he telegraphed an article from Petrograd to Kiev: "Nothing is lost, nothing is destroyed of what is necessary for the war. By contrast, we have received what we were lacking: Russia is now governed by people who love her."[49]

Sudden Opportunities

The outbreak of war between Russia and Austria-Hungary left the Ukrainian national movement in a difficult situation. Ukrainian activists both in Russia and in Habsburg-ruled Galicia rushed to declare their loyalty to their respective empires.[50] In the movement's main Russian-language journal, Symon Petliura acknowledged the tragic situation of a nation living on both sides of the front line but announced that all Ukrainians would "fulfill their duty as citizens of Russia"—in the hope of being rewarded with extended national rights after the war.[51] Nevertheless, the government immediately moved against the Ukrainian movement, closing down nearly all Ukrainian-language publications and exiling several activists to the interior provinces. The anti-Ukrainian campaign was exported to Galicia when Russia conquered the region in September 1914. The new governor-general Georgii Bobrinskii set up a repressive occupation regime based on the premise that Galicia was an inherently Russian territory and must be delivered of the Mazepist danger. Bobrinskii had Ukrainian organizations and schools closed down and nationalist activists deported. Russian nationalists and Orthodox clerics arrived from Russia to lobby for repressions against the local Uniate Church. Some of Russia's Ukrainian activists supported Galician refugees or sent protests to Petrograd, but Kiev's Ukrainian social life remained weak until the end of 1916.[52]

There is very little information about the wartime activities of the Shul'hyn-Ustymovych family, but it seems that its members tried to avoid involvement with the war. Although all three sons were of age for military service, only the youngest, Mykola, served in the imperial army, signing up for an artillery academy in Odessa and becoming a balloon observer. His brother Volodymyr remained in Kiev, where he led a circle of Ukrainian science and medicine students. The eldest son, Oleksander, graduated in 1915 but continued his research at Petrograd University. His wife Lidiia, a medical doctor, was working in a military hospital in Kiev.[53] His mother Liubov and sister Nadiia, like their counterparts in the Russian branch of the family, entered nursing service for wounded soldiers. Their hospital, operated by the Ukrainian club Rodyna, treated mostly soldiers from Ukraine, whom the nurses taught Ukrainian grammar.[54]

When the revolution broke out in late February 1917, Oleksander Shul'hyn was in Petrograd, where he had joined the youth group of the Society of Ukrainian Progressives (TUP). Although most TUP members sympathized with the Provisional Government, they dispatched Oleksander to the Soviet of Workers' and Soldiers' Deputies, where a group of Ukrainian soldiers had already formed. These soldiers elected Oleksander Shul'hyn as their president, even though unlike most of them, he was neither a Social Democrat nor a Socialist Revolutionary. Shul'hyn was more of an observer than an active participant in this key organization of the Russian revolution. The Soviet's minutes have preserved only one short speech in which Shul'hyn announced that the Ukrainians would fight for freedom alongside the Russians: "We are a part of the Russian state and now we do not have any wish to separate from you."[55]

On 23 March, Oleksander left Petrograd for Kiev, where the Ukrainian movement was beginning to gather its forces. Its main organ was the Central Rada, a body formed by the TUP leadership, Ukrainian socialist organizations, and representatives of students, soldiers, workers, and agricultural cooperatives. Mykhailo Hrushevs'kyi, the most respected Ukrainian intellectual, became the Rada's president.[56] Meanwhile, the city's revolutionary and Ukrainian forces embarked on the symbolic appropriation of Kiev's imperially marked urban space. A series of demonstrations filled the city's streets in March, and protesters toppled the statue of Petr Stolypin on the Duma square. Tens of thousands, among them many soldiers, attended a Ukrainian demonstration that displayed blue and yellow flags and greeted Hrushevs'kyi with enthusiastic ovations.[57]

Upon arriving in Kiev, Oleksander Shul'hyn made two memorable speeches. The first was at the TUP congress, just after Hrushevs'kyi had advocated the immediate organization of a Ukrainian Constituent Assembly and a rapid declaration of autonomy. Shul'hyn disagreed, insisting that autonomy ought to be achieved by moderate and loyal means, in coordination with Petrograd.[58] A few days later, he spoke at the Ukrainian National Congress in front of fifteen hundred delegates from peasant cooperatives, zemstvos, and cultural organizations. Conceptualizing Ukrainian politics within a Drahomanovite framework,

Shul'hyn argued that Ukraine's autonomy ought to be accompanied by the transformation of the entire empire into a federal republic. In a similar vein, the congress's resolution demanded broad national-territorial autonomy within the Russian republic. The National Congress was also meant to broaden the legitimacy of the Central Rada. It elected some 115 new members to represent cultural, regional, and professional organizations. Oleksander Shul'hyn joined both the Rada and the Little Rada—a smaller body that took care of everyday business—as a representative of the reestablished Radical-Democratic Party.[59]

Only twenty-seven years old, Shul'hyn embarked on a stellar career in Ukraine's emerging autonomous institutions. This unknown student activist, whom the Kievans had so far only recognized as Iakov Shul'gin's son, suddenly made a name for himself. His oratorical talent and youthful enthusiasm helped him play a leading role on Ukraine's revolutionary political scene. As he reported back to Petrograd, Oleksander was thrilled about the "electric agitation" of the Ukrainian political awakening. Free Ukraine would guarantee equal rights and tolerance to all nationalities, he assured the skeptical Russian progressives, and the slogans "Independent Ukraine" and "Ukraine for Ukrainians" belonged to a small minority of extremists.[60]

Taking into account the period's socialist trend, Oleksander Shul'hyn's Radical-Democratic Party was soon renamed the Ukrainian Party of Socialist-Federalists (UPSF). Shul'hyn supported the name change, stressing the need for a non-Marxist, evolutionary socialism to overcome economic conflicts.[61] A numerically small group without mass appeal, the UPSF nevertheless played an important role in the first months of the revolution because it included many of the Ukrainian movement's leading intellectuals. A significant exception was Mykhailo Hrushevs'kyi. The Central Rada president broke with his old companions and aligned himself with the Ukrainian Party of Socialist Revolutionaries (UPSR), which was dominated by very young students. The third major Ukrainian party was the Ukrainian Social Democratic Workers' Party (USDRP), a nationally inclined Marxist group led by the writer Volodymyr Vynnychenko and the journalist Symon Petliura.[62]

Over the spring, the Central Rada gradually turned from a nationalist interest group into Kiev's main revolutionary organ. Increasingly popular in the city, the Rada began to fill the power vacuum left by the fall of tsarism. In March, Kiev's liberals and moderate socialists had formed the Council of United Societal Organizations, a body that the Provisional Government recognized as its local representation. However, the

Rada leadership soon began to bypass the council and enter into direct relations with Petrograd. The Menshevik-dominated Kiev Workers' Soviet failed to acquire as much authority as its Petrograd counterpart, and the local Bolsheviks had even less mass support in this phase. According to one observer, "the strength of the Ukrainian movement lay mostly in the weakness of its opponents."[63] In the decisive first weeks of the revolution, the Ukrainian nationalists set up a well-functioning organization. Not least due to its socialist slogans, the Central Rada came to be perceived as the local embodiment of revolutionary power.

In mid-June, the Rada established a General Secretariat to serve as its executive body. Presided over by Volodymyr Vynnychenko, this "cabinet" included five Ukrainian SDs (Vynnychenko, Petliura, Borys Martos, Valentyn Sadovs'kyi, Ivan Steshenko), two Ukrainian SRs (Pavlo Khrystiuk and Mykola Stasiuk), one Socialist-Federalist (Serhii Iefremov), and one nonparty man (Khrystofor Baranovs'kyi). Two weeks later, an important step for an understanding with Petrograd and the non-Ukrainian population was made. The Rada's Second Universal (declaration) extended the Rada's membership to over eight hundred seats, of which almost a third were to be held by the national minorities. On 15 July, Oleksander Shul'hyn replaced his reluctant fellow party member Iefremov as general secretary for inter-nationality affairs. His first task was to defend the General Secretariat's provisional statute in the Rada. This document, which Oleksander (over-)enthusiastically announced as Ukraine's "first constitution," declared the General Secretariat to be the highest regional administrative organ, subordinate only to the Provisional Government in Petrograd and competent in nearly all political matters.[64] The Petrograd government did not accept the statute, but after a further round of negotiations, the governments in Kiev and Petrograd reached a precarious modus vivendi in August. The General Secretariat of the Central Rada became the recognized regional government for the provinces of Kiev, Poltava, Chernigov, Volhynia, and Podolia.[65]

One reason for the sudden emergence of the Central Rada as a regional power center was the popularity of Ukrainian slogans among the soldiers stationed in Kiev, who also formed a considerable contingent among the Rada delegates. It has been plausibly argued that the Great War favored the mobilization of Ukrainian national feeling among soldiers in the Russian army. The experience of cultural similarity in occupied Galicia, the repressions against Galicia's Ukrainian movement, and propaganda by the German-sponsored Union for the Liberation of Ukraine among war prisoners may all have strengthened soldiers' Ukrainian sympathies.[66] The formation of Ukrainian units in the Russian army in the summer of 1917 probably also drew some soldiers toward Ukrainian nationalism, even though others saw the Ukrainization of their units chiefly as a means to escape front service.[67]

However, the Central Rada's hold on power beyond Kiev was precarious at best. It had hardly any control over most rural regions and little contact with the local authorities. Nor was the peasantry as committed to the Ukrainian cause as some Ukrainian leaders later claimed.[68] The most thorough study of Ukraine's agrarian revolution to date has concluded that the majority of peasants cared most about their perceived economic needs and tended to identify with their village community rather than with any nation or class. The electoral victories of the Ukrainian Socialist Revolutionaries in autumn 1917 were most likely due to their agrarian program and their superior agitation in the countryside, not their demands for national autonomy and cultural Ukrainization. Given the socioethnic composition of Ukraine's population, in which most Ukrainian speakers were peasants and vice versa, it is clear that the revolution's national and social programs were intertwined. However, intellectual activists in Kiev tended to prioritize national issues, whereas most peasants cared more about the socioeconomic question of land redistribution.[69]

The creation of new power structures around the Rada offered unexpected opportunities for the city's Ukrainian nationalists. The vast majority of Kiev's professional intelligentsia, including most lawyers and academics, could not speak Ukrainian and were reluctant to learn it. Many were outright hostile to Ukrainian state-building.[70] Therefore, the small Ukrainian-speaking intelligentsia was direly needed to staff the emerging state. Volodymyr Vynnychenko later remembered the desperate search for cadres: "We needed thousands of experienced, educated, and nationally conscious people to occupy all the government posts. . . . There may be enough for the ministers, but then what? The directors, the clerks, the commissars, the tens of thousands of public servants—where to find them?"[71]

Such were the conditions that enabled young and unexperienced activists like Oleksander Shul'hyn to rise through the Rada's ranks. The General Secretariat's members were all between twenty-seven and forty-four years old; none of them had been higher bureaucrats or elected politicians. Out of nine general secretaries, six had worked as writers or journalists before the revolution; the remaining three had been active in the Ukrainian cooperative movement.[72] Three general secretaries had been nationally socialized as students in Kiev's Ukrainophile milieu (Steshenko, Vynnychenko, Iefremov); five had been members of the Revolutionary Ukrainian Party around 1905 (Vynnychenko, Petliura, Martos, Sadovs'kyi, Stasiuk). Overall, then, this was a committee of young male socialist intellectuals. When Oleksander Shul'hyn replaced Iefremov, he became the second-youngest member of the "cabinet." Determined and energetic, the young general secretary made an impression on more seasoned activists. "Another one who has grown with the revolution is O. Ia. Shul'hyn," one of them noted. "A bit of a loose cannon, but a great difference from what he used to be."[73] The prevalence of inexperienced youthful activists differentiates the Ukrainian events of 1917, for instance, from the Czechoslovak "national revolution" of 1918, which was led by middle-aged veterans of the Habsburg Empire's democratic, administrative, and military institutions.[74]

While Oleksander Shul'hyn pursued his career, his family provided cadres for the emerging Ukrainian bureaucracy and the cultural-educational sphere. Twenty-three-year-old Volodymyr Shul'hyn worked for the Kiev Provincial Commissariat and fulfilled minor assignments for his brother. Mykola Shul'hyn, a twenty-one-year-old student with no professional experience whatsoever, became Oleksander's personal secretary and later occupied posts at the Ukrainian Foreign Ministry.[75] It was thus not completely unfair if contemporaries criticized the Rada for staffing its offices with incompetent students and half-educated nationalists.[76] Politics and the bureaucracy were still male domains in the Ukrainian national movement of 1917—only twenty-one of the Rada's over eight hundred delegates were women—but female activists were prominent in the cultural and educational field.[77] Among these women were Liubov Shul'hyna and her daughter Nadiia. Both were involved in the foundation of the Taras Shevchenko Gymnasium, Kiev's first secondary school to teach in Ukrainian. Nadiia Shul'hyna, one of the few mathematicians in the Ukrainian movement, taught mathematics; her mother took care of the kindergarten. Nadiia also joined a commission that tried to elaborate a Ukrainian mathematical terminology and published a Ukrainian-language arithmetic textbook, which was printed in thirty-five thousand copies.[78] Faced with unexpected opportunities, the young Shul'hyns put their "nationalist education" to good use.

A telling counterexample is their uncle Volodymyr Naumenko. At age sixty-four in the spring of 1917, Naumenko was the doyen of Kiev's Ukrainian movement, a universally respected pedagogue and one of the

FIGURE 13. Volodymyr Shul'hyn and his bride Lidiia Tartakivs'ka wearing *vyshyvanky*, 1917. Ishchuk-Pazuniak private collection, courtesy of Olena Leontovych.

last survivors of the generation that had held up the Ukrainian banner under the Ems Ukaz. Naumenko experienced the fall of tsarism as a liberation after decades of oppression. In March, he was elected vice president of the Central Rada, a symbolic but highly honorable position.[79]

In private, however, Naumenko was appalled by what he called the Ukrainian movement's "method of seizure": "formerly we were hated by the Russian riffraff and the government, but now the best people of the Russian intelligentsia are beginning to hate us." Unwilling to enter into open conflict with the Rada, Naumenko decided to concentrate on "cabinet work."[80] In August, he was nominated to be curator of the Kiev School District. In an interview with *Kievlianin*, Naumenko stressed that the Ukrainization of Kiev's schools must be applied very cautiously. Ukrainian-language teaching could only be introduced once suitable teachers and textbooks were available, and Russian would still be taught as the "common state language" and "language of the brotherly nation." These views soon brought Naumenko into conflict with Ivan Steshenko, the general secretary for education, so that he quit his post after only three months.[81] After decades of cautious negotiation with the state, Naumenko was neither able nor willing to go along with the younger activists' aggressive course.

Other older Ukrainophiles also stood on the sidelines of events in 1917 or were simply pushed aside by younger men.[82] Petro Stebnyts'kyi, a longtime leader of Saint Petersburg's Ukrainian circles, felt alienated by the movement's "youthful zeal, extreme slogans, harsh positions" as early as March 1917. His friend Ievhen Chykalenko spent much of the year on his estate in Kherson province, feeling no inclination to participate in public life. His experience as a landowner convinced him that the peasants did not care about autonomy, that their goal was to gain as much land as possible, and that the nationalists misjudged the situation because they only met the politically conscious peasants who participated in congresses.[83] Mykhailo Hrushevs'kyi was almost the only fifty-year-old who played a decisive role in the Ukrainian revolution. Many Ukrainophiles of the older generation disliked both the Rada's socialist politics and its extremely rapid progress in the direction of autonomy and Ukrainization.

Toward Independent Ukraine

As general secretary for inter-nationality relations, Oleksander Shul'hyn was responsible for the Rada's peaceful coexistence with the country's non-Ukrainian communities. The three main nationalities envisaged by the General Secretariat were Ukraine's Jews, Poles, and Russians, but other groups could also apply for recognition. After Oleksander's nomination, vice-secretaries of Polish and Jewish affairs (Mieczysław

Mickiewicz and Moshe Zil'berfarb) were named. The vice secretariat of Great Russian affairs remained vacant.[84] Taking his task seriously, Shul'hyn repeatedly appealed to the population to treat non-Ukrainians fairly. When the first news of antisemitic pogroms reached Kiev in October, he issued a declaration "to the conscious citizenship of Ukraine," sharply condemning the violence: "We used to be oppressed, but we must not oppress anybody, for we know how hard it is to live under a yoke."[85] Similarly, Shul'hyn protested against the deposition of elected local officials because of their non-Ukrainian nationality: "The citizens of Ukraine must understand that all are equal in the Ukrainian People's Republic: rich and poor, Jew and Ukrainian, Pole and Great Russian." He also corresponded with local (possibly self-appointed) representatives of the national minorities, acknowledging the local national council of Mariupol's Greek population, assuring Kiev's Poles of his sympathy for the "brotherly Polish nation," or reminding the local authorities in a Volhynian town not to forbid Jewish traders to open their shops on Sunday.[86]

The centerpiece of the General Secretariat's nationalities policy was the law on national-personal autonomy, promised in autumn 1917 and finally passed by the Rada in January 1918. It allowed the Great Russian, Jewish, and Polish "nations" (and other groups that could gather ten thousand signatures) to form their own administrative organs, which would receive a share of the state budget and deal with the nationality's internal matters. Membership of each nationality was to be determined through nationality registers (*kadastry*), into which individuals could inscribe their names at will. The underlying principle of extraterritorial national autonomy was inspired by the writings of the Austro-Marxist theoretician Karl Renner, as Oleksander Shul'hyn later confirmed.[87] At least on paper, this was a very liberal minorities policy. However, since the Rada's power was already waning when the policy was promulgated, its provisions hardly took effect. Only the Jewish political parties managed to set up institutions to deal with educational matters and protection from pogroms; however, they were plagued by infighting and made no great impact on the life of Jewish communities.[88]

The main weakness of the Rada's nationalities policy was its definition of "minorities." Many Jewish (Zionist or diaspora nationalist) political leaders were ready to accept this designation and the corresponding rights. Without a realistic prospect of building their own nation-state, nonterritorial Jewish autonomy in a Ukraine federated with Russia suited their needs. The Polish case was more problematic.

Ukraine's Polish nationalists, while working with the Central Rada, were ultimately oriented toward Polish statehood. Moreover, most Polish leaders were landowners who stood to lose from the Rada's agrarian policies.[89] However, it was above all the self-defined Russians of Ukraine for whom the designation as a national minority was unacceptable. For decades, Russian nationalists had insisted that the Orthodox majority population of "Little Russia" was an integral part of the Russian nation. The acceptance of minority status would have signified their definitive defeat. As Vasilii Shul'gin wrote in April 1917, the only difference between Russians and Ukrainians was that the former spoke Russian while the latter used "Professor Hrushevs'kyi's dialect." To Shul'gin, the fact that most Kiev newspapers continued to be published in Russian after the end of censorship proved that most readers saw themselves as Russians.[90] Nor were Ukraine's Russian-speaking socialists—a group comprising people of Great Russian, Little Russian, and Jewish origin—interested in organizing as a national minority. These people tended to oppose the Ukrainians' nationality institutions as a danger for the "united revolutionary front."[91] It is thus no surprise that the Great Russian Vice-Secretariat never got off the ground. The post was occupied only in November (by the Trudovik Dmitrii Odinets), and no Russian nationality organization was formed.

Toward the end of the year, Oleksander Shul'hyn's field of duty shifted toward foreign policy. At first, this meant relations with representatives of the empire's nationalities beyond Ukraine—the potential members of the envisaged federation. In September, Oleksander spoke at the Congress of Russia's Peoples, a meeting of nationality representatives in Kiev, where he stressed the need for unity among all of Russia's democracies. He established friendly relations with representatives of the emerging Cossack, Caucasian, and Crimean republics, in the (ultimately futile) hope to set up a federation of Black Sea states.[92] This situation changed with the Bolshevik assumption of power in Petrograd on 25 October 1917. An analogous attempt in Kiev—directed against the army's general staff—failed and ended up strengthening the Rada's position, but the General Secretariat soon understood that it could not cooperate with Petrograd. On 7 November, the Rada issued its Third Universal, proclaiming the Ukrainian People's Republic (Ukraïns'ka Narodna Respublika, UNR) as an autonomous state extending over nine provinces. At the same time, it announced a radical social policy, promising the introduction of the eight-hour workday in Ukraine's factories and the passage of all land to the "laboring population" without compensation to the former owners.[93]

Over the following weeks, tensions between Kiev and Petrograd continued to mount. The Rada's General Secretariat resented the Bolsheviks' pretension to act as the government for all of the former empire and to represent all territories at armistice negotiations. The Bolsheviks, in turn, distrusted the Rada leaders for their "bourgeois" nationalism and their cooperation with the "counterrevolutionary" Don government. In December, the Soviet of People's Commissars sent an ultimatum to Kiev, demanding that the Rada end the "disorganization on the front," the disarmament of Soviet forces, and the right of passage for army units from the western front to the Don region. On 17 December, a Bolshevik-dominated Soviet Congress declared the foundation of the Ukrainian Socialist Soviet Republic in Kharkov, an industrial city near the Russian border, where the Bolsheviks found support among the workers.[94]

As a federation of nation-states on the former imperial territory became unlikely, Oleksander Shul'hyn found it necessary to enter into direct relations with other European states. A sympathizer of the Entente, he was opposed to a separate peace with Germany but had to recognize that Ukraine was incapable of continuing the war. His goal was thus to prepare for a general peace with French and British support. Over the autumn, he met with the consuls of several states allied with imperial Russia, including Italy, Romania, and the United States, and also Tomáš Masaryk, who was in Kiev to organize the Czechoslovak Legion.[95] France's "man on the spot," General Georges Tabouis, became a frequent visitor and tried to persuade Shul'hyn to continue the war effort. On 29 December, Tabouis was named commissar to the Ukrainian Republic by the French government. Meanwhile, the British government appointed John Picton Bagge as its representative in Ukraine, promising support against the Central Powers. The formerly half-private relations between Oleksander Shul'hyn and these diplomats almost turned into official interstate relationships. Shul'hyn partially achieved diplomatic recognition, and for a brief period it seemed as though Ukraine might be accepted by the Entente powers as a legitimate successor state to the defunct Russian Empire.[96]

However, as the Soviet of People's Commissars sent troops into Ukraine to support the Bolshevik government in Kharkov, military hostilities were imminent. The growing unrest in the countryside and the spontaneous demobilization of the front deprived the UNR of functioning troops. Invited by the Central Powers to join their armistice negotiations with the Bolsheviks, the General Secretariat dispatched a delegation to Brest-Litovsk.[97] Given the military danger, the UNR could hardly avoid getting involved in the talks. On 21 December 1917, Shul'hyn asked the cabinet to rename his office "General Secretariat of International Affairs" and make it officially responsible for relations with foreign states and the future members of the Russian federation. This was granted by Vynnychenko the following day—excluding the point about the future federation.[98]

Indeed, given the extremely strained relationship with Petrograd, the idea of a fully independent Ukraine was gaining popularity among the Rada leadership. Oleksander Shul'hyn still opposed it. A declaration of independence, he explained, would exacerbate the military conflict with the Bolsheviks and make Ukraine dependent on Germany, ultimately leading to a German occupation.[99] The decision was delayed, but on 9 (22) January 1918, the Rada issued its Fourth Universal, which declared Ukraine an independent state, formalizing a situation that had de facto existed for several weeks. With Bolshevik troops already advancing on Kiev, the Ukrainian parties met the decree without enthusiasm. The Rada's Jewish and Russian socialist delegates decisively opposed its promulgation.[100] Full independence was forced upon the UNR by the circumstances rather than actively sought by its leaders.[101]

The Fourth Universal transformed the general secretariats into ministries and officially made Oleksander Shul'hyn the first foreign minister of independent Ukraine. However, only one week later, Vynnychenko's ministers left their posts to a more left-wing cabinet. By this time, the Kiev Bolsheviks had started another uprising, and Soviet artillery troops were bombarding the city from across the Dnieper. Among others, Mykhailo Hrushevs'kyi's seven-story apartment building was hit by artillery fire and burned down.[102] The Rada government was considering evacuation to Volhynia. Having refused an offer to remain in the cabinet, Oleksander Shul'hyn used a teleprinting apparatus to advise the UNR delegation at Brest-Litovsk, which was negotiating a separate peace independently from the Bolsheviks. On 27 January (9 February) 1918, the Central Powers and the UNR signed the war's first peace treaty, by which Germany and Austria-Hungary recognized Ukraine's independence and promised military aid to the Central Rada. In return, the Ukrainian side was to deliver to its new allies a million tons of foodstuffs, to be paid for with manufactured goods.[103] Hours earlier, the Bolshevik forces took Kiev after days of heavy fighting. While the government fled to Zhitomir, Oleksander Shul'hyn remained in hiding in the city, staying at first with rich Russian friends, then with a Polish professor of zoology, and finally with an old policeman in the village of Pushcha-Voditsa.[104]

After only three weeks of Bolshevik rule, the Rada's ministers returned to Kiev in February, this time accompanied by German troops.[105] The Ukrainian socialist cabinet returned to power, albeit in an uneasy cohabitation with the occupying German army. Kiev's Russian nationalists were appalled, as were some Ukrainian activists, including Volodymyr Naumenko, who blamed the Rada for this "shameful day for Ukraine." Emerging from his hideout, Oleksander Shul'hyn made the tragic discovery that his brother Volodymyr had perished in the fight against the Bolsheviks. His student volunteer company had been ordered to the village of Kruty northeast of Kiev, where he was killed in combat against a much larger Bolshevik force.[106]

By the spring of 1918, Oleksander Shul'hyn's federalist convictions were crumbling under the impression of war and personal loss. Ukraine, he now wrote, was forced to defend itself against the "the wild hordes" of the Bolsheviks, the newest incarnation of both Muscovite despotism and Russia's "Asiatic" chaos: "History has forced us to choose the path of complete separation from anarchic Russia."[107] The revolution, Shul'hyn claimed, had revealed the "true face of the dark and half-savage people of Russia." At the same time, he still hoped that Ukraine would go "via independence toward federation," but this would require a new, non-Bolshevik government in Russia.[108] Formerly an idealistic federalist intent on retaining close Russian-Ukrainian ties, Shul'hyn had become a pragmatic independentist who doubted if such ties were even possible. If he had loathed the imperial state before, he now explained Russia's politics—both despotic and anarchic—as an outgrowth of the Russian people's innate shortcomings.

In April, Shul'hyn got an opportunity to return to the cabinet. Displeased with the government's socialist policies and hoping for more efficient grain deliveries, the German military leadership supported a coup to install General Pavel Skoropadskii (Pavlo Skoropads'kyi) as Hetman of the Ukrainian state. Skoropadskii appointed as his first prime minister ("Otaman of the Ministers' Council") none other than Shul'hyn's uncle Nikolai Ustimovich, an active member of the Ukrainian Cossack movement. Hoping to form a coalition between the Socialist-Federalists and more conservative forces, Ustimovich offered his nephew Oleksander and several other party members portfolios in

Figure 14. Nikolai Ustimovich and his wife Liubov' in full Cossack attire. Volodymyr Ianiv, ed., *Zbirnyk na poshanu Oleksandra Shul hyna (1889–1960)* (Paris, 1969), plate 18. Author's collection.

his ministry. However, Oleksander refused to work in what he perceived as a nonnational puppet regime. Ustimovich resigned almost immediately, and the Hetman formed a new cabinet including only one Ukrainian nationalist.[109]

Ustimovich's brief involvement in the Hetman's government was not a coincidence. Skoropadskii's regime appealed more to nostalgia and traditional regional patriotism than to modern nationalism, as is evident in the choice of the Cossack title "hetman." Skoropadskii himself was a descendant of an eighteenth-century Cossack leader, a former tsarist general, and a monarchist. His regime, as the novelist Mikhail Bulgakov famously wrote, had the flavor of an operetta. His German-supported government relied on the support of Ukraine's wealthy landowners rather than continuing the Rada's socialist agrarian policies.[110] All of this cannot have failed to please Oleksander's romantic uncle, who wore historical Cossack uniforms and had long dreamed of resuscitating the Cossack tradition, all the while remaining loyal to the tsar and the empire.[111] Oleksander Shul'hyn, by contrast, was a republican and an Entente sympathizer. Unwilling to join the Hetman's government, he soon turned his attention to diplomacy.

Conservative Politics amid Revolution

While the Ukrainian Shul'hyns rejoiced at the news of the February revolution, the opposite was true for their conservative Russian relatives. For Ekaterina Shul'gina, the tsar's abdication came as a tremendous shock, making her weep uncontrollably. When news reached Kiev that Vasilii Shul'gin had been directly involved in the dynasty's fall, his sixteen-year-old son Veniamin threatened to leave the family's "treacherous house."[112] Yet, despite the emotional turmoil that it caused the family, Kievlianin's first reactions to the change of leadership were cautiously optimistic. For Ekaterina Shul'gina, the February revolution was a "miracle": the formerly dark Russian masses, educated by their war experience, had toppled a chaotic government unable to wage the war.[113] She and her husband continued to view Russia's domestic upheaval through the lens of the ongoing war with Germany. It was in the hope of strengthening Russia's position in the war that Kievlianin offered its conditional support to the Provisional Government. Political disagreements had to be put aside, and only the outcome of the war would decide whether Russia was to be a monarchy or a republic.[114]

During the first weeks after the February revolution, Vasilii Shul'gin tried to influence events in Petrograd. According to his own memoirs, Shul'gin wanted to head the Petrograd Telegraph Agency but was fired when he sent out a political article on his first day. Pavel Miliukov, by contrast, wrote that Shul'gin could have joined the government but "preferred in this difficult minute for the fatherland to remain in his profession as a publicist."[115] For several weeks, Shul'gin worked as *Kievlianin*'s correspondent in the capital, contributing daily articles by telegraph. In a speech in April 1917, he admitted that the Duma's conservatives had contributed decisively to the fall of tsarism: "We cannot disavow this revolution. We have bound ourselves to it and bear moral responsibility for it." However, he continued, the two months since February had made him doubt his support for the revolution. Instead of working for the war effort, Petrograd's socialists were agitating against the government, the army, and the Allied powers. Taken separately, all these actions were but stupidities, Shul'gin concluded with an allusion to Miliukov's earlier speech, but together, they amounted to treason.[116]

As the first wave of optimism passed, Shul'gin was increasingly concerned about the chaos and destruction that the revolution might bring. In April, he painted a gloomy picture of the weeks to come: "They will do everything that the old authorities did. . . . The old authorities persecuted the non-Russian nationalities, now they will ridicule Russian feeling, blacken the Russian past, ruin Russian antiquity, customs, and traditions."[117] For Shul'gin, the socialists' basic mistake was that they tried to redistribute wealth without taking into account the healthy egoism underlying all economic activity. In order to channel this egoism into societal solidarity, he wrote, one had to start with the naturally altruistic circle of the family. From the family circle, solidarity would spread to the village, the region, and ultimately, the nation.[118] Like his father Pikhno, Shul'gin saw family solidarity and nationalism as two cornerstones of a functioning society—the more so in times of all-embracing turmoil.

Kievlianin, too, continued to rely on family solidarity. With Shul'gin still in Petrograd and the official editor Smakovskii terminally ill, the entire responsibility for the paper lay in the hands of two women. Lina Mogilevskaia took care of all administrative, organizational, and editorial duties. Ekaterina Shul'gina wrote political commentaries, either anonymously or as "Ezhov." The editorial office and family home on the corner of Kuznechnaia and Karavaevskaia Streets once more became a meeting point for Kiev's Russian nationalists, "a kind of club" where Lina Mogilevskaia received guests who came to "pour out their heart, take counsel, simply breathe in the *Kievlianin* atmosphere."[119] *Kievlianin*'s moderately reformist political line was more palatable to the readership in revolutionary times than the reactionary monarchism that had been so successful in the region before the war. This allowed the Shul'gins to reestablish their traditional influence in Kiev's monarchist and nationalist milieu, becoming what Ekaterina Shul'gina would later call "a sort of general staff for Russian Kiev."[120]

The Shul'gins soon identified Ukrainian nationalism as the main enemy on the local political stage, especially as Kiev's power center shifted toward the Central Rada. Vasilii Shul'gin lobbied the Provisional Government against the recognition of the Rada, attempting to convince Prime Minister L'vov that it did not express the true will of "South Russia." *Kievlianin* kept insinuating that the Ukrainians were in reality working for the German enemy. As the well-organized Ukrainians "stole Kiev," the Shul'gins saw their fears of Austro-German "Mazepist" intrigue confirmed.[121] Over the course of the year, they recognized the Bolshevik party as a second serious opponent—one that they increasingly portrayed as a Jewish force and simultaneously an instrument of German designs. Thus, Vasilii Shul'gin ultimately saw Ukrainian nationalists and Bolsheviks as two sides of the same German coin. While the "Mazepists" supposedly executed the "Prussian revolution" in Kiev, the Bolshevik revolution turned Petrograd into "Wilhelmsburg."[122]

Kievlianin analyzed local politics through the lens of all-imperial developments and their geopolitical implications. As early as March, Ekaterina Shul'gina (alias Ezhov) lamented that all "South Russians" would be forced to live in Ukraine, "a country that has never existed," and to learn a useless language. "How could such things come to pass? Well, Gentlemen, simply because there are in our region all kinds of Ukrainian organizations, but not a single *Russian* one! . . . A mass of people are hypnotized by 'Ukraine' and the Ukrainians. . . . In order to battle against this hypnosis, the South Russians must unite."[123] Thus, Shul'gina decided to organize the city's Russian national forces and overcome their prewar divisions. Many readers wrote to Ezhov, and one even suggested that "he" should become the political leader of Kiev's Russians. Unwilling to reveal her incognito, Shul'gina decided to gather like-minded individuals in a new nationalist group. *Kievlianin* soon announced the formation of the National Cultural-Political Society Rus'. Based in the *Kievlianin* editorial office, it would unite Kievans behind the war effort and advance "Common Russian" culture in the region.[124]

Shul'gina tried to make the Rus' Society an above-party group focused on national unity. As one contributor to *Kievlianin* put it, "Many of us have only recently felt that they are Russians. . . . The Russians have become unable to imagine their belonging to the Russian nationality independent of their commitment to some particular political creed."[125] However, in the face of the Ukrainians' "separatist and treacherous aspirations," Kiev's Russians could no longer afford to disagree: "Now there is something that must keep them together under their common national flag, something that does not allow for disagreement and dissent, that must force them to concentrate all their energy and will, all their ambition toward solidarity and agreement."[126] Once more, Kiev's Russian nationalists mobilized in reaction to a looming external threat. And again, what was presented as the achievement of national consciousness was in reality a political choice: a commitment to the reestablishment of a strong, centralized Russian state.

Revolutionary events increasingly politicized everyday life and involved ever broader segments of the population, including underage students.[127] At the Imperial Alexander Gymnasium, where Ekaterina Shul'gina's elder sons Vasilid and Veniamin were students, a council of class representatives was elected, and several national associations appeared. According to Shul'gina, her sons felt so offended by the ubiquity of Ukrainian, Polish, and Jewish flags in the city that they began to wear ribbons in the Russian national colors white, blue, and red. On 30 April, patriotic middle-school students staged a demonstration to express support for the army, the Allies, and the Provisional Government. Ekaterina Shul'gina, who was involved in the preparations, tried to dissuade the teenagers from using monarchist slogans. However, when one group displayed the Ukrainian slogan "Long Live the Free Federal Republic," some right-wing students unfurled a banner with the inscription "Constitutional Monarchy," and the situation escalated into a brawl.[128]

By the summer of 1917, Shul'gina had become an influential figure in Kiev's Russian nationalist milieu. The absence of many men due to the war forced women like her to fill key positions in political movements. However, remaining attached to the conventional gender norms she had already transgressed, Shul'gina consciously limited her own political possibilities. She assumed responsibility in the Rus' Society but kept hiding her published views behind a male pseudonym. Even though the Provisional Government had introduced female suffrage, she believed it inappropriate for herself to participate in the upcoming elections to the City Duma and the All-Russian Constituent Assembly.[129]

> I was ready to do everything necessary for the preparation of the elections, manage the upcoming campaign, but in no way could I become a member of the [City] Duma and even less of the Constituent Assembly. After all, . . . I was first and foremost a woman and, what is more, a nervous woman. In order to step behind the lectern, engage in a battle of words with your enemies, take and parry blows . . . one has to be born either as a man or as an entirely different woman.[130]

Shul'gina believed that Kiev's Russian nationalists needed a male leader, and her candidate for the job was her own husband, Vasilii. Their marriage, dysfunctional as a romantic relationship, thrived as a political partnership during the revolution. While Vasilii was still in Petrograd with his lover, Ekaterina worked hard to stabilize his reputation in Kiev. By uniting the Rus' Society with the Kiev Club of Russian Nationalists and a few smaller organizations, she managed to set up a "Nonparty Bloc of Russian Voters." The formation of a unified electoral bloc was facilitated by the fact that the extreme right did not dare to run for office in times of social upheaval. In the elections, Shul'gina hoped, their supporters would grudgingly vote for the nationalist ticket, despite their leaders' extreme distaste for *Kievlianin*. Still, it took all Ekaterina Shul'gina's "female craft" to mediate between the various disunited factions and the activists' "male vanities." She was supported by a few active Rus' Society members and by Anatolii Savenko, who had once more quit *Kievlianin* the year before but returned in 1917 to agitate tirelessly in Shul'gin's favor. As the Provisional Government moved ever further to the left, Vasilii Shul'gin no longer felt useful in Petrograd and let himself be persuaded to return to Kiev. After his arrival in July, he became the head of the pre-electoral committee.[131]

Rather than discuss potentially divisive subtleties, the bloc built its electoral campaign around the simple and vague idea of national "self-defense." Vasilii Shul'gin published a protest "Against the Forced Ukrainization of Southern Rus'." His proclamation was subsequently issued as a separate leaflet for readers to sign and send back. By September, eleven thousand Kievans had signed the protest.[132] By means of this campaign, Shul'gin mobilized potential voters well beyond monarchist circles, once more positioning *Kievlianin* as the center of national resistance to the Ukrainian "usurpers." Like 1905, 1917 was one of the "phases of extraordinary cohesion and moments of intensely felt collective solidarity" that are crucial to the short-term mobilization of nationalist feeling.[133] As people felt their cultural habits and social position to be threatened—"under siege," in Dmitrii Pikhno's words—the unambiguous group identification offered by nationalism became attractive. Faced with state collapse and national adversity, many Kievans agreed to display and defend their Russianness.

Drawing attention away from social antagonisms and principles of state organization to the question of nationality, the Shul'gins attempted to distract from the unpopularity of their monarchist views. As their opponents liked to remind them, they could hardly appeal to the previously disenfranchised segments of the population that were now entering the political stage. A leftist newspaper described their "Nonparty Bloc" as the barely disguised Black Hundreds, who had ruined the country under the old regime.[134] Kiev's socialists and Ukrainian nationalists also acted directly against their staunch opponents. During the attempted coup d'état of General Lavr Kornilov, with whom Shul'gin sympathized, a revolutionary committee arrested Shul'gin and temporarily stopped the publication of *Kievlianin*.[135] At the height of the electoral campaign, a group of Ukrainian soldiers occupied and demolished the editorial offices. Subsequently, a Bolshevik group requisitioned the premises to produce their own newspaper. Following negotiations with the Bolsheviks, *Kievlianin* recovered its offices and renewed publication after eighteen days.[136]

As far as electoral results go, the Shul'gins' 1917 campaign was a tremendous success. At a time when conservative parties were no longer active in most Russian cities, their ticket achieved a respectable number of votes in three subsequent elections, confirming their prewar successes under the conditions of unfettered democracy. In the City Duma elections of July 1917, their ticket received 14.08 percent (25,421) of the votes, ranking third after the socialist bloc and the Ukrainian SD and SR ticket—while Oleksander Shul'hyn's Ukrainian Socialist-Federalists finished at only 0.67 percent. This result made Vasilii Shul'gin and sixteen of his fellow campaigners City Duma delegates.[137] In the elections to the All-Russian Constituent Assembly in November, the Russian bloc got 19.74 percent (36,602 votes), the second-best result after the Ukrainian socialists and before the Bolsheviks. And when the elections to the Ukrainian Constituent Assembly were held in January 1918, the bloc achieved the best result of all tickets (29.47 percent or 25,428 votes, with much lower electoral participation). This made Vasilii Shul'gin the city's only delegate to this legislative body—a body that never actually met. Since the Ukrainian and Zionist parties similarly increased their share of votes over the three elections, while the Kadets and non-national socialists lost, one of Shul'gin's associates could note with satisfaction that "Kiev's population is increasingly grouped into nationalities rather than political parties." However, while Kiev confirmed its reputation as a "Russian island amid the Ukrainian sea," the Ukrainian socialists won a landslide victory in the surrounding provinces.[138]

Vasilii Shul'gin emerged as the recognized leader of Kiev's conservatives. Rather than try to turn the clock back, he and his family accepted the new realities of revolutionary democracy. They put their family newspaper to good use as a propaganda machine and managed to turn conservative fears and insecurities into political capital. Successful though their electoral campaigns were, they had little effect on subsequent events. On 26 January (8 February) 1918, the Bolsheviks took Kiev. The following night, Vasilii Shul'gin was arrested and taken to the Mariinskii Palace; later he was transferred to Luk'ianovka prison. Two weeks later, the Bolsheviks released him unharmed, possibly thanks to the protection of his Bolshevik colleagues in the City Duma and the SR mayor, Evgenii Riabtsov.[139] By this time, the Ukrainian Central Rada had signed the Brest-Litovsk treaty and was preparing to take back control with German support. Soon, the Bolshevik forces began to retreat eastward.

Vasilii Shul'gin saw his worst fears of German machinations come true. "A simply devilish situation has arisen," he wrote on 11 (24) February. In Shul'gin's eyes, both the "Russian-Jewish gang" of the Bolsheviks and the Ukrainians were puppets in a German master plan to divide Russia. The Germans had allowed the Bolsheviks to terrorize Kiev's population in order to alienate them from Russian culture; now they had ordered them to retreat so that the German troops would appear as saviors.[140] After almost a year of revolution, Vasilii Shul'gin was still unable to imagine actual popular support for the Ukrainian nationalists or the Bolsheviks. Throughout the civil war, he would deny the possibility of an alliance with the former against the latter.

The advent of Bolshevism, a common enemy that could have brought about a temporary understanding between Russian and Ukrainian nationalists, even widened the rift. Over several decades, an atmosphere of mutual distrust had arisen between them, as one perceived slight led to the next and both sides lost faith in the respectability of their opponents' intentions. The rapid sequence of events in 1917 accelerated this

FIGURE 15. Title page of Vasilii Shul'gin's new periodical *Malaia Rus'*, no. 2 (1918). Rather cynically, it depicts Mykhailo Hrushevs'kyi's apartment house, which was incinerated during the Bolshevik siege, as a torch. In the same issue, Ekaterina Shul'gina commented, "The sorcerer's damned nest has burned down." E., "To chto ia pomniu (Iz zhenskikh perezhivanii v dni tsarstvovaniia bol'shevikov)" (p. 86). Courtesy of the Ukrainian National Library in Kyiv.

dynamic, making any cooperation impossible. To the Russian nationalists, their Ukrainian counterparts were quintessential traitors that could never be trusted. As Ekaterina Shul'gina put it in November 1917, "Ukraine, the Ukrainians, the Ukrainian movement will always be hostile to everything Russian and to Russia and will willy-nilly . . . seek help, union, support, and sympathy from those who are also hostile to Russia and to everything Russian."[141] By early 1918, the Shul'gins saw the Bolsheviks as "Russian-Jewish" accomplices of the Ukrainians in a German plot, while for Oleksander Shul'hyn they epitomized both Russian chaos and Russian despotism.

With the arrival in Kiev of German troops, the Shul'gins—like their Ukrainian relative—interrupted their public activism. In a dramatic gesture of protest, they published "the last issue of *Kievlianin*," explaining that they had sworn loyalty to Russia's French and British allies and would not work under the protection of the enemy: "We may be your prisoners of war, but we will not be your friends as long as the war is going on."[142] The Shul'gins kept their word. During the entire German occupation, *Kievlianin* remained silent. As revolutionary politics were increasingly militarized, the Shul'gins' short-lived attempt at nationalizing the city through electoral politics found its end. They, too, had to continue their struggle by other means.

United and Indivisible

Over the spring and summer of 1918, anti-Bolshevik politicians swarmed into Kiev, where the Hetman's regime and the German occupiers tolerated various political tendencies. Some of them sought a stable environment, while others hoped for German support against the Bolsheviks. Several Kadets of the Kiev branch entered Skoropadskii's government. The Shul'gins' little white house on the corner of Kuznechnaia and Karavaevskaia Streets, by contrast, again became a center of opposition to the Ukrainian government. Ekaterina and Vasilii Shul'gin tried to form a new coalition of anti-German political forces, working with pro-Entente Kadets in Kiev and Moscow. However, their "Kiev National Center" remained ineffective.[143] As long as the German army buttressed the Hetman's dictatorial power, a handful of politicians and journalists could not challenge his regime. Still, as an Austrian officer's report shows, the Central Powers in Kiev took note of Vasilii Shul'gin: "An opponent to take seriously, since he is very intelligent."[144]

Unable to engage in electoral politics, Shul'gin chose conspiratorial methods in his crusade for the resurrection of the Russian state. Already in November 1917, he had visited Novocherkassk in the Don territory, where General Mikhail Alekseev, the former commander-in-chief of the Provisional Government, was beginning to raise an anti-Bolshevik force. Over the following months, Shul'gin recruited officers for Alekseev's endeavor and sent them from Kiev to the Don. After the arrival of the Germans, Shul'gin was contacted by Entente representatives in Kiev, the French officer Emile Henno and a British diplomat, who gave him 20,000 rubles. Shul'gin used this money to establish his private intelligence agency Azbuka (Alphabet), so called because its members used the letters of the Cyrillic alphabet as their code names. Politically, Azbuka continued *Kievlianin*'s anti-German, anti-Ukrainian, and anti-Bolshevik line. The group established contacts with like-minded forces all over the former empire, including French and British agents in Kiev and Moscow and General Alekseev's Volunteer Army, which had in the meantime been forced to move to the Kuban territory, east of Crimea. Connecting these groups with one another, Azbuka sent them regular reports about the political situation in Kiev and the mood of the population.[145]

The agency was organized along strictly vertical hierarchies, so that agents only reported to their immediate superiors. At the very top was Shul'gin (alias "Vedi"), and at first the agency centered on his private network of family and Kievan acquaintances. One of the most active agents was the ever-present Anatolii Savenko ("Az"). Shul'gin's lover Liubov' Popova played an important role in the background, preparing tiny copies of messages on pieces of film that she then rolled into cigarettes for the messengers to carry to Ekaterinodar or Moscow. Ekaterina Shul'gina sometimes stepped in when her husband was absent; their sons Vasilid and Veniamin worked as messengers. Over time, the organization recruited dozens of officers serving in the Volunteer Army, as well as Kadet politicians such as Igor' Demidov ("Buki") and Vasilii Stepanov ("Slovo").[146] Although Azbuka worked for the Volunteer Army, it never became its official organ. Shul'gin repeatedly tried and failed to integrate it into the army's organization. In 1919, he managed to attract subsidies from the army budget, but they amounted only to about 700,000 rubles (compared to the propaganda division's 25 million per quarter). Thus, Azbuka remained a private organization that "continued to reflect the views and personality of its creator."[147] When it acquired branches in various cities, this organization by "personal union" led to chaos, and Shul'gin had to cede part of his responsibilities.[148]

In July 1918, Vasilii Shul'gin was warned that the Skoropadskii government might arrest him and decided to leave Kiev for the Volunteer Army in Ekaterinodar, the capital of the Kuban territory.[149] Before leaving, Shul'gin performed a last public protest against the Hetmanate. The Hetman's cabinet had just passed a law on Ukrainian citizenship, which declared all subjects of the Russian Empire who were currently within Ukraine's borders to be Ukrainian citizens—unless they explicitly appealed to the authorities to be excluded.[150] Shul'gin did just that: Alongside Anatolii Savenko, his son Vasilid, and two more associates, he petitioned the regional government not to be counted as a Ukrainian citizen. He added a memorandum explaining that the Ukrainian state had no foundation in history. According to Shul'gin, all previous states on its territory had been Russian, and the very name "Ukraine" was just a synonym for *okraina*—"borderland"—thus proving that the region could never be an independent state. "As natural inhabitants of this region, . . . we do not want to renounce the glorious national name of our forebears, for which they have fought so much, and cannot turn into some kind of Ukrainians without kin and tribe: we were born Russians, and Russians we remain."[151] Shul'gin's categorical rejection of all Ukrainian terminology was more than political rhetoric: in his eyes, the defense of the "Russian name" was his family's ancestral mission.

In Ekaterinodar, Shul'gin's first move was to establish a newspaper, *Rossiia*, with the help of several Azbuka members. He planned to create a network of newspapers that would accompany the Volunteer Army's advance into Central Russia. One each was to be published in Ekaterinodar, Odessa, Kiev, and Kharkov, and one was to move along with the troops and end up in Moscow.[152] The great political question of the day was whether the Volunteer Army should openly declare itself a monarchist organization or stick to its previous position that only the Constituent Assembly was to choose Russia's future form of government. A majority of the army's officers were monarchists, but its leaders were anxious not to alienate progressive circles.[153] Vasilii Shul'gin, who had himself defended "nondecisionism" (*nepredreshenchestvo*) in 1917, now came out forcefully in favor of monarchy. Republicans, Shul'gin wrote, had ruined Russian statehood. Only the monarchists, with their disposition to subordinate themselves to hierarchy, were able to enforce discipline and order. However, Shul'gin continued, "the offended dynasty" would only return "once the entire people will be on its knees praying to God for the return of the bygone tsars."[154]

Shul'gin's articles angered General Anton Denikin, a man of liberal persuasions who would soon assume supreme command over the entire army. Still, he allowed Shul'gin to continue editing *Rossiia* and even granted him a subsidy from the army's budget. Shul'gin was also entrusted with drafting the statute of the Special Council, the Volunteer Army's civil administration. Once instituted, the Special Council was staffed by Kadet politicians and former bureaucrats but headed by the army's leading generals. Vasilii Shul'gin held a post without portfolio but soon found that dry administrative work with little real impact was not to his taste and stopped attending the meetings.[155]

In the last weeks of 1918, two terrible tragedies befell the Shul'gin family. In November, Vasilii Shul'gin traveled from Ekaterinodar to Iaşi (Jassy) in Romania with his secretary and lover Liubov' Popova. There, a conference of Russia's anti-Bolshevik forces had been called to discuss further plans after the German defeat in the World War. On the way, however, both contracted the Spanish flu, so that Shul'gin missed the conference's (fruitless) deliberations. After a few days of heavy illness, Popova died in Iaşi, leaving Shul'gin devastated to the point of considering suicide.[156] Three weeks later, on 1 (14) December 1918, the Shul'gins lost their eldest son Vasilid during the fall of the Hetman's government in Kiev. Faced with the imminent retreat of his German sponsors, Hetman Skoropadskii had embarked on a Russophile, federalist course, hoping to attract the support of Russian politicians and the Entente powers. Instead, he had provided the Ukrainian socialists with a pretext to begin an uprising and establish a Directory led by Vynnychenko and Petliura. Skoropadskii's forces, deprived of German support, consisted mostly of Russian officers, who hardly defended the city.[157] Nineteen-year-old Vasilid Shul'gin fought and died in a unit formed from gymnasium students. His commander had forgotten to order a retreat after the Hetman's capitulation. Having rejected Ukrainian citizenship, Vasilid was not subject to mobilization, but he volunteered to defend the city, held by a regime his family despised, against the even more loathed Ukrainian socialists. His death threw Ekaterina Shul'gina into despair; she blamed herself for having drawn her children into politics. Having buried her son, she retreated from public activism and left Kiev for Odessa.[158]

Meanwhile, Vasilii Shul'gin, barely recovered from his illness, had also reached Odessa, where he soon assumed an important role in local government. After the collapse of the Hetmanate, Petliura's Ukrainian forces had briefly taken Odessa, but a French intervention force arrived in the port only one week later. Shul'gin's old ally, the self-appointed "French consul" Emile Henno, reached an agreement with the local Volunteer Army commander Aleksei Grishin-Almazov, who drove the Ukrainians to the city's outskirts.[159] Communications with Ekaterino-dar were so bad that Grishin-Almazov almost had a free hand governing the city. Vasilii Shul'gin, whom both Henno and Grishin-Almazov trusted, advised the city government and gave it ideological backing via his new paper (again called *Rossiia*). Shul'gin told Grishin-Almazov to abolish the Ukrainian language and history classes introduced to Odessa's schools during the Hetmanate, and to offer "local studies" (*kraevedenie*) instead. Indeed, Grishin-Almazov removed the "Galician language" from curricula, introduced facultative classes in the "Little Russian language (Shevchenko's, Kotliarevskii's language)," and replaced "the history and geography of Ukraine" with "the history and geography of South Russia."[160]

Apart from such squabbles over terminology, Shul'gin advocated a strictly hostile policy toward Petliura's Ukrainian government. When the Entente proposed peace talks on the Prince Islands to reconcile the Volunteer Army and Petliura, Shul'gin wrote, "A feeling of almost physical disgust and revulsion comes over me at the thought of having to meet them somewhere and talk to them." Shul'gin believed that Petliura had added extreme socialist policies to the Ukrainians' treacherous pro-German separatism and accused him of inciting his soldiers to loot and kill civilians.[161] As he wrote to the Kadet politician Vasilii Maklakov, then in Paris as a diplomat, "The Ukrainians are the very same Bolsheviks, with all their methods of administration and terror, but with the free addition of the damned Ukrainian language, which nauseates everyone who has not been shot by the Galicians."[162]

While it is true that Petliura's troops created much disorder in 1919—above all by starting a horrible wave of antisemitic violence—Shul'gin's verdict misses the mark.[163] Petliura was a nationalist with Social Democratic leanings, certainly not a Bolshevik. Yet Shul'gin's radically anti-Ukrainian position was largely in line with that of the Volunteer Army's leadership. Its commander, General Denikin, was an ardent defender of "united and indivisible Russia," as were almost all the former imperial generals and liberal politicians that led the movement. The restoration of Russia's territorial unity and integrity was at the very core of the Volunteers' ideology, more important even than the defeat of Bolshevism.[164] The White leaders received much of their information about Ukraine and Ukrainian nationalism from the locals in their ranks, people like Shul'gin or Savenko. For instance, most Az-buka reports were written by Russian nationalists from Ukraine, whose political biases slipped into their (otherwise valuable) analyses.[165] Thus, the army's leaders and their "experts" on Ukrainian matters mutually confirmed each other's preconceived views of their opponents, preclud-ing any cooperation between the Volunteer Army and the Ukrainian governments.

Grishin-Almazov's regime in Odessa was short-lived. Both the Volunteer Army's headquarters in Ekaterinodar and the occupying French forces disapproved of its autonomy but lacked a clear plan for action. The French angered their erstwhile ally Shul'gin by closing down his newspaper because of his critique of their conciliatory diplo-macy. Shul'gin stopped publishing altogether, not without reminding the French that one year earlier he had already closed a newspaper—precisely out of loyalty to the Entente.[166] Shul'gin was also shocked by Grishin-Almazov's secret order to murder Odessa's Bolshevik leaders. While he did not pity the victims, whom he saw as the heirs of socialist terrorism, he disapproved of the secrecy and lawlessness of the proce-dure. At any rate, by March 1919, the Bolsheviks were besieging the city, and the French began to evacuate their army. Vasilii Shul'gin, his wife Ekaterina, and their two surviving sons left Odessa on a boat for Anapa on the Black Sea's northeastern shore. For five months, Shul'gin abstained almost entirely from politics and journalism. Serving in the White river fleet, he traveled across the Volunteer Army's Kuban, Don, and southern Volga territories.[167]

Propagandizing White Kiev

In the meantime, the tide turned for the Volunteer Army. Advancing from the Southeast into Ukraine, the Whites celebrated one victory after another, taking Kharkov in June, then Ekaterinoslav and Poltava. By August, they were advancing on Kiev.[168] Given the opportunity to come home, Vasilii Shul'gin returned to politics. During the march on Kiev, General Denikin signed a manifesto "To the Population of Little Russia," which Shul'gin later claimed was his own work.[169] While pro-claiming Russian the only official language, the manifesto announced the introduction of administrative decentralization and "respect for the peculiarities of local everyday life." Above all, it promised that the "Little Russian language" would be allowed in the press, in zemstvos, law courts, and private schools. Even state schools were permitted to teach "the Little Russian popular language in its classical examples." Such concessions would perhaps have appeased the prewar Ukraino- philes, but in order to convince the Ukrainian parties in 1919, they were too little, far too late. Nor did the Whites count on their support, for the manifesto repeated the accusation that Petliura was a German agent.[170]

On 17 (30) August 1919, just hours after the Bolsheviks had left, Pet- liura's Galician Army reached Kiev from the west. On the next morning, the Volunteer Army arrived from the east. After a brief skirmish, the Galicians agreed to leave the city to the Whites. Vasilii Shul′gin arrived by train on the following day; to his relief, he found the house intact and his sister Lina, who had remained in the city, alive and well.[171] Ac- cording to eyewitnesses, many Kievans welcomed both the Galicians and the Whites with flowers and national flags as liberators after the brutal rule of the Bolsheviks. The second period of Bolshevik govern- ment in Kiev, from February to August 1919, had been much more violent than the first. The Cheka, the Bolshevik secret police, had ar- rested, interrogated, and tortured thousands of Kievans, and killed at least three thousand of their prisoners.[172] Among the victims were sixty-eight members of the Kiev Club of Russian Nationalists, includ- ing Timofei Florinskii and Sergei Shchegolev, who had both published anti-Ukrainian treatises. Another victim was the elderly Ukrainophile Volodymyr Naumenko, apparently shot as punishment for his brief tenure as minister of education in the Hetman's last cabinet. The mur- der of this venerable scholar and pedagogue shocked many Kievans and came to be seen as emblematic of the Bolsheviks' senseless brutality. Lina Mogilevskaia and Vasilii Shul′gin, his distant in-laws and ideologi- cal opponents, were horrified.[173]

Only three days after the taking of Kiev, the Shul′gins renewed the publication of *Kievlianin*. This was possible thanks to donations from the population and a loan of 200,000 rubles that the Volunteer Army gave them as compensation when it invalidated the circulating Soviet money.[174] For the last time, the *Kievlianin* family managed to use its reputation and connections to acquire a position of influence in Kiev. Indeed, Vasilii Shul′gin opened the first issue with a reference to his ancestors' struggle for the city's Russianness. Quoting the words that Vitalii Shul′gin had written half a century earlier—"This land is Rus- sian, Russian, Russian"—he presented the Volunteer Army's arrival as a final return and a decisive moment in the civil war: "Yes, this land is Russian. We shall not give it away—neither to the Ukrainian traitors, who have covered it in shame, nor to the Jewish executioners, who have drenched it in blood."[175]

As this quotation indicates, Vasilii Shul'gin blamed the Bolsheviks' brutality on Kiev's Jewish population. His antisemitism reached its peak during the autumn of 1919. It is true that the Kiev Cheka was particularly ruthless in 1919; it is also true that people of Jewish origin were overrepresented in its ranks, constituting 64 or 75 percent of the Kiev Chekists, depending on the source. However, the Cheka treated Jewish Kievans no less brutally than its Orthodox victims, and a majority of Kiev's Jews had little sympathy for the Bolsheviks.[176] Still, Shul'gin held all Jews responsible. In order to make good for the damage done by Jewish socialists, he suggested, all Jews should voluntarily abandon politics. "We propose the Jews the minimal payment," Shul'gin added in a threatening tone. "Of course, the Jews will not listen to us and, of course, they will pay much more dearly."[177] Shul'gin's writings were in line with the mood among many in the Volunteer Army. Jewish diarists and memoirists recorded their unease in the weeks after the Whites' arrival, as antisemitic comments became increasingly frequent, and the word "Yid" (*zhid*) was "buzzing" through the streets of Kiev.[178]

The situation of Kiev's Jews worsened drastically in October 1919. On 1 (14) October, Bolshevik troops appeared on the western outskirts of the city. Amid the population's general panic, the city's White rulers began to evacuate across the Dnieper to Darnitsa on the eastern shore. Some fifty thousand Kievans joined this exodus to escape Bolshevik rule. Supported by underground fighters in the city, the Bolsheviks occupied parts of the city center, but the Volunteer Army held the bridgeheads. After three days of heavy fighting, they defeated the Red Army and returned to the city, followed by the civilian refugees. On 3 (16) October, a pogrom against the city's Jewish population began. In fashionable areas, officers entered the apartments of wealthy Jewish Kievans to extort money and jewelry. Because of their "businesslike" manner, the event became known as a "silent pogrom." In poorer neighborhoods, locals and soldiers pillaged Jewish shops and apartments, smashing to pieces what they could not carry off. They killed hundreds of civilians and raped dozens of Jewish women. Witnesses heard screams of fear resounding in the whole city. The army's generals issued proclamations condemning the pogroms but were neither capable of nor seriously committed to preventing them.[179]

When *Kievlianin* renewed publication a few days after the Darnitsa events, Vasilii Shul'gin published a short editorial titled "Torture by

Fear." Describing the "heart-rending yell" of the "Yids" during the pogrom, Shul'gin expressed his hope that this terrible experience would teach Russia's Jews a lesson: "Will they understand what it means to destroy a state that they have not built? . . . Will they understand what it means to incite class against class following the plan of the 'great teacher' Karl Marx?" Instead of accusing the pogromists, he insisted, the Jews must accept their fault and condemn the Jewish Bolsheviks. Shul'gin also gave credence to the rumor that Jews had fired shots at the army from their windows during the evacuation. The Jews, he explained, had destroyed Russia in their fanatical quest for equal rights; the socialists' "struggle against historical Russian statehood" had been "a Jewish national cause." At the same time, he worried that the pogroms would deprave the army and help the Jews by evoking pity.[180]

Shul'gin's reaction to the pogrom, while particularly harsh, was typical of his antisemitism. He rejected pogroms as a disorderly political method but agreed with the pogromists in assigning collective blame to all Jews for the actual and alleged deeds of some Jews. The article immediately prompted strong reactions, especially among Jewish intellectuals. The writer Il'ia Erenburg wrote a patriotic response, claiming that the painful experience of the pogrom had only strengthened his love for Russia, his only homeland. Most commentators, however, saw "Torture by Fear" as a cynical and distasteful piece of propaganda, and it contributed to Shul'gin's reputation as a particularly infamous antisemite.[181]

On the Ukrainian question, *Kievlianin* stuck to its long-established position. Shul'gin "tried to isolate what was natural and even useful in the Ukrainian movement, i.e. the seeds of healthy local patriotism, and delimit this local patriotism clearly from the completely nonlocal treachery."[182] The Volunteer Army granted Kiev's Ukrainian milieu the cultural liberties promised in Denikin's manifesto. Fourteen of the city's nineteen Ukrainian-language schools continued to function. The Ukrainian press was published relatively freely as long as it did not support independence or Petliura's Directory too openly. Some politically moderate Ukrainian journalists hoped for an agreement with the Whites against the common Bolshevik enemy.[183] *Kievlianin*, however, categorically rejected the possibility of such a compromise. Anatolii Savenko declared that there could not even be such a thing as "moderate Ukrainians": "What is a Ukrainian? It is a man . . . who has renounced the Russian name of his forefathers and the Russian nation and believes to belong to some distinct 'Ukrainian' nation. But can there be a moderate or an immoderate renunciation?"[184]

Yet, the *Kievlianin* editors knew that the main problem facing the Whites was neither the "Jewish question" nor the "Ukrainian question." More important was the old problem of rural landownership, on which the peasants' loyalty depended. Ukraine's peasants had seized many plots from the landlords since 1917 and feared that they would have to restitute them. While General Denikin was willing to strengthen peasant landownership at the expense of landlords, conservatives in his government diluted and delayed all measures to that effect. Alongside Bolshevik propaganda portraying the Whites as a reactionary force, this made most peasants distrust the Volunteers.[185] Vasilii Shul'gin, who had witnessed the peasants' impatience when they appropriated cattle at his Kurgany estate, was frustrated with the slow progress of land reform, writing as early as December 1918,

> For all his barbarism, our *muzhik* is healthy in soul and body and incredibly obstinate in his basic demands. Our noble landowners are weak in body and soul, and they have lost the healthy egoism of the proprietor, so strong in the English and the French. . . . But if we have to give away the land all the same, the question arises: Are we doing the right thing in postponing this issue until Russia's reconstruction? After all, the main obstacle to this reconstruction is precisely this damned land issue.[186]

Shul'gin's preferred solution, unsurprisingly, was to create a class of small homestead (*khutor*) proprietors, as his father Pikhno had advocated for decades. Only a strong Russian state, he told his (imagined) peasant readers, could guarantee them hereditary landownership.[187] In September 1919, Shul'gin's brother-in-law Aleksandr Bilimovich became Denikin's minister of agriculture and formed a commission to plan a land reform. The commission's proposal foresaw a period of two years for landowners to sell their land voluntarily. Thereafter, all plots exceeding 160 to 440 hectares (depending on the soil's quality) would be taken away, financially compensated, and sold to local peasants in plots of 10 to 50 hectares. If somewhat more radical than earlier plans, this project was still very much in Pikhno's and Stolypin's spirit. Even Denikin later acknowledged that it was "completely unsuitable as a means of struggle."[188] Ukraine's peasants would hardly have agreed to pay for land in 1919—but at any rate, Denikin lacked the time to implement the project.

By November, the Whites were almost as unpopular in Kiev as their predecessors had been. *Kievlianin*'s confrontational course did more harm than good to their cause. Since the city's commander, General Abram Dragomirov (the son of a former Kiev governor-general), was personally and politically close to Vasilii Shul'gin, many Kievans believed it was Shul'gin who dictated the government's nationalities policy.[189] This was not quite true, but it damaged the regime's prestige among all those who became the target of Shul'gin's vitriolic editorials. The geologist Vladimir Vernadskii (Volodymyr Vernads'kyi), a liberal with moderate Ukrainian sympathies, remarked that the local authorities tried to reproduce the rule of Alexander III, alienating Kiev's Jews, Ukrainians, and democrats. A Jewish student feared that the pogroms and *Kievlianin*'s antisemitism might drive Jewish artisans and petty bourgeois into the hands of the Bolsheviks. Even General Dragomirov criticized the newspaper's extremely anti-Ukrainian views, calling Anatolii Savenko a "narrow-minded fanatic of his idea, incapable of understanding any point of view except his own."[190]

As the Volunteers desperately tried to recruit soldiers, Kiev's population got the impression that they could not guarantee order, leading to demoralization, political apathy, and panicked rumors.[191] By late November, with the Red Army advancing again, it was clear that the Whites' days in Kiev were numbered. Having sent his family out of town, Vasilii Shul'gin and his Azbuka associates published a last issue of *Kievlianin*, in its highest-ever print run of seventy thousand copies. Shul'gin's final article called on "fathers and husbands" to stay and defend their city. However, even before it was published, Shul'gin recognized the hopeless situation and left Kiev and his family home, this time for good.[192]

With the evacuation of Kiev, the Shul'gins began an odyssey of narrow escapes, desperate military campaigns, and underground hideouts. Marching to the south or riding on extremely slow, overcrowded, and disease-ridden trains, Vasilii Shul'gin, his wife Ekaterina, and their two sons all made their way to Odessa. When this city also came under Red Army siege, the Shul'gins joined the westward march of the remaining White troops to the Romanian border. Having failed to enter Romania, they made their way back to Odessa, where Vasilii Shul'gin fell ill with typhus. In Bolshevik-held Odessa, the Cheka was looking for him, and Shul'gin repeatedly had to change his apartments and fake identities. Finally, in July 1920, he and his sons escaped by boat to the island of Tendra. From there, they made it to Crimea, the last bastion of the

Volunteer Army under its new leader, General Petr Vrangel'. Over the year 1920, Shul'gin became disillusioned with the White movement. As he witnessed troops committing antisemitic pogroms and looting the possessions of the locals, he felt that the Volunteer Army was losing its moral superiority. Yet Shul'gin was not in a position to influence policies or public opinion anymore. Like the rest of his family, he was fighting for his bare life.[193]

As the civil war became ever more brutal, the Shul'gin family suffered several more losses. Within a few months, three of Vasilii Shul'gin's (half) brothers perished. Pavel Pikhno died of typhus on the way to Odessa during the evacuation from Kiev in December 1919. In May 1920, the Odessan Cheka arrested Filipp Mogilevskii. Vasilii Shul'gin tried to arrange a prisoner exchange but could not save Mogilevskii from being shot. A few months later, Dmitrii Pikhno (jr.) was arrested and shot by the Cheka when the Bolsheviks took Crimea. Finally, Vasilii's and Ekaterina's second son Veniamin joined a Volunteer Army regiment in August 1920 and got lost in combat, never to be found again. His fate remains unknown to this day.[194]

When Vasilii Shul'gin tried to reach Odessa in a last, desperate attempt to free Filipp Mogilevskii, a storm blew his boat too far west, and he got stranded on the Romanian coast. From Romania, he traveled farther south, arriving in Constantinople by the end of the year. Just as the last Volunteer Army detachments were evacuating Crimea, Shul'gin involuntarily became an émigré. Ekaterina Shul'gina spent another year hiding anonymously in Odessa, working as a chambermaid and nanny. Once she was arrested and spent weeks in a Cheka prison. After several unsuccessful attempts to leave Odessa, she managed to cross the Soviet-Polish border in the winter of 1921–1922 and made it to the family's Volhynian estate at Kurgany, which had narrowly ended up in Poland. After almost five years of revolution and civil war, all surviving family members had joined the ranks of the Russian emigration.[195]

Vasilii Shul'gin's civil war activities have been assessed quite harshly by Western historians. According to Anna Procyk, Shul'gin's "almost pathological hatred of all Jews and Ukrainians . . . was responsible to no small degree for the strong antisemitism and Ukrainophobia that prevailed at Ekaterinodar."[196] Peter Kenez states that "Shulgin alone among the major figures of the anti-Bolshevik movement could be described as a proto-fascist. His passionate nationalism, his demagogy, his willingness to exploit antisemitism and his ability to experiment with unconventional methods of political warfare made him appear a modern figure among conservatives and reactionaries."[197] Both of these judgments require qualification. It is exaggerated to blame Shul'gin for the Volunteer Army's nationalist course, given that he never had any powers of decision. However, Shul'gin's analyses of the political situation were doubtless wrong and harmful to the White cause. By framing all Ukrainian nationalists as treacherous German hirelings, he discredited all possible cooperation with the region's only other significant anti-Bolshevik force. Misconstruing the Bolsheviks as a Jewish national party, he ignored the appeal of their radical socioeconomic slogans to the (Christian) masses. Shul'gin and his associates contributed to alienating the peasants, the Ukrainian nationalists, and the moderate urban Jews. But even if their writings influenced the mood in the army's ranks, their views largely chimed with preexisting prejudices and biases.[198]

As to Shul'gin's "proto-fascism," his skills at mass mobilization and his virulent antisemitism, reinforced by wartime resentment, certainly made him a right-wing demagogue of a modern type. He also subscribed to a cult of the army and of the strong leader (despite finding Denikin too liberal). In emigration, he would at one point come to admire Benito Mussolini and call himself a "Russian fascist."[199] For all his inflammatory rhetoric, however, Shul'gin never endorsed violence and looting as a political strategy. While he advocated a military dictatorship to restore order in the war-torn countryside, this was only a temporary option for him. Shul'gin longed for a restoration of the semi-constitutional Stolypinite monarchy rather than for a new, unfettered authoritarianism. Ultimately, he was too legitimist and conservative to be truly (proto-)fascist.[200] While the Shul'gins proved capable of adapting their political practices to the circumstances of revolution and civil war, their program lacked this flexibility. Based on private property, historically legitimate hierarchies, and state unity, their ideology was a product of the relatively calm late imperial period. In a time when any political force needed to win over the revolutionized peasants and the revolting soldiers, it failed to appeal to the masses.

Without Territory

Oleksander Shul'hyn did not quit politics altogether in the spring of 1918. In June, he took up work for the Hetmanate's Foreign Ministry under his friend Dmytro Doroshenko, the only committed Ukrainian nationalist in an otherwise conservative cabinet. Hetman Skoropadskii, brought to power by the Germans, sought to broaden his domestic appeal by forming a coalition of Ukraine's moderate elites. At various points, his supporters included older liberal Ukrainophiles who did not want a total break with Russian culture (Volodymyr Naumenko, Mykola Vasylenko, Vladimir Vernadskii), the socially conservative Ukrainian nationalists around the agrarian *Khliboroby* party (Dmytro Dontsov, Viacheslav Lypyns'kyi), and local monarchists with Ukrainophile sympathies, like Oleksander's uncle Ustimovich. Skoropadskii also relied on wealthy landowners, industrialists, and a few military men, all of whom hoped for socioeconomic stability and protection against land seizures. Finally, the Hetman could count on the temporary support of some Russian politicians—both liberals like Pavel Miliukov and extreme right-wingers—who saw a conservative Ukrainian state as a stepping-stone to the liberation of Russia from the Bolsheviks.[201]

This unstable and highly disparate coalition forced the Hetman to maneuver between Ukrainian nationalism and a Russophile federalist course. Still, the regime failed to attract several powerful forces in the region. The nationalist Ukrainian socialists disagreed with its landowner-friendly policies. The local Russian nationalists around Vasilii Shul'gin despised Ukrainian nationalism even in its conservative and federalist form. For the liberal and military circles gathered around the Volunteer Army, Russia's unity and an Entente orientation were not negotiable—although their worldview was in many ways similar to Skoropadskii's. Finally, the Bolsheviks and the peasant masses bitterly resented the government's pro-landowner policies and the brutal requisitions carried out by the occupying German troops.[202] The presence of so many powerful opponents doomed the Hetmanate to failure once the Germans retreated. But for several months in 1918, it seemed like the only viable Ukrainian political project, and many of its critics, including Oleksander Shul'hyn, agreed to give it temporary backing.

As part of the Brest-Litovsk system, the Ukrainian state had to establish diplomatic relations with all four Central Powers: Germany, Austria-Hungary, the Ottoman Empire, and Bulgaria. In the summer of 1918, Foreign Minister Doroshenko named Oleksander Shul'hyn ambassador to the smallest of these states, Bulgaria, to the satisfaction of the Bulgarian king Ferdinand, who wished to see a nationalist in the post.[203] Immediately after his arrival in Sofia, Shul'hyn received petitions from prisoners of war, former soldiers of the imperial Russian army who asked him to negotiate their release. "The Bulgarians are very kind to me," Shul'hyn reported back to Kiev, "but the prisoners—may God protect them. Horrible complaints from both Ukrainians and

Russians." Shul'hyn established good personal relations with King Ferdinand and ultimately got the Bulgarians to let thousands of prisoners leave for Odessa by boat.[204] Despite this success, the Austrian ambassador Count Otto Czernin noted patronizingly that "Mr. Schulgin . . . does not yet seem to be very well versed in the treatment of diplomatic questions."[205]

Meanwhile, it became increasingly clear that the Central Powers were losing the war and that Ukraine had to reorient itself toward the Entente. In October, the Bulgarians were the first of the Central Powers to capitulate. When the Hetman, in a last desperate bid for new allies, declared federation with Russia, Oleksander Shul'hyn resigned. As soon as the UNR Directory took power in Kiev, it appointed him to its delegation to the peace conference in Paris, where he arrived in March 1919.[206] Shul'hyn's appointment made sense. After one year of diplomatic work, he was already one of the UNR's more experienced diplomats; he was known as an Entente sympathizer and spoke good French. The delegation's head was the engineer Hryhorii Sydorenko. Among its members was Oleksander's university acquaintance Arnol'd Margolin, a Jewish lawyer from Kiev who had discovered his Ukrainian sympathies only in the course of the revolution. Several scholarly and legal advisers accompanied the delegation.[207]

The Ukrainian diplomats soon had to discover that most of the conference participants knew little to nothing about Ukraine and the Ukrainian national movement. "While every nation has been agitating for years," Oleksander Shul'hyn complained in a report to his government, "while the Czechs, Poles, Romanians, Yugoslavs, Greeks all had a mass of literature and squandered money in order to get the press behind them, we did not do anything, and the Paris delegation simultaneously had to provide the most elementary information about the issue and engage in real diplomatic work."[208]

Oleksander Shul'hyn tried to improve this state of affairs by composing an official memorandum to the conference's leaders. In line with the tendency of all delegations to demand as much land as conceivable, the memorandum began by outlining Ukraine's "ethnographic territory," including not only right-bank and left-bank Ukraine and the southern steppes but also East Galicia, Bukovina, Hungarian Transcarpathia, Kholm province, the Kuban territory, and parts of several other Russian provinces. Needless to say, many of these territories had never been under the control of the UNR. In a way, the memorandum confirmed its own claim that "Ukraine has no neatly defined natural limits." Shul'hyn went on to claim that the UNR had some fifty million inhabitants, of which 75 percent were Ukrainians, as against 9 percent Russians, 7.6 percent Jews, and 4 percent Poles. These numbers were roughly based on the prewar imperial census, which, however, had counted speakers of the "Little Russian dialect," not asked people to define themselves as "Ukrainians." Thus, the memorandum continued the time-honored tradition of both Russian and Ukrainian nationalists to claim all the territory's Orthodox peasants for their respective nations, regardless of their self-identification. A large section of the text was dedicated to economic questions. In much detail, it described the achievements and potential of Ukrainian agriculture, Ukraine's wealth of coal and iron ore, its sugar industry and cooperative movement—all in order to demonstrate that Ukraine could function as a "complete organism" unto itself.[209]

The memorandum's arguments, of course, were not new. Ukrainian nationalists had rehearsed them over decades while debating Russian intellectuals. Shul'hyn mustered the scholarly authority of the previous generation of Ukrainophiles to address a new audience: politicians from France, Britain, or the United States. His exposition of Ukrainian history relied heavily on the narratives of Antonovych and Hrushevs'kyi, stressing the continuity of Ukrainian statehood and the democratic struggle for independence. His description of Ukrainian geography was indebted to the geographer Stepan Rudnyts'kyi, with his focus on Ukraine's territorial unity and peculiarity.[210] Citing the work of his teacher Fedir Vovk, Shul'hyn explained that the Ukrainians formed a different anthropological type from the Russians, with darker hair and eyes, taller bodies, and rounder skulls. The text was replete with nineteenth-century clichés opposing Ukrainians' innate democratism to Russian authoritarianism and Polish feudalism. Shul'hyn even included the absurd claim, borrowed from Kostomarov, that "the Ukrainian people love trees and flowers, for which the Russian people feel an almost absolute indifference."[211]

Shul'hyn insisted that the UNR had always sought Entente support and unwillingly collaborated with the Germans only under the threat of mutinous soldiers and invading Bolsheviks. Of course, this was at best partially true. Shul'hyn himself was one of the few consistently pro-Entente politicians in the UNR; many of its leaders had repeatedly switched (and would keep switching) their orientation along with the changing military and geopolitical situation. The memorandum concluded by demanding a territory within Ukraine's ethnographic borders, "except for rare and insignificant corrections," which, unsurprisingly, always enlarged the territory.[212] While Shul'hyn's memorandum relied on the Wilsonian principle of self-determination and on learned demonstrations of Ukraine's separate nationhood, the UNR delegates also tried more pragmatic arguments in their meetings with Entente representatives. Independent Ukraine would pay up to 30 percent of imperial Russia's state debt, they claimed; it offered possibilities of investment for French and British companies; and it was the best bulwark against the advance of Bolshevism into Europe.[213]

Despite all these arguments, the UNR delegates mostly encountered ignorance and indifference in their conversations with the French, British, and American delegates. The conference's organizers never even considered making the UNR a conference participant. Shul'hyn and Margolin got to meet the French foreign minister Stephen Pichon and Prime Minister Georges Clemenceau. Both men were courteous but did not waver in their support of Denikin's White army and the new Polish state. By June 1919, Shul'hyn had little hope left. The Entente, he found, would only take the Ukrainians seriously if the plan to rebuild a strong Poland and Russia failed.[214]

In retrospect, the delegation's task was almost impossible. The Ukrainian amateur diplomats could not compete with the professionals in other delegations.[215] Even the White Russian delegation was headed by Sergei Sazonov, the former imperial foreign minister, and Vasilii Maklakov, the ambassador to France of the defunct Provisional Government. The Czech and Polish delegations relied on prominent émigrés in the West. Meanwhile, the Entente leaders lacked a clear plan for the former Russian Empire and could not even decide whether to throw their full force behind the White armies or to arrange themselves with the Bolsheviks.[216] They had little patience for the UNR delegation, which only seemed to further complicate matters. As the journalist Jean Xydias wrote, "In Paris, they only had a very vague idea of the Ukrainian movement; they knew that it was, to a certain extent, of German inspiration, and thus concluded that it had become insignificant due to Germany's defeat."[217]

The French were dedicated to the Polish cause. This inclined them against the Ukrainians because of the situation in East Galicia, where the recently formed West Ukrainian People's Republic competed with the revived Polish state. As Polish armies advanced through Galicia, their French allies secured the approval of the other great powers. By the autumn, Polish control of Galicia was a fact and had the Entente's backing. Other Entente clients also pretended to parts of the territory the UNR claimed. The Romanians had their eyes set on Bukovina and Bessarabia, while Czechoslovakia annexed Transcarpathia in the spring of 1919.[218] To make matters worse, the Ukrainian delegation was itself disunited. The Galician delegates saw the Poles as their main opponents, whereas the East Ukrainians prioritized the struggle against Bolsheviks and White Russians. Recalling this kind of infighting, Shul'hyn later said that it would have been better not to send any delegation at all rather than make such a bad impression on the French.[219]

Above all, however, the UNR's territory was continually shrinking as the proceedings in Paris went on. The Directory lost Kiev to the Bolsheviks and Odessa to the Whites in January 1919. It was driven out of Vinnitsa, its temporary capital, in March. By April, the Directory's cabinet was fleeing through Galicia in railway carriages, hounded by Polish troops and the Red Army from both sides. The UNR had become a government without territory. "As long as we cannot establish a certain order, nobody, and no delegation, will achieve recognition of Ukraine by the Entente," Oleksander Shul'hyn reported back to Ukraine.[220]

In September 1919, Oleksander Shul'hyn quit the UNR delegation and left for Czechoslovakia. He visited Ukraine for the last time in the summer of 1920 and reassumed his diplomatic activity in the autumn, when the UNR government dispatched him to the first assembly of the newly founded League of Nations in Geneva. In the meantime, the UNR's last hope of regaining its territories had been crushed. Abandoning claims to Eastern Galicia, Symon Petliura had concluded a military alliance with the Poles in April 1920. Their joint offensive brought them to Kiev, but the Bolsheviks soon took the city back and drove their opponents deep into Poland. Petliura's UNR went into exile in the West Galician town of Tarnów, where the Polish government interned its troops.[221] Pretending to represent Ukraine on the international stage, its diplomats competed with representatives of the West Ukrainian Republic, the supporters of Hetman Skoropadskii, a UNR splinter group in Vienna, and the diplomats of Soviet Ukraine.[222]

Oleksander Shul'hyn arrived in Geneva in November 1920. He hoped to persuade the representatives of smaller states, such as the Latin American republics, to procure the votes the UNR needed for admission to the League. The main obstacle, as he soon found out, was that the League's charter obliged member states to protect each other in case of military attacks. Given that the entire territory claimed by the UNR was held by other states, this was problematic.[223] On 25

November, Shul'hyn and his colleague Margolin were called to explain their cause before the responsible commission, headed by the Norwegian polar explorer Fridtjof Nansen. Nansen wanted the Ukrainians to prove the stability of their government, and Shul'hyn had to admit that they currently only held parts of right-bank Ukraine. Even this was an exaggeration, however. Days earlier, the last remainders of the UNR army had crossed the river Zbruch into Poland. All its former territory was controlled by the Soviet Ukrainian government that Shul'hyn called an "occupational military terrorist regime." Despite his assiduous lobbying, both the commission and the general assembly refused the UNR membership.[224]

By the summer of 1921, Shul'hyn was disillusioned with the prospects of Ukrainian diplomacy. As the Soviets and Poland concluded the Peace Treaty of Riga, partitioning the territory claimed by the UNR, his appeals to the French government went unheard. Rival Ukrainian diplomatic missions were fighting over funds that Skoropadskii had deposited in the German and Austrian state banks, and the UNR government in Tarnów was itself torn by disagreements. "The French government considers us émigrés at war with one another," Shul'hyn wrote to Symon Petliura; "the events of the last month confirm this opinion to some extent."[225] This was a realistic assessment. Like the members of Russia's White movement, Oleksander Shul'hyn and several thousands of Ukrainian nationalists had to accept emigration as their long-term destiny.

The First World War and the resulting breakdown of the Russian Empire exacerbated preexisting political tensions, including the conflict between Russian and Ukrainian nationalism. Ukraine's educated elites were forced to choose sides in the increasingly harsh competition between the two nation-building projects. As dedicated nationalists, the Shul'gins and Shul'hyns stuck to their earlier choices. However, the rapidly changing situation pushed them to radicalize their respective projects. Vasilii Shul'gin, despairing about the imperial bureaucracy, sought an alliance with the liberals in the national-democratic Progressive Bloc and even condoned the monarchy's demise to strengthen Russia's war effort. Later on, he resorted to highly divisive rhetoric against Ukrainian nationalists and allegedly Jewish Bolsheviks. Oleksander Shul'hyn and other Ukrainian activists abandoned their traditional federalism when the disintegration of central authority made Ukrainian independence appear as a more viable alternative.

Nationalism was not the cause of the empire's collapse. Rather, the state's implosion opened new possibilities of action for nationalists and strengthened centrifugal tendencies.[226] In Kiev, where the share of industrial workers was small, national democracy became a popular idiom of revolutionary politics. The Ukrainian parties managed to turn their Central Rada into the main organ of revolutionary power in the region. It attracted parts of the intelligentsia and many soldiers from the garrison, but also peasants who appreciated its radical stance on land reform. Oleksander Shul'hyn, and to a lesser extent his siblings, profited from the urgent need for cadres to staff the emerging Ukrainian institutions. Formerly an unknown student activist, Shul'hyn became a political leader thanks to his nationalist education, his rhetorical talent, and his energetic work. His Russian relatives, too, knew how to profit from their prewar resources. Kiev's Russian nationalists retained their popularity with the urban middle classes that had brought them electoral successes before 1914. Ekaterina Shul'gina and Vasilii Shul'gin adapted their family enterprise to revolutionary politics, becoming the only conservatives in the disintegrating empire to win an election.

However, both the Ukrainian People's Republic and the Russian nationalist alternative proved structurally too weak to ensure order in the long term. Over the following three years, both Russian and Ukrainian nationalists came up with various schemes for national reconstruction that were increasingly desperate and detached from reality. As Ukraine descended into a brutal and destructive civil war, the Shul'gins and Shul'hyns were no longer able to influence political events. Both family branches shared the worldview of a bourgeois intelligentsia, but in the years 1918 to 1920, revolutionary adventurers and military men took the initiative. Oleksander Shul'hyn's centrist policies had no chance of swaying the masses, and he took to diplomatic work instead. His career as a historian and political activist had not prepared him sufficiently for this task. As the government he represented abroad crumbled at home, his mission became hopeless. Vasilii Shul'gin initially had more success and repeatedly attained influential positions. Yet he too ultimately succumbed to military force. By 1920, he was fighting for survival, in the process losing half his family to war, disease, and political terror. One year later, both men were émigrés, soon to be followed by the other surviving family members.

Ukrainian and Russian nationalists lost the power struggle to a third contender, the Bolsheviks, whose radical program and ruthless methods made them superior in a time of general chaos and violence. Not the least reason for the nationalists' defeat was their inability to compromise and cooperate with one another. While the rural masses craved land and peace, which the Bolsheviks promised to deliver instantly, Russian and Ukrainian nationalists continued their arcane disputes over the region's correct name and historical identity. The brutality and the personal losses that both sides experienced in the civil war only deepened the ideological rift between them. A few years later, the onetime leader of the White army laconically juxtaposed the nationalists' theoretical battles against the population's continued indifference to nationalistic categories: "And the people? The people had extraordinarily little interest in their own historical genealogy. The theories and findings of [the Russian historian Vasilii] Kliuchevskii and of M. Hrushevs'kyi were equally unknown and foreign to them."[227]

CHAPTER 5

Living off the Past

Nationalists Write Their Lives in Interwar Europe

As the civil war in the former Russian Empire came to its close in the early 1920s, hundreds of thousands of Russian and Ukrainian political émigrés fled to Western and Central Europe. All the surviving members of the Shul'gin and Shul'hyn families settled outside the Soviet Union. The last to cross the border were Nadiia Shul'hyna and her mother Liubov. In 1923, they left Kiev for the newly independent Polish republic, ultimately settling in the Volhynian town of Rovno, where Nadiia began to teach at the Ukrainian gymnasium. Nadiia's brothers Oleksander and Mykola spent the 1920s between Paris and Prague.[1] Meanwhile, their Russian nationalist relatives were scattered throughout the émigré colonies of interwar Europe. Vasilii Shul'gin and Ekaterina Shul'gina repeatedly moved between countries, living at different times in Bulgaria, Germany, Czechoslovakia, France, and Yugoslavia.

In the "New Europe" of nation-states, the Russian and the Ukrainian emigration became extraterritorial societies unto themselves, each with its own social spaces and cultural institutions. Both emigrations gave rise to new political groups and parties, all rife with what one researcher has called "complicated and sterile political factionalism."[2] A crucial medium for émigré debates was autobiographical writing. Trying to make sense of the recent revolutionary cataclysm, thousands of people sat down to write their memoirs. For all of them, the revolution became the defining event of their biographies, a focal point in relation to which they defined their worldviews and political disagreements.[3] By reflecting on their roles in the revolutionary process, émigré memoirists tried to shape their image in the present and inscribe themselves into national histories. They continued a tradition of the Russian intelligentsia, among which it had long been common to "conceive of one's personal life as historical in nature, and to sculpt one's autobiography in order to make the self conform to the exigencies of historical progression."[4] Thus, autobiographical writing was both self-transformative and eminently political for nationalist émigrés.

Among these émigré authors were Oleksander Shul'hyn, Ekaterina Shul'gina, and Vasilii Shul'gin. All three of them penned substantial memoirs during the interwar period, using different writing strategies for different purposes. Oleksander Shul'hyn pretended to leadership in the Ukrainian emigration. For him, autobiographical writing was a means to construct a self-image as an unambiguously Ukrainian politician and intellectual, thereby bolstering his position in an emerging Ukrainian public sphere. Ekaterina Shul'gina's memoirs, by contrast, had a more self-therapeutic function. Struggling to cope with personal and political losses, she retrospectively tried to define a fitting societal role for herself as a conservative, nationalist woman. Finally, Vasilii Shul'gin used autobiographical texts for his political musings about recent history. The question around which all his writings turned was that of historical guilt for the Russian Empire's collapse. In different ways, then, all three of them continued to live in, and off, their prerevolutionary past.

Ukraine against Moscow

After the definitive defeat of the Ukrainian armies by the Bolsheviks, Oleksander Shul'hyn found himself in a rapidly changing political landscape. On the left, various groups of Ukrainian Social Democrats and Socialist Revolutionaries were formed, some of which sympathized and established contact with the Soviet state. On the moderate right, the former Hetman Skoropadskii headed a group that advocated an estate-based Ukrainian monarchy. The far-right ideologue Dmytro Dontsov pioneered Ukrainian integral nationalism, an authoritarian current that took inspiration from Italian fascism and became influential among the Ukrainian youth of East Galicia. A Galician group of war veterans, the Ukrainian Military Organization, employed terrorism in its fight against the Polish state.[5] In this increasingly polarized field, Symon Petliura's UNR government in exile tried to defend the middle ground. Abandoning their earlier socialist commitments, its supporters adopted a national-democratic ideology and proclaimed the need for Ukraine to develop along West European lines.[6]

As head of the UNR's mission in Paris and delegate to various international conferences, Oleksander Shul'hyn remained loyal to Symon Petliura, whom he idealized as the glorious and indisputable leader of the Ukrainian movement. Shul'hyn's devotion became even more ardent after Petliura's assassination by a presumptive Soviet agent in 1926.[7] Shortly before his death, Petliura had made Shul'hyn foreign minister of the exile government. In this capacity, Shul'hyn advocated an orientation toward France and her allies, despite the continued lack of interest on the French side.[8] Shul'hyn's Francophilia was linked to his admiration for the comparatively well-functioning parliamentary democracy of the French Third Republic, which he saw as the only viable model for his country's future. By contrast, he rejected fascism, finding it as unfit for "individualist" Ukraine as Soviet communism.[9]

Like a majority of East Ukrainian émigrés, Shul'hyn regarded the Soviet Union as Ukraine's main enemy. Describing Soviet rule in Ukraine as colonial oppression, he rejected its claim to represent Ukrainian nationhood and culture.[10] By contrast, most West Ukrainian political programs, whether in Polish Galicia or in the emigration, were directed against Poland. Oleksander Shul'hyn advocated peaceful relations with the Polish government and criticized the terror attacks perpetrated in Galicia by Ukrainian nationalists. This repeatedly drew the ire of West Ukrainian nationalists, who accused him of Polonophilia and of abandoning *sobornist'*, the unity of all Ukrainian territories. In such conflicts, Shul'hyn insisted that the UNR exile government was the only true successor to the defunct Ukrainian state, true to the principle that "the nation stands above class, the state stands above party."[11] In reality, of course, the UNR was only one of many factions in the highly fragmented sphere of émigré politics.[12]

This fragmentation and sectarianism has usually been described as a weakness of the Ukrainian emigration. In the words of one historian, the rivaling Ukrainian parties "fought one another as much as their national enemies."[13] However, the competition between parties was also a sign of success for the Ukrainian emigration, for it reflected the widened scope of Ukrainian politics abroad. If nearly all Ukrainian politicians up to 1917 had been socialists, or at the utmost liberal national democrats, the emigration came to include the entire political spectrum, with a whole series of conservative and right-wing formations taking shape in this period. Combined with the geographical detachment from Russia, this development made it possible to keep the most important debates within the Ukrainian émigré community instead of having to engage in feuds with Russian politicians.[14]

Thus, most of Oleksander Shul'hyn's political struggles during these years pitted him against other Ukrainians and revolved around the emigration's internal disagreements. True, there was occasional communication with some of the more conciliatory politicians in the Russian emigration; however, since the premise of Ukrainian independence was no longer negotiable for most Ukrainian exiles, very little could come of it. In 1921, for example, Shul'hyn was in contact with Vladimir Burtsev's Paris newspaper *Obshchee delo*, which at the time seemed open to cooperation between Russian and Ukrainian anti-Bolshevik forces. Yet Shul'hyn had little hope: "My real goal is that they no longer interfere with us, or at least interfere less. I hardly believe in the possibility of common action on the basis of the recognition of Ukrainian independence."[15] Two years later, Shul'hyn wrote that he was frequently talking to his Ukrainian political opponents, "and sometimes with the Russians, too (though very rarely)."[16]

Beyond his deep-rooted convictions, the emergence of a separate Ukrainian public sphere gave Oleksander Shul'hyn a concrete material incentive to present himself as an unambiguous Ukrainian. Having gone directly from the university into revolutionary politics, he had never completed his professional education. In the Shul'hyns' household, money was scarce during the entire interwar period.[17] The most promising source of income for Oleksander was employment by the Ukrainian political and cultural institutions that cropped up as several thousand nationalist Ukrainians settled in Western and Central Europe.[18] From 1923, he regularly traveled between Paris and Prague, where he continued his academic career as a history professor at the Ukrainian Free University, a new émigré institution supported by the Czechoslovak government.[19] Shul'hyn's claim to a leading position in émigré organizations relied solely on the role he had played in 1917. His former federalist views were well known in émigré circles and were occasionally used to criticize him as insufficiently nationalist.[20] Therefore, Shul'hyn needed to stress his patriotism and independentism on every occasion. Even though Ukrainian émigré institutions had very limited means, it was more promising to become a leader of the Ukrainian community than to compete with the much larger Russian emigration.[21] Thus, the financial hardships of Ukrainian political émigrés arguably contributed to their complete separation from the Russian emigration.

The interwar emigration in Western and Central Europe was the first purely Ukrainophone intellectual society, one that was hardly closer to Russians and Poles than to the Czech, German, or French societies surrounding it. The formation of separate Russian and Ukrainian émigré communities made it almost impossible to embrace an intermediate regionalist option, which had already eroded over previous decades. The noncommittal sympathy for Ukrainian culture, still characteristic of many liberals in the region before 1917, was a thing of the past. By associating with Ukrainian émigré organizations, one declared loyalty to the Ukrainian national project; by participating in Russian circles, one chose to ignore it.[22] And even though Oleksander Shul'hyn had been a Ukrainian nationalist since his youth, it was only in emigration, and in part through autobiographical writing, that he shed his last attachments to Russian culture—most notably, the Russian language—and completed his self-fashioning as an unambiguously Ukrainian politician.

Autobiographical writing had a distinctly political function in the Ukrainian interwar emigration, for the diverging interpretations of what had happened between 1917 and 1920 were a major source of political rivalries.[23] Oleksander Shul'hyn weighed in from the mid-1920s, publishing a few short reminiscences and obituaries in the weekly *Tryzub*, the unofficial organ of the UNR in Paris. It is in these articles that he began to develop his narrative of the revolution.[24] On the occasion of the revolution's tenth anniversary, he described the events of 1917 as a justified explosion of popular hatred against the tsarist government, albeit one that led to disaster. For Ukraine, Shul'hyn explained, the revolution had a double, ambiguous significance. On the one hand, it was the period when the Ukrainian nation achieved self-awareness and renewed its statehood; on the other hand, it was a time of ruin and endless suffering.[25] This interpretation of the revolution as a double-edged sword also informed his autobiographical monograph *L'Ukraine contre Moscou*, published in Paris in 1935.

Remarkably, Shul'hyn wrote his first major memoir in French. At the time of its publication, he was still foreign minister of the UNR in exile, and he likely saw it as part of the UNR's information and propaganda effort in France. At the same time, he must have been aware that

FIGURE 16.   Oleksander Shul'hyn in the interwar period. Ishchuk-Pazuniak private collection, courtesy of Olena Leontovych.

it would meet at least as much interest among the Ukrainian emigration. Shul'hyn promised his readers a "national confession" that would faithfully describe the historical facts, including the bitter truths. His account was to be impartial but personal, situating his own experience and his family's fate in a larger historical process: "I mix the tragedy of the nation and that of my family."[26] A trained historian, Shul'hyn was well aware that his memoirs were a contribution to the future historical narrative of the Ukrainian revolution. Therefore, he included French translations of several constitutional documents in his text. He also printed the full text of letters and speeches by the French envoy in Kiev, General Tabouis, assuring his French readership that these documents were "exactly tantamount to the recognition of Ukraine by France."[27]

In typically nationalist fashion, Shul'hyn conceptualized Ukrainian history as a three-stage process, from an earlier statehood via "denationalization" by a foreign absolutist empire to the "dawn" of the nation, initiated by the national "awakeners" of the nineteenth century. Arguing against the assumed Russophilia of his French audience, Shul'hyn insisted that prerevolutionary Russia had been a repressive and outdated multinational empire. Its breakup, he explained, was best understood in terms of the nationalities' rightful struggle against imperial domination. France and Germany had survived the war by relying on their population's national patriotism, whereas Russia and Austria-Hungary, "states not based on the patriotic spirit of a self-aware nation," had not.[28]

Turning to the history of the Ukrainian national movement, Shul'hyn reproduced a nationalist genealogy that was already widely recognized in the interwar period. Beginning with the writers Kotliarevs'kyi, Gogol', and Shevchenko, he stressed that Shevchenko's lyrical spirit did more for Ukrainian patriotism than the skeptical outlook represented by Gogol'. Via the Cyrillo-Methodians, Antonovych, and Drahomanov, Shul'hyn ended up in the early twentieth century. He praised Hrushevs'kyi and the great organizer Chykalenko, but opposed the old-fashioned patriotism of his uncle Naumenko to the "more ardent nationalism of the younger generation" active in the Revolutionary Ukrainian Party. The triumph of the national movement, to him, was the logical result of a gradually rising national consciousness: "The national idea was too natural to lose, the Ukrainian race too strong in its resistance against the attempts at Russification."[29]

Shul'hyn inscribed his own family into this national genealogy. The complete split between the family's two branches, in his view, was typical of "intellectual or aristocratic families among nations awakening to independence," with many similar cases among Czech or Polish families. For him, the Shul'gins had been a "russified Ukrainian family" before Iakov joined the Ukrainophiles. Similarly, his maternal grandfather Nikolai Ustimovich, a liberal nobleman who spoke Russian and French, had lacked attachment "to the natural elements of the people's national life." By contrast, Oleksander's maternal grandmother, the peasant-born Iefrosyniia Ustymovych, had been "Ukrainian in all the fibers of her being. Emanating from the people, she was profoundly attached to its life, to its habits." Thus, in contrast to the argument that this book has been making, Oleksander Shul'hyn read his parents' Ukrainian nationalism not as a conscious political choice but as a logical return to their true national identity. In the following generation, he wrote, family tradition protected the young from the influence of Russian high culture, keeping them "faithful to the national culture and spirit."[30]

This brief account of the family history mapped neatly onto the teleological scheme of national history, whereby Ukraine's earlier national culture was embodied by the grandmother's peasant lineage, the denationalizing imperial influence was represented by the grandfather and the grand-uncle Vitalii Shul'gin, and the role of national "awakeners" fell to Oleksander's parents. Finally, Oleksander and his siblings were equated with the "more ardent" nationalist generation of the early twentieth century. Shul'hyn thus presented a prehistory of the national revolution in 1917, setting the youngest generation up as its main actors. To some extent, then, the Ukrainian "generation of 1917" was formed retrospectively in the interwar period, in the process of constructing a collective memory of the revolution's events. Texts like Shul'hyn's contributed significantly to the perception of the revolution's actors as a completely nationalized generational cohort.

Moving on to 1917, Shul'hyn emphasized the elation of Petrograd's population among the chaos of the February revolution. The revolution, he admitted, had "truly sublime moments," making people believe in the future and fraternize with strangers, but the bitter disappointment followed soon. "History is brutal. Doubtless this must be so . . . in the moment when one volume of history ends and another one begins, in the moment when great empires fall and the birth of new nations announces itself."[31] In Shul'hyn's view, the revolution's rapid degeneration into anarchy and violence had deep roots in Russian culture. He presented the aftermath of the February revolution and his departure from Petrograd as the fateful moment of his definite break with Russian culture, implicitly moving his pro-independence turn forward by a year:

> One never forgets one's beginnings in life, and my best years are connected to the fog and cold of Petrograd. To be sure, I still recognize the profound qualities of my Russian masters, as well as their literary, artistic, or scientific value. But the more I have advanced in life, the more I have learned to understand the dangerous sides of Russian culture. . . . I do not feel any hatred for Russia, no more than for any other country, but I am nevertheless absolutely convinced that Ukraine's well-being depends on our capacity to create

a certain distance between ourselves and the Russians. . . . We cannot be bound forever to this immense nation, always afflicted by the most contagious illnesses: the spirit of nihilism, of anarchy, slackness, mysticism, the near-complete weakening of the will on which a people depends to live and conquer its place among the other nations of the world. We had to break with this organism which, from one extreme, absolute monarchism, threw itself into the abyss of Bolshevism.[32]

By leaving the capital of the crumbling empire for Kiev, Shul'hyn entered "a new world," where revolutionary disorder was counterbalanced by a newly found mass patriotism: "Like a fire that has long smoldered under the ashes and suddenly takes revenge by flaming up, Ukrainian national feeling appeared suddenly, unexpected, incomprehensible to the foreign observer."[33] Shul'hyn thus paralleled his own emancipation from Russian culture with Ukraine's political emancipation from "Muscovy," representing both as irreversible ruptures.

Shul'hyn formulated a dichotomy between internationalist Russia, where the revolution unleashed anarchy and disorder, and Ukraine, where the national principle guaranteed more constructive results. While the Ukrainians were about to realize their potential as a nation, the Russians could not escape "the brutality of a man that civilization has not yet tamed."[34] The tradition of contrasting allegedly inherent characteristics of the Russian and Ukrainian nations went back at least to the Ukrainophile folklorists of the 1830s.[35] Oleksander Shul'hyn's account, however, denied the Russians even the one positive attribute that Ukrainophiles had traditionally granted them: the capacity for state-building and creating order. Shul'hyn's view of Russia as a source of both chaos and despotism, first uttered in 1918, had hardened into the pathologizing stereotype of a "monster state," "too large to be a country like others," "always ill," and inhabited by people of an irredeemably "imperialist spirit."[36]

By the time Oleksander Shul'hyn was writing, several participants of the Ukrainian revolution had already published works on the revolutionary period. Volodymyr Vynnychenko had brought out his memoirs, and Pavlo Khrystiuk produced a multivolume documentary account. Dmytro Doroshenko had written both a memoir and an academic history of the Ukrainian revolution.[37] While the former two, in accordance with their left-wing politics, criticized the Ukrainian revolutionary leaders for their lack of social radicalism, the more conservative

Doroshenko blamed the Ukrainians' ultimate failure on their inability to build a well-functioning state. A centrist in politics, Oleksander Shul'hyn also assumed a moderate position in his assessment of the Central Rada. Deploring the fact that the Rada's "very advanced social reforms" had alienated the conservatives, he also wrote that it was forced to fulfill the "people's will" and pursue a leftist course during this period of revolutionary agitation.[38]

By focusing on 1917 and ending his account with the Bolshevik attack on Kiev, Shul'hyn evaded a clear judgment on the reasons for the defeat of Ukrainian statehood. Instead, his book concludes with the battle of Kruty in January 1918, the nation's "baptism by fire and blood," as he termed it.[39] Kruty also signified a personal catastrophe for him, namely the death of his brother Volodymyr. Remembering his brother's funeral, Shul'hyn wrote that this painful loss strengthened his emotional attachment to the national cause: "Ernest Renan was right: Mourning and pain bring people closer together than victories. National mourning deepens, even creates a feeling of unity, it reinforces a nation's will. Never perhaps have I felt as profoundly Ukrainian as in this moonlit spring night on the silvery shore of the Dnieper, eternal witness of our suffering, of our history."[40] Once more, Shul'hyn connected his feeling of national belonging directly to the emotional link of kinship, positing the family as an intermediate historical agent between the individual and the nation. That said, Shul'hyn himself remains a flat character in the text. He comes across as an ardently patriotic yet sensibly moderate politician, but we learn rather little about his personal emotions and motivations. The narrative voice is often impersonal, betraying the trained historian and his pretense to objectivity.[41] In a sense, Shul'hyn tried to write the nation's autobiography rather than his own.

Over the following years, the UNR's foreign political orientation remained decisive for Oleksander Shul'hyn's career within the exile government. As the Soviet Union, the UNR's main enemy, concluded a nonaggression treaty with Poland in 1932 and an alliance with France in 1935, Shul'hyn's pro-Entente stance became increasingly untenable. When the UNR leadership tried to move toward a German orientation in 1936, he relinquished his post as foreign minister. Politically isolated within the emigration, Shul'hyn felt betrayed by his former friends.[42] He temporarily quit politics to complete a study about Jean-Jacques Rousseau and his influence on the emergence of modern patriotism. Shul'hyn sympathized with the exiled Genevan philosopher, and when he wrote that "he who has never left his country, who never perceives the painful feeling of nostalgia, does not yet know the true love of his fatherland," he doubtless thought of his own situation, too.[43] When war broke out in 1939, the UNR leadership made Shul'hyn prime minister. After the Nazi invasion of France, he was imprisoned in Paris for half a year. In 1945, as the UNR's almost only consistent pro-Entente leader, Shul'hyn became foreign minister for a last time, but after another conflict with the UNR president, he definitely retreated from politics in 1946.[44] He spent the remainder of his life in Paris, working assiduously for Ukrainian cultural and educational institutions until his death in 1960.[45]

In Shul'hyn's Ukrainian-language childhood and youth memoirs, which he wrote in the 1950s, he foregrounded his family even more than in his 1935 book. In this text, Shul'hyn wanted to show "how step for step we overcame the surroundings, how we arrived at freedom and a steady national consciousness, how the preceding generations . . . changed the very circumstances through their ant-like work."[46] It is here that he completed his portrayal of the family as a shelter for Ukrainian culture under the Ems Ukaz. Perhaps his account was inspired by Rousseau, whose views on "national education" he had quoted approvingly in his 1937 monograph.[47] After several decades of political exile, Shul'hyn's memoirs must have struck a chord with Ukrainian émigré readers. Among widespread fears of "denationalization," they offered hope that patriotic families could cultivate their national heritage in private spaces and save it over a long period of exile. In line with the general picture of family harmony, Shul'hyn even found a few conciliatory words about his Russian nationalist relatives: "My father hated Vitalii [Shul'gin] for his views, and doubtless Vitalii paid him back in kind. Personally, however, beyond their diametrically opposed views, I now think that both of them were noble people and so was Vasyl' [Vasilii Shul'gin] in his own way."[48]

Political Anxieties

Writing was Ekaterina Shul'gina's preferred means to deal with the traumatic loss of two sons in the civil war. She began to write about her eldest son Vasilid immediately after his death in 1918 and continued even when living underground in Bolshevik Odessa.[49] In January 1922, she managed to flee Soviet Ukraine with the help of a young relative and a group of Jewish smugglers. When she made it to her Kurgany estate and was safe on the Polish side of the border, writing remained her central occupation. The Russian State Archive has preserved several notebooks that she filled in this period. They constitute a kind of introspective diary, replete with stream-of-consciousness-like invocations of her lost sons Vasilid and Veniamin, as well as desperate declarations of her love for Russia.[50]

In April 1922, Shul'gina moved to Prague, where she began to write more coherent autobiographical fragments. In 1924, she combined her sketches into a full-length memoir of the revolutionary and civil war period. A manuscript of over eight hundred pages, Shul'gina's memoir covers the period from her first initiation to politics to her successful escape from Soviet Odessa. Shul'gina probably never planned to publish her text in its entirety.[51] In her own opinion, the text was too intimate for publication during her lifetime. Immediately after finishing her draft, she sold the manuscript to the Prague Archive of the Russian emigration, which collected émigrés' memoirs of the revolutionary and civil war period. In his expertise for the archive, the historian Aleksandr Kizevetter found the text too focused on Shul'gina's personal and family life but nevertheless recommended it for purchase.[52]

In fact, the personal and the political were intimately connected for Shul'gina. In her text, whose title can be translated either as "Outline of My Political Experience" or as "Compendium of My Political Anxieties," Shul'gina paralleled her own political development with that of Russia as a whole. Her account starts in 1904–1905 with the appearance of the rift between a revolutionary, antinational intelligentsia and its counterrevolutionary, national opponents. The problem, Shul'gina wrote, was that the latter force mostly consisted of uneducated peasants, while "nationally thinking people" were scarce. She then went on to portray her father-in-law Dmitrii Pikhno as an idealized version of such a nationally thinking person, a "true representative of Russian democracy" with roots in the peasantry, whose worldview Ekaterina came to admire as she discovered her patriotism during the Russo-Japanese War. For Pikhno, she wrote, "every personal matter coincided with a public one and provoked an influx of energy."[53] This coincidence of (auto-)biography and national history frames the entire narrative structure of Shul'gina's memoir, from the initiation moment of 1904–1905, via the steady growth of the Duma years, to the culmination of 1917 and the civil war catastrophe.

To Shul'gina, the period following the 1905 revolution was a time of harmony in the family and of productive societal work in the state: "In his [Pikhno's] large family, there was not the smallest disagreement—he was the captain on a loyal boat, everyone assembled around him as a beloved leader." The tragedy of the Duma period, in Shul'gina's interpretation, lay in the mutual misunderstanding between the Kadets and Stolypin's followers. In her view, both sides were politically closer to each other than they believed, separated mostly by their attitude toward the monarchy. Furthermore, she stressed a geographical factor, noting that Stolypin had most support in Kiev, whereas the Kadets were a Moscow-Petersburg party.[54] This period ended in Shul'gina's account with the almost parallel catastrophes of Stolypin's death in 1911 and Dmitrii Pikhno's in the summer of 1913: "Stolypin was the last Russian ruler. After his death, Russia remained rudderless." Similarly, Pikhno's death left the family without its helmsman: "With the death of Dmitrii Ivanovich [Pikhno], our youth came to its end. . . . All worries and strains now fell onto us."[55] Fittingly, Shul'gina then moved on to describe two major political crises, first the local dispute over the Beilis affair, then the outbreak of the First World War in the following year.

The narrative climax of the memoirs, however, is the year 1917, when, for a couple of months, Ekaterina Shul'gina became a political activist in her own right. "Looking back now, I clearly see that all of us, in particular V.V. [Vasilii Shul'gin] and I, were dragged headlong into the revolutionary whirlwind," she wrote in 1923.[56] The metaphor of the "revolutionary whirlwind" is conventional and yet telling. In Shul'gina's retrospective interpretation, she had not striven for political agency but had been compelled to act by circumstances that drew her in like a force of nature. Shul'gina acknowledged that she and her husband were bound to the revolution, "entangled through some kind of threads and nerves," and the memoirs show that she took pride in the political and rhetorical skills that allowed her to play a central part in her group's electoral successes.[57] However, in the knowledge of the revolution's drastic consequences for state and family, she presented her political adventure as a path into tragedy. "I would never have chosen this type of occupation. . . . I ended up as a 'politician' and as a 'journalist' due to some conspiracy prepared by my fate."[58]

Thus, Shul'gina's "Compendium" was also a conservative woman's reflection on women's place in politics and in the national community. She emphasized that she could only become politically active by hiding her "female nature," her "female mask," as she also called it in an odd terminological reversal. Her pseudonym Aleksei Ezhov appears as a person completely different from herself: "Thinking as a male person,

I completely threw off everything specifically feminine. . . . It was almost a reincarnation."[59] Shul'gina's path into disaster, as she saw it in retrospect, began when she simultaneously transcended her unconditional monarchist loyalties and her traditional gender role. As she repeatedly wrote, she only engaged in politics for want of suitable men and stepped aside as soon as her husband returned to Kiev. While she did not categorically exclude women's participation in electoral politics, she played down her own scope of action.[60]

Covering the period from the end of 1917 to the civil war, Shul'gina presented herself first as an increasingly passive observer and then as a victim of the revolution. The victimhood narrative dominates the second part of her memoirs, beginning with the death of her eldest son Vasilid in the defense of Kiev against Petliura's troops: "The blow that I received on 1 December 1918 turned me into a cripple. It cut me off from the future; it destroyed my continuation on earth."[61] The text then narrates the disasters that befell Shul'gina and her family over the following three years: material poverty, heavy illness, the death of relatives and friends, her own arrest and imprisonment by the Odessa Cheka, and the disappearance of her second son Veniamin. The importance of this story, Shul'gina explained, was in the fact that her lost sons were "types of those Russian boys of this terrible period whose youthful chests took the shattering blow aimed at Russia."[62]

Shul'gina tried to bestow meaning on her loss by inscribing it into a larger tragedy of historical significance. Her memoirs draw a parallel between the loss of her family and the loss of Russia's prerevolutionary society and imperial state—a polity in which she was emotionally invested. The text bears the marks of a self-therapeutic effort to deal with her strong feelings of guilt for having "destroyed" her own family.[63] This guilt, in her mind, was linked to the transgression she believed herself to have committed by entering the masculine sphere of political activism. In one of her many letters to her surviving son Dmitrii, Shul'gina wrote that her alter ego Aleksei Ezhov, "a being with an almost masculine psychology," had alienated her from her family and deprived her sons of their mother.[64] Rejecting politics, she tried to adopt one of the historical roles that nationalist ideology foresaw for women: that of the suffering mother who willingly sacrifices her sons to the national cause. As she wrote in one of her early sketches, "Only for Her [Russia] I gave birth to my boys, in order to have something to give away, in order not to come with empty hands, in order to be able . . . to sacrifice to Her and for Her my blood and my flesh."[65] In a letter she even described her sons as "martyrs" who had "redeemed and washed their homeland with their blood."[66] The religiously tinged language betrays Shul'gina's wish to sacralize the nationalist cause for which her family had fought and died.

For while Shul'gina regretted her involvement in politics, she hardly questioned her nationalist ideology. She still read the civil war as a struggle between the Whites' national and the Reds' antinational dictatorship—the latter allegedly led by hateful Jews. She also had a simple explanation for Ukraine's failure to achieve lasting statehood, in contrast to Finland and the Baltic states: "because there is no separate Ukrainian nation, there is the Russian nation in its three branches." The successes of Ukrainian nationalism in the revolutionary period, Shul'gina explained, were only due to the "provincialism" of the rural "half-intelligentsia," who felt that they could play a much larger role in Ukrainian culture than in Russian culture.[67]

Still, Shul'gina admitted that the peasantry was perhaps less dedicated to Russian nationalism than she had once thought. With the wisdom of hindsight, it seemed to her that peasants had joined the Union of the Russian People mostly because they hoped that the tsar would reward them with land, just as they later understood the Ukrainian Republic as a "union" (*spilka*) for land distribution: "So they perceived 'Ukraine' and the 'Union of the Russian People' on the same level." In retrospect, then, even this committed nationalist suspected Ukraine's peasants of being a nationally indifferent mob driven by economic imperatives. While she questioned the national consciousness of the masses, however, she could not doubt their Russian national essence. To say that Ukraine's peasants were not Russians would have shattered the very foundations of her worldview: "For, if the Ukrainians are not renegades of the Russian nation, then we are renegades of the Ukrainian nation."[68]

In 1925, Shul'gina moved to Paris, having deposited all her manuscripts at the Prague Archive. In France, she worked as governess in a friend's family and occasionally contributed to the émigré press.[69] Her surviving letters from the period suggest that she never recovered from the trauma of losing two sons. Despite regular contact with her family and in-laws, Shul'gina was a lonely woman. In October 1923, she and her husband had got a divorce, many years after their factual separation. "At bottom, this has hardly changed our relations," Vasilii Shul'gin wrote to his ex-wife. "What has remained, will remain anyway. What has gone, has gone."[70] For Ekaterina, however, the divorce and her ex-husband's second marriage to the young Mariia Sedel'nikova appear to have aggravated her feeling of isolation.

In 1932, Shul'gina finally received a visa for Yugoslavia, where most of her remaining family was living at this point.[71] The young Yugoslav state was fairly open to White Russian émigrés, hiring many of them as professional, academic, and military cadres.[72] Shul'gina's widowed brother-in-law Aleksandr Bilimovich was a professor of economics at the University of Ljubljana. Her son Dmitrii had married the Bilimoviches' daughter Tat'iana (his first cousin) and studied road engineering in Ljubljana. Ekaterina's former husband Vasilii Shul'gin and her sister-in-law Lina Mogilevskaia were also in Yugoslavia. Ekaterina Shul'gina settled first in Ljubljana and then in Belgrade with Lina Mogilevskaia. Two years later, in April 1934, Lina alerted the Belgrade city council to the disappearance of her sister-in-law. After a few days, Ekaterina Shul'gina's dead body was found in Pančevo, near Belgrade. She had drowned herself in the Danube. Lina Mogilevskaia remained in Belgrade until 1945, when, eighty years old, she, too, committed suicide for unknown reasons.[73]

Who Is to Blame?

The family's tragedies of the civil war were no less traumatic for Vasilii Shul'gin than for his wife. In 1921, he identified loss as the defining condition of the Russian emigration: "All of us have some most heavy sorrow—sons lost in battle, fathers or mothers shot by the Cheka, husbands vanished without a trace, close ones carried away by epidemics."[74] Stranded in Constantinople with thousands of other Russian émigrés, Shul'gin set his hopes on General Vrangel', the leader of the Volunteer Army who had evacuated his troops from Crimea to Gallipoli near Constantinople. Only if the emigration was united around this leader, he believed, did it have a chance of ever returning to the lost homeland.[75] Although Shul'gin briefly took part in an abortive attempt to form an émigré government led by Vrangel', he no longer engaged in party politics. Unlike other prerevolutionary parties, the Russian Nationalists never established an exile organization. Neither did Shul'gin want to head a monarchist group, since many right-wingers still resented his role in the tsar's abdication.[76]

In 1921, Shul'gin traveled from Constantinople to Bulgaria. From there, he attempted to reach Crimea by boat in order to find his son Veniamin and his brother Dmitrii. Shul'gin made it to the Crimean shore but had to return without results, and later learned that his brother was already dead.[77] In the spring of 1922 he traveled on to Prague, and at the end of the same year moved to Berlin. Finally, in the autumn of 1923, he made it to Paris. Shul'gin's itinerary over these years—from Constantinople via the Balkans and Central Europe to France—was a typical geographical trajectory of the White Russian emigration.[78]

In material terms, Vasilii Shul'gin continued to live off his own and his family's past. After a few months of poverty, he found two sources of income. His Volhynian estate at Kurgany, bought by Dmitrii Pikhno in 1905, had narrowly ended up on the Polish side of the Soviet-Polish border after the Treaty of Riga, as had Lina Mogilevskaia's estate. The long-term failure of Pikhno's economic Russification plan, ironically, saved the estates from confiscation by the communists. This allowed the Shul'gins to lease them to a Polish-Catholic in-law, Wacław Kamiński. When the Kurgany mill began to make profits, Kamiński paid Shul'gin half of its income, amounting to over 1,000 US dollars per year—enough to survive in France and later to finance a good life in Yugoslavia.[79] Shul'gin's second source of income was writing. Throughout the 1920s, he contributed political feuilletons to the Russian émigré press. He also began to publish his memoirs, earning a meager additional income of about 250 dollars per year.[80]

Like his wife Ekaterina, Vasilii Shul'gin had taken up autobiographical writing after a loss. Immediately after the death of his lover Liubov' Popova in November 1918, he began to process his grief in a diary, integrating reflections on happier times he had spent with her. After his flight abroad, he initiated a more systematic autobiographical project. Shul'gin's first two memoirs treated the seminal years 1905, 1917, and 1920: *The Year 1920* and *The Days* were first serialized in Petr Struve's journal *Russkaia mysl'* in 1921 and 1922–1923, respectively.[81] Shul'gin's plan was to continue the memoir work on two more levels. One memoir was to cover the entire State Duma period and the remaining bits of the civil war, while the other one was meant to describe his private life.[82] To some extent, he fulfilled his plan, producing two more volumes on the civil war period, but neither of them was published during the interwar period. He also continued to write the multivolume memoir *War without Peace*. Covering the entire period between 1914 and 1918, this text centered on Shul'gin's tragic relationship with Liubov' Popova and was not meant to be published during his own or his son's lifetime.[83]

The revolution and the collapse of the tsarist state stood at the heart of Shul'gin's memoirs. The one issue that animated all of these texts, and even much of his private correspondence, was the Herzenian question "Who is to Blame?" Unlike his ex-wife, Shul'gin made no attempt at a teleological, bildungsroman-like interpretation of his own trajectory. Instead, following the conventions of (male) political memoirs, he presented himself as a somewhat detached protagonist and an ironical, often polemical observer of important events. Deriving interpretative authority from personal experience, Shul'gin's memoirs were political-historical pamphlets, an attempt to inscribe his own memories and opinions into the historical record.[84] As he wrote in a letter, he was "writing for posterity, in order to preserve the past, for I am horrified when I see how fast everything, even very recent experiences, evaporates from human memory and consciousness."[85] A different letter of the period stated Shul'gin's didactic intention even more explicitly: "I am writing all kinds of memoirs, so that our descendants will not repeat the stupidities that we have committed."[86]

Shul'gin's first autobiographical volume treated the most recent past. Written in 1921, it traced Shul'gin's and the Volunteer Army's path into military defeat and emigration. Shul'gin advanced a moral explanation for the catastrophe of the year 1920. According to him, the Whites defended high ideals. They were supposed to be honest, chivalrous, just, polite, religious, and patriotic, abhorring needless cruelty, looting, excess, and class hatred. However, he went on to describe what he had witnessed during the campaigns of 1920: irregular army units replacing official regiments, officers looting the civilian population, soldiers persecuting innocent Jews, officers self-administering justice instead of handing perpetrators over to court-martials. The Whites had become "gray and dirty." This brutalization through the conditions of the civil war, for Shul'gin, was the reason for the defeat of the Volunteer Army. By losing their moral superiority over the Bolsheviks, the Whites had forfeited their right to victory.[87]

Despite long passages detailing Shul'gin's adventurous escapes from the Bolsheviks, the volume offered little by way of consolation or heroic narrative. Covering a period when the Whites were already losing the civil war, it told their story in elegiac tone as the hopeless cause of "former people." Yet, it closed on a twistedly optimistic note. Over years of fighting, Shul'gin claimed, the Red Army had adopted both the Whites' original discipline and its goal of a united, indivisible Russia. Soon, the Bolsheviks would come around to the autocratic form of government: "The White Idea will win in any case."[88] The book made an immediate impression on the Russian emigration. For some, as for Shul'gin's sister Lina, his merciless account of the White defeat was very painful reading.[89] Shul'gin's critical tone appealed to his Soviet enemies, and already in 1922, his book was republished in Moscow. Apparently, the Soviet censors interpreted it as a deconstruction of the White movement by its own ideologue.

Shul'gin's second memoir, *The Days*, took a more long-term perspective, focusing on the decisive historical moments of the October days in 1905 and of the February revolution. The chronology of this book posits a direct continuity from 1905 to 1917 and portrays the history of Russian constitutionalism as a path into chaos and destruction. The book begins with Shul'gin's account of the demonstration in Kiev on 18 October 1905 and the ensuing antisemitic pogrom, then moves directly to November 1916 and the February revolution. The book's structure is thus defined by the retrospective knowledge of the revolution, leaving little room for a positive assessment of the semiconstitutional experiment: "There you have the 'Russian constitution.' . . . It began with a Jewish pogrom and ended in the destruction of the dynasty." Shul'gin insisted that this outcome was foreseeable, praising his father Dmitrii Pikhno as one of "the few people who, from the Alpha (1905), directly determined the Omega (1917) of the Russian revolution."[90]

What connects 1905 and 1917 in Shul'gin's narrative is an extremely negative portrayal of the masses. By rising in revolution during the Japanese war, Shul'gin wrote, the population had betrayed Russia: "We hated this kind of people and laughed at their despicable rage." At the sight of the protesting masses during the Feburary revolution, he continued, "the old hatred, the hatred of the year 1905, flowed into my head." In his descriptions of a blindly violent mass of "neobarbarians" or "Scythians," Shul'gin hardly differentiated between revolutionary demonstrations and the counterrevolutionary pogroms of October 1905. Casting aside his semi-democratic views of the war period, he claimed to have understood "that only the language of machine guns was comprehensible to the street mob and that only lead could chase the unleashed wild beast back into its den. . . . Alas, this wild beast was . . . His Majesty, the Russian people!"[91] It is the contemptuous tone in passages like these that led Shul'gin's critic, the Soviet journalist David Zaslavskii, to describe him as "a nobleman, an aristocrat, a white-handed intellectual among the Black Hundreds."[92]

The decisive difference between 1905 and 1917, in Shul'gin's view, was that military officers and patriots still understood the tsar in 1905, whereas nobody cared to save the autocracy anymore twelve years later.

His disdain for the masses went along with a biting critique of the empire's elites: the incapable ministers of the last tsarist cabinets—"really good for nothing"—but equally the Russian intelligentsia. The latter, in Shul'gin's view, had neglected practical and material progress in their starry-eyed utopianism: "It was much more fun to create 'world' literature, transcendental ballet, and anarchist theories."[93] Shul'gin repeatedly complained about the "atrophied will" of the ruling class, which he believed to result from the "extreme degeneration of the Russian intelligentsia."[94] Writing to his friend, the former Kadet politician Vasilii Maklakov, he expressed the hope that the brutal experience of the civil war period would harden the "effeminate" educated elites.[95] There are echoes of fin-de-siècle biologism and degeneration theory in Shul'gin's concern about the elite's lack of willpower and "neurasthenia." It is also conceivable that these fears had deeper psychological roots linked to his family's problematic intimate life.[96]

At the same time, Shul'gin continued to single out Russia's Jewish population as the prime culprits of the Bolshevik revolution. He made his most comprehensive statement on the Jewish theme in 1929. When the Jewish émigré journalist Solomon Poliakov called on "honest antisemites" to explain their views, Shul'gin wrote a three-hundred-page pamphlet titled *What We Do Not Like about Them*. According to the pamphlet, the obsessive desire of Russia's Jews to achieve equal rights had made them a destructive element in Russian society. They had fueled the 1899 student protests, the defeatist demonstrations of 1905, the press campaigns against the autocracy, and the February revolution. This tendency, in Shul'gin's view, had culminated in the Bolshevik party, which he understood as a tool for Jewish interests: "Not all Jews are communists; not all communists are Jews; but the influence of Jews in the Communist Party is inversely proportional to their number in Russia." Jews were the "backbone" and "brain" of the Communist Party and thus the main culprits of what Shul'gin called a "Russian pogrom." Like parents for their children, all Jews bore a collective ethnic responsibility for the destructive force and hatred against Russia that that their nationality had allegedly brought forth.[97] Shul'gin's pamphlet followed a line of argumentation that he had developed ten years earlier; beyond that, it bore a clear resemblance to Dmitrii Pikhno's comments on Jewish participation in the revolution of 1905.[98]

Shul'gin's conviction that a Jewish minority was capable of holding sway over the much larger Russian population was directly linked to his highly pessimistic view of the Russians themselves. Shul'gin dealt in absolutes, opposing the Jews' essential national strength to what he called the Russians' "'anyhowness' [koe-kakstvo], i.e. negligence, inaccuracy, carelessness."[99] The Jews were "bees," strong-willed, hardworking, and distinguished by a unique instinctive ethnic solidarity; the Russians were "bulls," an obedient herd in need of a strong leader. Therefore, the national struggle between Russians and Jews was inevitable: the former would always try to build a state based on strong leadership; the latter would always seek to destroy it. However, Shul'gin explained, Bolshevism had only become possible because it spoke to the darkest traits of the Russian national character, too: "Bolshevism, the child of *Asiatic immoderacy* is within all of us Russians to some degree or other."[100] Thus, in Shul'gin's view, Bolshevism was a symptom of both the Russians' and the Jews' inherent shortcomings. In an unpublished article he wrote in 1925, Shul'gin even reduced the entire revolution to a "clash of three races: the diseased Russian one, . . . the active German one, which insisted on advancing to the east and driving out the lazy and feminine Slavic race from the world's most fertile plain and, finally, the Jewish one, which was ripe for a gigantic predatory leap onto the spine of a nation sickened by the fight."[101]

Who, then, was to blame for the revolution after all? Shul'gin gave a summary answer in his private notes. The main cause, he wrote, was the great war against Germany, caused by the Germans' imperialism and their allegedly Nietzschean philosophy of rule by force. However, he also named several minor reasons: the unsuccessful war against Japan in 1904–1905, the peasants' destructive obsession with land redistribution, the intelligentsia's and the nationalities' "unnatural fury" against a benevolent and reforming state, the Jews' exaggerated anger about their limited rights, and, not least, the absence of a stronger tsar.[102] However, these explanations should not be seen as Shul'gin's definite judgment. In his countless writings of the interwar period, he never ceased to meditate on the revolution's causes, stressing different factors at various times. Shul'gin's manner of thought was too unsystematic and associative to produce a logically consistent explanatory scheme for the empire's collapse. What is characteristic, however, is that he always blamed the revolution on external factors and the autocracy's opponents. Although Shul'gin flirted with more modern political systems (both constitutional monarchy and fascism), he never considered the possibility that the autocracy itself was to blame for its inability to introduce effective reforms.

Strikingly, Shul'gin's memoirs of the 1920s accorded little attention to the Ukrainian issue. He treated Ukrainian nationalism as an

epiphenomenon, never as a cause of the revolution. Despite the existence of a significant Ukrainian presence in emigration, Shul'gin still
insisted that the Ukrainian national movement lacked any broad support and was a foreign invention—either German, Austrian, Polish, or
even Swedish—to split the Russian nation.[103] Perhaps, having discredited the Ukrainian nationalists as an insignificant political sect for
many years, Shul'gin thought it inappropriate to accord them pride of
place as a major factor in the empire's downfall.

While Oleksander Shul'hyn used the family's history as backdrop for
his account of national history, Vasilii Shul'gin hardly cared to confront
the split within his wider family. In 1929, however, Maklakov asked
Shul'gin about his Ukrainian namesake, motivating him to explain
the family history. For Vasilii, Iakov Shul'gin had been an "ungrateful
adoptee" who left his uncle's house to join a group of heretics: "Thus,
in the completely Russian or Little Russian Shul'gin family, . . . a first
apostate appeared—'Iasha the Turncoat.'" Led into ruin by his greedy
revolutionary friends, the "bad Ukrainian and bad revolutionary" Iakov
later established the family's Ukrainized branch. The family's bifurcation proved that the Ukrainian question was not a conflict between two
nationalities but an "internal quarrel" between those in the Southwest
of Russia who wanted to keep their Russian nationality and those who
wished to relinquish it.[104] Thus, Vasilii Shul'gin's interpretation of the
family history was diametrically opposed to Oleksander Shul'hyn's. If
Oleksander portrayed Iakov's turn to Ukrainophilism as a (re)discovery
of his true national essence, Vasilii described it with religious connotations as a denial of his roots and his family. The worldviews of Russian
and Ukrainian nationalists—similar in certain ways but irreconcilable
in the core issue—were long beyond the point where compromise was
possible.

By this time, Shul'gin was no longer the influential émigré publicist
he had been in the early 1920s. His reputation had suffered greatly
from the affair surrounding a sensational trip he had made to the Soviet Union in 1925-1926. Still hoping to find his lost son Veniamin,
Shul'gin had agreed to a proposal from a group of people he believed to
be members of a secret anti-Soviet underground. He crossed the Soviet
border illegally and spent three months in Kiev, Moscow, and Leningrad. After his return, Shul'gin published the book *Three Capitals*, in
which he enthusiastically described a reawakening Russian population
that hated its Bolshevik rulers and was preparing to overthrow them.
The New Economic Policy, he believed, was beginning to undermine

communist society. Luxury consumption and class differentiations were reappearing, and antisemitism was on the rise among the Russian majority. Shul'gin was relieved that he hardly heard any Ukrainian spoken in Kiev and complained about the many Jews he encountered in Moscow. Overall, he found, Russia had changed less than most émigrés thought: "Everything is as it used to be, just worse." If he had formerly set his hopes on the emigration, Shul'gin now believed that the inhabitants of Soviet Russia would soon free themselves.[105]

However, only months after the publication of his book, Shul'gin learned that he had been the victim of a Soviet counterintelligence operation. His entire trip had been organized and monitored by agents of the Soviet intelligence agency GPU. They had fed him information he wanted to hear, and even proofread the manuscript of his book.[106] Having exposed himself to the emigration's mockery and criticism, Shul'gin decided to follow "the very wise political habit . . . of going into retirement after a 'failure' . . . at least temporarily."[107] He and his second wife Mariia spent the following three years in Southern France, then moved to Yugoslavia, where they ultimately settled down in Sremski Karlovci north of Belgrade. There, Vasilii Shul'gin largely abstained from political work, although he did give some lectures for an organization of far-right anti-Soviet youth, the National Labor Alliance of the New Generation.[108] Isolated from emigration circles and bored by his work in a construction company, Shul'gin felt rather lonely. As he wrote to his ex-wife, "I am a stranger to the Russian emigration, for I cannot share its malignity, and I am a stranger to the nations among which I must live, because I am too old to find a 'second fatherland.'"[109]

When the Second World War broke out, Vasilii Shul'gin was sixty-one. He remained in Sremski Karlovci during the occupation by the fascist Croatian Ustaša state, neither collaborating with the occupiers nor opposing them. When the Red Army took the city in October 1944, the Soviet military counterintelligence agency SMERSH arrested Shul'gin and brought him to Moscow. He was imprisoned in the Lubianka and, after lengthy interrogations, convicted and sentenced to twenty-five years of prison. He spent nine years incarcerated in the Central Russian city of Vladimir, alongside German generals and other former White émigrés. Owing to Nikita Khrushchev's "Thaw," Shul'gin was released in 1956 and allowed to live in Vladimir. In old age, he achieved a certain fame within the Soviet Union, especially after appearing in the 1965 film *Pered sudom istorii* (*Facing the Judgment of History*), which was loosely based on his memoirs. Artists and dissidents like Aleksandr

Solzhenitsyn or Mstislav Rostropovich traveled to Vladimir to meet a living fossil of the imperial period. Shul'gin died in 1976 at the age of ninety-eight.[110]

Over all these years, autobiographical writing remained Shul'gin's most important occupation. In prison, he filled thousands of handwritten pages with rambling recollections of his youth in rural Volhynia.[111] Once he was released from prison, Shul'gin continued to dictate memoirs to various acquaintances. His late accounts of political events, compiled at a time when he believed his unpublished interwar works to be lost, are often strikingly close to the earlier versions, developing similar narratives and chains of association.[112] This suggests that Shul'gin's intense autobiographical reflection more or less fixed his memories and interpretations already in the 1920s. Living in the Soviet Union, of course, Shul'gin had to scale down his antisemitic and anti-Ukrainian rhetoric. Yet, despite a certain willingness to compromise with the Soviet authorities, his late memoirs give one the impression that he stuck to the worldview that he had formed at the turn of the century under his father's influence.[113]

Like many Ukrainian and Russian political émigrés in the interwar period, the surviving members of the Shul'gin/Shul'hyn family lived off their past in a double sense. Economically, they depended on incomes related to their earlier biographies, whether in the form of royalties from the publication of memoirs, rent for estates bought before the revolution, or salaries for jobs at émigré institutions. Psychologically, they continued to understand their own place in society in relation to the values and categories of the pre-emigration period. Many émigrés used autobiographical writing to reflect on their political choices and their country's fate, allowing them to inscribe their personal experiences into national histories. Most memoirists saw the years of revolution and civil war as the culmination of their own lives and of their nation's recent history, a moment when earlier experiences converged in an enormous upheaval that, in turn, defined all that was to follow.

All three protagonists of this chapter downplayed their personal agency in their memoirs, subsuming it under much more significant historical processes. Ekaterina Shul'gina felt that by engaging in politics, she had unduly transgressed the feminine sphere and contributed to her family's misfortune. Her memoirs became an attempt to reinterpret her role as that of a patriotic mother who sacrificed her beloved sons to the nation. Neither was Vasilii Shul'gin too keen on stressing his own role in the empire's downfall. Instead, he distilled in his memoirs a series of explanations for the revolution, several of which were based in the purported essential shortcomings of the Russian and Jewish ethnicities. While he harshly criticized the imperial elites all the way up to the tsar himself, Shul'gin remained steadfast in his belief that autocracy was the most suitable system to govern Russia. Finally, for Oleksander Shul'hyn, his own trajectory symbolized the Ukrainian nation's "reawakening" to independence. Just as he himself had broken free from Russia's seductive but harmful culture, Ukraine as a whole had (temporarily) shed the oppressive tutelage of its powerful neighbor. Ukrainians' national sentiment and healthy individualism—embodied in Shul'hyn's family—had allegedly protected them from the inherently Russian sins of anarchism and barbarism until the Bolsheviks brought them back into Ukraine.

Oleksander Shul'hyn's account of a Ukrainian nation that had emancipated itself from Russia was, of course, a one-sided nationalist interpretation of recent history. However, with respect to the Ukrainian political emigration, there was some truth to it. Severed from the Russian state, the Ukrainian émigrés, for the first time, created a purely Ukrainophone public sphere. For all their political differences and quarrels, they now socialized and debated almost exclusively with people who shared the premise of Ukrainian independence. In turn, Russian nationalist émigrés—even those who, like the Shul'gins, came from "Little Russia"—were less interested in the Ukrainian question than previously. Perceiving it as a minor factor in the national catastrophe, they tended to ignore their Ukrainian rivals in emigration.

The autobiographical practices of nationalist émigrés contributed decisively to this separation. The Russian and Ukrainian emigration constituted themselves as separate milieus not least on the basis of diverging collective memories regarding the revolutionary period. Both literally and figuratively, Ukrainian and Russian nationalists of the interwar period spoke different languages. The emergence of separate Russian and Ukrainian cultural-political spheres forced émigrés to make a choice for one camp or the other. Russia and much of Ukraine remained united under Soviet rule, but in the interwar emigration, the Ukrainian and the Russian paths were no longer intertwined.

Conclusion

On 19 February 2016, Kyiv's mayor Vitalii Klichko promulgated a decree renaming a street in the city's outlying Sviatoshyn district—hitherto named after a Soviet army commander—in honor of Volodymyr Shul'hyn.[1] The South Ukrainian city of Kropyvnyts'kyi, the former Elisavetgrad, where the Shul'hyns lived for a few years in the 1890s, has had a Shul'hyn Family Street since 2015.[2] And although Oleksander Shul'hyn is much less famous than other politicians of his generation, Ukrainian historians and media occasionally remember him as the "founder" or "father of Ukrainian diplomacy."[3] As independent Ukraine engages in "decommunization" and nationalizing memory politics, the Ukrainian Shul'hyns have entered the country's national-historical pantheon as minor deities.

Understandably, the Ukrainian state has little interest in memorializing the other, self-defined Russian, half of the family. One of them, Vasilii Shul'gin, has become a well-known historical figure in Russia, where his role in the revolution and civil war is remembered by history buffs and professional historians alike.[4] Shul'gin's popularity has been greatly enhanced by his cultural legacy: his colorful memoirs, several volumes of which have recently been (re)published, and his charming performance in the 1965 Soviet film *Facing the Judgment of History*. His complex biography and ambiguous personality—the monarchist who attended the monarch's abdication, the demagogue who scorned mass politics, the antisemite who defended the Jew Beilis—continue to fascinate readers. To date, nobody has seriously tried to promote Shul'gin's rather incoherent ideas as a fitting ideological program for Russian nationalism in the twenty-first century, even though eerie echoes of his writings can be heard in the pseudo-historical arguments used by Vladimir Putin and his minions to justify their war against Ukraine.[5]

Historical memory of the Shul'gin/Shul'hyn family, then, is as divided as the family itself. Still, the family's history is full of reminders that the clear-cut separation between Ukrainian and Russian nationhood is a relatively recent phenomenon. When Iakiv Shul'ha first moved to Kiev around 1830, one could easily be a Ukrainian (Little Russian) and a Russian at the same time. When his son Vitalii Shul'gin evoked a "Russian, Russian, Russian" Kiev, this did not exclude a strong consciousness of the region's peculiarities that set it apart from Central Russia. While Vitalii's nephew Iakov Shul'gin rubbed shoulders with Kiev's Ukrainophile milieu, he simultaneously served the Russian imperial state. And even though Iakov's children were socialized as Ukrainian patriots, they still received an education from Russian-language institutions and might well have found a place in imperial society, had not the revolution of 1917 offered an opportunity for separate Ukrainian statehood.

And yet, entangled and multilayered loyalties gradually gave way to ideas of unambiguous national identity, either Russian or Ukrainian. To understand this bifurcation of the Kiev intelligentsia, one needs to reverse a common assumption about the nature of nationalism. According to this assumption, which Jeremy King has termed "ethnicism," nationalism arises when people become conscious of their ethnicity and begin to politicize it. King criticizes "ethnicism" as a tautological genealogy, "an attempt to explain who joined which national movement. When an individual became national in a German sense, that was because he or she belonged to the German ethnic group."[6] Against ethnicism, this book argues that nationalism among nineteenth-century Kiev intellectuals was a conscious choice of path, one conditioned by their socioeconomic backgrounds and by the political projects that they embraced: state-sponsored modernization and imperial autocracy in Dmitrii Pikhno's case, peasant-oriented Ukrainophile socialism in Iakov Shul'gin's. Only subsequently did these activists self-fashion themselves into members of their chosen national-cultural communities.

In the long term, choices of path created path dependencies. The children of nationalists grew up in households that conveyed a clear sense of national belonging, an idea of (monarchist, conservative) Russianness or of (oppositional, populist) Ukrainianness. As the conservative Little Russian and the Ukrainophile milieu grew apart and solidified into unambiguously nationalist political camps, it became less likely for members of the young generation to choose a different national affiliation. This does not mean that the transfer of national self-identification from one generation to another was free of conflict. Some children of activists were indifferent to their parents' national politics; others contested or radicalized their visions of the nation. Even such a dedicated Ukrainian nationalist as Oleksander Shul'hyn only finalized his self-Ukrainization in the interwar period, using autobiographical writing to purge vestiges of his attachment to Russian culture. By the early twentieth century, however, national belongings in the Kiev intelligentsia were clearly less fluid and flexible than they had been a few decades earlier.

In a somewhat schematic way, the Ukrainian-Russian divergence among Kiev's patriotic intelligentsia may be periodized into five phases. The middle of the nineteenth century was characterized by the emergence of separate Ukrainophile and pro-imperial Little Russian discourses, each with their own cultural assumptions and political legitimation strategies. The decades after the Ems Ukaz of 1876 saw two separate milieus emerge, as activists gathered in private among their ideological peers. In the semiconstitutional post-1905 decade, separate Ukrainian and Russian nationalist newspapers, clubs, cultural associations, and, to some extent, political parties were established—but debates and disputes between the two camps continued. During the revolution and civil war, the Ukrainian-Russian conflict was militarized as each side acquired concrete state-building projects and military formations. Finally, the interwar emigration saw the rise of distinct Ukrainian and Russian public spheres that tended to ignore one another, while exchange and interaction continued in Soviet Ukraine itself. Throughout these phases, each camp's ideology evolved relatively slowly, whereas practices were radically transformed in a changing legal-political environment.[7]

During the first phase, and on occasion until much later, Ukrainophile and pro-imperial Little Russian activists engaged in a negotiation process, trying to find common ground between their respective visions of the national community. Since their projects targeted the same peasant population, their short-term goals often coincided. In the long run, however, their objectives were too different to permit a stable agreement. The conservative Little Russians wanted to use the state to strengthen the economic and social position of the local Orthodox peasantry. Education was to assimilate the peasants to Russian culture, which, in turn, would reinforce state power in the region. Meanwhile, the Ukrainophiles wanted to strengthen the peasantry by accommodating local cultural peculiarities; therefore, the imperial state needed to be federalized and democratized. Neither side was truly prepared to compromise, and particularly the Little Russians did not hesitate to use against their opponents the political leverage that their affinity with the state ideology gave them.

Thus, the diverging relationship with Russia's imperial state was the pivotal difference between Russian and Ukrainian nationalists. Imperial loyalty and Russian nationalism enabled Little Russians such as Dmitrii Pikhno to climb the social ladder while assimilating into Russian elite culture. Unlike the elites of other peripheral regions, they were automatically accepted as Russians in the national sense if they supported the imperial project. Ukrainophiles like Iakov Shul'gin, by contrast, were highly critical of the state and could become subject to repression. Fully aware that the police were watching them, they tried to exploit gray areas in the legislation. Their precarious situation forced them to remain politically moderate, and many Ukrainophiles turned to cautious gradualism. Paradoxically, however, the near-complete prohibition of Ukrainian-language public activism under the Ems Ukaz meant that even purely cultural work came to be seen as a political challenge to the regime. Still, very few people in the Ukrainian movement seriously believed in Ukrainian independence before 1914, and when it suddenly became a realistic option three years later, some activists were shocked by the rapid development. Ultimately, it was neither the (dubious) nationalism of the revolutionary masses nor the purported radicalism of the younger activist generation that caused the Ukrainian People's Republic to declare independence. Rather, the breakdown of the imperial order created a vacuum of power that the young Ukrainian leaders were better prepared to fill than other local actors. In reaction to the Ukrainians' successes, Russian nationalists mobilized well among Kiev's urban population and among army officers, but their vision, like Ukrainian nationalism, failed to appeal sufficiently to the rural masses.

For, of course, the story told in this book is one of educated urban elites. From what we can tell, national modes of thought penetrated

Ukraine's popular masses, at best, superficially before the First World War. Despite rivaling nationalist claims to the majority population, most peasants did not declare a clear national allegiance, and in candid moments, both Russian and Ukrainian nationalists admitted as much. More research is needed to understand the appeal of nationalism—or the lack thereof—to the lower classes of Ukraine: the Volhynian peasants who voted for conservative Russian nationalists in 1907 but for socialist Ukrainian nationalists in 1917; the urban workers who came from the Ukrainian-speaking countryside but were supposedly subject to quick Russification; the soldiers of the imperial army who welcomed the Ukrainization of their units in 1917 but were not willing or able to defend the UNR in the civil war. Detailed studies of local lower-class milieus could confirm (or refute) the anecdotal evidence which suggests that the nationalization of the popular masses in Ukraine was much slower than that of the urban intelligentsia. More biographical research on educated activists—in particular, on nationalist women—may yield further insights into the rise of nationalism as a political ideology aiming to embrace all domains of life.

This study suggests that private and family life were important settings for the nationalization of the intelligentsia in the Russian Empire. Family loyalty could reinforce national loyalties, but the two could also clash, as when Iakov Shul'gin broke with his uncle during the quarrel surrounding the Kiev Geographical Society. The precise political function of a family hinged on its relationship with the imperial state. To the Ukrainophile Shul'hyn-Ustymovych clan, the family along with its private spaces appeared as a cultural refuge safe from the grasp of the state. It served as a locus of political and national socialization for their children and for the Ukrainophile milieu surrounding them. For their loyalist relatives, by contrast, the family was a model of an ideal and harmonious patriarchal society. The Pikhno-Shul'gins used their family as an organizational and economic network around which they built their patriotic family business. Finally, the family played a role in the memorialization of its members' contributions to national history, presented as an intermediate social unit connecting the individual to the imagined community of the nation.

The political functions of the family were particularly important for women. In the Russian Empire, state service was an exclusively male domain, and so was electoral politics when it came into existence after 1905. Nationalism, however, permeated all social domains and thus bestowed political significance on the domestic sphere, which was seen as inherently feminine. Family structures, thus, simultaneously constrained and enabled women's political agency.[8] In the Ukrainophile milieu, which was confined to domestic spaces after the Ems Ukaz of 1876, women like Liubov Shul'hyna occupied a central place. They were responsible for educating the next generation in a "national spirit," they often knew the "mother tongue" better than their husbands, and they were not forced to lead their husbands' double life between private nationalist commitment and professional loyalty to the empire. Meanwhile, the tight and unconventional family circle of the Pikhno-Shul'gins, while ideologically committed to traditional gender roles, made it possible for the family's women to become involved in political newspaper work. Like so many prerevolutionary certainties, the exclusion of women from public politics came to an end in 1917. Although only few women were elected to high office, the "revolutionary whirlwind" drew in even such nonfeminist nationalist women as Ekaterina Shul'gina.

The family history of the Shul'gins and Shul'hyns, although extraordinary in many ways, is emblematic of the historical experience of the region's elites. For Ukraine has been both: a cultural space unto itself, distinct from both its Polish and Russian neighbors, and a part of the Russian Empire, whose imperial elite culture exerted a strong pull on—and was in turn shaped by—Ukraine's educated classes. As Eastern Europe fell under the spell of the powerful political force of nationalism, this duality resulted in harsh conflicts among the region's Orthodox intelligentsia. Educated men and women perceived a political need to create homogeneous national collectives, either Russian or Ukrainian, leaving ever less space for the ambiguous and multilayered loyalties that had once prevailed among them. The nationalist struggle for the population's hearts and minds led to vicious debates and, ultimately, to military conflicts, in which members of the region's intelligentsia fought and died on different sides. In this sense, the story of the Shul'gin/Shul'hyn family exemplifies the tragedy of Ukraine, but also the enduring political vitality of its society.

Notes

Introduction

First epigraph from V. Shul'gin to V. Maklakov, 12 February 1929, in *Spor o Rossii: V. A. Maklakov–V. V. Shul'gin, perepiska 1919–1939 gg.*, ed. O. V. Budnitskii (Moscow: ROSSPEN, 2012), 298, emphasis in original. Second epigraph from Alexandre Choulguine, *L'Ukraine contre Moscou (1917)* (Paris: Alcan, 1935), 21.

1. M. A. Bulgakov, *Belaia gvardiia. Master i Margarita* (1925; repr., Minsk: Uradzhai, 1988), 16.

2. Serhii Iefremov, "Dorohoiu tsinoiu. Iasnii pam'iaty Volodymyra Shul'hyna," *Nova Rada*, 7 (20) March 1918, 1; "Pokhoron studentiv-sichovykiv," ibid., 3.

3. "Oni ne poluchili prikazaniia," *Kievlianin*, 1 (14) December 1919, 1.

4. Strictly speaking, Vasilid was not biologically related to Volodymyr because his father was an illegitimate child.

5. Vladimir Putin, "On the Historical Unity of Russians and Ukrainians," 12 July 2021, http://en.kremlin.ru/events/president/news/66181 (last accessed on 2 May 2022).

6. Andreas Kappeler, *Russland und die Ukraine: Verflochtene Biographien und Geschichten* (Vienna: Böhlau, 2012), 348. See, by way of comparison, Michael Werner and Bénédicte Zimmermann, "Penser l'histoire croisée: Entre empirie et réflexivité," *Annales. Histoire, Sciences Sociales* 58, no. 1 (2003): 7–36.

7. According to the 1897 census, East Slavs ("Russians") formed a two-thirds majority of the empire's population, with 44.31 percent Great Russians, 17.81 percent Little Russians, and 4.68 percent Belorussians. See David Saunders, "Russia's Ukrainian Policy (1847–1905): A Demographic Approach," *European History Quarterly* 25, no. 2 (1995): 181–208; Vera Tolz, *Russia: Inventing the Nation* (London: Arnold, 2001), 209–32.

8. Brian J. Boeck, "What's in a Name? Semantic Separation and the Rise of the Ukrainian National Name," *Harvard Ukrainian Studies* 27, no. 1/4 (2004–2005): 33–65.

9. A. L. Kotenko, O. V. Martyniuk, and A. I. Miller, "Maloross," in *"Poniatiia o Rossii": K istoricheskoi semantike imperskogo perioda*, ed. A. I. Miller, D. A. Sdvizhkov, and I. Shirle (Moscow: Novoe literaturnoe obozrenie, 2012), 2:392–443.

10. O. N. Tobilevich, ed., *Russkie govory na Ukraine* (Kyiv: Naukova dumka, 1982); Michael Moser, "Geschichte und Gegenwart des Russischen in der Ukraine: Ein Überblick," *Die Welt der Slaven* 67, no. 2 (2022): 393–423.

11. Both nation-building projects found adherents among the Orthodox clergy. See Ricarda Vulpius, *Nationalisierung der Religion: Russifizierungspolitik und ukrainische Nationsbildung 1860–1920* (Wiesbaden: Harrassowitz, 2005).

12. Even in Austrian Galicia, where most Ukrainian speakers were Greek Catholics, the All-Russian project offered a powerful alternative to Ukrainian nationalism. See Anna Veronika Wendland, *Die Russophilen in Galizien: Ukrainische Konservative zwischen Österreich und Russland, 1848–1915* (Vienna: Verlag der Österreichischen Akademie der Wissenschaften, 2001).

13. In Ernest Gellner's terms, their resistance to social entropy was fairly weak. See Ernest Gellner, *Nations and Nationalism* (1983; repr., Malden, MA: Blackwell, 2006), 63–71.

14. Andreas Kappeler, "Mazepintsy, Malorossy, Khokhly: Ukrainians in the Ethnic Hierarchy of the Russian Empire," in *Culture, Nation, and Identity: The Ukrainian-Russian Encounter, 1600–1945*, ed. Andreas Kappeler et al. (Toronto: Canadian Institute of Ukrainian Studies, 2003), 173–74.

15. Andreas Kappeler, "Ukrainische und russische Nation: Ein asymmetrisches Verhältnis," in *Die Ukraine: Prozesse der Nationsbildung*, ed. Andreas Kappeler (Cologne: Böhlau, 2011), 191–201.

16. Stefan Berger and Alexei Miller, eds., *Nationalizing Empires* (Budapest: Central European University Press, 2015).

17. Miroslav Hroch, *Social Preconditions of National Revival in Europe: A Comparative Analysis of the Social Composition of Patriotic Groups among the Smaller European Nations* (Cambridge: Cambridge University Press, 1985); Andreas Kappeler, *Der schwierige Weg zur Nation: Beiträge zur neueren Geschichte der Ukraine* (Cologne: Böhlau, 2003), 70–87.

18. Despite the popularity of (post-)colonial terminology in some recent scholarship, most analyses of nineteenth-century Ukraine as a Russian colony obscure more than they enlighten. In contrast to the classical examples of postcolonial theory, Ukraine was considered part of the extended imperial metropole and of the core nation by the empire's elites. While exoticizing descriptions of Ukraine and its peasants (*khokhly*) are reminiscent of a colonial gaze, the same goes for the elites' patronizing views of the Great Russian peasantry and, for that matter, Parisians' depictions of rural Southern France. See Eugen Weber, *Peasants into Frenchmen: The Modernization of Rural France, 1870–1914* (Stanford, CA: Stanford University Press, 1976), 3–12.

19. Alexei Miller, *The Ukrainian Question: The Russian Empire and Nationalism in the Nineteenth Century* (Budapest: Central European University Press, 2003).

20. Faith Hillis, *Children of Rus': Right-Bank Ukraine and the Invention of a Russian Nation* (Ithaca, NY: Cornell University Press, 2013).

21. Serhiy Bilenky, *Romantic Nationalism in Eastern Europe: Russian, Polish, and Ukrainian Political Imaginations* (Stanford, CA: Stanford University Press, 2012).

22. Johannes Remy, *Brothers or Enemies: The Ukrainian National Movement and Russia, from the 1840s to the 1870s* (Toronto: University of Toronto Press, 2016).

23. A biographical approach has proven fruitful in the imperial context, yielding new insights into how empires functioned "on the ground." See Martin Aust and Frithjof Benjamin Schenk, eds., *Imperial Subjects: Autobiographische Praxis in den Vielvölkerreichen der Romanovs, Habsburger und Osmanen im 19. und*

frühen 20. Jahrhundert (Cologne: Böhlau, 2015); Tim Buchen and Malte Rolf, eds., *Eliten im Vielvölkerreich: Imperiale Biographien in Russland und Österreich-Ungarn (1850–1918)* (Berlin: De Gruyter Oldenbourg, 2015). On critical biography-writing see Pierre Bourdieu, "L'illusion biographique," *Actes de la recherche en sciences sociales*, no. 62–63 (1986): 69–72; Hans Erich Bödeker, "Biographie: Annäherungen an den gegenwärtigen Forschungs- und Diskussionsstand," in *Biographie schreiben*, ed. Hans Erich Bödeker (Göttingen: Wallstein Verlag, 2003), 9–63; Levke Harders, "Legitimizing Biography: Critical Approaches to Biographical Research," *Bulletin of the German Historical Institute*, no. 55 (2014): 49–56.

24. Rogers Brubaker, *Nationalism Reframed: Nationhood and the National Question in the New Europe* (Cambridge: Cambridge University Press, 1996), 7, 24.

25. Rogers Brubaker, *Ethnicity without Groups* (Cambridge, MA: Harvard University Press, 2004), 10–12, 46–48. See also Alexander Maxwell, "Nationalism as Classification: Suggestions for Reformulating Nationalism Research," *Nationalities Papers* 46, no. 4 (2017): 539–55.

26. Jeremy King, *Budweisers into Czechs and Germans: A Local History of Bohemian Politics, 1848–1948* (Princeton, NJ: Princeton University Press, 2002); Eagle Glassheim, *Noble Nationalists: The Transformation of the Bohemian Aristocracy* (Cambridge, MA: Harvard University Press, 2005); Pieter M. Judson, *Guardians of the Nation: Activists on the Language Frontiers of Imperial Austria* (Cambridge, MA: Harvard University Press, 2006); Tara Zahra, *Kidnapped Souls: National Indifference and the Battle for Children in the Bohemian Lands, 1900–1948* (Ithaca, NY: Cornell University Press, 2009); Alexander Maxwell, *Choosing Slovakia: Slavic Hungary, the Czechoslovak Language, and Accidental Nationalism* (London: Tauris Academic Studies, 2009); Pieter M. Judson, *The Habsburg Empire: A New History* (Cambridge, MA: Belknap Press of Harvard University Press, 2016), esp. chap. 6. The only study to apply a similar set of questions to nineteenth-century Ukraine so far is Hillis, *Children of Rus'*.

27. See Tara Zahra's programmatic article, "Imagined Noncommunities: National Indifference as a Category of Analysis," *Slavic Review* 69, no. 1 (2010): 93–119.

28. Several examples from two very different regions are mentioned in Kate Brown, *A Biography of No Place: From Ethnic Borderland to Soviet Heartland* (Cambridge, MA: Harvard University Press, 2004); Mark R. Baker, *Peasants, Power, and Place: Revolution in the Villages of Kharkiv Province, 1914–1921* (Cambridge, MA: Harvard University Press, 2016). See also Christine Worobec, "Conceptual Observations on the Russian and Ukrainian Peasantries," in *Culture, Nation, and Identity: The Ukrainian-Russian Encounter, 1600–1945*, ed. Andreas Kappeler et al. (Toronto: Canadian Institute of Ukrainian Studies, 2003), 256–76.

29. See the forum on national indifference in the Russian Empire in *Kritika: Explorations in Russian and Eurasian History* 20, no. 1 (2019): 7–72.

30. Jerzy Stempowski, *W dolinie Dniestru. Pisma o Ukrainie* (1941; repr., Warsaw: Towarzystwo "Więź," 2014), 6–7.

31. Some partial exceptions deal with literary figures: Edyta M. Bojanowska, *Nikolai Gogol: Between Ukrainian and Russian Nationalism* (Cambridge, MA: Harvard University Press, 2007); Iaroslav Hrytsak, *Ivan Franko and His Community*

(Edmonton: Canadian Institute of Ukrainian Studies, 2018); Yuliya Ilchuk, *Nikolai Gogol: Performing Hybrid Identity* (Toronto: University of Toronto Press, 2021); see also Kappeler, *Russland und die Ukraine.*

32. Rogers Brubaker and Frederick Cooper, "Beyond 'Identity,'" in Brubaker, *Ethnicity without Groups*, 28–63.

33. See Anne McClintock, "Family Feuds: Gender, Nationalism and the Family," *Feminist Review*, no. 44 (1993): 61–80.

34. See John Randolph, *The House in the Garden: The Bakunin Family and the Romance of Russian Idealism* (Ithaca, NY: Cornell University Press, 2007); Barbara Alpern Engel, *Breaking the Ties That Bound: The Politics of Marital Strife in Late Imperial Russia* (Ithaca, NY: Cornell University Press, 2011); Katherine Pickering Antonova, *An Ordinary Marriage: The World of a Gentry Family in Provincial Russia* (New York: Oxford University Press, 2013); and the extensive literature review in Katharina Kucher and Alexa von Winning, "Privates Leben und öffentliche Interessen: Adlige Familie und Kindheit in Russlands langem 19. Jahrhundert," *Jahrbücher für Geschichte Osteuropas* 63, no. 2 (2015): 233–55.

35. Alexa von Winning, *Intimate Empire: The Mansurov Family in Russia and the Orthodox East, 1855–1936* (Oxford: Oxford University Press, 2022), 11.

36. John Randolph, "'That Historical Family': The Bakunin Archive and the Intimate Theater of History in Imperial Russia, 1780–1925," *Russian Review* 63, no. 4 (2004): 574–93; Kucher and von Winning, "Privates Leben," 248.

37. The "national split" among the Shul'gin/Shul'hyn family was particularly conspicuous but not unique in the Kiev intelligentsia. Comparable cases include the Storozhenko and Grushevskii/Hrushevs'kyi families. A famous case of a split Polish-Ukrainian clan from Galicia is the Szeptycki/Sheptyts'kyi family. On microhistory see Jill Lepore, "Historians Who Love Too Much: Reflections on Microhistory and Biography," *Journal of American History* 88, no. 1 (2001): 129–44; Matti Peltonen, "Clues, Margins, and Monads: The Micro-Macro Link in Historical Research," *History and Theory* 40, no. 3 (2001): 347–59.

38. While it would be impossible to read all the roughly sixteen thousand editions of *Kievlianin*, I have consulted over a thousand issues. For the paper's early years, the index in M. K. Shul'gina, ed., *"Kievlianin" pod redaktsiei Vitaliia Iakovlevicha Shul'gina (1864–1878)* (Kiev: Universitetskaia tipografiia I.I. Zavadskago, 1880) has been invaluable.

39. Vasilii Shul'gin wrote his first memoirs in the early interwar period: V. V. Shul'gin, *1920 g.: Ocherki* (Sofia: Rossiisko-bolgarskoe knigoizdatel'stvo, 1921); V. V. Shul'gin, *Dni* (Belgrade: Knigoizdatel'stvo M. A. Suvorin i Ko. "Novoe Vremia," 1925). A second group of texts was written in the 1920s and recently published: V. V. Shul'gin, *1919 god*, ed. A. A. Chemakin, 2 vols. (Moscow: Kuchkovo pole, 2018); V. V. Shul'gin, *1921 god*, ed. A. A. Chemakin (Moscow: Kuchkovo pole, 2018). A voluminous unpublished memoir is held at OR IMLI RAN, f. 604, ed. khr. 179–85; two more, composed in prison during the early 1950s, are in RGALI, f. 1337, op. 4, d. 54–58. Finally, Shul'gin's late autobiographical texts have been published in two volumes: V. V. Shul'gin, *Poslednii ochevidets: Memuary, ocherki, sny*, ed. N. N. Lisovoi (Moscow: OLMA-Press, 2002); V. V. Shul'gin, *Teni, kotorye prokhodiat*, ed. R. G. Krasiukov (Saint Petersburg: Nestor-Istoriia, 2012).

40. E. G. Shul'gina, *Konspekt moikh politicheskikh perezhivanii (1903–1922)*, ed. A. A. Chemakin (Moscow: Fond Sviaz' Epokh, 2019); Choulguine, *L'Ukraine contre Moscou*; Oleksander Shul'hyn, "Uryvky iz spohadiv," in *Zbirnyk na poshanu Oleksandra Shul'hyna (1889–1960)*, ed. Volodymyr Ianiv (Paris, 1969), 199–308.

41. See Volker Depkat, "Autobiographie und die soziale Konstruktion von Wirklichkeit," *Geschichte und Gesellschaft* 29, no. 3 (2003): 441–76.

42. Collection R-5974 in the State Archive of the Russian Federation (GARF) comes closest, containing numerous sketches, memoirs, and letters written by Vasilii Shul'gin and Ekaterina Shul'gina. It has made its way to Moscow from the interwar Russian Historical Archive Abroad in Prague, which Czechoslovakia donated to the Soviet Union in 1948.

43. D. I. Zaslavskii, *Rytsar' monarkhii Shul'gin* (Leningrad: Knizhnie novinki, 1927).

44. V. G. Makarov, A. V. Repnikov, and V. S. Khristoforov, eds., *Tiuremnaia odisseia Vasiliia Shul'gina: Materialy sledstvennogo dela i dela zakliuchennogo* (Moscow: Russkii put', 2010); D. I. Babkov, *Gosudarstvennye i natsional'nye problemy v mirovozzrenii V. V. Shul'gina v 1917–1939 godakh* (Moscow: ROSSPEN, 2012); A. S. Puchenkov, *Ukraina i Krym v 1918–nachale 1919 goda: Ocherki politicheskoi istorii* (Moscow: Nestor-Istoriia, 2013); S. Iu. Rybas, *Vasilii Shul'gin: Sud'ba russkogo natsionalista* (Moscow: Molodaia gvardiia, 2014).

45. Olivier Perrin, ed., *Alexandre Choulguine (1889–1960)* (Paris: Académie internationale libre des sciences et des lettres, 1961); Volodymyr Ianiv, ed., *Zbirnyk na poshanu Oleksandra Shul'hyna (1889–1960)*, *Zapysky Naukovoho Tovarystva im. Shevchenka* 186 (Paris, 1969); Emre Akyndzhy, "Hromads'ko-politychna ta dyplomatychna diial'nist' Oleksandra Shul'hyna (1889-1960)" (PhD diss., Pereiaslav-Khmel'nyts'kyi, Derzhavnyi pedahohichnyi universytet imeni Hryhoriia Skovorody, 2015); Valentyna Piskun, ed., *Oleksandr Shul'hyn v ukraïns'komu derzhavotvorenni ta mizhnarodnii politytsi* (Kyiv: Instytut ukraïns'koï arkheohrafiï ta dzhereloznavstva im. M. S. Hrushevs'koho, 2016).

46. On the family's Russian branch see the memoir by Olga Matich, a direct descendant: *Zapiski russkoi amerikanki: Semeinye khroniki i sluchainye vstrechi* (Moscow: Novoe literaturnoe obozrenie, 2017); as well as Faith Hillis, "Making and Breaking the Russian Empire: The Case of Kiev's Shul'gin Family," in *Eliten im Vielvölkerreich: Imperiale Biographien in Russland und Österreich-Ungarn (1850–1918)*, ed. Tim Buchen and Malte Rolf (Berlin: De Gruyter Oldenbourg, 2015), 179-98. On the Ukrainian branch see Olena Leontovych, *Shul'hyny: Bat'ky, dity, onuky* (Ternopil': Navchal'na knyha—Bohdan, 2012); S. I. Shevchenko, *Shul'hyny: Inhul's'ka storinka* (Kirovohrad: Imeks-LTD, 2012).

47. V. B. Liubchenko, "Kyïvs'ki Shul'hiny: Natsional'no rozdilena rodyna v istoriï Ukraïny," *Ukraïns'ka biohrafistyka: Zbirnyk naukovych prats'* 2 (1999): 153-62.

1. At the Crossroads

1. V.A., "Kiev," *Kievlianin*, 15 May 1865, 2.

2. The best study of the midcentury socioethnic situation is Daniel Beauvois, *The Noble, the Serf and the Revizor: The Polish Nobility between Tsarist*

Imperialism and the Ukrainian Masses (1831–1863) (Chur, Switzerland: Harwood Academic, 1991).

3. Zenon E. Kohut, *Russian Centralism and Ukrainian Autonomy: Imperial Absorption of the Hetmanate, 1760s–1830s* (Cambridge, MA: Harvard Ukrainian Research Institute, 1988).

4. *Vitalii Iakovlevich Shul'gin: Nekrolog i rechi, proiznesennyia nad grobom* (Kiev: Universitetskaia tipografiia I. I. Zavadskago, 1879), 4–7. Both Iakov's father and grandfather were called Ignatii Shul'ga (Ihnatyi Shul'ha). In 1785, a man of this name, probably his grandfather, was one of Nezhin's two mayors. See L. V. Lesyk, "Do pytannia evoliutsiï mis'koho samovriaduvannia na prykladi mista Nizhyna," *Literatura ta kul'tura Polissia: Zbirnyk naukovykh prats'* 70 (2012): 59.

5. *Vitalii Iakovlevich Shul'gin: Nekrolog*, 4–6; G. K. Gradovskii, "Vitalii Iakovlevich Shul'gin (biograficheskii ocherk)," in *"Kievlianin" pod redaktsiei Vitaliia Iakovlevicha Shul'gina (1864–1878)*, ed. M. K. Shul'gina (Kiev: Universitetskaia tipografiia I. I. Zavadskago, 1880), 1–2.

6. "Spisok parafiian Preobrazhenskoi Tserkvi, g. Nezhin," 1788, DAChO, f. 679, op. 1, spr. 573, ark. 56–56zv; "Ispovedal'naia rospis' Preobrazhenskoi Tserkvi, g. Nezhin," 1809, DAChO, f. 679, op. 1, spr. 507, ark. 62–62zv. Around 1800, these two urban estates were still mutually permeable. See Alison K. Smith, *For the Common Good and Their Own Well-Being: Social Estates in Imperial Russia* (New York: Oxford University Press, 2015), 41–43.

7. Elise Kimerling Wirtschafter, *Social Identity in Imperial Russia* (DeKalb: Northern Illinois University Press, 1997), 47.

8. *Vitalii Iakovlevich Shul'gin: Nekrolog*, 4.

9. Denis Sdvižkov, *Das Zeitalter der Intelligenz: Zur vergleichenden Geschichte der Gebildeten in Europa bis zum Ersten Weltkrieg* (Göttingen: Vandenhoeck & Ruprecht, 2006), 160.

10. V. Shcherbina, "Iz semeinago arkhiva. II. Stikhotvoreniia Evstafiia Petrovicha Rudykovskago (1784–1851)," *Kievskaia starina*, no. 5 (1892): 204; Shul'hyn, "Uryvky iz spohadiv," 227.

11. Hillis, "Making and Breaking," 180–82.

12. Michael F. Hamm, *Kiev: A Portrait, 1800–1917* (Princeton, NJ: Princeton University Press, 1993), 24, 62–69; Serhiy Bilenky, *Imperial Urbanism in the Borderlands: Kyiv 1800–1905* (Toronto: University of Toronto Press, 2018), 169–98.

13. *Vitalii Iakovlevich Shul'gin: Nekrolog*, 6–7.

14. V. Shul'gin to M. Maksimovich, 8 December 1859, IR NBUV, f. III, od. zb. 6066, ark. 1.

15. Patricia Grimsted Kennedy, "Archeography in the Service of Imperial Policy: The Foundation of the Kiev Archeographic Commission and the Kiev Central Archive of Early Record Books," *Harvard Ukrainian Studies* 17, no. 1–2 (1993): 27–44.

16. Bilenky, *Romantic Nationalism*, 270–86.

17. Miller, *Ukrainian Question*, 52. For Hroch's scheme see Hroch, *Social Preconditions*.

18. Diverse orientations toward Russia existed in the regional elites long before the emergence of Ukrainian nationalism. Among the left-bank gentry around 1800, Zenon Kohut distinguishes between assimilationists and

more localist—but equally loyal—traditionalists. See Kohut, *Russian Centralism*, 258–76.

19. *Vitalii Iakovlevich Shul'gin: Nekrolog*, 8–12.

20. Shcherbina, "Iz semeinago arkhiva," 194–99, 211, 214–15.

21. V. Shcherbina, "Iz semeinago arkhiva. II. Stikhotvoreniia Evstafiia Petrovicha Rudykovskago (1784–1851)," *Kievskaia starina*, no. 7 (1892): 55–59, 64, 69–70.

22. V. Shul'gin to E. Rudykovs'kyi, 19 October 1846, IR NBUV, f. I, od. zb. 7729.

23. Bilenky, *Romantic Nationalism*, 287–99; Remy, *Brothers or Enemies*, 25–28.

24. P. A. Zaionchkovskii, *Kirillo-Mefodievskoe obshchestvo (1846–1847)* (Moscow: Izdatel'stvo Moskovskogo Universiteta, 1959), 125–32.

25. Miller, *Ukrainian Question*, 53.

26. See his footnote to P. Iva-nko, "Shevchenko, Maksimovich i Kostomarov pered istoricheskim (?) sudom Kulisha," *Kievlianin*, 8 March 1875, 3.

27. V. Ia. Shul'gin, *Iugozapadnyi krai v poslednee dvadtsatipiatiletie* (Kiev: Universitetskaia tipografiia, 1864), 44. The quotation is from a Shevchenko poem.

28. V. Ia. Shul'gin, *O sostoianii zhenshchin v Rossii do Petra Velikago* (Kiev: Tipografiia I. Val'nera, 1850), v, xxv–xxvii.

29. V. G. Avseenko, "Shkol'nye gody. Otryvki iz vospominanii 1852–1863," *Istoricheskii vestnik* 4 (1881): 717; *Vitalii Iakovlevich Shul'gin: Nekrolog*, 13–16; Gradovskii, "V. Ia. Shul'gin," 7.

30. Shul'gin, *Teni*, 35; Bilenky, *Imperial Urbanism*, 175, 317–20.

31. "Zapiski iz universitetskoi zhizni (1860–1864)," *Kievlianin*, 13 August 1864, 1–2; continued in *Kievlianin*, 25 August 1864, 1–2; Mykhailo Drahomanov, *Narodni shkoly na Ukrajini sered zhyt't'a i pys'menstva v Rossiji* (Geneva: H. Georg, 1877), 19–22; Ihnat Zhytets'kyi, "Kyïvs'ka Hromada za 60-kh rokiv," *Ukraïna. Naukovyi dvokhmisiachnyk ukraïnoznavstva* 26, no. 1 (1928): 93–94.

32. Volodymyr Antonovych, "Memoirs," in *Fashioning Modern Ukraine: Selected Writings of Mykola Kostomarov, Volodymyr Antonovych and Mykhailo Drahomanov*, ed. Serhiy Bilenky (Toronto: Canadian Institute of Ukrainian Studies, 2013), 187–236.

33. B. S. Poznanskii, "Vospominaniia," *Ukrainskaia zhizn'*, no. 3 (1913): 15–24. On Ukrainophile tendencies among Polish-speaking students see also K. P. Mikhal'chuk, "Iz ukrainskago bylogo," *Ukrainskaia zhizn'*, no. 8–10 (1914): 70–85; Johannes Remy, "National Aspect of Student Movements in St. Vladimir's University of Kiev 1855–1863," *Skhid-Zakhid: Istoryko-Kul'turolohichnyi Zbirnyk* 7 (2005): 248–73.

34. B. S. Poznanskii, "Vospominaniia," *Ukrainskaia zhizn'*, no. 5 (1913): 44; Zhytets'kyi, "Kyïvs'ka Hromada," 94–95, 102–4, 122–24.

35. Miller, *Ukrainian Question*, 75–90; Michael Moser, "Osnova and the Origins of the Valuev Directive," *East/West: Journal of Ukrainian Studies* 4, no. 2 (2017): 39–95.

36. N. Kostomarov, "Dve russkiia narodnosti," *Osnova*, no. 3 (1861): 33–80; V. B. Antonovich, "Moia ispoved'. Otvet panu Padalitse," *Osnova*, no. 1 (1862): 83–96. Both texts are translated in Bilenky, *Fashioning Modern Ukraine*, 134–74, 241–52.

37. Bilenky, *Fashioning Modern Ukraine*, 162–74.

38. Bilenky, 251.

39. The classic account of the January Uprising is Stefan Kieniewicz, *Powstanie styczniowe* (Warsaw: Państwowe Wydawnyctwo Naukowe, 1972); on Kiev and the right-bank provinces see 39–42, 175–77, 297–300, 497–502.

40. Hamm, *Kiev*, 74–76.

41. Theodore R. Weeks, *Nation and State in Late Imperial Russia: Nationalism and Russification on the Western Frontier, 1863–1914* (DeKalb: Northern Illinois University Press, 1996), 96–99; Witold Rodkiewicz, *Russian Nationality Policy in the Western Provinces of the Empire (1863–1905)* (Lublin: Scientific Society of Lublin, 1998), 58–67, 133–38; Alexei Miller and Mikhail Dolbilov, "'The Damned Polish Question': The Romanov Empire and the Polish Uprisings of 1830–1831 and 1863–1864," in *Comparing Empires: Encounters and Transfers in the Long Nineteenth Century*, ed. Jörn Leonhard and Ulrike von Hirschhausen (Göttingen: Vandenhoeck & Ruprecht, 2011), 446–49. On the Northwest see M. D. Dolbilov, *Russkii krai, chuzhaia vera: Etnokonfessional'naia politika imperii v Litve i Belorussii pri Aleksandre II* (Moscow: Novoe literaturnoe obozrenie, 2010), 227ff.

42. Miller, *Ukrainian Question*, 97–115, quotation 263–64; Rodkiewicz, *Russian Nationality Policy*, 199–201.

43. "Metricheskaia kniga dannaia v Staro-Kievskuiu Georgievskuiu Tserkov'," 1860, TsDIAK, f. 127, op. 1012, spr. 3293, ark. 252zv–254; *Vitalii Iakovlevich Shul'gin: Nekrolog*, 27–29; Gradovskii, "V. Ia. Shul'gin," 7–8.

44. V. Shul'gin to the Kiev Assembly of Noble Deputies, 4 January 1861, DAKO, f. 782, op. 1, spr. 13427, ark. 45; "Ob uvol'nenii professora Shul'gina ot sluzhby pri universitete," 1862, DAK, f. 16, op. 301, spr. 228.

45. A. V. Romanovich-Slavatinskii, "Moia zhizn' i akademicheskaia deiatel'nost' 1832–1882 gg.," *Vestnik Evropy* 5 (1903): 190.

46. "Protokoly zasedanii Soveta. 27-go marta 1864 goda (Dopolnenie)," *Universitetskiia izvestiia*, no. 5 (1864): 15–29; Gradovskii, "V. Ia. Shul'gin," 10–11.

47. Gradovskii, "V. Ia. Shul'gin," 14–15.

48. N. Annenkov to F. Witte, 23 April 1864, TsDIAK, f. 707, op. 30, spr. 150, ark. 1.

49. *Vitalii Iakovlevich Shul'gin: Nekrolog*, 30. Later, the subsidy was paid by the Ministry of Popular Enlightenment. See TsDIAK, f. 707, op. 261 (1875), spr. 16.

50. Andreas Renner, *Russischer Nationalismus und Öffentlichkeit im Zarenreich 1855–1875* (Cologne: Böhlau, 2000), 159, 168–72. On the interdependence of state and civil society see Joseph Bradley, *Voluntary Associations in Tsarist Russia: Science, Patriotism, and Civil Society* (Cambridge, MA: Harvard University Press, 2009), 13–15, 259–65.

51. Starozhil [S. G. Iaron], *Kiev v vos'midesiatykh godakh* (Kiev: Tipografiia "Petr Barskii v Kieve," 1910), 64.

52. "Ob"iavlenie," 1864, TsDIAK, f. 707, op. 30, spr. 150, ark. 4.

53. "Kiev," *Kievlianin*, 1 July 1864, 2.

54. "Nashi nezavisimye," *Kievlianin*, 1 July 1864, 2. Unfortunately, I have not found any copies of the caricature.

55. Shul'gin, *Iugozapadnyi krai*, 14. This text was serialized in *Kievlianin* over the summer of 1864.

56. Shul'gin, *Iugozapadnyi krai*, 58–108. For a more balanced view of Bibikov's attempts to ease the peasants' burden see Beauvois, *Noble, the Serf and the Revizor*, 26–40.

57. Shul'gin, *Iugozapadnyi krai*, 253–54.

58. M. Iuzefovich, "Kiev," *Kievlianin*, 28 September 1865, 1.

59. See, for instance, V.A., "Kiev," *Kievlianin*, 15 May 1865, 1–2; V.A., "Kiev," *Kievlianin*, 25 January 1866, 1–2.

60. Weeks, *Nation and State*, 31–33; see also Renner, *Russischer Nationalismus*, 185–273.

61. Darius Staliūnas, *Making Russians: Meaning and Practice of Russification in Lithuania and Belarus after 1863* (Amsterdam: Rodopi, 2007), 57–70.

62. "Kiev," *Kievlianin*, 22 September 1864, 1–2; Z.S., "Kiev," 19 November 1864, 1–2.

63. John D. Klier, "Kievlianin and the Jews: A Decade of Disillusionment, 1864–1873," *Harvard Ukrainian Studies* 5, no. 1 (1981): 94–95.

64. "Kiev," *Kievlianin*, 14 July 1864, 1–2.

65. "Kiev," *Kievlianin*, 26 November 1864, 1–2.

66. Mykhailo Drahomanov, "Avtobiograficheskaia zametka," in *Literaturno-publitsystychni pratsi* (Kyiv: Naukova dumka, 1970), 1:41–45; "Avstro-rus'ki spomyny (1867–1877)," ibid., 2:156–64. On the Temporary Pedagogical School see Shul'gin, *Iugozapadnyi krai*, 228–32.

67. M. P. Dragomanov, "Kiev," *Kievlianin*, 3 August 1865, 1–2.

68. Drahomanov, *Narodni shkoly*, 46–48. The article in question is "Pedagogicheskoe znachenie malorusskago iazyka," *Sankt-Peterburgskiia vedomosti*, 8 April 1866, 1–2.

69. "Kiev," *Kievlianin*, 14 April 1866, 1–2; "Kiev," *Kievlianin*, 16 April 1866, 2.

70. M. Iuzefovich, "Kiev," *Kievlianin*, 23 April 1866, 1–2; "Kiev," *Kievlianin*, 21 May 1866, 1–2. This controversy led to a first administrative inquiry into Drahomanov's views. See "Delo o Privat Dotsente Dragomanove," TsDIAK, f. 707, op. 261 (1866), spr. 35.

71. "Kiev," *Kievlianin*, 7 May 1866.

72. *Kievlianin*, 25 August 1866, 2.

73. A. A. Teslia, *"Istinno russkie liudi": Istoriia russkogo natsionalizma* (Moscow: RIPOL klassik, 2019), 159–60.

74. V. Antonovych to M. Drahomanov, 27 May 1875, in *Arkhiv Mykhaila Drahomanova. Tom 1: Lystuvannia Kyïvs'koï staroï hromady z M. Drahomanovym (1870–1895 rr.)*, ed. Roman Smal'-Stots'kyi (Warsaw: Ukraïns'kyi naukovyi instytut, 1937), 7.

75. Volodymyr Shcherbyna, "Pamiaty Iakova Shul'hyna," *Zapysky Ukraïns'koho Naukovoho Tovarystva v Kyïvi* 10 (1912): 5–6.

76. Avseenko, "Shkol'nye gody," 718.

77. V. I. Shcherbyna, "Z kolyshn'oho zhyttia Kyïvs'koho universytetu. Spomyny staroho studenta," n.d., IR NBUV, f. 179, od. zb. 889, ark. 20–26.

78. "Vstupna lektsiia V. B. Antonovycha u Kyïvs'komu universyteti sv. Volodymyra," in *Syn Ukraïny: Volodymyr Bonifatiiovych Antonovych*, ed. Viktor Korotkyi and Vasyl' Ul'ianovs'kyi (Kyiv: Zapovit, 1997), 1:383–84.

79. Shcherbyna, "Z kolyshn'oho zhyttia," IR NBUV, f. 179, od. zb. 889, ark. 24–26.

80. "Spomyny pro Kyïvs'kyi Universytet 1868–1872 rokiv," n.d., IR NBUV, f. 317, od. zb. 56, ark. 48–51; V. S. Chevazhevskii, "Iz proshlago Kievskago universiteta i studencheskoi zhizni (1870–1875 g.)," *Russkaia starina* 150, no. 4–6 (1912): 563–69. On Ziber see Kappeler, *Der schwierige Weg zur Nation*, 181–94.

81. Two sources mention this incident: Diary entry for 12 March 1875, O. F. Kistiakivs'kyi, *Shchodennyk (1874–1885) u dvokh tomakh* (Kyiv: Naukova dumka, 1994–1995), 1:43; S. Podolinskii to V. Smirnov, 17 May 1875, in *"Vpered!" 1873–1877: Materialy iz arkhiva Valeriana Nikolaevicha Smirnova*, ed. Boris Sapir (Dordrecht: Reidel, 1970), 2:444.

82. "Stara Hromada (spohady)," n.d., IR NBUV, f. I, od. zb. 49600, ark. 4–4zv.

83. Drahomanov, "Avstro-rus'ki spomyny," 214. On radicals' negative views of the Ukrainophiles' "boring endeavors that nobody needed" see Lev Deich, "M. P. Dragomanov v izgnanii," *Vestnik Evropy*, no. 10 (1913): 204.

84. Oleksandr Riabinin-Skliarevs'kyi, "Kyïvs'ka Hromada 1870-kh r.r.," *Ukraïna. Naukovyi dvokhmisiachnyk ukraïnoznavstva* 21, no. 1–2 (1927): 144.

85. A. L. Kotenko, "Etnohrafichno-statystychna ekspeditsiia P. Chubyns'koho v pivdenno-zakhidnyi krai," *Ukraïns'kyi istorychnyi zhurnal*, no. 3 (2014): 128–51.

86. F. Volkov, "P. P. Chubinskii. Otryvki iz lichnykh vospominanii," *Ukrainskaia zhizn'*, no. 1 (1914): 45–47. The history of the KGS is covered in great detail in Fedir Savchenko, *Zaborona ukraïnstva 1876 r.* (1928; repr., Munich: Wilhelm Fink Verlag, 1970).

87. P. Antonovich to A. Shirinskii-Shikhmatov, 19 July 1875, TsDIAK, f. 707, op. 261 (1875), spr. 17, ark. 17zv; Savchenko, *Zaborona ukraïnstva*, 14–16; Miller, *Ukrainian Question*, 158–59.

88. "Ekspeditsiia geograficheskago obshchestva dlia izsledovaniia iugozapadnago kraia," *Kievlianin*, 5 July 1869, 1–2.

89. "N. V. Lysenko kak kontsertant i kompozitor," *Kievlianin*, 25 April 1872, 1–2.

90. *Kievlianin*, 17 February 1873, 1–2; "Eshche o Iugozapadnom otdele Imperatorskago russkago geograficheskago Obshchestva," *Kievlianin*, 20 February 1873, 1–2.

91. "Iubilei Mikhaila Aleksandrovicha Maksimovicha," *Kievlianin*, 16 September 1871, 1–2; continued in *Kievlianin*, 18 September 1871, 1–3; *Kievlianin*, 21 September 1871, 1–2. It is symbolically fitting that Maksimovich died in November 1873, just before the conflict between *Kievlianin* and the Ukrainophiles came to a head.

92. Aleksandr Grushevskii, "Iz zhizni kievskago ukrainskago kruzhka 1870 gg.," *Ukrainskaia zhizn'*, no. 11–12 (1915): 33–34.

93. Shcherbyna, "Pamiaty Iakova Shul'hyna," 7; Shcherbyna, "Z kolyshn'oho zhyttia," IR NBUV, f. 179, od. zb. 889, ark. 30–31.

94. Ben Eklof and Tatiana Saburova, *A Generation of Revolutionaries: Nikolai Charushin and Russian Populism from the Great Reforms to Perestroika* (Bloomington: Indiana University Press, 2017), 39–72.

95. Ia. Shul'gin to M. Hrushevs'kyi, 17 January 1899, TsDIAK, f. 1235, op. 1, spr. 873, ark. 262.

96. Antonovych, "Memoirs," in Bilenky, *Fashioning Modern Ukraine*, 205, 208–9; Drahomanov, "Avstro-rus'ki spomyny," 151–55.

97. See their letters in Smal'-Stots'kyi, *Arkhiv Mykhaila Drahomanova*, 5–44.

98. V. P. Naumenko, "Otryvki vospominanii detstva," n.d., IR NBUV, f. I, od. zb. 47080, ark. 7; A. Rusov, "Kak ia stal chlenom 'Gromady,'" *Ukrainskaia zhizn'*, no. 10 (1913): 40–41; Sofiia Rusova, "Moï spomyny rr. 1861–1879," *Za sto lit* 2 (1928): 135.

99. Hrytsak, *Ivan Franko*, 67, 74, 134ff.

100. A. Khatchenko, "Iurii Iurievich Tsvetkovskii, kak obshchestvennyi deiatel'," *Ukrainskaia zhizn'*, no. 7–8 (1913): 102.

101. Mykhailo Drahomanov, "Antrakt z istoriï ukraïnofil'stva (1863–1872)," in *Vybrane* (Kyiv: Lybid', 1991), 224.

102. Drahomanov spelled out his views in his programmatic article "Literatura rosiis'ka, velykorus'ka, ukraïns'ka i halyts'ka," in *Literaturno-publitsystychni pratsi*, 1:80–220, first published in 1873–1874 under pseudonym in the Galician journal *Pravda* (and thus not subject to Russian censorship).

103. G. V. Kas'ianov and A. I. Miller, *Rossiia–Ukraina: Kak pishetsia istoriia* (Moscow: Rossiiskii gosudarstvennyi gumanitarnyi universitet, 2011), 183–84.

104. "Flag prikryvaet gruz," *Kievlianin*, 28 September 1874, 1–2.

105. "Novaia malorusskaia opera," *Kievlianin*, 2 February 1874, 1.

106. "Shalosti vzroslykh detei," *Kievlianin*, 7 September 1874, 1–2. In fact, Gogol' himself had used such terminology in the story's first version. See Bojanowska, *Nikolai Gogol*, 266–67.

107. *Kievlianin*, 29 August 1874, 1–2; *Kievlianin*, 17 September 1874, 1–2.

108. *Kievlianin*, 3 October 1874, 1; "Gde tonko, tam i rvetsia," *Kievlianin*, 21 November 1874, 1; "Nedorazumeniia po povodu odnodnevnoi perepisi v Kieve," *Kievskii telegraf*, 29 January 1875, 1–2; continued in *Kievskii telegraf*, 31 January 1875, 1–2.

109. *Vydumki "Kievlianina" i pol'skikh gazet o malorusskom patriotizme* (Kiev: Kievskii telegraf, 1874), 21–22, 28, 89–90.

110. Konstantin Voskresenskii, "Arkheologicheskii s"ezd," *Kievlianin*, 22 August 1874, 1–2.

111. M. Dragomanov, "Pis'mo k redaktoru 'Kievlianina,'" *Kievlianin*, 12 September 1874, 1–3; "Literaturnye priemy redaktora 'Kievlianina,'" *Kievskii telegraf*, 11 October 1874, 2–3; "K sozhaleniiu, eshche raz po vsem nadoevshemu delu," *Kievlianin*, 15 October 1874, 4. See also Fabian Baumann, "Vid spivpratsi do konfrontatsiï: Mykhailo Drahomanov, rodyna Shul'ginykh i rozbrat u seredovyshchi kyïvs'koï intelihentsiï," forthcoming in *Spadshchyna: Literaturne dzhereloznavstvo, tekstolohiia* 16.

112. "Khitroumnomu Odisseiu 'Kievskago Telegrafa,'" *Kievlianin*, 22 March 1875, 2.

113. Savchenko, *Zaborona ukraïnstva*, 61–64, 145–47.

114. P. Antonovich to A. Shirinskii-Shikhmatov, 5 July 1875, TsDIAK, f. 707, op. 261 (1875), spr. 18, ark. 22zv; P. Antonovich to A. Shirinskii-Shikhmatov, 19 July 1875, TsDIAK, f. 707, op. 261 (1875), spr. 17, ark. 15–15zv.

115. "Ot vykhodiashchikh sotrudnikov," *Kievskii telegraf*, 30 July 1875, 2.

116. The entire text is printed in Savchenko, *Zaborona ukraïnstva*, 372–81.

117. For a detailed account of the origins and execution of the Ems Ukaz see Miller, *Ukrainian Question*, 179–97.

118. Drahomanov, "Avtobiograficheskaia zametka," 1:61–63; Shcherbyna, "Z kolyshn'oho zhyttia," IR NBUV, f. 179, od. zb. 889, ark. 31.

119. Miller, *Ukrainian Question*, 201; Remy, *Brothers or Enemies*, 217.

120. Diary entry for 11 March 1876, Kistiakivs'kyi, *Shchodennyk*, 1:118.

121. V. Berenshtam to M. Drahomanov, 12/24 August 1876, in Smal'-Stots'kyi, *Arkhiv Mykhaila Drahomanova*, 59.

122. The term "Little Russian" came to designate locals loyal to Russian culture and the empire precisely during the 1860s and 1870s. See Kotenko, Martyniuk, and Miller, "Maloross," 2:418–24.

123. Savchenko, *Zaborona ukraïnstva*, 374.

124. Miller, *Ukrainian Question*, 141–45, 161–62, 201–2; V. S. Shandra, *Heneral-hubernatorstva v Ukraïni: XIX–pochatok XX st.* (Kyiv: Natsional'na akademiia nauk Ukraïny, 2005), 310–15; Hillis, *Children of Rus'*, 87–89.

125. See, for instance, Christopher Ely, *Underground Petersburg: Radical Populism, Urban Space, and the Tactics of Subversion in Reform-Era Russia* (DeKalb: Northern Illinois University Press, 2016), 118–35.

126. Franco Venturi, *Roots of Revolution: A History of the Populist and Socialist Movements in Nineteenth Century Russia* (London: Weidenfeld & Nicolson, 1964), 565; see also Vladimir Debogorii-Mokrievich, *Vospominaniia* (Saint Petersburg: Knigoizdatel'stvo "Svobodnyi trud," 1906), 111–31; P. B. Aksel'rod, *Perezhitoe i peredumannoe* (Berlin: Izdatel'stvo Z. I. Grzhebina, 1923), 106–25.

127. Savchenko, *Zaborona ukraïnstva*, 380.

128. P. Zhytets'kyi to M. Drahomanov, 13 February 1873, in Smal'-Stots'kyi, *Arkhiv Mykhaila Drahomanova*, 130–31.

129. Savchenko, *Zaborona ukraïnstva*, 106–8; Miller, *Ukrainian Question*, 162–63.

130. "Shalosti vzroslykh detei," *Kievlianin*, 7 September 1874, 1–2; "Malen'kim-velikim liudiam," *Kievlianin*, 5 November 1874, 1.

131. See "Segobochnym i togobochnym avtokhtonam," *Kievlianin*, 4 May 1874, 1–2.

132. This metaphor is inspired by Viktor Shklovskii's comments on the sequence of generations in literature: "The inheritance does not pass from father to son, but from uncle to nephew." What he meant is that a new generation of prominent writers emerges among the successors of a previously minor group, not within the formerly dominant school. See Viktor Shklovskii, *O teorii prozy* (Moscow: Izdatel'stvo "Federatsiia," 1929), 227.

133. Savchenko, *Zaborona ukraïnstva*, 78, 274.

134. Ie. V. Paikova, "Volodymyr Naumenko (1852–1919)," *Ukraïns'kyi istorychnyi zhurnal*, no. 6 (1998): 91; Shul'gin, *1919 god*, 114. Iakov's middle sister Aleksandra got married to the director of the Simferopol state bank. The oldest sister, Nadezhda, may have died as a teenager.

135. Diary entry for 8 March 1876, Kistiakivs'kyi, *Shchodennyk*, 1:111.

136. Ia. Shul'gin to N. Bunge, 5 October 1892, GARF, f. 102, op. 90, d. 853, l. 50.

137. Shcherbyna, "Pamiaty Iakova Shul'hyna," 5; Shul'hyn, "Uryvky iz spohadiv," 230.

138. Similarly, Mikhail Iuzefovich's son Boris would play an important role in the consolidation of Russian nationalist political organizations in the early twentieth century.

139. This situation was comparable to Austrian Galicia, where Russophiles and Ukrainophiles engaged in similar cultural and organizational work, albeit for different motives. See Wendland, *Die Russophilen in Galizien*, 572-73.

140. Andreas Kappeler, *Russland als Vielvölkerreich: Entstehung, Geschichte, Zerfall* (Munich: C. H. Beck, 1992), 183-91.

141. Gary B. Cohen, "Nationalist Politics and the Dynamics of State and Civil Society in the Habsburg Monarchy, 1867-1914," *Central European History* 40, no. 2 (2007): 241-78.

142. Brian Porter, *When Nationalism Began to Hate: Imagining Modern Politics in Nineteenth-Century Poland* (New York: Oxford University Press, 2000).

2. Niche Nationalism

1. E. Sedlaczek to Count G. Kálnoky von Kőröspatak, 6 September 1893, published in Dmytro Doroshenko, "Ukraïns'kyi rukh 1890-kh rokiv v osvitlenni avstriis'koho konsulia v Kyievi," in *Z mynuloho. Zbirnyk*, vol. 1 (Warsaw: Ukraïns'kyi naukovyi instytut, 1938), 63-64.

2. See, for instance, Orest Subtelny, *Ukraine: A History* (Toronto: University of Toronto Press, 1988), 283ff.; Iaroslav Hrytsak, *Narys istoriï Ukraïny: Formuvannia modernoï ukraïns'koï natsiï XIX–XX stolittia* (Kyiv: Heneza, 1996), 71ff.; Paul R. Magocsi, *A History of Ukraine: The Land and Its Peoples*, 2nd ed. (Toronto: University of Toronto Press, 2010), 400-404, 407.

3. Historians have long recognized that private and domestic spaces were important settings of political debate throughout the nineteenth century, and that it is thus impossible to draw a strict dividing line between the private and public spheres. For my discussion, I define "private life" as all social practices that take place inside family homes and are only accessible by personal invitation, as opposed to press debates, public associations, or bureaucratic higher-level politics. See Jeff Weintraub, "The Theory and Politics of the Public/Private Distinction," in *Public and Private in Thought and Practice: Perspectives on a Grand Dichotomy*, ed. Jeff Weintraub (Chicago: University of Chicago Press, 1997), 1-42; K. D. Reynolds, *Aristocratic Women and Political Society in Victorian Britain* (Oxford: Clarendon, 1998), 154-55.

4. "O syne kollezhskago sovetnika politicheskom ssyl'nom Iakove Nikolaeve Shul'gine, Protokol No. 2," 1882, GARF, f. 112, op. 1, d. 559, l. 17ob.

5. Shcherbyna, "Z kolyshn'oho zhyttia," IR NBUV, f. 179, od. zb. 889, ark. 31; Deich, "M. P. Dragomanov v izgnanii"; Myhkailo Hrushevs'kyi, *Z pochyniv ukraïns'koho sotsiialistychnoho rukhu. Mykh. Drahomanov i zhenevs'kyi sotsiialistychnyi hurtok.* (Vienna: Institut sociologique ukrainien, 1922), 59-63, 75-81; Monika Bankowski, "'Kleinrussischer Separatist' oder 'russischer Nihilist'? M. P. Drahomanov und die Anfänge der ukrainischen Emigration in der

Schweiz," in *Asyl und Aufenthalt: Die Schweiz als Zuflucht und Wirkungsstätte von Slaven im 19. und 20. Jahrhundert*, ed. Monika Bankowski et al. (Basel: Helbing & Lichtenhahn, 1994), 107–38.

6. Ia. N. [Shul'gin] to V. N. [Smirnov], 28 February 1876, in *Lysty Mykhaila Drahomanova do redaktoriv rosiis'koho sotsiial'no-revoliutsiinoho vydania "Vpered" (1876–1878)*, ed. Mykhailo Pavlyk (Lemberg: Drukarnia I. Aikhel'bergera, 1910), 13–19.

7. Liudmyla Myshchenko, "Z mynuloho stolittia. Spomyny," *Za sto lit* 4 (1929): 109–10. The French police file is in APP, BA 196. I thank Faith Hillis for providing this document.

8. Iu. Tsvitkovs'kyi to M. Drahomanov, 7 July 1877, in Smal'-Stots'kyi, *Arkhiv Mykhaila Drahomanova*, 222–29.

9. Oleksandr Riabinin-Skliarevs'kyi, "Z revoliutsiinoho ukraïns'koho rukhu 1870-kh rokiv: Odes'ka hromada 1870-kh rokiv," *Ukraïna. Naukovyi dvokhmisiachnyk ukraïnoznavstva* 19, no. 5 (1926): 117–37; Sofiia Iehunova-Shcherbyna, "Odes'ka Hromada kintsia 70-kh rokiv (spomyny)," *Za sto lit* 2 (1928): 189–99.

10. Riabinin-Skliarevs'kyi, "Z revoliutsiinoho ukraïns'koho rukhu," 126; Shul'hyn, "Uryvky iz spohadiv," 234.

11. A. Zheliabov to M. Drahomanov, 12 May 1880, in M. P. Dragomanov, *K biografii A. I. Zheliabova* (Geneva: Imprimerie de La Parole Libre, 1882), 5, 10–15.

12. See Ely, *Underground Petersburg*, 7–11.

13. S. I. Svitlenko, *Narodnytstvo v Ukraïni 60–80-kh rokiv XIX stolittia: Teoretychni problemy dzhereloznavstva ta istoriï* (Dnipropetrovs'k: Navchal'na Knyha, 1999).

14. Iu. A. Safronova, "Vovlechenie v politicheskoe: Revoliutsionnoe narodnichestvo 1870-kh godov kak soobshchestvo chitatelei," *Vestnik permskogo universiteta* 41, no. 2 (2018): 65–74.

15. V. D. Novitskii, *Iz vospominanii zhandarma* (1929; repr., Moscow: Izdatel'stvo Moskovskogo Universiteta, 1991), 87.

16. "Svod ukazanii, dannykh nekotorymi iz arestovannykh po delam o gosudarstvennykh prestupleniiakh (Mai 1880 goda)," *Byloe*, no. 6 (1907): 120–21; Aksel'rod, *Perezhitoe i peredumannoe*, 108–9. On "conspiratorial apartments" see Ely, *Underground Petersburg*, 185–92.

17. Novitskii, *Iz vospominanii zhandarma*, 129.

18. "Kopii pokazanii Bogoslovskogo A. A. i Zabramskogo A. I.," 6 March 1880, TsDIAK, f. 442, op. 830, spr. 41a, ark. 20zv–22zv; "Svod ukazanii," 152; Riabinin-Skliarevs'kyi, "Kyïvs'ka Hromada," 147.

19. See Claudia Verhoeven, *The Odd Man Karakozov: Imperial Russia, Modernity, and the Birth of Terrorism* (Ithaca, NY: Cornell University Press, 2009), 33–38.

20. "Spravka na Shul'gina Iakova Nikolaevicha," November 1879, GARF, f. 109, op. 230, d. 10116, ll. 1–2.

21. "Spravka na Shul'gina Iakova Nikolaevicha," ll. 7, 12.

22. Venturi, *Roots of Revolution*, 635–38.

23. Oleksandr Riabinin-Skliarevs'kyi, "Z revoliutsiinoho ukraïns'koho rukhu 1870-kh rr. v dobu tymchasovykh heneral-hubernatoriv," *Za sto lit*, no. 1 (1927): 156.

24. E. Totleben to M. Chertkov, 27 November 1879, TsDIAK, f. 442, op. 829, spr. 416, ark. 15zv–16zv.

25. See Katy Turton, *Family Networks and the Russian Revolutionary Movement, 1870–1940* (London: Palgrave Macmillan, 2018), 93–99.

26. "O syne kollezhskago sovetnika Shul'gine," GARF, f. 112, op. 1, d. 559, l. 17.

27. N. Bunge to V. Plehve, 8 February 1882; A. Shcherbina to I. Durnovo, 21 October 1882; medical report, 20 January 1883, GARF, f. 102, op. 90, d. 853, ll. 3–3ob, 20, 24.

28. Medical report; I. Durnovo to the Eniseisk Governor, 12 March 1883, GARF, f. 102, op. 90, d. 853, ll. 24–26.

29. Ia. Shul'gin and L. Shul'hyna to P. Zhytets'kyi, 28 March 1890, IR NBUV, f. I, od. zb. 49056.

30. Ia.Sh., "Osvěta na Ukraině," *Zoria*, no. 20 (1885): 235. The article was part of a longer text on Ukraine's political situation, which, however, the journal's editor Ivan Franko refused to publish. Unfortunately, I have not been able to locate the manuscript. See I. Franko to M. Drahomanov, 4 November 1885, in Ivan Franko, *Zibrannia tvoriv u p'iatdesiaty tomakh* (Kyiv: Naukova dumka, 1976–1986), 48:566.

31. Copy of V. Novitskii's report to Kiev University, 6 September 1884, TsDIAK, f. 707, op. 262 (1887), spr. 3, ark. 2–4. Testimony against Iakov Shul'gin is found in TsDIAK, f. 385, op. 1, spr. 132 and TsDIAK, f. 442, op. 830, spr. 41a.

32. Ia. Shul'gin to V. Vel'iaminov-Zernov, 15 November 1888, TsDIAK, f. 707, op. 262 (1887), spr. 3, ark. 7–12.

33. Ia. Shul'gin to N. Bunge, 5 October 1892; N. Shebeko to N. Bunge, 19 December 1892, GARF, f. 102, op. 90, d. 853, l. 49–51ob.

34. "Formuliarnyi spisok o sluzhbe Ia. N. Shul'gina," DAK, f. 108, op. 94, spr. 346, ark. 1zv; Shul'hyn, "Uryvky iz spohadiv," 239, 252.

35. Police report, 25 January 1900; report by V. Novitskii, 31 October 1901, GARF, f. 102, op. 90, d. 853, ll. 65, 67ob.

36. Ia. Shul'gin to D. Sipiagin, 31 December 1901, GARF, f. 102, op. 90, d. 853, ll. 73–74.

37. V. Novitskii to the Police Department, 20 January 1902, GARF, f. 102, op. 90, d. 853, l. 77–78ob.

38. Shul'hyn, "Uryvky iz spohadiv," 230, 253.

39. Similar cases are discussed in Barbara Alpern Engel, *Mothers and Daughters: Women of the Intelligentsia in Nineteenth-Century Russia* (Cambridge: Cambridge University Press, 1983), 176; Turton, *Family Networks*, 19.

40. "Formuliarnyi spisok o sluzhbe Ia. N. Shul'gina," DAK, f. 108, op. 94, spr. 346, ark. 1–4zv.

41. Paustovskii describes Iakov Shul'gin as a "meek and gentle old man," whose illness caused occasional bouts of fury: Konstantin Paustovskii, *Povest' o zhizni* (Moscow: Sovetskaia Rossiia, 1966), 1:274–76.

42. Shul'hyn, "Uryvky iz spohadiv," 256.

43. Myhkailo Hrushevs'kyi, "Pamiaty Iakova Shul'hyna," *Zapysky Naukovoho Tovarystva im. Shevchenka* 107 (1912): 5.

44. On the remaining Drahomanovite student circles see Mariia Berenshtam-Kistiakovs'ka, "Ukraïns'ki hurtky v Kyïvi druhoï polovyny 1880-ykh ta pochatku 1890-ykh rokiv," *Za sto lit* 3 (1928): 206–25.

45. Porter, *When Nationalism Began to Hate*, 43–74; Norman Davies, *Heart of Europe: The Past in Poland's Present* (Oxford: Oxford University Press, 2001), 148–51, 179–85.

46. Teslia, *Istinno russkie liudi*, 236–37.

47. Diary entry for 2 March 1884, Kistiakivs'kyi, *Shchodennyk*, 2:455.

48. Stara Hromada to M. Drahomanov, [1886?], translated in Bilenky, *Fashioning Modern Ukraine*, 401.

49. P. Antonovich to A. Shirinskii-Shikhmatov, 19 July 1875, TsDIAK, f. 707, op. 261 (1875), spr. 17, ark. 14zv.

50. Diary entry for 12 February 1880, Kistiakivs'kyi, *Shchodennyk*, 2:73.

51. In 1881–1882, the newspaper *Trud* also occasionally expressed Ukrainian sympathies. See Starozhil, *Kiev v vos'midesiatykh godakh*, 51.

52. Maryna Paliienko, *"Kievskaia starina" u hromads'komu ta naukovomu zhytti Ukraïny (kinets' XIX–pochatok XX st.)* (Kyiv: Tempora, 2005), 1:33–34.

53. On the Lebedintsevs' peculiar brand of local patriotism see Heather Coleman, "History, Faith, and Regional Identity in Nineteenth-Century Kyiv: Father Petro Lebedyntsev as Priest and Scholar," in *The Future of the Past: New Perspectives on Ukrainian History*, ed. Serhii Plokhy (Cambridge, MA: Harvard University Press, 2016), 333–62.

54. Quoted in Paliienko, *Kievskaia starina*, 1:157–58.

55. Paliienko, *Kievskaia starina*, 1:99–100; Kappeler, *Der schwierige Weg zur Nation*, 131, 144–46.

56. Ihnat Zhytets'kyi, "'Kievskaia starina' sorok rokiv tomu," *Za sto lit* 3 (1928): 141; Hillis, *Children of Rus'*, 101, 104.

57. Paliienko, *Kievskaia starina*, 1:47–63.

58. Monika Baár, *Historians and Nationalism: East-Central Europe in the Nineteenth Century* (Oxford: Oxford University Press, 2010), 57.

59. V. B. Antonovich, "N. I. Kostomarov, kak istorik," *Kievskaia starina*, no. 5 (1885): xxxiii.

60. See Bohdan Klid, "Volodymyr Antonovych: Ukrainian Populist Historiography and the Cultural Politics of Nation Building," in *Historiography of Imperial Russia: The Profession and Writing of History in a Multinational State*, ed. Thomas Sanders (Armonk, NY: M. E. Sharpe, 1999), 390n25.

61. Dmitrii Bagalei and Vasilii Danilevich were at Kharkov University, Ivan Linnichenko and Oleksandr Hrushevs'kyi at Odessa, Mitrofan Dovnar-Zapol'skii at Kiev. Not all of them were enthusiastic Ukrainophiles; Linnichenko, for instance, championed All-Russian unity.

62. See Baár, *Historians and Nationalism*, 64ff.

63. Olga Andriewsky, "The Russian-Ukrainian Discourse and the Failure of the 'Little Russian Solution,'" in *Culture, Nation, and Identity: The Ukrainian-Russian Encounter, 1600–1945*, ed. Andreas Kappeler et al. (Toronto: Canadian Institute of Ukrainian Studies, 2003), 203–7.

64. V. Antonovich, "Kiev, ego sud'ba i znachenie s XIV po XVI stoletie (1362–1569)," *Kievskaia starina*, no. 1 (1882): 1–48, quotation 35. In reading

late medieval Lithuania as an East Slavic state, Antonovych (without acknowledging it) followed in the footsteps of the Russian historian Nikolai Ustrialov. See Teslia, *Istinno russkie liudi*, 94–112.

65. In 1895, *Kievskaia starina* initiated a competition for a synthetic history of Ukraine. Its winner was a female historian, Aleksandra Efimenko, but the journal's editors were not quite happy with her *History of the Ukrainian People*, which was only published in 1906. See Kappeler, *Russland und die Ukraine*, 214–25.

66. Volodymyr Antonovych had previously refused the position and recommended his student instead. See Serhii Plokhy, *Unmaking Imperial Russia: Mykhailo Hrushevsky and the Writing of Ukrainian History* (Toronto: University of Toronto Press, 2005), 39–40.

67. Plokhy, 95–116.

68. Kappeler, *Der schwierige Weg zur Nation*, 141–43; Paliienko, *Kievskaia starina*, 1:65–70, 161–66.

69. Diary entry for 11 June 1895, Serhii Iefremov, *Shchodennyk. Pro dni mynuli (spohady)*, ed. Ihor Hyrych (Kyiv: Tempora, 2011), 113.

70. V. Naumenko, "Knizhnaia rech′ u malorossov i rusinov," *Kievskaia starina*, no. 1 (1899): 135–42.

71. T. Florinskii, "Neskol′ko slov o malorusskom iazyke (narechii) i noveishikh popytkakh usvoit′ emu rol′ organa nauki i vysshei obrazovannosti," *Kievlianin*, 1 December 1899, 2.

72. V. Naumenko, "Reshen-li prof. T. D. Florinskim vopros o knizhnoi malorusskoi rechi?," *Kievskaia starina*, no. 1 (1900): 130.

73. Ievhen Chykalenko, *Spohady (1861–1907)* (1925; repr., New York: Ukr. vil′na akademiia nauk u SShA, 1955), 368–69; Olga Andriewsky, "The Politics of National Identity: The Ukrainian Question in Russia, 1904–1912" (PhD diss., Harvard University, 1991), 64–71, 79–84.

74. *Ob otmene stesnenii malorusskago pechatnago slova* (Saint Petersburg: Tipografiia imperatorskoi akademii nauk, 1905), 25.

75. George Y. Shevelov, *The Ukrainian Language in the First Half of the Twentieth Century (1900–1941): Its State and Status* (Cambridge, MA: Harvard Ukrainian Research Institute, 1989), 36; Fabian Baumann, "The Debate on Ukrainian Identities in the Duma and the Russian Press, 1905–1914" (M.Phil thesis, University of Oxford, 2014), 31–33.

76. V. Naumenko to Ie. Chykalenko, 9 April 1900, IR NBUV, f. I, od. zb. 35635, ark. 1b.

77. V. Naumenko to S. Iefremov, 11 April 1902, IL NANU, f. 120, od. zb. 375, ark. 1.

78. Zhytets′kyi, "Kievskaia starina," 144.

79. Paliienko, *Kievskaia starina*, 1:45. The same donors kept the Ukrainian-language daily *Rada* going after 1906.

80. Plokhy, *Unmaking Imperial Russia*, 26–27.

81. Magocsi, *History of Ukraine*, 307–17. A recent assessment stresses the religious aspect of the violence: Barbara Skinner, "Borderlands of Faith: Reconsidering the Origins of a Ukrainian Tragedy," *Slavic Review* 64, no. 1 (2005): 88–116.

82. V. B. Antonovich, *Izsledovanie o gaidamachestve po aktam 1700–1768 g.* (Kiev: Universitetskaia tipografiia I. I. Zavadskago, 1876).

83. Taras Shevchenko, *Haidamaky. Poema* (1841; repr., Saint Petersburg: Drukarnia P. A. Kulisha, 1861).

84. Ia. Shul'gin, "Ocherk kolievshchiny po neizdannym i izdannym dokumentam 1768 i blizhaishikh gg.," *Kievskaia starina*, no. 2 (1890): 185–220; no. 3 (1890): 381–418; no. 4 (1890): 22–52; no. 5 (1890): 268–306; no. 6 (1890): 409–26; no. 7 (1890): 1–21; no. 8 (1890): 192–223.

85. Shul'gin, "Ocherk kolievshchiny," 2:188–89.

86. Shul'gin, "Ocherk kolievshchiny," 2:220; 3:385–87, 409–10, 417–18; 4:27, 30–31. The text uses the derogatory term *zhid* for Jews, but this probably reflects the Polish and Ukrainian of the sources rather than the author's prejudice.

87. Shul'gin, "Ocherk kolievshchiny," 5:272, 283, 297.

88. Shul'gin, "Ocherk kolievshchiny," 2:197–99, 7:10ff., 8:210.

89. Tadeusz Korzon, "Nowa książka o koliszczyźnie," *Kwartalnik historyczny*, no. 3 (1892): 527–40, quotation 540. Iakov's response is Ia. Shul'gin, " 'Pravda' o koliivshchine pol'skago istorika g. Korzona," *Kievskaia starina*, no. 1 (1893): 126–60.

90. Kotenko, Martyniuk, and Miller, "Maloross," 2:415.

91. As in the only seemingly pleonastic expression "the South Russian Ukrainian population." Shul'gin, "Ocherk kolievshchiny," 8:192.

92. On Iakov's worries about censorship see Ia. Shul'gin to E. Kivlitskii, 15 July 1890, IR NBUV, f. III, od. zb. 9467, ark. 2–2zv.

93. Ia. Shul'gin to D. Sipiagin, 31 December 1901, GARF, f. 102, op. 90, d. 853, l. 74. Emphasis in the original.

94. Iakiv Shul'hyn, *Nacherk koliïvshchyni na pidstavi vydanykh i nevydanykh dokumentiv 1768 i blyzshykh rokiv* (Lemberg: Rus'ka istorychna biblioteka, 1898), i–iv.

95. L.Ch. [Iakov Shul'gin], "Ukraïna pislia 1654 roku," *Zapysky Naukovoho Tovarystva im. Shevchenka* 29 (1899): 1–13; 30 (1899): 14–67.

96. Hrushevs'kyi, "Pamiaty Iakova Shul'hyna," 7. One section, dealing with the reemergence of serfdom in Ukraine, appeared in a Petersburg journal in 1887. Long abolished by that time, serfdom was a more acceptable object for historical criticism than the curtailment of Ukrainian autonomy. See Ia. Shul'gin, "Razvitie krepostnogo prava v Malorossii XVII–XVIII vv.," *Severnyi vestnik*, no. 6 (1887): 50–64.

97. See Martin Rohde, *Nationale Wissenschaft zwischen zwei Imperien: Die Ševčenko-Gesellschaft der Wissenschaften, 1892–1918* (Göttingen: V&R unipress, 2022), 80, 87–88.

98. Serhy Yekelchyk, "The Nation's Clothes: Constructing a Ukrainian High Culture in the Russian Empire, 1860–1900," *Jahrbücher für Geschichte Osteuropas* 49, no. 2 (2001): 230–39.

99. Shul'hyn, "Uryvky iz spohadiv," 204, 227.

100. In 1862, a neighbor had denounced Ustimovich for hosting a dinner for three thousand recently freed serfs. Dressed in peasant costume, he had told them

not to pay for their land since it rightfully belonged to them anyway. Upon his arrest, Ustimovich confirmed the accusations and presented a memorandum on the peasant question. He seems to have escaped punishment because he was declared insane. Amazingly, his memorandum actually reached the minister of internal affairs Valuev. See "O vnushenii krest'ianam nepovinovenii pomeshchikom Poltavskoi guber. Ustimovichem," 1862, GARF, f. 109, op. 202, d. 154.

101. Colonel Bashin to V. von Plehve, 27 August 1882, GARF, f. 102, op. 78, d. 522, l. 2.

102. Shul'hyn, "Uryvky iz spohadiv," 218-21.

103. Shul'hyn, "Uryvky iz spohadiv," 201, 207-9, 221-22.

104. Alexandre Choulguine, *L'Ukraine contre Moscou (1917)* (Paris: Alcan, 1935), 17.

105. Shul'hyn, "Uryvky iz spohadiv," 243.

106. Ia. Shul'gin to M. Hrushevs'kyi, 12 December 1901, TsDIAK, f. 1235, op. 1, spr. 848, ark. 15.

107. Shul'hyn, "Uryvky iz spohadiv," 243-44.

108. Eric J. Hobsbawm, *Nations and Nationalism since 1780: Programme, Myth, Reality* (Cambridge: Cambridge University Press, 1990), 112. See also Ihor Hyrych, "Ukraïns'ka mova v zhytti diiachiv natsional'no-vyzvol'noho rukhu Naddniprianshchyny XIX-poch. XX st.," *Kyïvs'ka starovyna*, no. 2 (2012): 51-67.

109. Chykalenko, *Spohady*, 298-99. It is a bit surprising that the Shul'hyns' in-laws, the Naumenko family, are not on Chykalenko's list, given Volodymyr Naumenko's well-documented excellent command of Ukrainian. Possibly the ever-cautious Naumenko did not wish to compromise his position as a schoolteacher or his wife Vera had never learned the language.

110. Mykola Galagan, *Z moikh spomyniv* (L'viv: Chervona kalyna, 1930), 1:81-83.

111. Shul'hyn, "Uryvky iz spohadiv," 260.

112. Olena Pchilka, *Opovidannia z avtobiohrafiieiu* (Kharkiv: Rukh, 1930), 30.

113. Nadiia Shul'hyna-Ishchuk, "Spohad," n.d., Ishchuk-Pazuniak Private Collection, 1; Shul'hyn, "Uryvky iz spohadiv," 219, 248-50.

114. Shul'hyn, "Uryvky iz spohadiv," 262. See, by way of comparison, Catriona Kelly, *Children's World: Growing Up in Russia, 1890–1991* (New Haven, CT: Yale University Press, 2007), 455ff.

115. Remy, *Brothers or Enemies*, 221.

116. Shul'hyn, "Uryvky iz spohadiv," 261.

117. Heidrun Zettelbauer, *"Die Liebe sei Euer Heldentum": Geschlecht und Nation in völkischen Vereinen der Habsburgermonarchie* (Frankfurt am Main: Campus, 2005), 215, 221, 226.

118. Chykalenko, *Spohady*, 299.

119. Serhii Shelukhyn, "Ukraïnstvo 80-kh rokiv i moï znosyny z Iv. Frankom," *Literaturno-naukovyi visnyk*, no. 7-8 (1926): 271-73.

120. Shul'hyn, "Uryvky iz spohadiv," 243. On the political selection of partners see Hrytsak, *Ivan Franko*, 295.

121. Heorhii Kas'ianov, *Ukraïns'ka intelihentsiia na rubezhi XIX–XX stolit': Sotsial'no-politychnyi portret* (Kyiv: Lybid', 1993), 46.

122. McClintock, "Family Feuds," 66.

123. Choulguine, *L'Ukraine contre Moscou*, 21, 23-24.

124. The binary opposition between two parents' characters is a trope that has also been identified in the autobiographies of Russian priests' sons: Laurie Manchester, *Holy Fathers, Secular Sons: Clergy, Intelligentsia, and the Modern Self in Revolutionary Russia* (DeKalb: Northern Illinois University Press, 2008), 111.

125. Partha Chatterjee, "The Nationalist Solution of the Women's Question," in *Recasting Women: Essays in Indian Colonial History*, ed. Kumkum Sangari and Sudesh Vaid (New Brunswick, NJ: Rutgers University Press, 1990), 238-39.

126. Ute Planert, "Vater Staat und Mutter Germania: Zur Politisierung des weiblichen Geschlechts im 19. und 20. Jahrhundert," in *Nation, Politik und Geschlecht: Frauenbewegungen und Nationalismus in der Moderne*, ed. Ute Planert (Frankfurt am Main: Campus, 2000), 44.

127. See, by way of comparison, Engel, *Mothers and Daughters*, 191-98; Martha Bohachevsky-Chomiak, *Feminists despite Themselves: Women in Ukrainian Community Life, 1884-1939* (Edmonton: Canadian Institute of Ukrainian Studies, 1988), xxii.

128. Diary entry for 3 May 1883, Kistiakivs'kyi, *Shchodennyk*, 2:416; Myshchenko, "Z mynuloho stolittia," 146. Ukraine's "lexicographic revolution"—a crucial element of nineteenth-century nationalism according to Benedict Anderson—lagged several decades behind other European languages. See Benedict Anderson, *Imagined Communities: Reflections on the Origin and Spread of Nationalism*, rev. ed. (1983; repr., London: Verso, 2006), 71-75.

129. Oleksander Lotots'kyi, *Storinky mynuloho* (1932-1934; repr., [Bound Brook, NJ]: Vyd. ukraïns'koï pravoslavnoï tserkvy v SShA, 1966), 1:169-70. According to Lotots'kyi, a policeman once came in during Antonovych's lecture, upon which Antonovych immediately changed the topic to speak about (unsuspicious) archaeological excavations, while the landlady treated the policeman to a glass of wine and a bribe.

130. Lotots'kyi, *Storinky mynuloho*, 1:171-72, 196; Chykalenko, *Spohady*, 111-12, 310-11, 326-27; Bohachevsky-Chomiak, *Feminists despite Themselves*, 35; Shul'hyn, "Uryvky iz spohadiv," 229, 254.

131. N. Vasilenko, "V. P. Naumenko i 'Kievskaia starina,'" 1919, printed in Paliienko, *Kievskaia starina*, 1:182.

132. Here I follow those historians who assert that a "cult of domesticity" inspired by Western bourgeois models took root in late nineteenth-century Russia at least as an ideal. See Engel, *Breaking the Ties*, 160-68.

133. On the Russian home as a "stage for modern self-creation and performance" see Randolph, *House in the Garden*, 5.

134. On the Ukrainophiles' use of "national dress" see Serhy Yekelchyk, "The Body and National Myth: Motifs from the Ukrainian National Revival in the Nineteenth Century," *Australian Slavonic and East European Studies* 7, no. 2 (1993): 31-59.

135. Letter excerpt, I. Steshenko to S. Iurkevich, 27 February 1892, GARF, f. 102, op. 226, d. 707, l. 4.

136. Galagan, *Z moïkh spomyniv*, 1:83.

137. Shul'hyn, "Uryvky iz spohadiv," 252.

138. Shul'hyn, "Uryvky iz spohadiv," 229, 299–302, 307.

139. "Iz ukrainofil'skago lageria," *Kievlianin*, 19 August 1908, 3.

140. V. Antonovych to F. Vovk, 11 January 1891, in Marko D. Antonovych, "Nedrukovani lysty V. B. Antonovycha do F. K. Vovka (z arkhivu VUAN)," *Ukraïns'kyi istoryk*, no. 1–4 (1988): 158–59.

141. Chykalenko, *Spohady*, 241–42; Iefremov, *Shchodennyk. Pro dni mynuli*, 431–32.

142. Information on addresses comes from various editions of the annual address book *Adresnaia i spravochnaia kniga Ves' Kiev* (Kiev: Izdanie M. L Radominskago [et al.], 1899–1915).

143. Chykalenko, *Spohady*, 291.

144. Report by gendarme agent M. Zhelezniak, 2 July 1900, published in Paliienko, *Kievskaia starina*, 1:168.

145. Mayhill C. Fowler, "'A Theatrical Mecca': The Stages of Kyiv in 1907," in *Modernism in Kyiv: Jubilant Experimentation*, ed. Irena R. Makaryk (Toronto: University of Toronto Press, 2010), 35–42; Natan M. Meir, *Kiev, Jewish Metropolis: A History, 1859–1914* (Bloomington: Indiana University Press, 2010), 194.

146. Shul'hyn, "Uryvky iz spohadiv," 230; Shul'gin, *Teni*, 37.

147. Report by V. Novitskii, 15 March 1886, GARF, f. 102, op. 226, d. 707, l. 2.

148. M. Lysenko to H. Kovalenko-Kolomats'kyi, 5 May 1897, in Mykola Lysenko, *Lysty*, ed. O. Lysenko (Kyiv: Mystetstvo, 1964), 284.

149. Police report, 3 October 1899, GARF, f. 102, op. 97, d. 4118, l. 1aob.

150. Police report to the Kiev governor, 16 February 1902, GARF, f. 102, op. 97, d. 4118, l. 18.

151. Shul'hyn, "Uryvky iz spohadiv," 211–14. Leontovich's older brother Ivan was a centrist politician and a member of the State Council from 1906 to 1911; his younger brother Volodymyr was a Ukrainian-language writer and became involved in the Ukrainian national movement.

152. Shul'hyn, "Uryvky iz spohadiv," 214–18.

153. On the "limited relevance of ethnicity to everyday social experience" see Rogers Brubaker et al., *Nationalist Politics and Everyday Ethnicity in a Transylvanian Town* (Princeton, NJ: Princeton University Press, 2006), esp. chap. 6, quotation 206.

154. See Shul'hyn, "Uryvky iz spohadiv," 250, 267.

155. Gary B. Cohen, *The Politics of Ethnic Survival: Germans in Prague, 1861–1914*, 2nd ed. (West Lafayette, IN: Purdue University Press, 2006), 34, 250, 267; King, *Budweisers*, 101–11, 127–29.

156. Chykalenko, *Spohady*, 353–90, 427–29; Andriewsky, "Politics of National Identity," 14–35, 128–34; Mariya Melentyeva, "Liberals and the Ukrainian Question in Imperial Russia, 1905–1917," *Revolutionary Russia* 33, no. 2 (2020): 151–71.

157. Andriewsky, "Politics of National Identity," 175–226. For Andriewsky, "the impact of the caucus on the Ukrainian national movement . . . was immediate and profound" (221), imbuing the activists with confidence in the political viability of Ukrainian nationalism.

158. Diary entry for 14 February 1909, Ievhen Chykalenko, *Shchodennyk (1907–1917)* (Kyiv: Tempora, 2011), 56. See also Andrii Danylenko, "The

'Doubling of Hallelujah' for the 'Bastard Tongue': The Ukrainian Language Question in Russian Ukraine, 1905-1916," in *The Battle for Ukrainian: A Comparative Perspective*, ed. Michael S. Flier and Andrea Graziosi (Cambridge, MA: Harvard Ukrainian Research Institute, 2017), 73-78.

159. Diary entry for 31 May 1910, Chykalenko, *Shchodennyk (1907-1917)*, 110.

160. V. Naumenko to S. Ponomarev, 28 November 1909, RGALI, f. 402, op. 1, d. 207, l. 12ob.

161. In 1908-1911, Naumenko was again investigated for Ukrainophile activism. He escaped consequences thanks to the support of his students' parents and his excellent reputation as a pedagogue. See "Delo o Direktore chastnoi muzhskoi gimnazii v Kieve Vladimire Pavloviche Naumenko," 1908-1911, TsDIAK, f. 442, op. 858, spr. 139.

162. Serhii Iefremov, "Iak povstav Hrinchenkiv slovnyk," in *Slovnyk ukraïns'koï movy*, ed. Borys Hrinchenko, 3rd ed., vol. 2 (Kyiv: Horno, 1927), v-xxiv.

163. Olga Andriewsky, "The Making of the Generation of 1917: Towards a Collective Biography," *Journal of Ukrainian Studies* 29, no. 1-2 (2004): 21.

164. N. D. Horodnia, "Oleksandr Shul'hin (1889-1960) iak predstavnyk novoï heneratsiï ukraïns'koï natsional'noï elity pershoï polovyny XX stolittia," *Visnyk Kyïvs'koho natsional'noho universytetu imeni Tarasa Shevchenka*, no. 80-81 (2005): 11.

165. Galagan, *Z moïkh spomyniv*, 1:83.

166. "Promova O. Shul'hyna na iuvileinykh zborakh u N'iu-Iorku," 1959, in Ianiv, *Zbirnyk na poshanu O. Shul'hyna*, 176. See also Shul'hyn, "Uryvky iz spohadiv," 304.

167. Jan Křen, *Die Konfliktgemeinschaft: Tschechen und Deutsche 1780-1918* (Munich: R. Oldenbourg Verlag, 1996), 184.

168. Ie. Chykalenko to P. Stebnyts'kyi, 19 September 1909, IR NBUV, f. III, od. zb. 52923, ark. 4.

169. Ie. Chykalenko to P. Stebnyts'kyi, 9 March 1910, IR NBUV, f. III, od. zb. 54935, ark. 1zv.

170. V. Vynnychenko to Ie. Chykalenko, 23 July 1912, in Ievhen Chykalenko and Volodymyr Vynnychenko, *Lystuvannia 1902-1929 roky* (Kyiv: Tempora, 2010), 224-26.

171. See Kas'ianov, *Ukraïns'ka intelihentsiia*, 69-96.

172. Kotenko, Martyniuk, and Miller, "Maloross," 2:430-31.

173. Iefremov, *Shchodennyk. Pro dni mynuli*, 532-36.

174. Shul'hyn, "Uryvky iz spohadiv," 284-85.

175. Shul'hyn, "Uryvky iz spohadiv," 265, 275-76.

176. Ia. Shul'gin to F. Vovk, 10 April 1908, NAIA NANU, f. 1, V/4637, ark. 2.

177. Choulguine, *L'Ukraine contre Moscou*, 24; Shul'hyn, "Uryvky iz spohadiv," 285, 291-92, 295-97.

178. See Richard Stites, *The Women's Liberation Movement in Russia: Feminism, Nihilism, and Bolshevism, 1860-1930* (Princeton, NJ: Princeton University Press, 1978), 82-83, 168-74.

179. "Shul'gin Aleksandr Iakovlevich," TsGIA SPb, f. 14, op. 3, d. 52119, ll. 10, 16, 33; Shul'hyn, "Uryvky iz spohadiv," 279.

180. O. Shul'hyn to F. Vovk, 4 April 1911, NAIA NANU, f. 1, V/4642, ark. 2zv.

181. On the concept of "national science" see Rohde, *Nationale Wissenschaft*, 172–211.

182. Marina Mogilner, *Homo Imperii: A History of Physical Anthropology in Russia* (Lincoln: University of Nebraska Press, 2013), 94–98.

183. F. Volkov, "Ukraintsy v antropologicheskom otnoshenii," *Ukrainskii vestnik*, no. 7 (1906): 418–26. Already in the 1860s, Franciszek Duchiński had written that Ukrainians were racially purer Slavs than Russians. Vovk's innovation was the attempt to prove this claim by means of biological indicators. See Ivan L. Rudnytsky, *Essays in Modern Ukrainian History*, ed. Peter L. Rudnytsky (Edmonton: Canadian Institute of Ukrainian Studies, 1987), 188–90.

184. Thus, Mykhailo Hrushevs'kyi cited Vovk's studies in the 1913 edition of his *History of Ukraine-Rus'*. The intertwining of racial-biological and national-cultural categories was characteristic of the period's scholarship, and biological determinism was not necessarily more rigid than the essentialized conception of national cultures. See Vera Tol'ts, "Diskursy o rase: Imperskaia Rossiia i 'Zapad' v sravnenii," in *Poniatiia o Rossii* (Moscow: Novoe literaturnoe obozrenie, 2012), 2:145–93.

185. O. Shul'hyn to F. Vovk, 5 June and 3 August [1910], NAIA NANU, f. 1, V/4643 and V/4650. On this expedition see my forthcoming article with Martin Rohde.

186. L. Strutyns'ka-Sadovs'ka, "Ukraïns'ki hromady u vyshchykh zhinochykh peterburz'kykh shkolakh (1912-1917)," in *Z mynuloho. Zbirnyk*, vol. 2 (Warsaw: Ukraïns'kyi naukovyi instytut, 1939), 110–22; Lotots'kyi, *Storinky mynuloho*, 2:69, 102, 111–12.

187. Lotots'kyi, *Storinky mynuloho*, 2:77, 127, 134–44.

188. Strutyns'ka-Sadovs'ka, "Ukraïns'ki hromady," 120.

189. N. P. Antsiferov, *Iz dum o bylom: Vospominaniia* (Moscow: Feniks, 1992), 190–91, 193.

190. Panas Fedenko, "Dmytro Chyzhevs'kyi (4 kvitnia 1894-18 kvitnia 1977): Spomyn pro zhyttia i naukovu diial'nist'," *Ukraïns'kyi istoryk*, no. 1–3 (1978): 106.

191. Antsiferov, *Iz dum o bylom*, 193.

192. Letter excerpt, O. Shul'hyn to L. Shul'hyna, 16 November 1910, GARF, f. 102, op. 240, d. 59, ch. 51lB, l. 59. On these protests see Susan K. Morrissey, *Heralds of Revolution: Russian Students and the Mythologies of Radicalism* (New York: Oxford University Press, 1998), 206–11.

193. See A. Shul'gin, "Byl-li kapitalisticheskii stroi vo frantsuzskoi promyshlennosti XVIII v.?," *Russkoe bogatstvo*, no. 8-10 (1917): 129–60.

194. O. Shul'hyn to F. Vovk, 1 January 1915, NAIA NANU, f. 1, V/4648, ark. 1.

195. Alexei Miller, "The Role of the First World War in the Competition between Ukrainian and All-Russian Nationalism," in *The Empire and Nationalism at War*, ed. Eric Lohr et al. (Bloomington, IN: Slavica, 2014), 76–77.

196. Diary entry for 17 September 1910, Chykalenko, *Shchodennyk (1907–1917)*, 126.

197. Diary entry for 30 October 1912, Chykalenko, *Shchodennyk (1907–1917)*, 246; Dmytro Doroshenko, *Moï spomyny pro davnie-mynule (1901–1914 roky)* (Winnipeg: Tryzub, 1949), 152, 163.

198. John-Paul Himka, "Young Radicals and Independent Statehood: The Idea of a Ukrainian Nation-State, 1890–1895," *Slavic Review* 41, no. 2 (1982): 219–35; Iaroslav Hrytsak, "Do henezy ideï politychnoï samostiinosti Ukraïny," *Ukraïna: Kul'turna spadshchyna, natsional'na svidomist', derzhavnist'* 1 (1992): 119–43.

199. Writing in his private diary, Ievhen Chykalenko insisted that except for a minuscule group around Mykola Mikhnovs'kyi, nobody was thinking of an independent Ukrainian state. Diary entry for 25 November 1911, Chykalenko, *Shchodennyk (1907–1917)*, 186.

200. Serhy Yekelchyk has remarked that Ukrainian nationalism therefore eludes the Hrochian periodization into a cultural stage A and a political stage B. Yekelchyk, "Nation's Clothes," 231.

201. See Philipp Ther, "'Imperial Nationalism' as Challenge for the Study of Nationalism," in *Nationalizing Empires*, ed. Stefan Berger and Alexei Miller (Budapest: Central European University Press, 2015), 588.

202. The centrality of such "collective events" for the constitution of generational groups as communities of shared experience was already acknowledged in Karl Mannheim's classical treatise. As newer research has shown, the retrospective image of a coherent generational community is often constructed through collective narratives about dramatic events. See Karl Mannheim, "Das Problem der Generationen," 1928, in *Wissenssoziologie* (Berlin: Luchterhand, 1970), 552–55; Ulrike Jureit, "Generation, Generationalität, Generationenforschung," *Docupedia Zeitgeschichte*, 2010, http://docupedia.de/zg/jureit_generation_v1_de_2010 (last accessed 2 November 2022).

3. Patriarchs and Patriots

1. "Posluzhnoi spisok ordinarnago professora Dmitriia Ivanovicha Pikhno," DAK, f. 16, op. 465, spr. 4806, ark. 16zv; "Avtobiografiia Vasiliia Vital'evicha Shul'gina," 1932, HIA, 33003, box 19, folder 37, l. 45.

2. Shul'gina, *Konspekt*, 48; L. Volkov, "Iz vospominanii o D. I. Pikhno," *Moskovskiia vedomovsti* no. 184, 1913.

3. O. I. Levyts'kyi, "Pro V. B. Antonovicha," 1912, IR NBUV, f. I, od. zb. 8076, ark. 5; V. V. Shul'gin, "Muka," 1951–1952, RGALI, f. 1337, op. 4, d. 54, ll. 29ob–31ob.

4. A. D. Bilimovich and N. M Tsytovich, *Pamiati D. I. Pikhno* (Saint Petersburg: Senatskaia tipografiia, 1913), 5–6; Shul'hyn, "Uryvky iz spohadiv," 230.

5. Chevazhevskii, "Iz proshlago Kievskago universiteta," 565.

6. Diary entry for 7 December 1876, Kistiakivs'kyi, *Shchodennyk*, 1:243.

7. *Kievlianin*, 9 June 1895, 2.

8. Ekaterina Pravilova, *A Public Empire: Property and the Quest for the Common Good in Imperial Russia* (Princeton, NJ: Princeton University Press, 2014), 6–7.

9. Diary entries for 18 November 1876, 20 December 1876, and 21 January 1877, Kistiakivs'kyi, *Shchodennyk*, 1:226, 1:260, 1:316.

10. Diary entry for 9 November 1876, Kistiakivs'kyi, *Shchodennyk*, 1:211.

11. V. Naumenko to Ia. Shul'gin, 12 February 1876, in Smal'-Stots'kyi, *Arkhiv Mykhaila Drahomanova*, 171.

12. Matich, *Zapiski russkoi amerikanki*, 46. It can now be definitively confirmed that Pikhno was Vasilii Shul'gin's biological father. Oleksandr Kistiakivs'kyi hinted at it as early as September 1879 (Kistiakivs'kyi, *Shchodennyk*, 1:544), and the rumor has since surfaced frequently. According to Olga Matich, the granddaughter of Vasilii's older sister Alla, Pikhno's fatherhood has always been an open secret in the family. Vasilii Shul'gin himself always stuck to the "official" genealogy. However, in the autobiographical notes he compiled in a Soviet prison—a text not intended for publication—he once mentioned Pikhno as "my stepfather, who was in reality my biological father." Shul'gin, "Muka," 1952, RGALI, f. 1337, op. 4, d. 56, l. 1190b.

13. *Kievlianin*, 1 January 1879, 1.

14. Diary entry for 24 August 1880, Kistiakivs'kyi, *Shchodennyk*, 2:256.

15. D. Pikhno to A. Suvorin, n.d. [1880?], RGALI, f. 459, op. 1, d. 3317, ll. 1ob–2.

16. D. Pikhno to T. Filippov, 7 November 1883, GARF, f. 1099, op. 1, d. 2404, l. 1.

17. Liudmyla Staryts'ka-Cherniakhivs'ka, "Dvadtsiat' p'iat' rokiv ukraïns'koho teatra (Spohady ta dumky)," *Ukraïna* 4, no. 10 (1907): 49–55.

18. D. Pikhno to A. Suvorin, n.d. [1880?], RGALI, f. 459, op. 1, d. 3317, l. 3ob; D. Pikhno to S. Ponomarev, 11 April 1881, RGALI, f. 402, op. 1, d. 237, l. 5.

19. "Otnositel'no priobreteniia stepeni doktora politseiskago prava D. I. Pikhno," 1888, DAK, f. 16, op. 327, spr. 36, ark. 24–25; Francis W. Wcislo, *Tales of Imperial Russia: The Life and Times of Sergei Witte, 1849–1915* (Oxford: Oxford University Press, 2011), 96.

20. See Frithjof Benjamin Schenk, *Russlands Fahrt in die Moderne: Mobilität und sozialer Raum im Eisenbahnzeitalter* (Stuttgart: F. Steiner, 2014), 37–118.

21. R. G. Krasiukov, "Kievliane Mogilevskie—vnebrachnye deti Dmitriia Ivanovicha Pikhno (1853-1913)," *Izvestiia russkogo genealogicheskogo obshchestva* 18 (2006): 48. On laws against incest see Laura Engelstein, *The Keys to Happiness: Sex and the Search for Modernity in Fin-de-Siècle Russia* (Ithaca, NY: Cornell University Press, 1992), 42–48.

22. S. Iu. Vitte, *Iz arkhiva S. Iu. Vitte: Vospominaniia*, ed. B. V. Anan'ich (Saint Petersburg: D. Bulanin, 2003), 1:149. I have not found any evidence for Witte's claim that Pikhno married Lina and that his goal was to secure her inheritance. Lina's private letters suggest a close relationship between the couple, despite frequent quarrels.

23. Krasiukov, "Kievliane Mogilevskie," 46.

24. L. Mogilevskaia [Shul'gina] to M. Krestovskaia, 21 October 1891, RGALI, f. 2174, op. 1, d. 104, l. 6.

25. L. Mogilevskaia to M. Krestovskaia, March 1897, RGALI, f. 2174, op. 1, d. 104, ll. 26–28; Shul'gin, *Teni*, 43.

26. Evg. Shol'p, "D. I. Pikhno," *Kievskaia mysl'*, 30 June 1913; "Dmitrii Ivanovich Pikhno (Nekrolog)," ibid.

27. L. Volkov, "Iz vospominanii o D. I. Pikhno," *Moskovskiia vedomovsti*, no. 184, 1913.

28. Starozhil, *Kiev v vos'midesiatykh godakh*, 90; A. E. Kaufman, *Druz'ia i vragi evreev. 1. D. I. Pikhno* (Saint Petersburg: Knigoizdatel'stvo "Pravda," 1907), 31; S. Bogdanov, "Sel'skokhoziaistvennyia zaslugi D. I. Pikhno," *Kievlianin*, 7 August 1913, 2.

29. Bilimovich and Tsytovich, *Pamiati D. I. Pikhno*, 11; Iefremov, *Shchodennyk. Pro dni mynuli*, 413–14.

30. Joachim Zweynert, *Eine Geschichte des ökonomischen Denkens in Russland: 1805–1905* (Marburg: Metropolis-Verlag, 2002), 296–303.

31. E. E. Kartavtsov, *Obrusenie zemlevladeniia v iugo-zapadnom krae* (Kiev: Universitetskaia tipografiia I. I. Zavadskago, 1877), 89, 116–37.

32. Daniel Beauvois, *La bataille de la terre en Ukraine 1863–1914: Les Polonais et les conflits socio-ethniques* (Lille: Presses universitaires, 1993), 70–71, 258–65.

33. Starozhil, *Kiev v vos'midesiatykh godakh*, 3–11; Hamm, *Kiev*, 42, 103; Bilenky, *Imperial Urbanism*, 267.

34. Meir, *Kiev, Jewish Metropolis*, 106–22, 160–64; Hillis, *Children of Rus'*, 117–34; Bilenky, *Imperial Urbanism*, 200–229.

35. Hillis, *Children of Rus'*, 135–36.

36. Meir, *Kiev, Jewish Metropolis*, 51–57; John D. Klier, *Russians, Jews, and the Pogroms of 1881–1882* (Cambridge: Cambridge University Press, 2011), 34–37, 135–37, 145–46.

37. Kaufman, *D. I. Pikhno*, 10–28, 31. Kaufman links this temporary mitigation of Pikhno's antisemitism to his "intimate friendship" with the Jewish millionaire Brodskii, who, he claims, helped Pikhno to buy estates.

38. *Kievlianin*, 14 April 1903, 1.

39. D. I. Pikhno, *Vliianie nekotorykh ekonomicheskikh uslovii na sel'skoe khoziaistvo* (Kiev: Tipografiia T-va I. N. Kushnerev, 1901), 7–8, 15.

40. "Glavneishiia nuzhdy russkago sel'skago khoziaistva," *Kievlianin*, 16 March 1902, 2; continued in *Kievlianin*, 18 March 1902, 1–2; 24 March 1902, 2–3; 28 March 1902, 2; 1 April 1902, 1–2.

41. See Heinz-Dietrich Löwe, *Antisemitismus und reaktionäre Utopie: Russischer Konservatismus im Kampf gegen den Wandel von Staat und Gesellschaft, 1890–1917* (Hamburg: Hoffmann & Campe, 1978), 23–29.

42. "Ob ekonomicheskikh zadachakh 'Zapadno-russkago obshchestva,'" *Kievlianin*, 3 February 1912, 3.

43. Starozhil, *Kiev v vos'midesiatykh godakh*, 52.

44. Shul'gin, "Muka," RGALI, f. 1337, op. 4, d. 54, ll. 94–95ob. See Rodkiewicz, *Russian Nationality Policy*, 73.

45. Shul'gin, "Muka," RGALI, f. 1337, op. 4, d. 56, l. 139; Matich, *Zapiski russkoi amerikanki*, 30.

46. Shul'gina, *Konspekt*, 48–49.

47. Shul'gin, *Poslednii ochevidets*, 194–96; Shul'gin, "Muka," 1952, RGALI, f. 1337, op. 4, d. 55, l. 143ob; ibid., d. 56, ll. 198–200.

48. Shul'gina, *Konspekt*, 50–51; Shul'gin, "Muka," 1952, RGALI, f. 1337, op. 4, d. 57, ll. 106ob–108. See also the typesetters' emotional obituary for Pikhno in *Kievlianin*, 31 July 1913, 2.

49. Bilimovich and Tsytovich, *Pamiati D. I. Pikhno*, 6; Shul'gina, *Konspekt*, 85; V. V. Shul'gin, "Med," 1952, RGALI, f. 1337, op. 4, d. 60, ll. 68ob–70ob.

50. Shul'gina, *Konspekt*, 55–56; Shul'gin, "Muka," RGALI, f. 1337, op. 4, d. 56, ll. 183–84, 188–91.

51. V. V. Shul'gin, "Vospominaniia V. V. Shul'gina o vyborakh na Ukraine v I i II Gosudarstvennuiu Dumu," n.d., GARF, f. R-5974, op. 1, d. 306, l. 51. "Russian" here refers to local Volhynian peasants, not to Great Russians.

52. L. Shul'gina to M. Krestovskaia, 27 November 1890, RGALI, f. 2174, op. 1, d. 104, l. 3.

53. Shul'gin, "Muka," RGALI, f. 1337, op. 4, d. 56, ll. 175–180ob, 244ob–253ob, 260–277ob. An official report confirms this incident: Ostrog District police captain to Kiev governor-general, 10 December 1905, TsDIAK, f. 442, op. 855, spr. 391G, ark. 193

54. A similar retrospective idealization of the rural social order is characteristic of Polish émigré memoirs. See Beauvois, *La bataille de la terre*, 144–45.

55. Shul'gina, *Konspekt*, 82.

56. See Shul'gin, "Muka," RGALI, f. 1337, op. 4, d. 54, l. 229ff.

57. Shul'gina, *Konspekt*, 304.

58. Shul'gin, "Muka," RGALI, f. 1337, op. 4, d. 56, l. 68.

59. Robert Edelman, *Gentry Politics on the Eve of the Russian Revolution: The Nationalist Party, 1907–1917* (New Brunswick, NJ: Rutgers University Press, 1980), 16–19, 58–59; Roberta T. Manning, *The Crisis of the Old Order in Russia: Gentry and Government* (Princeton, NJ: Princeton University Press, 1982), 11–20; Rodkiewicz, *Russian Nationality Policy*, 81.

60. Vitte, *Iz arkhiva S. Iu. Vitte*, 1:153.

61. For instance, *Kievlianin*, 4 January 1904, 2. For these articles, a British weekly praised Pikhno as "perhaps the most daring and outspoken of all Russian editors." See "Russian Newspapers of To-day and the Men Who Run Them," *Sphere*, 22 April 1905, 82.

62. I. A. Sikorskii, "Kharakteristika trekh osnovnykh chelovecheskikh ras—chernoi, zheltoi i beloi," *Kievlianin*, 29 February 1904, 3.

63. *Kievlianin*, 19 May 1905, 1–2; *Kievlianin*, 6 July 1904, 2; *Kievlianin*, 19 August 1905, 1. For a concise account of the war and the societal reactions see Abraham Ascher, *The Revolution of 1905* (Stanford, CA: Stanford University Press, 1988–1992), 1:43–53.

64. "Bol'noi vopros," *Kievlianin*, 9 March 1904, 1–3; "Novyi zakon o evreiakh," *Kievlianin*, 27 August 1904, 1–2; *Kievlianin*, 30 October 1904, 1–2.

65. Ascher, *Revolution of 1905*, 1:127–74, 194–207.

66. "Smuta nashikh dnei," *Kievlianin*, 18 February 1905, 1; continued in *Kievlianin*, 19 February 1905, 1–2; "Chto delat' s vyshchimi uchebnymi zavedeniiami?," *Kievlianin*, 11 March 1905, 1–2.

67. "Organizatsiia radikal'noi partii," *Kievlianin*, 7 April 1905, 1–2; continued in *Kievlianin*, 8 April 1905, 1–2; *Kievlianin*, 5 July 1905, 1.

68. *Kievlianin*, 28 June 1905, 1–2; "Surovyia predosterezheniia," *Kievlianin*, 29 June 1905, 2.

69. "Dobryi sovet evreiam," *Kievlianin*, 6 May 1905, 1–2; "Meropriiatiia po tsarstvu pol'skomu," *Kievlianin*, 22 June 1905, 1–2.

70. Only in December, the paper offered biting comments on Ukrainian political groups, characteristically calling them a "Judaizing" sect: "Ukrainsko-revoliutsionnaia programma," *Kievlianin*, 8 December 1905, 2.

71. Hamm, *Kiev*, 178–86. The arrest of thirty RUP agitators in September 1905 further weakened the Ukrainians. See Faith Hillis, "Between Empire and Nation: Urban Politics, Community, and Violence in Kiev, 1863–1907" (PhD diss., Yale University, 2009), 350.

72. "Uchrezhdenie Gosudarstvennoi Dumy," *Kievlianin*, 10 August 1905, 2; Hamm, *Kiev*, 184–85; Ascher, *Revolution of 1905*, 1:178–80, 211–29.

73. *Kievlianin*, 20 October 1905, 1–2. On antisemitic rumors see Hillis, *Children of Rus'*, 157–67. As Hillis points out, the veracity of these accounts is impossible to determine.

74. *Kievlianin*, 20 October 1905, 2.

75. For details on the October pogrom see Hamm, *Kiev*, 189–96; Meir, *Kiev, Jewish Metropolis*, 122–28; Victoria Khiterer, *Jewish City or Inferno of Russian Israel? A History of the Jews in Kiev before February 1917* (Boston: Academic Studies, 2016), 273–79.

76. Meir, *Kiev, Jewish Metropolis*, 133–34.

77. *Kievlianin*, 20 October 1905, 1–2.

78. Klier, *Russians, Jews*, 132–50.

79. D. Pikhno to S. Witte, 17 December 1905, RGIA, f. 1622, op. 1, d. 458, ll. 3–3ob.

80. Shul'gin, *Dni*, 12, 15–16. According to the factory inspectorate, the typesetters remained quiet because they had shorter work hours due to the paper's exemption from preliminary censorship. Hillis, "Between Empire and Nation," 322–23.

81. A. Savenko, "Dumy i nastroeniia CLXXXIX. Pamiati uchitelia," *Kievlianin*, 31 July 1913, 2. Pikhno's collected editorials from October to December 1905 were republished in a volume titled "Under Siege": D. I. Pikhno, *V osade: Politicheskiia stat'i* (Kiev: Tipografiia T-va I. N. Kushnerev, 1905).

82. *Kievlianin*, 10 December 1905, 1.

83. Pikhno, *V osade*, 62–68, 138–42, 222, 253–61, 272.

84. "Rokovoe nedorazumenie," *Kievlianin*, 24 November 1905, 1.

85. See *Kievlianin*, 20 November 1905, 4, and many of the following editions. Only one such letter is preserved in the newspaper's archives: O. Chubina to *Kievlianin*, 20 December 1905, TsDIAK, f. 296, op. 1, spr. 27, ark. 149–50.

86. "Iz pisem v redaktsiiu," *Kievlianin*, 26 November 1905, 2.

87. "Iz pisem v redaktsiiu," *Kievlianin*, 6 November 1905, 3; 8 November 1905, 3; 10 November 1905, 2; 26 November 1905, 2; 1 December 1905, 2; 3 December 1905, 3.

88. See Pikhno, *V osade*, 178–80, 254.

89. Pikhno, *V osade*, 1.

90. Mikhail Loukianov, "Conservatives and 'Renewed Russia,' 1907–1914," *Slavic Review* 61, no. 4 (2002): 763; George Gilbert, *The Radical Right in Late Imperial Russia: Dreams of a True Fatherland?* (London: Routledge, 2016), 40.

91. Don C. Rawson, *Russian Rightists and the Revolution of 1905* (Cambridge: Cambridge University Press, 1995), 21–72.

92. For instance, Paul Bushkovitch, "What Is Russia? Russian National Identity and the State, 1500–1917," in *Culture, Nation, and Identity: The Ukrainian-Russian Encounter, 1600–1945*, ed. Andreas Kappeler et al. (Toronto: Canadian Institute of Ukrainian Studies, 2003), 158–60.

93. M. N. Luk'ianov, "'Rossiia—dlia russkikh' ili 'Rossiia—dlia russkikh poddannykh'? Konservatory i natsional'nyi vopros nakanune pervoi mirovoi voiny," *Otechestvennaia istoriia*, no. 2 (2006): 36–46.

94. Loukianov, "Conservatives and 'Renewed Russia,'" 764–66.

95. On the (originally structuralist) distinction between marked and unmarked national categories see Brubaker et al., *Nationalist Politics and Everyday Ethnicity*, 211–12.

96. See Brubaker, *Ethnicity without Groups*, 144–45.

97. Teodor Shanin, *Revolution as a Moment of Truth: Russia, 1905–07* (London: Macmillan, 1986), 184.

98. Shul'gina, *Konspekt*, 240.

99. V. V. Shulgin, *The Years: Memoirs of a Member of the Russian Duma, 1906–1917*, trans. Tanya Davis (New York: Hippocrene, 1984), 4.

100. Shul'gin, *Teni*, 44–49; Hillis, "Between Empire and Nation," 276. A poem mocking Pikhno as "the loyal slave of the Orthodox tsar" is preserved in "K delu o volnenii studentov Kievskogo universiteta," 1899, RGIA, f. 1410, op. 2, d. 53, l. 25.

101. V. V. Shul'gin, *Prikliuchenia kniazia Voronetskago. V strane svobod* (Kiev: Tipografiia T-va I. N. Kushnerev, 1914).

102. V. V. Shul'gin, *Nedavnie dni* (Kharkov: Tipografiia "Mirnyi Trud," 1910), 102–3. Twelve years later, Shul'gin rewrote this text into an unambiguously autobiographical report: Shul'gin, *Dni*, 5–54.

103. Shul'gin, *Dni*, 33.

104. Shul'gina, *Konspekt*, 37–40.

105. Shul'gina, *Konspekt*, 43, 108.

106. Hillis, *Children of Rus'*, 182–92; Ol'ha Martyniuk, "Rosiis'kyi natsionalizm iak sotsial'no-politychnyi fenomen u vybornomu protsesi pravoberezhnoï Ukraïny (1906–1912 rr.)" (PhD diss., Kyiv, Kyïvs'kyi politekhnichnyi instytut im. Ihoria Sikors'koho, 2016), 55–64.

107. Letter excerpt, Iu. Kulakovskii to A. Kulakovskii, 10 March 1906, GARF, f. 102, op. 265, d. 60, l. 99; "Rezul'taty izbiraniia vyborshchikov v Gosudarstvennuiu Dumu po g. Kievu," *Kievlianin*, 23 March 1906, 3.

108. See, among many others, the editorials in *Kievlianin*, 5 May 1906, 1; *Kievlianin*, 31 May 1906, 1–2.

109. Rawson, *Russian Rightists*, 98–103, 194.

110. "Otravlennaia Rossiia," *Kievlianin*, 30 August 1906, 2; "K vyboram v Gosudarstvennuiu Dumu," *Kievlianin*, 31 January 1907, 2–3; Hillis, *Children of Rus'*, 199–205; Rawson, *Russian Rightists*, 98.

111. Martyniuk, "Rosiis'kyi natsionalizm," 66.

112. For Shul'gin's account see Shul'gin, *Poslednii ochevidets*, 34–59. A slightly abridged English version is in Shulgin, *Years*, 3–27.

113. *Kievlianin*, 10 February 1907, 4; M. M. Boiovich, ed., *Chleny Gosudarstvennoi Dumy (portrety i biografii). Vtoroi sozyv 1907–1912 g.* (Moscow: Tipografiia T-va I. D. Sytina, 1907), 40–52; *Gosudarstvennaia duma. Ukazatel' k stenograficheskim otchetam. Vtoroi sozyv* (Saint Petersburg: Gosudarstvennaia tipografiia, 1907), 32–33.

114. Shul'gin, "Vospominaniia o vyborakh," GARF, f. R-5974, op. 1, d. 306, l. 12. In September 1906, Shul'gin had still united Russian and Polish nobles at a landowners' congress in a resolution demanding an electoral law organized along the lines of estate. See D. A. Kotsiubinskii, *Russkii natsionalizm v nachale XX stoletiia: Rozhdenie i gibel' ideologii Vserossiiskogo natsional'nogo soiuza* (Moscow: ROSSPEN, 2001), 187.

115. Martyniuk, "Rosiis'kyi natsionalizm," 87–89.

116. Ascher, *Revolution of 1905*, 2:274–78.

117. *Gosudarstvennaia duma. Vtoroi sozyv. Stenograficheskie otchety* (Saint Petersburg: Gosudarstvennaia tipografiia, 1908), session 2, part 1, cols. 1142–43, 1554, 1563; session 2, part 2, cols. 744–46, 1013–16.

118. *Kievlianin*, 15 March 1907, 1. See also the editorials on 2 March, 17 March, 21 March, and many more in the following weeks.

119. Shulgin, *Years*, 44–47.

120. "Rossiia dlia russkikh!," *Kievlianin*, 6 June 1907, 2.

121. Imperial order, 23 March 1907; report to the treasury, 5 April 1907, RGIA, f. 1162, op. 6, d. 415, ll. 1ob, 18.

122. Dominic Lieven, *Russia's Rulers under the Old Regime* (New Haven, CT: Yale University Press, 1989), 27, 61.

123. Kaufman, *D. I. Pikhno*, 7; "Konchina D. I. Pikhno," *Russkoe slovo*, no. 175, 1913; Alexandra Korros, *A Reluctant Parliament: Stolypin, Nationalism, and the Politics of the Russian Imperial State Council, 1906–1911* (Lanham, MD: Rowman & Littlefield, 2002), 95, 141.

124. Geoffrey A. Hosking, *The Russian Constitutional Experiment: Government and Duma, 1907–1914* (Cambridge: Cambridge University Press, 1973), 41–45.

125. M. M. Boiovich, ed., *Chleny Gosudarstvennoi Dumy (portrety i biografii). Tretii sozyv 1907–1912 g.* (Moscow: Tipografiia T-va I. D. Sytina, 1908), 40–52.

126. "Novyi zakon o krest'ianskom zemlevladenii," *Kievlianin*, 14 November 1906, 2; D. I. Pikhno, *Raskrepochshenie krest'ianskoi zemli* (Kiev: Tipografiia T-va I. N. Kushnerev, 1908).

127. Bernard Pares, "The Second Duma," *Slavonic Review* 2, no. 4 (1923): 43.

128. Shulgin, *Years*, 50–51.

129. *Sbornik kluba russkikh natsionalistov*, 5 vols. (Kiev: Tipografiia T-va I. N. Kushnerev, 1909-1913); T. V. Kal'chenko, *Kievskii klub russkikh natsionalistov: Istoricheskaia entsiklopediia* (Kiev: Kievskie vedomosti, 2008). On the club's social composition see Edelman, *Gentry Politics*, 89; Hillis, *Children of Rus'*, 217; Martyniuk, "Rosiis'kyi natsionalizm," 108-10, 234. While Edelman describes the southwestern Nationalists as a party of rural gentry interest, Hillis emphasizes their urban constituency. Martynyuk points out that many Nationalists (like the Shul'gins) were both rural landlords and urban professionals. The railway administrators were likely invited to bolster numbers.

130. Hosking, *Russian Constitutional Experiment*, 97-106; Edelman, *Gentry Politics*, 93-102.

131. Shulgin, *Years*, 92-93.

132. In 1903, the government had introduced appointed ("margarine") zemstvos in the western provinces, which the local elites largely ignored. See M. D. Dolbilov and A. I. Miller, eds., *Zapadnye okrainy Rossiiskoi imperii* (Moscow: Novoe literaturnoe obozrenie, 2006), 275.

133. *Gosudarstvennyi sovet. Stenograficheskie otchety. Sessiia chetvertaia* (Saint Petersburg: Gosudarstvennaia tipografiia, 1909), cols. 1933-41; see also D. I. Pikhno, *Predstavitel'stvo Zapadnoi Rusi v Gosudarstvennom sovete* (Kiev: Tipografiia T-va I. N. Kushnerev, 1909). The proposal may have been influenced by the recent Moravian compromise of 1905. See Shul'gin, *Poslednii ochevidets*, 131.

134. Edelman, *Gentry Politics*, 83-86; Hillis, *Children of Rus'*, 70-71.

135. V. V. Shul'gin, *Vybornoe zemstvo v iugo-zapadnom krae* (Kiev: Tipografiia T-va I. N. Kushnerev, 1909), 46-60.

136. Abraham Ascher, *P. A. Stolypin: The Search for Stability in Late Imperial Russia* (Stanford, CA: Stanford University Press, 2001), 335-36.

137. *Gosudarstvennaia duma. Tretii sozyv. Stenograficheskie otchety* (Saint Petersburg: Gosudarstvennaia tipografiia, 1908-1912), session 3, part 4, cols. 953, 956.

138. *Gosudarstvennyi sovet. Stenograficheskie otchety. Sessiia shestaia* (Saint Petersburg: Gosudarstvennaia tipografiia, 1911), cols. 767-69.

139. *Sbornik kluba russkikh natsionalistov*, 3:127.

140. Hosking, *Russian Constitutional Experiment*, 116-46; Edelman, *Gentry Politics*, 106-10, 116-27; Ascher, *P. A. Stolypin*, 330-62; Korros, *Reluctant Parliament*, 189-207.

141. Edelman, *Gentry Politics*, 136-39, 190-91.

142. Police Report on the Ukrainophile Movement, n.d., GARF, f. 102, op. 118, d. 204, t. 1, ll. 146-47.

143. Letter excerpt, V. Shul'gin to G. Rein, 21 September 1912, GARF, f. 102, op. 265, d. 576, l. 204.

144. Edelman, *Gentry Politics*, 153-57; Martyniuk, "Rosiis'kyi natsionalizm," 135-45, 158-62.

145. See Iuliia Polovynchak, *Hazeta "Kievlianin" i ukrainstvo: Dosvid natsional'noï samoidentyfikatsiï* (Kyiv: Natsional'na biblioteka Ukraïny im. V. I. Vernads'koho, 2008), 39-45, 62-67.

146. A. Savenko, "Zametki DLXVI," *Kievlianin*, 26 July 1908, 2; A. Savenko, "Zametki DCCCXCIII," *Kievlianin*, 13 April 1910, 2; Andriewsky, "Politics of National Identity," 266-68, 279-84. The Ukrainians mocked Stolypin's circular for classifying them as "aliens" and thus involuntarily recognizing them as non-Russians.

147. Andriewsky, "Politics of National Identity," 271-75. A typical article connecting Ukrainian nationalism and geopolitics is A. Savenko, "Zametki DCLXXV," *Kievlianin*, 7 February 1909, 3.

148. *Sbornik kluba russkikh natsionalistov*, 4-5:262.

149. A. Savenko, "Dumy i nastroeniia XVIII. Gde glavnyi vrag?," *Kievlianin*, 17 November 1911, 2; V. Shul'gin, "Ukraina," *Kievlianin*, 4 January 1912, 3.

150. A. Savenko, "Dumy i nastroeniia XXIV," *Kievlianin*, 11 December 1911; *Sbornik kluba russkikh natsionalistov*, 4-5:133-44; S. N. Shchegolev, *Ukrainskoe dvizhenie, kak sovremennyi etap iuzhnorusskago separatizma* (Kiev: Tipografiia T-va I. N. Kushnerev, 1912); A. V. Storozhenko, *Proiskhozhdenie i sushchnost' ukrainofil'stva* (Kiev: Tipografiia "S. V. Kul'zhenko," 1912); I. A. Sikorskii, *Russkie i ukraintsy (Glava iz etnologicheskago katekhizisa)* (Kiev: Tipografiia "S. V. Kul'zhenko," 1913). On Shchegolev see Baumann, "Debate on Ukrainian Identities," 61-68.

151. O. Belousenko [Lotots'kyi], "Lex Pichniana," *Ukrainskaia zhizn'*, no. 5 (1912): 30-42.

152. Letter excerpt, A. Savenko to V. Kovalevskii, 20 October 1911, GARF, f. 102, op. 265, d. 510, l. 53.

153. Colonel A. Shredel' to N. Kharlamov, 12 January 1912, GARF, f. 102, op. 118, d. 204, t. 1, ll. 79-79ob. Shredel' called Savenko "an enthusiastic writer of the feuilleton type who has sinned against truth more than once."

154. Police Report on the Ukrainophile Movement, GARF, f. 102, op. 118, d. 204, t. 1, ll. 146, 157, 167; report by General-Major Rykovskii, 13 May 1914, GARF, f. 102, op. 118, d. 204, t. 2, l. 70ob. The reports from other Ukrainian *guberniias*, collected in the same archival file, show very little concern.

155. Diary entry for 15 October 1912, Chykalenko, *Shchodennyk (1907–1917)*, 243. According to Chykalenko, the name was intentionally misleading, since Ukrainian *rodyna* (stressed on the second syllable) is spelled the same way as Russian *rodina* (stressed on the first syllable), meaning "homeland," which suggests a Russian patriotic society.

156. P. B. Struve, "Obshcherusskaia kul'tura i ukrainskii partikuliarizm (Otvet Ukraintsu)," *Russkaia mysl'*, no. 1 (1912): 65-86, quotation 84; see also Andriewsky, "Politics of National Identity," 419-45.

157. See V. Sadovskii, "Ukrainskii vopros v tret'ei Dume," *Ukrainskaia zhizn'*, no. 3 (1912): 17-27; Dm. Dontsov, "Eshche o russkom liberalizme," *Ukrainskaia zhizn'*, no. 10 (1912): 84-88; S. Petliura, "Iz russkoi pechati," *Ukrainskaia zhizn'*, no. 3 (1913): 69-74.

158. *Sbornik kluba russkikh natsionalistov*, 4-5:220.

159. A. Savenko, "Zametki DXXV," *Kievlianin*, 15 May 1908, 2; *Gosudarstvennaia duma. Tretii sozyv*, session 3, part 1, col. 3056. In the Duma, the right often let peasant deputies from Ukraine speak against Ukrainian demands. See, for

instance, S. Bogdanov, "Ukrainskii separatizm v Gosudarstvennoi Dume," *Kievlianin*, 31 December 1909, 2.

160. Bojanowska, *Nikolai Gogol*, challenges this reading.

161. Kotenko, Martyniuk, and Miller, "Maloross," 2:431–36.

162. Minutes of Kiev Club meeting on 30 July 1912, *Sbornik kluba russkikh natsionalistov*, 4–5:29.

163. Letter excerpt, A. Savenko to N. Savenko, 26 March 1913, GARF, f. 102, op. 265, d. 922, l. 621.

164. L. Mogilevskaia to M. Krestovskaia, 29 May 1903 and 5 November 1904, RGALI, f. 2174, op. 1, d. 104, ll. 55–59. Filipp Mogilevskii later married Mariia Merkulova's sister Elena.

165. See V. V. Shul'gin, "Kurgany," in "Voina bez mira," 1936–1937, OR IMLI RAN, f. 604, ed. khr. 183. Shul'gin's memoirs usually refer to Liubov' Popova by her preferred pseudonym Dar'ia Vasil'evna Danilevskaia.

166. L. Mogilevskaia to M. Krestovskaia, March 1905, RGALI, f. 2174, op. 1, d. 104, ll. 59–61; Shul'gin, "Muka," RGALI, f. 1337, op. 4, d. 56, ll. 151ob–167ob; Matich, *Zapiski russkoi amerikanki*, 86.

167. "Poslanie s togo sveta V. Ia. Shul'gina M. V. Iuzefovichu," 1879, TsDIAK, f. 849, op. 1, spr. 91, ark. 2.

168. Vitte, *Iz arkhiva S. Iu. Vitte*, 1:148.

169. Quoted in Ievhen Chykalenko, *Shchodennyk 1919–1920* (Kyiv: Vydavnytstvo imeni Oleny Telihy, 2005), 287.

170. L. Shul'gina to M. Krestovskaia, 27 November 1890, RGALI, f. 2174, op. 1, d. 104, l. 4.

171. L. Mogilevskaia to M. Krestovskaia, 29 May 1903, RGALI, f. 2174, op. 1, d. 104, l. 55.

172. L. Mogilevskaia to M. Krestovskaia, 1895, RGALI, f. 2174, op. 1, d. 104, l. 13.

173. Deborah Cohen, *Family Secrets: Shame and Privacy in Modern Britain* (New York: Oxford University Press, 2013), 196.

174. L. Mogilevskaia to M. Krestovskaia, January 1900, RGALI, f. 2174, op. 1, d. 104, l. 43.

175. L. Mogilevskaia to M. Krestovskaia, 4 February 1899, RGALI, f. 2174, op. 1, d. 104, l. 37.

176. L. Mogilevskaia to M. Krestovskaia, 9 August 1905, RGALI, f. 2174, op. 1, d. 104, ll. 64–65. See also D. Pikhno to M. Krestovskaia, 30 August 1905, RGALI, f. 2174, op. 1, d. 80, ll. 8–9.

177. Shul'gin, *Teni*, 44; Shul'gina, *Konspekt*, 60.

178. Brubaker, *Ethnicity without Groups*, 10.

179. L. Mogilevskaia to M. Krestovskaia, 5 November 1904, RGALI, f. 2174, op. 1, d. 104, l. 58; Shul'gin, *Teni*, 18, 99; Matich, *Zapiski russkoi amerikanki*, 108–9; Shul'gina, *Konspekt*, 71–73, 78–81.

180. Letter excerpt, L. Mogilevskaia to D. Pikhno, 9 February 1911, GARF, f. 102, op. 265, d. 478, l. 5; letter excerpt, D. Pikhno to L. Mogilevskaia, 30 March 1913, GARF, f. 102, op. 265, d. 922, l. 646.

181. Shul'gina, *Konspekt*, 61–62, 71, 76, 114–16.

182. Pikhno called Savenko a "blockhead" (*bolvan*); for Shul'gin, he was a "neurasthenic" with an "impossible character": letter excerpt, D. Pikhno to L. Mogilevskaia, 30 March 1913, GARF, f. 102, op. 265, d. 922, l. 646; Shul'gin, *Teni*, 148; Shul'gina, *Konspekt*, 106.

183. Shul'gina, *Konspekt*, 46; Evg. Shol'p, "D. I. Pikhno," *Kievskaia mysl'*, 30 June 1913.

184. Letter excerpt, D. Pikhno to L. Mogilevskaia, 24 October 1911, GARF, f. 102, op. 265, d. 510, l. 94. On the competition between newspapers and political parties over public opinion see Louise McReynolds, *The News under Russia's Old Regime: The Development of a Mass-Circulation Press* (Princeton, NJ: Princeton University Press, 1991), 199.

185. See Gilbert, *Radical Right*, 177–79; Jitka Malečková, "The Importance of Being National," in *Czech Feminisms: Perspectives on Gender in East Central Europe*, ed. Iveta Jusová and Jiřina Šiklová (Bloomington: Indiana University Press, 2016), 57. On the women's rights movement see Rochelle Goldberg Ruthchild, *Equality and Revolution: Women's Rights in the Russian Empire, 1905–1917* (Pittsburgh: University of Pittsburgh Press, 2010).

186. Matich, *Zapiski russkoi amerikanki*, 9.

187. Edelman, *Gentry Politics*, 39–42.

188. See Shulgin, *Years*, 37–39.

189. Richard Wortman, *Scenarios of Power: Myth and Ceremony in Russian Monarchy* (Princeton, NJ: Princeton University Press, 1995–2000), 2:407–9.

190. Dominic Lieven, "Empires and Their Core Territories on the Eve of 1914: A Comment," in *Nationalizing Empires*, ed. Stefan Berger and Alexei Miller (Budapest: Central European University Press, 2015), 647–60.

191. "Pol'skaia deputatsiia v Peterburge," *Kievlianin*, 6 March 1905, 2.

192. "Ottsy i deti," *Kievlianin*, 31 August 1905, 1.

193. D. Pikhno to M. Krestovskaia, 30 August 1905, RGALI, f. 2174, op. 1, d. 80, l. 8.

194. "Smuta nashikh dnei," *Kievlianin*, 19 February 1905, 3.

195. McClintock, "Family Feuds," 63.

196. Robert Weinberg, *Blood Libel in Late Imperial Russia: The Ritual Murder Trial of Mendel Beilis* (Bloomington: Indiana University Press, 2014); Hans Rogger, *Jewish Policies and Right-Wing Politics in Imperial Russia* (Berkeley: University of California Press, 1986), 40–55; Hillis, *Children of Rus'*, 244–52; 262–68.

197. "Chastnoe razsledovanie po delu ob ubiistve Andreia Iushchinskago," *Kievlianin*, 30 May 1912, 3; Shul'gina, *Konspekt*, 92–93.

198. Hillis, *Children of Rus'*, 256–57.

199. "Kiev, 29 iiulia," *Rech'*, 30 July 1913.

200. *Kievlianin*, 27 September 1913, 1.

201. Excerpt from anonymous letter to *Kievlianin*, 22 October 1913, GARF, f. 102, op. 265, d. 912, l. 6; Shul'gina, *Konspekt*, 101–2.

202. Quoted in Shulgin, *Years*, 112.

203. Shulgin, *Years*, 113–19; Shul'gina, *Konspekt*, 101–8; Hillis, *Children of Rus'*, 265–68.

204. *Kievlianin*, 25 September 1913, 2.

205. "Antisemitizm," *Kievlianin*, 15 October 1913, 2.

206. This is a constant in Shul'gin's otherwise fluctuating antisemitism. For a very critical analysis see Victoria Khiterer, "Vasilii Shul'gin and the Jewish Question: An Assessment of Shul'gin's Anti-Semitism," *On the Jewish Street* 1, no. 2 (2011): 137–63; for a more generous view see Bruce Adams, "The Extraordinary Career of Vasilii Shul'gin," *Revolutionary Russia* 5, no. 2 (1992): 193–220.

207. Edelman, *Gentry Politics*, 179–89.

208. Hosking, *Russian Constitutional Experiment*, 182ff.; S. M. San'kova, *Russkaia partiia v Rossii: Obrazovanie i deiatel'nost' vserossiiskogo natsional'nogo soiuza (1908–1917)* (Orel: S. V. Zenina, 2006), 127–29, 201–4.

209. In 1913, the print run of *Kievlianin* fell to ten thousand, then rose back to sixteen thousand during the war. Meanwhile, the more modern liberal daily *Kievskaia mysl'* sold up to eighty thousand copies. See "Prilozhenie k otchetu po periodicheskoi pechati," 1915, TsDIAK, f. 295, op. 1, spr. 579, ark. 55–58.

4. Triumph and Tragedy

1. Peter Holquist, *Making War, Forging Revolution: Russia's Continuum of Crisis, 1914–1921* (Cambridge, MA: Harvard University Press, 2002).

2. While an increasing number of detailed studies are available, the revolutionary period in Ukraine awaits an up-to-date synthesis. The most complete English-language political history is still John Reshetar, *The Ukrainian Revolution, 1917–1920: A Study in Nationalism* (Princeton, NJ: Princeton University Press, 1952). On the historiography see John-Paul Himka, "The National and the Social in the Ukrainian Revolution: The Historiographical Agenda," *Archiv für Sozialgeschichte* 34 (1994): 95–110; Christopher Gilley, "Untangling the Ukrainian Revolution," *Studies in Ethnicity and Nationalism* 17, no. 3 (2017): 326–38.

3. Orlando Figes, *A People's Tragedy: The Russian Revolution 1891–1924* (London: Jonathan Cape, 1996), 698.

4. On Russia's path into the war see Christopher Clark, *The Sleepwalkers: How Europe Went to War in 1914* (London: Allen Lane, 2012); Dominic Lieven, *Towards the Flame: Empire, War and the End of Tsarist Russia* (London: Allen Lane, 2015).

5. *Kievlianin*, 20 July 1914, 1. On the Russian public's pro-Polish turn in 1914 see Melissa K. Stockdale, *Mobilizing the Russian Nation: Patriotism and Citizenship in the First World War* (Cambridge: Cambridge University Press, 2016), 169–76.

6. *Kievlianin*, 23 July 1914, 1.

7. *Kievlianin*, 24 July 1914, 1; "Pol'skii narod," *Kievlianin*, 29 July 1914, 1.

8. Eric Lohr, "The Russian Press and the 'Internal Peace' at the Beginning of World War I," in *A Call to Arms: Propaganda, Public Opinion, and Newspapers in the Great War*, ed. Troy R. E. Paddock (Westport, CT: Praeger, 2004), 91–113; Stockdale, *Mobilizing the Russian Nation*, 15–44.

9. "Zaria novoi zhizni," *Kievlianin*, 3 August 1914, 3; *Kievlianin*, 27 September 1914, 1.

10. "Pol'skiia nastroeniia," *Kievlianin*, 18 January 1915, 2; A. Savenko, "Mysli i vpechatleniia CCVI. Avtonomiia Pol'shi," *Kievlianin*, 26 July 1915, 3.

11. "'Ukrainskii' puf," *Kievlianin*, 23 November 1914, 3.

12. *Kievlianin*, 10 August 1915, 1.

13. See Eric Lohr, *Nationalizing the Russian Empire: The Campaign against Enemy Aliens during World War I* (Cambridge, MA: Harvard University Press, 2003), 25–27. In 1916, Vasilii Shul'gin wrote against the confiscation of German colonists' land, stressing that many of them were fighting in the Russian army. See V. Shul'gin, "Kolonisty ili soldaty?," *Kievlianin*, 1 July 1916, 1–2.

14. "Varvary," *Kievlianin*, 13 August 1914, 1; A. Savenko, "Mysli i vpechatleniia CLXXXII. Kto glavnyi prestupnik," *Kievlianin*, 5 April 1915, 2.

15. A. Ezhov, "Dlia budushchago rascheta," *Kievlianin*, 6 January 1915, 3; Shul'gina, *Konspekt*, 121–23.

16. Eric Lohr, "War Nationalism," in *The Empire and Nationalism at War*, ed. Eric Lohr et al. (Bloomington, IN: Slavica, 2014), 91–107.

17. Shul'gina, *Konspekt*, 123.

18. "Rossiia i Bolgariia," *Kievlianin*, 31 March 1915, 1; A. Savenko, "Mysli i vpechatleniia CLXXIV. Bolgary i 'ukraintsy,'" *Kievlianin*, 5 April 1915, 2.

19. V. V. Shul'gin, "Voina bez mira," 1931, OR IMLI RAN, f. 604, ed. khr. 179, ll. 18–46, 127–64; Shulgin, *Years*, 136–46.

20. Shul'gina, *Konspekt*, 123–25; Olena Betlii, "Kiev—gorod problemnykh identichnostei," in *Goroda imperii v gody Velikoi voiny i revoliutsii: Sbornik statei*, ed. Alexei Miller and Dmitrii Chernyi (Moscow: Nestor-Istoriia, 2017), 280.

21. A. Ezhov, "Vpechatleniia. Kak oni stradaiut," *Kievlianin*, 13 December 1914, 2.

22. Laurie S. Stoff, *Russia's Sisters of Mercy and the Great War: More Than Binding Men's Wounds* (Lawrence: University Press of Kansas, 2015), 174–86.

23. Shul'gin, "Voina bez mira," OR IMLI RAN, f. 604, ed. khr. 179, l. 219. On such semipublic organizations see Holquist, *Making War, Forging Revolution*, 4; Joshua A. Sanborn, *Imperial Apocalypse: The Great War and the Destruction of the Russian Empire* (Oxford: Oxford University Press, 2014), 155–57.

24. Shul'gin, "Voina bez mira," OR IMLI RAN, f. 604, ed. khr. 185, ll. 10–11, 50–53; Edelman, *Gentry Politics*, 210–12, 217–18; A. V. Glushkov, "Gazeta 'Kievlianin' i progressivnye natsionalisty, 1915–1917 gody," *Vestnik permskogo universiteta* 18, no. 1 (2012): 271–77.

25. Michael F. Hamm, "Liberal Politics in Wartime Russia: An Analysis of the Progressive Bloc," *Slavic Review* 33, no. 3 (1977): 453–55.

26. Shul'gin, "Voina bez mira," OR IMLI RAN, f. 604, ed. khr. 185, l. 67; Edelman, *Gentry Politics*, 213.

27. Löwe, *Antisemitismus und reaktionäre Utopie*, 156–63.

28. A. Savenko, "Mysli i vpechatleniia CCXIV. Eshche o dumskom bloke," *Kievlianin*, 3 September 1915, 1–2; V. Shul'gin, *Kievlianin*, 1 September 1915, 1.

29. Tsuyoshi Hasegawa, *The February Revolution, Petrograd, 1917: The End of the Tsarist Regime and the Birth of Dual Power*, rev. ed. (Leiden: Brill, 2017), 35. Shul'gin's insolent behavior at a meeting with Goremykin—he recommended that the prime minister resign—may have contributed to the Duma's prorogation.

30. *Kievlianin*, 4 September 1915, 1; A. Savenko, "Mysli i vpechatleniia CCXVI. Kto vinovniki smuty," *Kievlianin*, 10 September 1915, 1–2; A. Savenko, "Mysli i vpechatleniia CCXXXII. Protiv Rossii ili protiv rezhima," *Kievlianin*, 5 November 1915, 2; V. Shul'gin, "Dvorianin fon-Pavlov," *Kievlianin*, 7 December 1915, 1–2.

31. Letter excerpt, V. Shul'gin to E. Shul'gina, 11 December 1915, GARF, f. 102, op. 265, d. 1040, l. 2209.

32. Shul'gin, "Voina bez mira," OR IMLI RAN, f. 604, ed. khr. 185, ll. 88–94; Hasegawa, *February Revolution*, 25–27.

33. Hamm, "Liberal Politics," 159–61; Löwe, *Antisemitismus und reaktionäre Utopie*, 170–79.

34. V. Shul'gin, "Neblagodarnoe delo," *Kievlianin*, 23 October 1915, 1–2.

35. V. Shul'gin, "Razmyshleniia vslukh," *Kievlianin*, 24 March 1916, 1; A. Ezhov, "Vpechatleniia. Vechnyi zhid," *Kievlianin*, 19 December 1915, 1.

36. V. Shul'gin, "Pol'skiia dela," *Kievlianin*, 6 August 1916, 2, continued in *Kievlianin*, 7 August 1916, 1.

37. Hasegawa, *February Revolution*, 53–55.

38. *Gosudarstvennaia duma. Chetvertyi sozyv. Stenograficheskie otchety* (Saint Petersburg: Gosudarstvennaia tipografiia, 1913–1917), session 5, cols. 67–71.

39. Shul'gina, *Konspekt*, 158.

40. V. Shul'gin, "Dekabristy 1916 g.," *Kievlianin*, 17 December 1916, 1.

41. Hasegawa, *February Revolution*, 138–42, 159–70.

42. *Kievlianin*, 9 January 1917, 2; V. Shul'gin, *Kievlianin*, 14 January 1917, 1; V. Shul'gin, *Kievlianin*, 11 February 1917, 1. See also his Duma speech of 17 February 1917 in *Gosudarstvennaia duma. Chetvertyi sozyv*, session 5, cols. 1495–1501.

43. See, for example, *Kievlianin*, 31 January 1917, where the entire lead article is missing.

44. V. Shul'gin to Grand Duke Nikolai Mikhailovich, 15 February 1917, GARF, f. 670, op. 1, d. 349, l. 6.

45. The negotiations are described in Hasegawa, *February Revolution*, 349–81.

46. Hasegawa, 487–93, 549–61, 606–12. Vasilii Shul'gin's account is in Shul'gin, *Dni*, 264–306.

47. See, for instance, V. Shul'gin, *Kievlianin*, 15 February 1917, 1.

48. Shul'gin, *Dni*, 163, 175, 181, 241.

49. "Stat'ia V. Shul'gina," *Kievlianin*, 5 March 1917, 3.

50. Magocsi, *History of Ukraine*, 493.

51. "Voina i ukraintsy," *Ukrainskaia zhizn'*, no. 7 (1914): 3–7.

52. Dmytro Doroshenko, *Istoriia Ukraïny 1917–1923 rr.* (1930–1932; repr., Kyiv: Tempora, 2002), 1:29, 33–36; Mark von Hagen, *War in a European Borderland: Occupations and Occupation Plans in Galicia and Ukraine, 1914–1918* (Seattle: University of Washington Press, 2007), 23–41.

53. "Lichnoe delo studenta Shul'gina N. Ia.," DAK, f. 16, op. 464, spr. 12026, ark. 6–13; O. Shul'hyn to F. Vovk, 9 July 1915, NAIA NANU, f. 1, V/4649, ark. 1zv; V. Shul'hyn to F. Vovk, 11 January 1916, NAIA NANU, f. 1, V/4653; "Mykola Shul'hyn (nekrolog)," *Tryzub*, no. 2–3 (1932): 13–14.

54. In 1915, Liubov Shul'hyna hosted Galician hostages that the Russian army had brought to Kiev. One of these men, Roman Ishchuk, ended up

marrying Nadiia Shul'hyna. Nadiia Shul'hyna-Ishchuk, "Do storinok istoriï ukraïns'koho shkil'nytstva (spohad)," in *125 rokiv Kyïvs'koï ukraïns'koï akademi-chnoï tradytsiï 1861–1986*, ed. Marko D. Antonovych (New York, 1993), 555–56; Leontovych, *Shul'hyny*, 32, 35.

55. P. V. Volobuev, ed., *Petrogradskii sovet rabochikh i soldatskikh deputatov v 1917 godu: Dokumenty i materialy* (Leningrad: Nauka, 1991), 1:319; Choulguine, *L'Ukraine contre Moscou*, 37–38, 57–58.

56. Choulguine, *L'Ukraine contre Moscou*, 82; Doroshenko, *Istoriia Ukraïny*, 1:52.

57. Stefan Mashkevich, *Kiev 1917–1920. Vol 1: Proshchanie s imperiei (mart 1917–ianvar' 1918)* (Kharkiv: Folio, 2019), 43–56.

58. Choulguine, *L'Ukraine contre Moscou*, 107–10.

59. I. V. Khmil', *Na shliakhu vidrodzhennia ukraïns'koï derzhavnosti (Ukraïns'kyi natsional'nyi konhres-z'ïzd 6–8 kvitnia 1917 r.)* (Kyiv: Instytut istoriï Ukraïny NAN, 1994), 24, 27, 47–51.

60. Aleksandr Shul'gin, "Ukrainskii narod i vserossiiskaia revoliutsiia," *Russkoe bogatstvo*, no. 4–5 (1917): 276–88.

61. Svitlana Ivanyts'ka, "Oleksandr Iakovych Shul'hyn—lider ta ideoloh ukraïns'koï partiï sotsialistiv-federalistiv," in Piskun, *Oleksandr Shul'hyn*, 41–42. The Ukrainian SR Pavlo Khrystiuk later described the Socialist-Federalists as "typical Ukrainian Kadets," and indeed, most of them were liberal democrats rather than socialists. See Pavlo Khrystiuk, *Zamitky i materiialy do istoriï ukraïns'koï revoliutsiï* (Vienna: Institut sociologique ukrainien, 1921–1922), 2:29.

62. Reshetar, *Ukrainian Revolution*, 51–52.

63. A. A. Gol'denveizer, "Iz kievskikh vospominanii," *Arkhiv russkoi revoliutsii* 6 (1922): 164–69, 176–78.

64. Minutes of the Little Rada session of 16 July 1917, in V. F. Verstiuk et al., eds., *Ukraïns'ka Tsentral'na Rada: Dokumenty i materialy u dvokh tomakh* (Kyiv: Naukova dumka, 1996–1997), 1:181–82; Choulguine, *L'Ukraine contre Moscou*, 120–24.

65. On the negotiations see D. Ia. Bondarenko, "Vremennoe pravitel'stvo i problema avtonomii Ukrainy (iiul'–oktiabr' 1917 g.)," *Otechestvennaia istoriia*, no. 1 (2006): 54–64.

66. Mark von Hagen, "The Great War and the Mobilization of Ethnicity in the Russian Empire," in *Post-Soviet Political Order: Conflict and State Building*, ed. Barnett Rubin and Jack Snyder (London: Routledge, 1998), 34–57.

67. Serhy Yekelchyk, "Bands of Nation Builders? Insurgency and Ideology in the Ukrainian Civil War," in *Empires at War: 1911–1923*, ed. Robert Gerwarth and John Horne (Oxford: Oxford University Press, 2012), 111–14. See also Khrystiuk, *Zamitky i materiialy*, 1:48–55; A. I. Denikin, *Ocherki russkoi smuty* (Paris: J. Povolsky [et al.], 1921–1926), vol. 1, pt. 2, 129–33.

68. For instance Khrystiuk, *Zamitky i materiialy*, 1:42–46.

69. Baker, *Peasants, Power, and Place*, esp. 77–89. See also Graham Tan, "Village Social Organisation and Peasant Action: Right-Bank Ukraine during the Revolution 1917–1923" (PhD diss., London, School of Slavonic and East European Studies, 1999). In right-bank Ukraine, the agrarian revolution was

sometimes accompanied by ethnicized violence against (Polish) landlords and (Jewish) townspeople. For an early account of pogrom-like riots see "Rozrukhy na Ukraïni," *Nova Rada*, 4 October 1917, 1.

70. Gol'denveizer, "Iz kievskikh vospominanii," 196–97.

71. Volodymyr Vynnychenko, *Vidrodzhennia natsiï* (Kyiv: Vydavnytstvo Dzvin, 1920), 1:256. On the Rada's relations with the bureaucracy see Stephen Velychenko, *State Building in Revolutionary Ukraine: A Comparative Study of Governments and Bureaucrats, 1917–1922* (Toronto: University of Toronto Press, 2011), 66–104.

72. Khrystiuk, *Zamitky i materiialy*, 1:17; Doroshenko, *Istoriia Ukraïny*, 1:86–87.

73. A. Nikovs'kyi to Ie. Chykalenko, 20 September 1917, in Ievhen Chykalenko and Andrii Nikovs'kyi, *Lystuvannia 1908–1921 roky* (Kyiv: Tempora, 2010).

74. Judson, *Habsburg Empire*, 433–36.

75. See "Chornovi zamitki, zapysy, bloknoty ministra A. Ia. Shul'hina," 1917–1918, TsDAVO, f. 2592, op. 1, spr. 101, ark. 73, 76; "Mykola Shul'hyn (nekrolog)," 13.

76. Velychenko, *State Building in Revolutionary Ukraine*, 86.

77. O. V. Onishchenko, "Zhinky v Ukraïns'kii Tsentral'nii Radi," *Literatura ta kul'tura Polissia: Zbirnyk naukovykh prats'* 85 (2016): 81–90.

78. Shul'hyna-Ishchuk, "Do storinok istoriï," 557–60; Doroshenko, *Istoriia Ukraïny*, 2:254. The textbook is Nadiia Shul'hyna-Ishchuk, *Zadachnyk do systematychnoho kursu arytmetyky*, 2 vols. (Kiev: Vydannia tovarystva shkil'noï osvity, 1917–1918).

79. V. Naumenko, "Dumy starika-ukraintsa o momente," *Kievskaia mysl'*, 14 March 1917, 1–2; Doroshenko, *Istoriia Ukraïny*, 1:52.

80. V. Naumenko to P. Stebnyts'kyi, 1 June 1917, IR NBUV, f. III, od. zb. 52546, ark. 1zv; V. Naumenko to F. Vovk, 19 June 1917, NAIA NANU, f. 1, V/3278, ark. 1zv.

81. N., "Novyi popechitel' uchebnago okruga ob ukrainizatsii shkoly (Beseda)," *Kievlianin*, 25 August 1917, 2; "Ostavlenie V. P. Naumenko dolzhnosti popechitelia uchebnago okruga," *Kievlianin*, 29 November 1917, 2.

82. V. F. Verstiuk et al., *Narysy istoriï ukraïns'koï revoliutsiï 1917–1921 rokiv* (Kyiv: Naukova dumka, 2011–2012), 1:99–103.

83. P. Stebnyts'kyi to Ie. Chykalenko, 11 March 1917; Ie. Chykalenko to P. Stebnyts'kyi, 2 April 1917, 27 June 1917, and 1 August 1917, all in Ievhen Chykalenko and Petro Stebnyts'kyi, *Lystuvannia 1901–1922 roky* (Kyiv: Tempora, 2008), 483, 489–90, 496, 505.

84. Matityahu Mintz, "The Secretariat of Internationality Affairs (Sekretariiat Mizhnatsional'nykh Sprav) of the Ukrainian General Secretariat (1917–1918)," *Harvard Ukrainian Studies* 6, no. 1 (1982): 25–42; Henry Abramson, *A Prayer for the Government: Ukrainians and Jews in Revolutionary Times, 1917–1920* (Cambridge, MA: Harvard University Press, 1999), 54–59.

85. "Do svidomoho hromadianstva Ukraïny," 18 October 1917, in Verstiuk et al., *Ukraïns'ka Tsentral'na Rada*, 1:354.

86. "Chornovi zamitki A. Ia. Shul'hina," TsDAVO, f. 2592, op. 1, spr. 101, ark. 16; "Pro okhoronu prav natsional'nykh menshostei na Ukraïni," 1917, TsDAVO, f. 2592, op. 1, spr. 31, ark. 1–14.

87. Choulguine, *L'Ukraine contre Moscou*, 154; see also Börries Kuzmany, "'Perekhresna istoriia' zakonu pro natsional'no-personal'nu avtonomiiu UNR: Peretikannia ideï vid avstro-marksystiv cherez ievreis'kyi Bund do revoliutsiinoï Ukraïny," in *Revoliutsiia, derzhavnist', natsiia: Ukraïna na shliakhu samostverdzhennia (1917–1921 rr.)*, ed. V. F. Verstiuk (Kyiv: Instytut istoriï Ukraïny NAN Ukraïny, 2017), 261–67. The law is printed in Verstiuk et al., *Narysy istoriï ukraïns'koï revoliutsiï*, 2:99–101.

88. Abramson, *Prayer for the Government*, 67–78.

89. Abramson, 38–39; R. G. Simonenko, "National'no-kul'turnaia avtonomiia na Ukraine v 1917–1918 godakh," *Voprosy istorii*, no. 1 (1997): 50–63; Marcel Radosław Garboś, "Revolution and the Defence of Civilization: Polish Visions of Nationhood, Property and Territory in Right-Bank Ukraine (1917–22)," *Slavonic and East European Review* 96, no. 3 (2018): 469–506.

90. V. Shul'gin, "Po telegrafu iz Petrograda," *Kievlianin*, 18 April 1917, 1.

91. Doroshenko, *Istoriia Ukraïny*, 1:198.

92. Minutes of the Congress of Russia's Peoples, 8 September 1917, in Verstiuk et al., *Ukraïns'ka Tsentral'na Rada*, 1:290; Choulguine, *L'Ukraine contre Moscou*, 185–87; Mintz, "Secretariat of Internationality Affairs," 28.

93. Reshetar, *Ukrainian Revolution*, 82–91.

94. Reshetar, 90–97; Khrystiuk, *Zamitky i materiialy*, 2:77–91.

95. Choulguine, *L'Ukraine contre Moscou*, 165–68, 180–84.

96. For Shul'hyn's account and relevant documents see Alexandre Choulguine, *L'Ukraine, la Russie et les puissances de l'Entente* (Bern, 1918), 31–41, 50–57. See also Wolodymyr Kosyk, *La politique de la France à l'égard de l'Ukraine, mars 1917–février 1918* (Paris: Publications de la Sorbonne, 1981), 164–66, 174, 182, 205–6; Caroline Milow, *Die ukrainische Frage 1917–1923 im Spannungsfeld der europäischen Diplomatie* (Wiesbaden: Harrassowitz, 2002), 76–80.

97. Borislav Chernev, *Twilight of Empire: The Brest-Litovsk Conference and the Remaking of East-Central Europe, 1917–1918* (Toronto: University of Toronto Press, 2017), 123–25.

98. O. Shul'hyn to General Secretariat, 21 December 1917, TsDAVO, f. 1063, op. 3, spr. 1., ark. 129–30. On the link between Ukrainian diplomacy and the move toward independentism see "Na mezhynarodnii shliakh," *Nova Rada*, 23 December 1917, 2.

99. General Secretariat meeting of 26 December 1917, in Verstiuk et al., *Ukraïns'ka Tsentral'na Rada*, 2:68, 70.

100. Khrystiuk, *Zamitky i materiialy*, 2:102–6; Doroshenko, *Istoriia Ukraïny*, 1:192–98.

101. See also Plokhy, *Unmaking Imperial Russia*, 72–87.

102. Khrystiuk, *Zamitky i materiialy*, 2:124–26; Mashkevich, *Kiev 1917–1920*, 370–423.

103. Choulguine, *L'Ukraine contre Moscou*, 198–203; Oleh S. Fedyshyn, *Germany's Drive to the East and the Ukrainian Revolution, 1917–1918* (New Brunswick, NJ: Rutgers University Press, 1971), 60–86; Chernev, *Twilight of Empire*, 126–38.

104. Choulguine, *L'Ukraine contre Moscou*, 207–12. It is a striking detail that Shul'hyn's hosts and benefactors all somehow represented the prerevolutionary imperial order.

105. For a biased but informative account of the first Bolshevik occupation see Konstantin Bel'govskii, "Letopis': Bor'ba s bol'shevikami," *Malaia Rus'*, no. 2 (1918): 3–30.

106. V. P. Naumenko, "Pro perebuvannia nimtsiv na Ukraïni," 1 March 1918, IR NBUV, f. I, od. zb. 47083, ark. 1; Oleksander Shul'hyn, "Lyst do redaktsiï," *Nova Rada*, 20 February (5 March) 1918, 2. The battle of Kruty was soon celebrated as a central heroic moment of the Ukrainian revolution and is remembered to this day, resulting, for instance, in a major 2019 motion picture.

107. Oleksander Shul'hyn, *Polityka (derzhavne budivnytstvo Ukraïny i mizhnarodni spravy): Statti, dokumenty, promovy* (Kyiv: Drukar', 1918), 34–39.

108. Oleksander Shul'hyn, "Samostiina ukraïns'ka derzhava i federalizm," *Nova Rada*, 23 March (5 April) 1918, 2; Oleksander Shul'hyn, "Trahediia rosiis'koho intelihenta," *Nova Rada*, 15 (28) April 1918, 2.

109. "Lyst M. Ustymovycha," *Nova Rada*, 26 April (9 May) 1918, 3; Pavlo Skoropads'kyi, *Spohady (kinets' 1917–hruden' 1918)*, ed. Iaroslav Pelens'kyi (Kyiv: Instytut ukraïns'koï arkheohrafiï ta dzhereloznavstva im. M. S. Hrushevs'koho NAN Ukraïny, 1995), 138, 149, 159–61.

110. Bulgakov, *Belaia gvardiia*, 33. On the Hetmanate see Doroshenko, *Istoriia Ukraïny*, vol. 2; Taras Hunczak, "The Ukraine under Hetman Pavlo Skoropadsky," in *The Ukraine, 1917–1921: A Study in Revolution*, ed. Taras Hunczak (Cambridge, MA: Harvard Ukrainian Research Institute, 1977), 61–81; Fedyshyn, *Germany's Drive*, 133–94; Frank Golczewski, *Deutsche und Ukrainer 1914–1939* (Paderborn: Schöningh, 2010), 298–360.

111. Ustimovich was probably murdered by insurgents in December 1918 while traveling as director of Ukraine's state horse-breeding farm. See Shul'hyn, "Uryvky iz spohadiv," 217.

112. Shul'gina, *Konspekt*, 166, 186.

113. A. Ezhov, "Vpechtleniia. Svoboda," *Kievlianin*, 10 March 1917, 1.

114. This argument is outlined in V. Shul'gin, "Po telegrafu iz Petrograda," *Kievlianin*, 16 April 1917, 1. See also his speech in *Kievlianin*, 6 May 1917, 3.

115. Shul'gin, *Teni*, 127–30; P. N. Miliukov, *Istoriia vtoroi russkoi revoliutsii* (Sofia: Rossiisko-bolgarskoe knigoizdatel'stvo, 1921–1923), 1:46.

116. "Torzhestvennoe zasedanie Gosudarstvennoi Dumy," *Kievlianin*, 29 April 1917, 4.

117. V. Shul'gin, "Po telegrafu iz Petrograda," *Kievlianin*, 6 April 1917, 1.

118. V. Shul'gin, "Etap," *Russkaia svoboda* no. 10–11 (1917), reprinted in V. V. Shul'gin, *"Belye mysli": Publitsistika 1917–1920 gg.*, ed. A. A. Chemakin (Moscow: Kuchkovo pole, 2020), 121–25.

119. Shul'gina, *Konspekt*, 156–57, 168–69, 175, quotation 230.

120. E. G. Shul'gina, "Rukopis' povesti '1917 god,'" 1923, GARF, f. R-5974, op. 2, d. 69, l. 90.

121. N. S–ko, "Strannye edinomyshlenniki," *Kievlianin*, 18 May 1917, 1; V. Shul'gin, "Po telegrafu iz Petrograda," *Kievlianin*, 2 June 1917, 1; *Kievlianin*, 20 June 1917, 1–2; V. Shul'gin, "Po telegrafu iz Petrograda," *Kievlianin*, 22

June 1917, 1; *Kievlianin*, 1 July 1917, 1. See also Ivan Basenko, "The 'German Intrigue' as an Element of the Anti-Ukrainian Campaign: A Case Study of Kyiv's Russian Language Press, 1914–18," *East/West: Journal of Ukrainian Studies* 5, no. 2 (2018): 149–73. Despite German financial support for Ukrainian agitation among POWs, the topic's leading researcher has concluded that in 1917, "neither Berlin nor Vienna had any definite plans" concerning Ukraine: Fedyshyn, *Germany's Drive*, 41.

122. V. Shul'gin, "Po telegrafu iz Petrograda," *Kievlianin*, 27 May 1917; V. Shul'gin, "Kto trebuet," *Kievlianin*, 19 October 1917, 1; V. Shul'gin, *Kievlianin*, 28 October 1917, 1.

123. A. Ezhov, "Vpechatleniia. Budushchee," *Kievlianin*, 31 March 1917, 1–2.

124. A. Ezhov, "Vpechatleniia. Rus'," *Kievlianin*, 23 April 1917, 3; Shul'gina, *Konspekt*, 173–74, 182.

125. K.B., "Chuvstvo natsional'nosti," *Kievlianin*, 1 May 1917, 1–2.

126. *Kievlianin*, 24 June 1917, 1.

127. See, by way of comparison, Matthias Neumann, "Mobilizing Children: Youth and the Patriotic War Culture in Kiev during World War I," in *Russia's Home Front in War and Revolution, 1914–22. Book 2: The Experience of War and Revolution*, ed. Sarah Badcock et al. (Bloomington, IN: Slavica, 2016), 273–300.

128. "Manifestatsiia russkoi uchashcheisia molodezhi," *Kievlianin*, 2 May 1917, 1; Shul'gina, *Konspekt*, 195–210. Kiev's leading leftist newspaper sharply condemned the "dark figures" who had abused "children" to display counterrevolutionary views. See Vsevolod Chagovets, "Dobrye pastyri," *Kievskaia mysl'*, 2 May 1917, 1.

129. On female suffrage see Ruthchild, *Equality and Revolution*, 218–35.

130. Shul'gina, "1917 god," GARF, f. R-5974, op. 2, d. 69, ll. 112–13.

131. "Mestnyia izvestiia," *Kievlianin*, 11 July 1917; Shul'gina, *Konspekt*, 175–79, 183, 222; Shul'gin, *Teni*, 51, 139, 148; Vl. Lazarevskii, "Ob ushedshikh druz'iakh," *Chasovoi* 129–30 (1934), 38.

132. V. Shul'gin, "Protiv nasil'stvennoi ukrainizatsii Iuzhnoi Rusi," *Kievlianin*, 18 July 1917, 1–2; "Ot redaktsii," *Kievlianin*, 8 September 1917, 2.

133. Brubaker, *Ethnicity without Groups*, 12.

134. "Za kogo golosovat'?," *Kievskaia mysl'*, 22 July 1917, 1.

135. "Arest V. V. Shul'gina," *Kievlianin*, 31 August 1917, 1; *Kievlianin*, 3 September 1917, 1.

136. "Nashim chitateliam," *Kievlianin*, 19 November 1917, 2.

137. "Rezul'taty vyborov v Kievskuiu gorodskuiu dumu," *Kievlianin*, 27 July 1917, 2.

138. Maloross, "Natsional'noe samoopredelenie stolitsy ukrainskoi respubliki," *Malaia Rus'*, no. 1 (1918): 56–57; Steven L. Guthier, "The Popular Base of Ukrainian Nationalism in 1917," *Slavic Review* 38, no. 1 (1979): 38.

139. For Vasilii Shul'gin's account of his imprisonment see V. Shul'gin, "Dvorets i tiur'ma," *Malaia Rus'*, no. 2 (1918): 33–82; for that of Ekaterina Shul'gina, E., "To, chto ia pomniu (Iz zhenskikh perezhivanii v dni tsarstvovaniia bol'shevikov)," *Malaia Rus'*, no. 2 (1918): 83–110.

140. "Vypiski iz dnevnika V. V. Shul'gina," 1918, GARF, f. R-5974, op. 1, d. 25a, l. 1.

141. A. Ezhov, "Amnistiia," *Kievlianin*, 21 November 1917, 1.

142. V. Shul'gin, *Kievlianin*, 25 February (10 March) 1918, 1.

143. Puchenkov, *Ukraina i Krym*, 88–122; V. M. Levitskii, "Bor'ba na Iuge," 1923, ibid., 142–43.

144. General-Major Waldstätten to the Austrian Foreign Ministry, 3 (16) April 1918, in Theophil Hornykiewicz, *Ereignisse in der Ukraine 1914–1922, deren Bedeutung und historische Hintergründe* (Horn, Germany: Ferdinand Berger, 1966–1969), 1:384.

145. "Dokladnaia zapiska V. V. Shul'gina ot 5 sentiabria 1918," in V. G. Bortnevskii, ed., "K istorii osvedomitel'noi organizatsii 'Azbuka,'" *Russkoe proshloe* 4 (1993): 162–65; Shul'gin, *Teni*, 190–93. Many Azbuka reports are preserved in the Vrangel' collection (27001) at the Hoover Institution Archives. On the formation of the Volunteer Army see Peter Kenez, *Civil War in South Russia, 1918: The First Year of the Volunteer Army* (Berkeley: University of California Press, 1971).

146. E. A. Efimovskii, "V russkom Kieve v 1918 godu: Politicheskie siluety," in *Stat'i* (Paris, 1994), 137; Shul'gin, *Teni*, 191–93. A list of 110 members is in Bortnevskii, "K istorii osvedomitel'noi organizatsii," 181–85.

147. Viktor Bortnevski, "White Intelligence and Counter-intelligence during the Russian Civil War," *Carl Beck Papers in Russian & East European Studies* 1108 (1995): 20–22; Peter Kenez, *Civil War in South Russia, 1919–1920: The Defeat of the Whites* (Berkeley: University of California Press, 1977), 66.

148. V. Stepanov to V. Shul'gin, 9 (22) January 1919, HIA, 27001, box 33, folder 41, l. 1.

149. V. V. Shul'gin, "Voina bez mira," n.d., OR IMLI RAN, f. 604, ed. khr. 182, l. 314.

150. Doroshenko, *Istoriia Ukraïny*, 2:108–11.

151. "Zapiska ob otkaze V. V. Shul'gina ot ukrainskogo poddanstva," 21 July (3 August) 1918, in V. V. Shul'gin, *Rossiia, Ukraina, Evropa: Izbrannye raboty*, ed. A. V. Repnikov (Moscow: Sodruzhestvo "Posev," 2015), 170–78, quotation 174.

152. V. V. Shul'gin, "Voina bez mira," OR IMLI RAN, f. 604, ed. khr. 183, ll. 23–24, 45. At several points in 1918–1920, "Shul'ginian" newspapers (variously called *Rossiia*, *Velikaia Rossiia*, or *Edinaia Rus'*) were indeed published in Ekaterinodar, Odessa, Rostov-on-Don, Kursk, Novorossiisk, and Sevastopol'. While Shul'gin was not always present, they regularly reprinted his articles. See D. I. Babkov, "Politicheskaia publitsistika V. V. Shul'gina v period grazhdanskoi voiny i emigratsii," *Voprosy istorii*, no. 3 (2008): 96–97.

153. Kenez, *Civil War, 1918*, 151–52.

154. *Monarkhisty. Stat'i V. V. Shul'gina i A.* (Ekaterinodar: Izdatel'stvo "Rossiia," 1918), 3–6, 8.

155. Shul'gin, "Voina bez mira," OR IMLI RAN, f. 604, ed. khr. 183, ll. 46–52; Kenez, *Civil War, 1918*, 192–201.

156. A copy of his brokenhearted diary is preserved in "Voina bez mira," 1918–1919, OR IMLI RAN, f. 604, ed. khr. 184. On the Jassy conference see Anna Procyk, *Russian Nationalism and Ukraine: The Nationality Policy of the Volunteer Army during the Civil War* (Toronto: Canadian Institute of Ukrainian Studies, 1995), 88–93.

157. Reshetar, *Ukrainian Revolution*, 197–204.

158. Azbuka report by "Az" [A. Savenko], "Kak i pochemu proizoshlo pad-enie Kieva," 21 December 1918, HIA, 27001, box 40, folder 20, ll. 199–206; "Oni ne poluchili prikazaniia," *Kievlianin*, 1 (14) December 1919, 1; Shul'gina, *Konspekt*, 362–65.

159. Kenez, *Civil War, 1919–1920*, 181–82. On Henno, a rather shady character, see Pascal Fieschi, "L'intervention française à Odessa (décembre 1918–mars 1919) vue à travers l'action du 'Consul de France,' Emile Henno," *Cahiers slaves* 14 (2016): 161–72.

160. "Prikaz odesskago voennago gubernatora Grishina-Almazova," *Rossiia (Odesskoe izdanie)*, 17 (30) January 1919, 4; Shul'gin, *1919 god*, 1:109–11.

161. V. Shul'gin, "Nasledniki Miasoedova," *Rossiia (Odesskoe izdanie)*, 17 (30) January 1919, 1: V. Shul'gin, "Otkrytoe pis'mo V. V. Shul'gina k g. Petliure," *Rossiia (Odesskoe izdanie)*, 9 (22) January 1919, 1.

162. V. Shul'gin to V. Maklakov, 2 (15) February 1919, HIA, 27001, box 31, folder 19, ll. 2–3.

163. For recent assessments see Christopher Gilley, "Beyond Petliura: The Ukrainian National Movement and the 1919 Pogroms," *East European Jewish Affairs* 47, no. 1 (2017): 45–61; Jeffrey Veidlinger, *In the Midst of Civilized Europe: The Pogroms of 1918–1921 and the Onset of the Holocaust* (New York: Metropolitan Books, 2021), 93–164.

164. Kenez, *Civil War, 1919–1920*, 150–53; Procyk, *Russian Nationalism and Ukraine*, 165.

165. For example, Savenko rather implausibly reported on Hetman Skoropadskii's "passionate hatred of Russia" or called the very moderate Volodymyr Naumenko a "partisan of forced school Ukrainization." See Azbuka report by "Az" [A. Savenko], n.d., HIA, 27001, box 35, folder 11, l. 195; Azbuka report by "Az," 2 (15) November 1918, HIA, 27001, box 35, folder 13, l. 304.

166. V. Shul'gin, "Ot redaktsii gazety Rossiia," *Rossiia (Odesskoe izdanie)*, 8 February 1919, 1; Kenez, *Civil War, 1919–1920*, 183–91.

167. Shul'gina, *Konspekt*, 380–84; Shul'gin, *1919 god*, 1:242–45, 2:7–41.

168. Kenez, *Civil War, 1919–1920*, 37–40.

169. Shul'gin, *1919 god*, 2:52. Denikin (*Ocherki russkoi smuty*, 5:142) does not name Shul'gin among the text's authors, but its style and content incline me to believe Shul'gin's version. Compare his programmatic note of October 1918, published in A. S. Puchenkov, *Natsional'naia politika generala Denikina (vesna 1918–vesna 1920 g.)*, 2nd ed. (Moscow: Nauchno-politicheskaia kniga, 2016), 33–37.

170. "Naseleniiu Malorossii," *Kievlianin*, 21 August (3 September) 1919, 1.

171. Stefan Mashkevich, *Dva dnia iz istorii Kieva: 30–31 avgusta 1919* (Kyiv: Varto, 2010); Shul'gin, *1919 god*, 2:103–6.

172. L. L-aia, "Ocherki zhizni v Kieve v 1919–20 gg.," *Arkhiv russkoi revoliutsii* 3 (1921): 216; Gol'denveizer, "Iz kievskikh vospominanii," 258; Thomas Chopard, *Le martyre de Kiev: 1919. L'Ukraine en révolution entre terreur soviétique, nationalisme et antisémitisme* (Paris: Vendémiaire, 2015), 127–51.

173. Gol'denveizer, "Iz kievskikh vospominanii," 251–52; Shul'gin, *1919 god*, 2:113–15.

174. V. Shul'gin, "Promin'," *Kievlianin*, 7 (20) November 1919, 1.

175. V. Shul'gin, "Oni vernulis'," *Kievlianin*, 21 August (3 September) 1919, 1.

176. Oleg Budnitskii, *Russian Jews between the Reds and the Whites, 1917–1920* (Philadelphia: University of Pennsylvania Press, 2012), 107–8; Chopard, *Le martyre de Kiev*, 118–20. The categorization of Bolshevik activists by religion or ethnicity is problematic, since many of them were internationalists and atheists who would have rejected such a description.

177. V. Shul'gin, "Poeticheskaia vol'nost'," 18 (31) September 1919, 1.

178. L-aia, "Ocherki zhizni v Kieve," 217; Gol'denveizer, "Iz kievskikh vospominanii," 260–61; diary entry for 9 (22) August 1919, Nelli Ptashkina, *Dnevnik 1918–1920* (Paris: Russkoe knigoizdatel'stvo Ia. Povolotskago i Ko, 1922), 300; diary entry for 19 August (1 September) 1919, "Dnevnik i vospominaniia kievskoi studentki (1919-20 g.g.)," *Arkhiv russkoi revoliutsii* 15 (1924): 229.

179. Budnitskii, *Russian Jews*, 255–57, 262–63; Chopard, *Le martyre de Kiev*, 202–12; Olena Boiko, *Narysy zhyttia Kyieva. 1919 rik: Polityka i povsiakdennist'* (Kyiv: Instytut istoriï Ukraïny NAN Ukraïny, 2015), 102–8.

180. V. Shul'gin, "Pytka strakhom," *Kievlianin*, 8 (21) October 1919, 1; V. Shul'gin, "Pogromshchiki," *Kievlianin*, 9 (22) October 1919, 1; V. Shul'gin, *Kievlianin*, 12 (25) October 1919. On stories about Jews shooting from their windows, a recurring antisemitic civil war myth, see Budnitskii, *Russian Jews*, 245–47.

181. Gol'denveizer, "Iz kievskikh vospominanii," 269; Zaslavskii, *Rytsar' monarkhii Shul'gin*, 61–62. Erenburg's article is reprinted in Shul'gin, *1919 god*, 2:433–34n337.

182. Shul'gin, *1919 god*, 2:167.

183. Boiko, *Narysy zhyttia Kyieva*, 121–39.

184. An. Savenko, "Zametki IX," *Kievlianin*, 29 September (12 October) 1919, 1.

185. Kenez, *Civil War, 1919–1920*, 86–94; Baker, *Peasants, Power, and Place*, 140–50.

186. Quoted in Denikin, *Ocherki russkoi smuty*, 5:155. On the Kurgany peasants see Shul'gina, *Konspekt*, 270–72.

187. V. Shul'gin, "Selianam," *Kievlianin*, 25 August (7 September) 1919, 1; V. Shul'gin, "Zemli i voli," *Kievlianin*, 24 October (6 November) 1919, 1.

188. Denikin, *Ocherki russkoi smuty*, 4:225; V. G. Medvedev, "Agrarnoe zakonodatel'stvo generala A. I. Denikina," *Gosudarstvo i pravo*, no. 8 (2015): 86–94.

189. Puchenkov, *Natsional'naia politika generala Denikina*, 222.

190. Diary entry for 22 October (4 November) 1919, V. I. Vernadskii, *Dnevniki 1917–1921*, ed. M. Iu. Sorokina (Kyiv: Naukova dumka, 1994–1997), 1:176; diary entry for 21 October (3 November) 1919, "Dnevnik i vospominaniia kievskoi studentki," 235; A. Dragomirov to A. Denikin, 20 October (2 November) 1919, quoted in Puchenkov, *Natsional'naia politika generala Denikina*, 223.

191. Boiko, *Narysy zhyttia Kyieva*, 109, 113–14.

192. V. Shul'gin, "Kak sdelali poliaki . . .," *Kievlianin*, 3 (16 December) 1919, 1; Shul'gin, *1919 god*, 2:336-47.

193. Shul'gin, *1920 g.*

194. Shul'gin, *1920 g.*, 213-14, 252; Shul'gina, *Konspekt*, 421-24; Shul'gin, *1921 god*, 295; A. A. Chemakin, "'Krymskaia ekspeditsiia' V. V. Shul'gina i kniga '1921 god,'" ibid., 11-12. According to Shul'gin, Veniamin (Lialia) died in a mental asylum in Vinnitsa around 1925; however, this information is based on little more than what a fortune-teller told him. See Shul'gin, *Teni*, 356.

195. Shul'gin, *1920 g.*, 237-45, 251; Shul'gina, *Konspekt*, 473-599. The Shul'gins' youngest son Dmitrii had left Crimea as a sailor of the White navy. Lina Mogilevskaia was in Belgrade, Alla Bilimovich and her husband in Ljubljana. See L. Mogilevskaia to V. Shul'gin, 1 January 1921, GARF, f. R-5974, op. 1, d. 58.

196. Procyk, *Russian Nationalism and Ukraine*, 171.

197. Kenez, *Civil War, 1919-1920*, 66.

198. The antisemitic stereotype of Jewish disloyalty that the Volunteer Army inherited from the imperial army is a central theme in Budnitskii, *Russian Jews*.

199. V. V. Shul'gin, *Tri stolitsy: Puteshestvie v krasnuiu Rossiiu* (Berlin: Knigoizdatel'stvo "Mednyi vsadnik," 1927), 421-22.

200. V. Shul'gin, *Kievlianin*, 26 November (9 December) 1919, 1. See Rogger, *Jewish Policies and Right-Wing Politics*, 232.

201. Doroshenko, *Istoriia Ukraïny*, 2:43-49; Velychenko, *State Building in Revolutionary Ukraine*, 117-18; Puchenkov, *Ukraina i Krym*, 107-22; Trevor Erlacher, *Ukrainian Nationalism in the Age of Extremes: An Intellectual Biography of Dmytro Dontsov* (Cambridge, MA: Harvard Ukrainian Research Institute, 2021), 138-47.

202. Kenez, *Civil War, 1918*, 236-40; Baker, *Peasants, Power, and Place*, 91-121.

203. Dmytro Doroshenko, *Moï spomyny pro nedavnie-mynule (1914-1920)* (1923-1924; repr., Munich: Ukraïns'ke vydavnytstvo, 1969), 272-73.

204. "Iz shchodennyka Ukraïns'koï posol's'koï misiï v Sofiï," 24 July (6 August) 1918, TsDAVO, f. 3766, op. 1, spr. 117, ark. 3-4; O. Shul'hyn to D. Doroshenko, 5 August (23 July) 1918, TsDAVO, f. 3766, op. 3, spr. 1, ark. 32; Arkadii Zhukovs'kyi, "Politychna i hromads'ka diial'nist' Oleksandra Shul'hyna," in Ianiv, *Zbirnyk na poshanu O. Shul'hyna*, 27.

205. O. Czernin to Count Burián, 28 (15) August 1918, in Hornykiewicz, *Ereignisse in der Ukraine*, 3:612-13.

206. "Curriculum Vitae," 1921, in Piskun, *Oleksandr Shul'hyn*, 179; Oleksander Shul'hyn, "Pizno," *Tryzub*, no. 6 (1935): 2-5.

207. Arnol'd Margolin, *Ukraina i politika Antanty (Zapiski evreia i grazhdanina)* (Berlin: Izdatel'stvo S. Efron, 1921), 134-35; Thomas Chopard, "Identifier, légitimer, stigmatiser: Les matériaux de la délégation ukrainienne à la Conférence de la Paix de Paris (1918-1920)," *Matériaux pour l'histoire de notre temps* 113-114, no. 1-2 (2014): 180-85.

208. "Vidchyt pro diial'nist' v Paryzhi O. Shul'hyna," September 1919, in Piskun, *Oleksandr Shul'hyn*, 180.

209. *Mémoire sur l'indépendance de l'Ukraine présenté à la conférence de la paix par la délégation de la République ukrainienne* (Paris, 1919), 9–11, 17–19, 65–106. Shul'hyn also published two shorter brochures with similar arguments: Alexandre Choulguine, *Les problèmes de l'Ukraine: La question ethnique—la culture nationale—la vie économique—la volonté du peuple* (Paris: Société des Éditions Louis Michaud, 1919); *Chronologie des principaux événements en Ukraine de 1917 à 1919* (Paris: Bureau ukrainien de presse, 1919).

210. See Guido Hausmann, "Das Territorium der Ukraine: Stepan Rudnyc'kyjs Beitrag zur Geschichte räumlich-territorialen Denkens über die Ukraine," in *Die Ukraine: Prozesse der Nationsbildung*, ed. Andreas Kappeler (Cologne: Böhlau, 2011), 145–58; Rohde, *Nationale Wissenschaft*, 369–87.

211. *Mémoire sur l'indépendance*, 15, 22–23, 31–35.

212. *Mémoire sur l'indépendance*, 111, 117.

213. "Vidchyt pro diial'nist'," 184–85.

214. Margolin, *Ukraina i politika Antanty*, 143–54; minutes of the delegation meeting on 6 June (24 May) 1919, TsDAVO, f. 1429, op. 5, spr. 14, ark. 7.

215. In Shul'hyn's and Margolin's opinion, particularly Sydorenko was not up to the task. Historian Frank Golczewski concurs. See minutes of the delegation meeting on 20 (7) June 1919, TsDAVO, f. 1429, op. 5, spr. 14, ark. 45; Margolin, *Ukraina i politika Antanty*, 134, 160; Golczewski, *Deutsche und Ukrainer*, 367.

216. Margaret MacMillan, *Peacemakers: The Paris Conference of 1919 and Its Attempt to End War* (London: John Murray, 2001), 71–91.

217. Jean Xydias, *L'intervention française en Russie 1918–1919: Souvenirs d'un témoin* (Paris: Les Éditions de France, 1927), 162.

218. Reshetar, *Ukrainian Revolution*, 229–30, 272–85, 294–98.

219. Doroshenko, *Moï spomyny pro nedavnie-mynule*, 491–92.

220. "Vidchyt pro diial'nist'," 183. "Without Territory" was the title of a book about the UNR in exile that Oleksander Shul'hyn published in 1934. There, he remembered a rhyme from 1919 mocking the Directory's loss of significance: "In the carriage the Directory, under the carriage its territory . . ." (U vahoni Dyrektoriia, pid vahonom terytoriia . . .). See Oleksander Shul'hyn, *Bez terytoriï: Ideolohiia ta chyn Uriadu U.N.R. na chuzhyni* (Paris: Mech, 1934), 110.

221. "Curriculum Vitae," 179; Reshetar, *Ukrainian Revolution*, 299–311.

222. On the confusion that the competing Ukrainian legations provoked among Western diplomats see Milow, *Die ukrainische Frage*, 172–81; Golczewski, *Deutsche und Ukrainer*, 364–66.

223. O. Shul'hyn to A. Margolin, 15 November 1920; O. Shul'hyn to A. Nikovs'kyi, 18 November 1920, in Piskun, *Oleksandr Shul'hyn*, 194–97.

224. Minutes of the meeting of sub-commission C of the League of Nations assembly's commission V, 25 November 1920; O. Shul'hyn to A. Nikovs'kyi, 7 December 1920 and 24 December 1920, in Piskun, *Oleksandr Shul'hyn*, 207–29.

225. O. Shul'hyn to S. Petliura, 11 August 1921, in Piskun, *Oleksandr Shul'hyn*, 257.

226. Alexei Miller, "The Collapse of the Romanov Empire," in *The Oxford Handbook of the Ends of Empire*, ed. Thomas Martin and Andrew S. Thompson (Oxford: Oxford University Press, 2018), 185–88.

227. Denikin, *Ocherki russkoi smuty*, 5:145.

5. Living off the Past

1. Leontovych, *Shul'hyny*, 38. During the Second World War, Nadiia and her family moved to Germany, and after the war, to the United States, where she died in 1979. Mykola Shul'hyn died in Paris in 1931.

2. Marc Raeff, *Russia Abroad: A Cultural History of the Russian Emigration, 1919–1939* (Oxford: Oxford University Press, 1990), 9. The Russian emigration has been researched more intensely than its Ukrainian counterpart. Besides Raeff's classical study see also Robert H. Johnston, *New Mecca, New Babylon: Paris and the Russian Exiles, 1920–1945* (Montreal: McGill–Queen's University Press, 1988); Catherine Andreyev and Ivan Savický, *Russia Abroad: Prague and the Russian Diaspora, 1918–1938* (New Haven, CT: Yale University Press, 2004). On Ukrainian émigrés see V. P. Troshchyns'kyi, *Mizhvoienna ukraïns'ka emihratsiia v Ievropi iak istorychne i sotsial'no-politychne iavyshche* (Kyiv: Intel, 1994); Nadia Zavorotna, *Scholars in Exile: The Ukrainian Intellectual World in Interwar Czechoslovakia* (Toronto: University of Toronto Press, 2020).

3. Dittmar Dahlmann, "Krieg, Bürgerkrieg, Gewalt: Die Wahrnehmung des Ersten Weltkriegs und des Bürgerkriegs in der russischen Emigration und in der Sowjetunion in der Zwischenkriegszeit," in *Der verlorene Frieden: Politik und Kriegskultur nach 1918*, ed. Jost Dülffer and Gerd Krumeich (Essen: Klartext-Verlag, 2002), 91–100; Korine Amacher et al., eds., *Personal Trajectories in Russia's Great War and Revolution, 1914–22: Biographical Itineraries, Individual Experiences, Autobiographical Reflections* (Bloomington, IN: Slavica, 2021).

4. Jochen Hellbeck, introduction to *Autobiographical Practices in Russia— Autobiographische Praktiken in Russland*, ed. Jochen Hellbeck and Klaus Heller (Göttingen: V&R unipress, 2004), 14.

5. Alexander J. Motyl, *The Turn to the Right: The Ideological Origins and Development of Ukrainian Nationalism, 1919–1929* (Boulder, CO: East European Monographs, 1980). On the politics of the Ukrainian emigration see also Christopher Gilley, *The "Change of Signposts" in the Ukrainian Emigration: A Contribution to the History of Sovietophilism in the 1920s* (Stuttgart: ibidem-Verlag, 2009); Golczewski, *Deutsche und Ukrainer*, 361ff.; Myroslav Shkandrij, *Ukrainian Nationalism: Politics, Ideology, and Literature, 1929–1956* (New Haven, CT: Yale University Press, 2015); Erlacher, *Ukrainian Nationalism in the Age of Extremes*, 159ff.

6. Jan Jacek Bruski, *Petlurowcy: Centrum Państwowe Ukraińskiej Republiki Ludowej na wychodźstwie (1919–1924)* (Cracow: Arcana, 2000).

7. See his lengthy defense of Petliura, in which he attempted to blame the 1919 pogroms on the Red Army and Denikin's forces: Alexandre Choulguine, *L'Ukraine et le cauchemar rouge: Les massacres en Ukraine* (Paris: J. Tallandier, 1927).

8. Shul'hyn, *Bez terytoriï*, contains Shul'hyn's account of his activities in this capacity.

9. Oleksander Shul'hyn, "Reaktsiia chy demokratiia?," *Tryzub*, no. 4–5 (1928): 12–15; Shul'hyn, *Bez terytoriï*, 45–46. Despite his antifascist views, Shul'hyn praised Mussolini as a great statesman in a 1933 article: Oleksander Shul'hyn, "Problemy suchasnoï polityky," *Tryzub*, no. 32 (1933): 11.

10. Shul'hyn, *Bez terytoriï*, 7, 154–55.

11. Oleksander Shul'hyn, "Na partiini temy," *Tryzub*, no. 13–14 (1928): 5. See also Oleksander Shul'hyn, "V al'bom 'natsionalistam,'" *Tryzub*, no. 37 (1929): 3–6; "Peredzvony," *Tryzub*, no. 46 (1930): 2–4; "Krapky nad 'I,'" *Tryzub*, no. 18 (1931): 10–13; "Prokliati pytannia," *Tryzub*, no. 1 (1931): 5–10.

12. Troshchyns'kyi, *Mizhvoienna ukraïns'ka emihratsiia*, 97–98.

13. Motyl, *Turn to the Right*, 22. See also Reshetar, *Ukrainian Revolution*, 324–28.

14. This even applies to the Sovietophiles, who participated in the same debates as other Ukrainian émigrés and had more contacts with Soviet Ukraine than with Soviet Russia. See Gilley, *"Change of Signposts,"* 397.

15. O. Shul'hyn to A. Nikovs'kyi, 28 November 1921, TsDAVO, f. 3696, op. 2, spr. 30, ark. 83.

16. O. Shul'hyn to L. and I. Shishmanov, 22 November 1923, in A. M. Iakimova, "Lystuvannia Oleksandra Shul'hyna z rodynoiu Shyshmanovykh u 1922–1923 rokakh," *Sums'kyi istoryko-arkhivnyi zhurnal*, no. 16–17 (2012): 53.

17. Oleksander's wife Lidiia, having completed her medical studies in Russia, was able to earn money as a pediatrician and as French lecturer at the Ukrainian Free University.

18. While some Ukrainian authors claim that the Ukrainian emigration included over one hundred thousand people, Frank Golczewski contends that the number of "nationally conscious" Ukrainians was probably much lower. See Golczewski, *Deutsche und Ukrainer*, 427–30.

19. Shul'hyn was disappointed with the university's academic quality and described the émigrés as "gloomy, sad people." O. Shul'hyn to L. and I. Shishmanov, 22 November 1923, in Iakimova, "Lystuvannia Oleksandra Shul'hyna," 54. On the Ukrainian Free University see Symon Narizhnyi, *Ukraïns'ka emigratsiia: Kul'turna pratsia ukraïns'koï emigratsiï mizh dvoma svitovymy viinamy* (Prague: Knihtisk, 1942), 119–36; Zavorotna, *Scholars in Exile*, 29–52.

20. See Margolin, *Ukraina i politika Antanty*, 163, 165.

21. This argument is related, in essence, to Ernest Gellner's remarks about economic incentives for peripheral ("Ruritanian") elites to embrace nationalism rather than assimilate into an imperial majority culture. See Gellner, *Nations and Nationalism*, 59–61.

22. See Mykola Soroka, "On the Other Side: The Russian-Ukrainian Encounter in Displacement, 1920–1939," *Nationalities Papers* 37, no. 3 (2009): 327–48.

23. Motyl, *Turn to the Right*, 5.

24. Oleksander Shul'hyn, "Elementy ukraïns'koï derzhavnosty v 1917 r.," *Tryzub*, no. 31 (1926): 6–9, and no. 32 (1926): 13–16; "Idealy i diisnist'," *Tryzub*, no. 4 (1927): 4–6; "Storinky spomyniv (na smert' Iana Bratianu)," *Tryzub*, no. 46 (1927): 6–10; "Ie. Kh. Chykalenko, iak hromads'kyi diiach," *Tryzub*, no. 29–30 (1929): 23–29.

25. Oleksander Shul'hyn, "Rosiis'ka revoliutsiia ta Ukraïna," *Tryzub*, no. 16 (1927): 13–16.

26. Choulguine, *L'Ukraine contre Moscou*, ix–x.

27. Choulguine, 172–75.

28. Choulguine, 3–7, 66.

29. Choulguine, 8–16, 30–37.

30. Choulguine, 21–25.

31. Choulguine, 53.

32. Choulguine, 82–83.

33. Choulguine, 84, 91.

34. Choulguine, 79, 103.

35. Remy, *Brothers or Enemies*, 16–18, 98.

36. Choulguine, *L'Ukraine contre Moscou*, ix–x, 190.

37. Vynnychenko, *Vidrodzhennia natsiï*; Khrystiuk, *Zamitky i materiialy*; Doroshenko, *Moï spomyny pro nedavnie-mynule*; Doroshenko, *Istoriia Ukrainy*.

38. Choulguine, *L'Ukraine contre Moscou*, 101, 147, 167.

39. Choulguine, 191.

40. Choulguine, 216.

41. See Sidonie Smith and Julia Watson, *Reading Autobiography: A Guide for Interpreting Life Narratives*, 2nd ed. (Minneapolis: University of Minnesota Press, 2010), 13–15.

42. O. Shul'hyn to L. Chykalenko, 15 January 1937, in Piskun, *Oleksandr Shul'hyn*, 358.

43. Alexandre Choulguine, "Les origines de l'esprit national moderne et Jean-Jacques Rousseau," *Annales de la société Jean-Jacques Rousseau* 26 (1937): 100.

44. Golczewski, *Deutsche und Ukrainer*, 729; Ievhen Vrets'ona, "Spohad pro Oleksandra Shul'hyna," in Ianiv, *Zbirnyk na poshanu O. Shul'hyna*, 88.

45. On Shul'hyn's postwar activities and writings see the essays in Perrin, *Alexandre Choulguine (1889–1960)*; Ianiv, *Zbirnyk na poshanu O. Shul'hyna*.

46. Shul'hyn, "Uryvky iz spohadiv," 258. These memoirs (which remained incomplete owing to the author's death) were first serialized in the Munich monthly *Ukraïn'ska literaturna hazeta* in 1957–1960.

47. The passage that Shul'hyn quoted (from the *Considerations on the Government of Poland*) reads, "It is education that must give souls their national shape and direct their opinions and tastes in such a way that they will be patriotic by inclination, by passion, by necessity." Choulguine, "Les origines de l'esprit national," 204.

48. Shul'hyn, "Uryvky iz spohadiv," 230.

49. E. Shul'gina to D. Shul'gin, 17 March 1931, ARS, SI AS 1021, folder 5, letter 24.

50. E. G. Shul'gina, "Vozvrashchenie," 23 March 1922, GARF, f. R-5974, op. 2, d. 15, and others.

51. A part of the text was once meant to appear in one of Vasilii Shul'gin's books. See E. G. Shul'gina, "Konspekt moikh politicheskikh perezhivanii (1903–1919 g.)," 1924, GARF, f. R-5974, op. 2, d. 11a, l. 94.

52. A. A. Chemakin, "Ekaterina Grigor'evna Shul'gina i ee 'Konspekt,'" in Shul'gina, *Konspekt*, 22–25. I generally use this recently published version of Shul'gina's memoirs but occasionally cite earlier, differing drafts.

53. Shul'gina, *Konspekt*, 31, 45, 49.

54. Shul'gina, 58, 108–9.

55. Shul'gina, 80, 100.

56. Shul'gina, "1917 god," GARF, f. R-5974, op. 2, d. 69, l. 9.

57. Shul′gina, *Konspekt*, 165.

58. Shul′gina, "1917 god," GARF, f. R-5974, op. 2, d. 69, l. 56.

59. Shul′gina, "1917 god," ll. 52, 56.

60. Such strategies to "depoliticize" one's own actions have been also described in the case of nationalist women elsewhere. See, for instance, Zettelbauer, *Die Liebe sei Euer Heldentum*, 451.

61. Shul′gina, *Konspekt*, 362.

62. Shul′gina, 313.

63. See, for instance, her notes in Shul′gina, "Vozvrashchenie," GARF, f. R-5974, op. 2, d. 15, l. 35. On the self-therapeutic function of autobiographical writing ("scriptotherapy") see Smith and Watson, *Reading Autobiography*, 29, 250; Ulrich Schmid, *Ichentwürfe: Russische Autobiographien zwischen Avvakum und Gercen* (Zurich: Pano Verlag, 2000), 377–78.

64. E. Shul′gina to D. Shul′gin, 17 March 1931, ARS, SI AS 1021, folder 5, letter 24.

65. E. G. Shul′gina, "Novyi zavet," 11 February 1922, GARF, f. R-5974, op. 2, d. 11v, l. 3.

66. E. Shul′gina to E. Efimovskii, 30 June 1922, HIA, 2012C6, box 1, folder 16.

67. Shul′gina, *Konspekt*, 298, 303, 392.

68. Shul′gina, 63, 299.

69. Lukáš Babka, Anastasia Kopřivová, and Lidiia Petrusheva, eds., *Russkii zagranichnyi istoricheskii arkhiv v Prage—dokumentatsiia* (Prague: Národní knihovna České republiky, 2011), 174; Matich, *Zapiski russkoi amerikanki*, 257.

70. V. Shul′gin to E. Shul′gina, 8 November 1923, GARF, f. R-5974, op. 2, d. 130, l. 22ob.

71. See her documents in ARS, SI AS 1021, folder 4.

72. Vladimir A. Tesemnikov, "Belgrad: Die russische Emigration in Jugoslawien," in *Der grosse Exodus: Die russische Emigration und ihre Zentren 1917 bis 1941*, ed. Karl Schlögel (Munich: C. H. Beck, 1994), 89–91.

73. L. Mogilevskaia to Belgrade City Council, 26 April 1934, ARS, SI AS 1022, folder 1; Shul′gin, *Teni*, 53–55, 63, 72–73, 84–86, 576–77n9; Matich, *Zapiski russkoi amerikanki*, 86.

74. V. Shul′gin, "Russkie zagranitsei," *Zarnitsy*, no. 3 (1921): 5.

75. V. Shul′gin to V. Maklakov, 9 March 1921, in Budnitskii, *Spor o Rossii*, 55–59; "Otkrytoe pis′mo V. V. Shul′gina P. N. Miliukovu," *Zarnitsy* no. 5 (1921), 3–5.

76. Makarov, Repnikov, and Khristoforov, *Tiuremnaia odisseia*, 235–36; Shul′gin, *1921 god*, 130, 216–20.

77. On this trip see M. D. Shul′gina, "Po chernomu moriu," in Shul′gin, *1921 god*, 243–96. Vladimir Lazarevskii, who reached the Soviet Union with this boat, subsequently organized Ekaterina Shul′gina's flight to Poland.

78. Karl Schlögel, "Einleitung: Die Zentren der Emigration," in *Der grosse Exodus: Die russische Emigration und ihre Zentren 1917 bis 1941*, ed. Karl Schlögel (Munich: C. H. Beck, 1994), 14.

79. "Svodka arendnoi platy V. V. Shul′ginu za imenie Kurgany ot 1925 po 1934 god vkliuchitel′no," ARS, SI AS 1021, folder 4; Shul′gin, *Teni*, 87.

80. Babkov, "Politicheskaia publitsistika," 97–99.

81. An influential voice in the first years of the emigration, *Russkaia mysl'* moved along with its editor, from Sofia (1921) to Prague (1922) and then Berlin (1923), an itinerary roughly corresponding to Vasilii Shul'gin's movement. See M. A. Kolerov, "Russkaia Mysl' (1921–1927). Rospis' soderzhania," *Issledovaniia po istorii russkoi mysli* 1 (1997): 287–317.

82. V. Shul'gin to V. Maklakov, 29 June 1922, in Budnitskii, *Spor o Rossii*, 94–95.

83. See "Predpolagaemym naslednikam i izdateliam rukopisi Vasiliia Vitalevicha Shul'gina ego posmertnoe pis'mo," 24 February 1941, OR IMLI RAN, f. 604, ed. khr. 182.

84. See Smith and Watson, *Reading Autobiography*, 33.

85. V. Shul'gin to V. Maklakov, 2 August 1923, in Budnitskii, *Spor o Rossii*, 132.

86. Quoted in A. A. Chemakin, "Istoriia odnoi knigi, ili dolgii put' '1919 goda' k chitateliu," in Shul'gin, *1919 god*, 1:25.

87. Shul'gin, *1920 g.*, 8–10, 12, 275.

88. Shul'gin, 7, 262–66, 277.

89. L. Mogilevskaia to V. Shul'gin, 19.12.[1921], GARF, f. R-5974, op. 1, d. 158 ll. 102–102ob.

90. Shul'gin, *Dni*, 5, 309.

91. Shul'gin, 57, 163, 175, 205.

92. Zaslavskii, *Rytsar' monarkhii Shul'gin*, 16.

93. Shul'gin, *Dni*, 74–75, 262.

94. Shul'gin, *1921 god*, 68, 88.

95. V. Shul'gin to V. Maklakov, 9 March 1921, in Budnitskii, *Spor o Rossii*, 55.

96. See Matich, *Zapiski russkoi amerikanki*, 49–52.

97. V. V. Shul'gin, *"Chto nam v nikh ne nravitsia . . .": Ob Antisemizisme v Rossii* (Paris: Russia minor, 1929), 5–6, 50, 144–48, 156–80. On such antisemitic myths in interwar Europe see Paul A. Hanebrink, *A Specter Haunting Europe: The Myth of Judeo-Bolshevism* (Cambridge, MA: Belknap Press of Harvard University Press, 2018).

98. Yuri Slezkine stresses the novelty of this comprehensive understanding of ethnic responsibility; however, Shul'gin's views are unmistakeably rooted in the family tradition. See Yuri Slezkine, *The Jewish Century* (Princeton, NJ: Princeton University Press, 2004), 181.

99. V. V. Shul'gin, "Po povodu odnoi stat'i," 1925, in Budnitskii, *Spor o Rossii*, 233.

100. Shul'gin, *Chto nam v nikh ne nravitsia*, 107–27, 171, emphasis in original.

101. Shul'gin, "Po povodu odnoi stat'i," 239.

102. Shul'gin, "Voina bez mira," OR IMLI RAN, f. 604, ed. khr. 182, ll. 153–61.

103. Shul'gin, *Chto nam v nikh ne nravitsia*, 110–12; Shul'gin, "Voina bez mira," OR IMLI RAN, f. 604, ed. khr. 181, ll. 61–64. Shul'gin gave more attention to the Ukrainian question in his political press articles and in two

brochures of the late 1930s, one of which compared Adolf Hitler's *Anschluss* of Austria with the "reunification" of Ukraine and the Russian Empire in 1654. See V. V. Shul'gin, *Anshluss i my!* (Belgrade: Izdanie N. Z. Rybinskago, 1938); V. V. Shul'gin, *Ukrainstvuiushchie i my!* (Belgrade: Izdanie N. Z. Rybinskago, 1939); Babkov, *Gosudarstvennye i natsional'nye problemy*, 168–208.

104. V. Shul'gin to V. Maklakov, 12 February 1929, in Budnitskii, *Spor o Rossii*, 296–98. In old age, like vice versa, Vasilii Shul'gin found something nice to say about Oleksander Shul'hyn: "According to those who have met him, he was a charming man." Shul'gin, *Teni*, 37.

105. Shul'gin, *Tri stolitsy*, 51, 148–49, 258, 414.

106. Basil Shulgin, "How I Was Hoodwinked by the Bolsheviks," *Slavonic Review* 6, no. 18 (1928): 505–19. On the emigration's reaction see Lazar' Fleishman, *V tiskach provokatsii: Operatsiia "Trest" i russkaia zarubezhnaia pechat'* (Moscow: Novoe literaturnoe obozrenie, 2003).

107. V. Shul'gin to P. Struve, 29 October 1927, HIA, 85018, box 136, folder 14, l. 8.

108. Makarov, Repnikov, and Khristoforov, *Tiuremnaia odisseia*, 190–94. See Johnston, *New Mecca*, 151–53, on the fascist and Nazi affinities of the National Labor Alliance.

109. V. Shul'gin to E. Shul'gina, 10 October [1931?], ARS, SI AS 1022, folder 1.

110. For a good overview over Shul'gin's late years see V. G. Makarov, A. V. Repnikov, and V. S. Khristoforov, "Vasilii Vital'evich Shul'gin: Shtrikhi k portretu," in Makarov, Repnikov, and Khristoforov, *Tiuremnaia odisseia*, 5–132.

111. Shul'gin, "Muka," "Med," RGALI, f. 1337, op. 4, d. 54–61.

112. See Shul'gin, *Poslednii ochevidets*; Shul'gin, *Teni*.

113. Some of Shul'gin's late texts include some pro-Soviet views, and there has been debate over the degree to which he accepted Soviet power. Given the inconsistency of his thought, it is no surprise that contemporaries' memories of his private statements differ greatly. As Russian researchers have rightly pointed out, many of Shul'gin's visitors seem to have heard from him precisely what they wished to hear. Makarov, Repnikov, and Khristoforov, "V. V. Shul'gin: Shtrikhi k portretu," 89.

Conclusion

1. Decree of Kyiv Mayor V. Klichko, 19 February 2016, http://kievcity. gov.ua/done_img/f/РКМГ-125-1-19022016.PDF (last accessed on 10 January 2022).

2. Iurii Mativos, "Vulytsi Kirovohrada: Povernennia Shul'hinykh," 21 April 2015, http://akulamedia.com/vulitsi-kirovograda-povernennja-shulginih-foto (last accessed on 10 January 2022).

3. For instance, Shevchenko, *Shul'hyny*, 55; Alla Lazareva, "Stratehiia chitkykh kordoniv," 21 January 2018, https://m.tyzhden.ua/publication/207879 (last accessed on 10 January 2022).

4. In 2011, a Russian court legally rehabilitated Shul'gin, concluding that he had never collaborated with the Nazis and that his conviction by the

Stalinist judiciary had been a case of politically motivated repression. See Makarov, Repnikov, and Khristoforov, *Tiuremnaia odisseia*, 305–8.

5. Fabian Baumann, "Einseitiger Einheitswunsch—Putins neueste Geschichtslektion," *Religion und Gesellschaft in Ost und West*, no. 9 (2021): 3–5.

6. Jeremy King, "The Nationalization of East Central Europe: Ethnicism, Ethnicity, and Beyond," in *Staging the Past: The Politics of Commemoration in Habsburg Central Europe, 1848 to the Present*, ed. Maria Bucur and Nancy M. Wingfield (West Lafayette, IN: Purdue University Press, 2001), 124.

7. Therefore this periodization, focusing on milieus and political practices, differs somewhat from Omelian Pritsak's and John Reshetar's geographical-ideological periodization of Ukrainian nationalism, Ivan Lysiak-Rudnytsky's social-ideological scheme, and Paul Robert Magocsi's tripartite periodization into a heritage-gathering, an organizational, and a political stage. See Serhy Bilenky, "The Ukrainian National Movement in the Nineteenth Century: Context, Timing, Issues," in *Fashioning Modern Ukraine*, xviii–xxix.

8. See von Winning, *Intimate Empire*, 104–41.

BIBLIOGRAPHY

Archival Sources

Archives de la Préfecture de Police (APP), Paris

BA 196: Cabinet du préfet, affaires générales

Arhiv Republike Slovenije (ARS), Ljubljana

SI AS 1021: Šulgin Dimitrij
SI AS 1022: Šulgin Katarina

Derzhavnyi arkhiv Chernihivs'koï oblasti (DAChO), Chernihiv

Fond 679: Chernigovskaia dukhovnaia konsistoriia

Derzhavnyi arkhiv mista Kyieva (DAK), Kyiv

Fond 16: Kievskii Universitet Sv. Vladimira
Fond 98: Kievskaia chastnaia progimnaziia G. A. Val'kera
Fond 108: Kievskaia pervaia gimnaziia

Derzhavnyi arkhiv Kyïvs'koï oblasti (DAKO), Kyiv

Fond 782: Kievskoe dvorianskoe deputatskoe sobranie

Gosudarstvennyi arkhiv Rossiiskoi Federatsii (GARF), Moscow

Fond 102: Departament politsii Ministerstva vnutrennykh del
Fond 109: Tret'e otdelenie Sobstvennoi Ego Imperatorskogo Velichestva kantseliarii
Fond 112: Osoboe prisutstvie Senata dlia suzhdeniia del o gosudarstvennykh prestupleniiakh
Fond 539: V. V. Vodovozov
Fond 670: Nikolai Mikhailovich, Velikii Kniaz'
Fond 1099: T. I. Filippov
Fond R-5827: A. I. Denikin
Fond R-5974: V. V. Shul'gin, E. G. Shul'gina

Hoover Institution Archives (HIA), Stanford

27001: P. N. Vrangel' collection
33003: M. D. Vrangel' collection
79083: P. B. Struve papers

85018: G. P. Struve papers
2012C6: E. A. Efimovskii papers

Instytut literatury im. T. G. Shevchenka Natsional'noï akademiï nauk
Ukraïny, arkhiv rukopysiv (IL NANU), Kyiv

Fond 23: B. S. Poznans'kyi
Fond 28: O. P. Kosach
Fond 120: S. O. Iefremov

Instytut rukopysu Natsional'noï biblioteky Ukraïny imeni V. I. Vernads'koho
(IR NBUV), Kyiv

Fond I: Literature collection
Fond III: Correspondence collection
Fond 21: Iu. A. Iavorskii
Fond 57: N. Kh. Bunge
Fond 86: I. P. Zhytets'kyi
Fond 179: A. I. Stepovich
Fond 208: V. P. Naumenko
Fond 209: A. A. Tulub
Fond 317: S. O. Iefremov

Naukovyi arkhiv Instytutu arkheolohiï Natsional'noï akademiï nauk Ukraïny
(NAIA NANU), Kyiv

Fond 1: F. K. Vovk

Otdel rukopisei Instituta mirovoi literatury im. A. M. Gor'kogo Rossiiskoi
akademii nauk (OR IMLI RAN), Moscow

Fond 604: V. V. Shul'gin

Rossiiskii gosudarstvennyi arkhiv literatury i iskusstva (RGALI), Moscow

Fond 395: A. N. Pypin
Fond 402: S. I. Ponomarev
Fond 637: D. D. Iazykov
Fond 1337: Kollektsiia vospominanii i dnevnikov
Fond 2174: M. V. Krestovskaia

Rossiiskii gosudarstvennyi istoricheskii arkhiv (RGIA), Saint Petersburg

Fond 1162: Gosudarstvennaia kantseliariia Gosudarstvennogo soveta
Fond 1410: Veshchestvennye dokazatel'stva po delam Ministerstva iustitsii
Fond 1622: S. Iu. Vitte

Tsentral'nyi derzhavnyi arkhiv vyshchykh orhaniv vlady ta upravlinnia
Ukraïny (TsDAVO), Kyiv

Fond 1063: Ukraïns'ka Tsentral'na Rada, Heneral'nyi sekretariat
Fond 1429: Kantseliariia dyrektoriï Ukraïns'koï Narodnoï Respubliky

Fond 2592: Narodne Ministerstvo sprav zakordonnykh Ukraïns'koï
    Narodnoï Respubliky
Fond 3696: Ministerstvo zakordonnykh sprav Ukraïns'koï Narodnoï
    Respubliky
Fond 3766: Ministerstvo zakordonnykh sprav Ukraïns'koï Derzhavy

Tsentral'nyi derzhavnyi istorychnyi arkhiv Ukraïny, m. Kyïv (TsDIAK), Kyiv

Fond 127: Kievskaia dukhovnaia konsistoriia
Fond 293: Kievskii tsenzurnyi komitet
Fond 295: Kievskii vremennyi komitet po delam pechati
Fond 296: Redaktsiia gazety "Kievlianin"
Fond 385: Zhandarmskoe upravlenie g. Odessy
Fond 442: Kantseliariia Kievskogo, Podol'skogo i Volynskogo
    General-Gubernatora
Fond 707: Kantseliiariia popechitelia Kievskogo uchebnogo okruga
Fond 832: Antonovychi
Fond 849: V. S. Ikonnikov
Fond 1235: Hrushevs'ki

Tsentral'nyi gosudarstvennyi istoricheskii arkhiv Sankt-Peterburga (TsGIA
    SPb), Saint Petersburg

Fond 14: Imperatorskii Petrogradskii Universitet

Ishchuk-Pazuniak Private Collection, Philadelphia
Olga Matich Private Collection, Berkeley

Newspapers

Kievlianin	Kiev, 1864–1919
Kievskaia mysl'	Kiev, 1906–1918
Kievskii telegraf	Kiev, 1859–1876
Moskovskiia vedomosti	Moscow, 1756–1917
Nova Rada	Kiev, 1917–1919
Rech'	Saint Petersburg, 1906–1918
Rossiia (Odesskoe izdanie)	Odessa, 1919
Russkoe slovo	Moscow, 1895–1918
Sankt-Peterburgskiia vedomosti	Saint Petersburg, 1727–1917

Journals

Arkhiv russkoi revoliutsii	Berlin, 1921–1937
Byloe	Saint Petersburg, 1906–1907
Chasovoi	Paris, 1929–1936
Hromada	Geneva, 1878–1882
Istoricheskii vestnik	Saint Petersburg, 1880–1917
Kievskaia starina	Kiev, 1882–1906

Kwartalnik historyczny	Lemberg, 1887–1939
Malaia Rus'	Kiev, 1918
Osnova	Saint Petersburg, 1861–1862
Russkoe bogatstvo	Saint Petersburg, 1876–1918
Russkaia mysl'	Moscow, 1880–1918
Russkaia starina	Saint Petersburg, 1870–1918
Severnyi vestnik	Saint Petersburg, 1885–1898
Sphere	London, 1900–1964
Tryzub	Paris, 1925–1940
Ukraïna	Kiev, 1907
Ukraïna	Kiev, 1924–1930
Ukrainskaia zhizn'	Moscow, 1912–1917
Ukrainskii vestnik	Saint Petersburg, 1906
Universitetskiia izvestiia	Kiev, 1861–1917
Vestnik Evropy	Moscow, 1866–1918
Vpered!	London, 1873–1877
Zapysky Ukraïns'koho Naukovoho Tovarystva	Kiev, 1908–1918
Zapysky Naukovoho Tovarystva im. Shevchenka	Lemberg, 1892–1937
Zarnitsy	Constantinople and Sofia, 1921
Za sto lit	Kiev, 1927–1930
Zoria	Lemberg, 1880–1897

Stenographic Reports and Document Collections

Babka, Lukáš, Anastasia Kopřivová, and Lidiia Petrusheva, eds. *Russkii zagranichnyi istoricheskii arkhiv v Prage—dokumentatsiia*. Prague: Národní knihovna České republiky, 2011.

Gosudarstvennaia duma. Vtoroi sozyv. Stenograficheskie otchety. 2 vols. Saint Petersburg: Gosudarstvennaia tipografiia, 1908.

Gosudarstvennaia duma. Ukazatel' k stenograficheskim otchetam. Vtoroi sozyv. Saint Petersburg: Gosudarstvennaia tipografiia, 1907.

Gosudarstvennaia duma. Tretii sozyv. Stenograficheskie otchety. 18 vols. Saint Petersburg: Gosudarstvennaia tipografiia, 1908–1912.

Gosudarstvennaia duma. Ukazatel' k stenograficheskim otchetam. Tretii Sozyv. Saint Petersburg: Gosudarstvennaia tipografiia, 1908.

Gosudarstvennaia duma. Chetvertyi sozyv. Stenograficheskie otchety. 12 vols. Saint Petersburg: Gosudarstvennaia tipografiia, 1913–1917.

Gosudarstvennyi sovet. Stenograficheskie otchety. Sessiia chetvertaia. Saint Petersburg: Gosudarstvennaia tipografiia, 1909.

Gosudarstvennyi sovet. Stenograficheskie otchety. Sessiia shestaia. Saint Petersburg: Gosudarstvennaia tipografiia, 1911.

Hornykiewicz, Theophil. *Ereignisse in der Ukraine 1914–1922, deren Bedeutung und historische Hintergründe*. 4 vols. Horn, Germany: Ferdinand Berger, 1966–1969.

Makarov, V. G., A. V. Repnikov, and V. S. Khristoforov, eds. *Tiuremnaia odisseia Vasiliia Shul'gina: Materialy sledstvennogo dela i dela zakliuchennogo*. Moscow: Russkii put', 2010.

"Svod ukazanii, dannykh nekotorymi iz arestovannykh po delam o gosu-darstvennykh prestupleniiakh (Mai 1880 goda)." *Byloe*, no. 6 (1907): 118-60.

Verstiuk, V. F., O. D. Boiko, Iu. M. Hamrets'kyi, and H. M. Mykhailychenko, eds. *Ukraïns'ka Tsentral'na Rada: Dokumenty i materialy u dvokh tomakh.* 2 vols. Kyiv: Naukova dumka, 1996-1997.

Volobuev, P. V., ed. *Petrogradskii sovet rabochikh i soldatskikh deputatov v 1917 godu: Dokumenty i materialy.* 5 vols. Leningrad: Nauka, 1991.

Published Books, Pamphlets, Memoirs, Diaries, and Correspondence

Adresnaia i spravochnaia kniga Ves' Kiev. Kiev: Izdanie M. L Radominskago [et al.], 1899-1915.

Aksel'rod, P. B. *Perezhitoe i peredumannoe.* Berlin: Izdatel'stvo Z. I. Grzhebina, 1923.

Antonovich, V. B. *Izsledovanie o gaidamachestve po aktam 1700–1768 g.* Kiev: Universitetskaia tipografiia I. I. Zavadskago, 1876.

Antonovych, Marko D. "Nedrukovani lysty V. B. Antonovycha do F. K. Vovka (z arkhivu VUAN)." *Ukraïns'kyi istoryk*, no. 1-4 (1988): 148-64.

Antsiferov, N. P. *Iz dum o bylom: Vospominaniia.* Moscow: Feniks, 1992.

Avseenko, V. G. "Shkol'nye gody. Otryvki iz vospominanii 1852-1863." *Istoricheskii vestnik* 4 (1881): 707-34.

Berenshtam-Kistiakovs'ka, Mariia. "Ukraïns'ki hurtky v Kyïvi druhoï polovyny 1880-ykh ta pochatku 1890-ykh rokiv." *Za sto lit* 3 (1928): 206-25.

Bilenky, Serhiy, ed. *Fashioning Modern Ukraine: Selected Writings of Mykola Kostomarov, Volodymyr Antonovych and Mykhailo Drahomanov.* Toronto: Canadian Institute of Ukrainian Studies, 2013.

Bilimovich, A. D., and N. M. Tsytovich. *Pamiati D. I. Pikhno.* Saint Petersburg: Senatskaia tipografiia, 1913.

Boiovich, M. M., ed. *Chleny Gosudarstvennoi Dumy (portrety i biografii). Vtoroi sozyv 1907–1912 g.* Moscow: Tipografiia T-va I. D. Sytina, 1907.

———. *Chleny Gosudarstvennoi Dumy (portrety i biografii). Tretii sozyv 1907–1912 g.* Moscow: Tipografiia T-va I. D. Sytina, 1908.

Bortnevskii, V. G., ed. "K istorii osvedomitel'noi organizatsii 'Azbuka.'" *Russkoe proshloe* 4 (1993): 160-93.

Budnitskii, O. V., ed. *Spor o Rossii: V. A. Maklakov–V. V. Shul'gin, perepiska 1919–1939 gg.* Moscow: ROSSPEN, 2012.

Bulgakov, M. A. *Belaia gvardiia. Master i Margarita.* 1925. Reprint, Minsk: Uradzhai, 1988.

Chevazhevskii, V. S. "Iz proshlago Kievskago universiteta i studencheskoi zhizni (1870-1875 g.)." *Russkaia starina* 150, no. 4-6 (1912): 555-85.

Choulguine, Alexandre [Oleksander Shul'hyn]. *L'Ukraine, la Russie et les puissances de l'Entente.* Bern, 1918.

———. *Les problèmes de l'Ukraine: La question ethnique—la culture nationale—la vie économique—la volonté du peuple.* Paris: Société des Éditions Louis Michaud, 1919.

———. *L'Ukraine et le cauchemar rouge: Les massacres en Ukraine.* Paris: J. Tallandier, 1927.

——. *Vers l'indépendance de l'Ukraine: Étude sur l'évolution politique du pays*. Paris: Association ukrainienne pour la Société des Nations, 1930.

——. *L'Ukraine contre Moscou (1917)*. Paris: Alcan, 1935.

——. "Les origines de l'esprit national moderne et Jean-Jacques Rousseau." *Annales de la société Jean-Jacques Rousseau* 26 (1937): 7–283.

Chronologie des principaux événements en Ukraine de 1917 à 1919. Paris: Bureau ukrainien de presse, 1919.

Chykalenko, Ievhen. *Spohady (1861–1907)*. 1925. Reprint, New York: Ukr. vil'na akademiia nauk u SShA, 1955.

——. *Shchodennyk 1919–1920*. Kyiv: Vydavnytstvo imeni Oleny Telihy, 2005.

——. *Shchodennyk (1907–1917)*. Kyiv: Tempora, 2011.

——. *Shchodennyk (1918–1919)*. Kyiv: Tempora, 2011.

Chykalenko, Ievhen, and Andrii Nikovs'kyi. *Lystuvannia 1908–1921 roky*. Kyiv: Tempora, 2010.

Chykalenko, Ievhen, and Petro Stebnyts'kyi. *Lystuvannia 1901–1922 roky*. Kyiv: Tempora, 2008.

Chykalenko, Ievhen, and Volodymyr Vynnychenko. *Lystuvannia 1902–1929 roky*. Kyiv: Tempora, 2010.

Debogorii-Mokrievich, Vladimir. *Vospominaniia*. Saint Petersburg: Knigoizdatel'stvo "Svobodnyi trud," 1906.

Deich, Lev. "M. P. Dragomanov v izgnanii." *Vestnik Evropy*, no. 10 (1913): 201–26.

——. "Ukrainskaia i obshcherusskaia emigratsiia." *Vestnik Evropy*, no. 8 (1914): 209–33.

——. *Za Polveka*. Berlin: Izdatel'stvo "Grani," 1923.

Denikin, A. I. *Ocherki russkoi smuty*. 5 vols. Paris: J. Povolsky [et al.], 1921–1926.

"Dnevnik i vospominaniia kievskoi studentki (1919–20 g.g.)." *Arkhiv russkoi revoliutsii* 15 (1924): 209–53.

Doroshenko, Dmytro. "Ukraïns'kyi rukh 1890-kh rokiv v osvitlenni avstriis'koho konsula v Kyievi." In *Z mynuloho. Zbirnyk*, 1:59–70. Warsaw: Ukraïns'kyi naukovyi instytut, 1938.

——. *Moï spomyny pro davnie-mynule (1901–1914 roky)*. Winnipeg: Tryzub, 1949.

——. *Moï spomyny pro nedavnie-mynule (1914–1920)*. 1923–1924. Reprint, Munich: Ukraïns'ke vydavnytstvo, 1969.

——. *Istoriia Ukraïny 1917–1923 rr*. 2 vols. 1930–1932. Reprint, Kyiv: Tempora, 2002.

Dragomanov, M. P. *K biografii A. I. Zheliabova*. Geneva: Imprimerie de La Parole Libre, 1882.

Drahomanov, Mykhailo. *Narodni shkoly na Ukrajini sered zhyt't'a i pys'menstva v Rossiji*. Geneva: H. Georg, 1877.

——. *Literaturno-publitsystychni pratsi*. Kyiv: Naukova dumka, 1970.

——. *Vybrane*. Kyiv: Lybid', 1991.

Efimovskii, E. A. "V russkom Kieve v 1918 godu: Politicheskie siluety." In *Stat'i*, 129–37. Paris, 1994.

Fedenko, Panas. "Dmytro Chyzhevs'kyi (4 kvitnia 1894–18 kvitnia 1977): Spomyn pro zhyttia i naukovu diial'nist'." *Ukraïns'kyi istoryk*, no. 1–3 (1978): 102–18.

Franko, Ivan. *Zibrannia tvoriv u p'iatdesiaty tomakh*. 50 vols. Kyiv: Naukova dumka, 1976–1986.

Galagan, Mykola. *Z moïkh spomyniv*. 2 vols. L'viv: Chervona kalyna, 1930.

Gol'denveizer, A. A. "Iz kievskikh vospominanii." *Arkhiv russkoi revoliutsii* 6 (1922): 161–303.

Gradovskii, G. K. "Vitalii Iakovlevich Shul'gin (biograficheskii ocherk)." In *"Kievlianin" pod redaktsiei Vitaliia Iakovlevicha Shul'gina (1864–1878)*, edited by M. K. Shul'gina, 1–19. Kiev: Universitetskaia tipografiia I. I. Zavadskago, 1880.

Hrushevs'kyi, Myhkailo. "Pamiaty Iakova Shul'hyna." *Zapysky Naukovoho Tovarystva im. Shevchenka* 107 (1912): 5–9.

——. *Z pochyniv ukraïns'koho sotsiialistychnoho rukhu. Mykh. Drahomanov i zhenevs'kyi sotsiialistychnyi hurtok*. Vienna: Institut sociologique ukrainien, 1922.

Iakimova, A. M. "Lystuvannia Oleksandra Shul'hyna z rodynoiu Shyshmanovykh u 1922–1923 rokakh." *Sums'kyi istoryko-arkhivnyi zhurnal*, no. 16–17 (2012): 45–64.

Ianiv, Volodymyr, ed. *Zbirnyk na poshanu Oleksandra Shul'hyna (1889–1960)*. Paris, 1969 (=*Zapysky Naukovoho Tovarystva im. Shevchenka* 186).

Iefremov, Serhii. "Iak povstav Hrinchenkiv slovnyk." In *Slovnyk ukraïns'koï movy*, edited by Borys Hrinchenko, 3rd ed., 2:v–xxiv. Kyiv: Horno, 1927.

——. *Shchodennyk. Pro dni mynuli (spohady)*. Edited by Ihor Hyrych. Kyiv: Tempora, 2011.

Iehunova-Shcherbyna, Sofiia. "Odes'ka Hromada kintsia 70-kh rokiv (spomyny)." *Za sto lit* 2 (1928): 189–99.

Ikonnikov, V. S., ed. *Biograficheskii slovar' professorov i prepodovatelei Imperatorskago Universiteta Sv. Vladimira (1834–1884)*. Kiev: Tipografiia Imperatorskago Universiteta Sv. Vladimira, 1884.

Kartavtsov, E. E. *Obrusenie zemlevladeniia v iugo-zapadnom krae*. Kiev: Universitetskaia tipografiia I. I. Zavadskago, 1877.

Kaufman, A. E. *Druz'ia i vragi evreev. 1. D. I. Pikhno*. Saint Petersburg: Knigoizdatel'stvo "Pravda," 1907.

Khrystiuk, Pavlo. *Zamitky i materiialy do istoriï ukraïns'koï revoliutsiï*. 4 vols. Vienna: Institut sociologique ukrainien, 1921–1922.

Khudozhestvenno-literaturnyi al'manakh "Kievlianka." Kiev: Tipo-Litografiia I. N. Kushnereva, 1884.

Kistiakivs'kyi, O. F. *Shchodennyk (1874–1885) u dvokh tomakh*. 2 vols. Kyiv: Naukova dumka, 1994–1995.

Konys'kyi, Oleksandr. "Dumky i pomitky." *Zapysky Naukovoho Tovarystva im. Shevchenka* 265 (2013): 387–450.

Korotkyi, Viktor, and Vasyl' Ul'ianovs'kyi, eds. *Syn Ukraïny: Volodymyr Bonifatiiovych Antonovych*. 3 vols. Kyiv: Zapovit, 1997.

L-aia, L. "Ocherki zhizni v Kieve v 1919–20 gg." *Arkhiv russkoi revoliutsii* 3 (1921): 210–33.

L. Ch. [Iakov Shul'gin]. "Ukraïna pislia 1654 roku." *Zapysky Naukovoho Tovarystva im. Shevchenka* 29 (1899): 1–13; 30 (1899): 14–67.

Leontovych, Volodymyr. "Spohady pro moï zustrichi z ukraïns'kymi diiachami starshoho pokolinnia." In *Zibrannia tvoriv*, 3:303–35. Kyiv: Sfera, 2005.

Lotots'kyi, Oleksander. *Storinky mynuloho*. 4 vols. 1932–1934. Reprint, [Bound Brook, NJ]: Vyd. ukraïns'koï pravoslavnoï tserkvy v SShA, 1966.

Lysenko, Mykola. *Lysty*. Edited by O. Lysenko. Kyiv: Mystetstvo, 1964.

Margolin, Arnol'd. *Ukraina i politika Antanty (Zapiski evreia i grazhdanina)*. Berlin: Izdatel'stvo S. Efron, 1921.

Mémoire sur l'indépendance de l'Ukraine présenté à la conférence de la paix par la délégation de la République ukrainienne. Paris, 1919.

Miliukov, P. N. *Istoriia vtoroi russkoi revoliutsii*. 3 vols. Sofia: Rossiisko-bolgarskoe knigoizdatel'stvo, 1921–1923.

Myshchenko, Liudmyla. "Z mynuloho stolittia. Spomyny." *Za sto lit* 4 (1929): 106–60.

Novitskii, V. D. *Iz vospominanii zhandarma*. 1929. Reprint, Moscow: Izdatel'stvo Moskovskogo Universiteta, 1991.

Ob otmene stesnenii malorusskago pechatnago slova. Saint Petersburg: Tipografiia imperatorskoi akademii nauk, 1905.

Pares, Bernard. "The Second Duma." *Slavonic Review* 2, no. 4 (1923): 36–55.

Paustovskii, Konstantin. *Povest' o zhizni*. 2 vols. Moscow: Sovetskaia Rossiia, 1966.

Pavlyk, Mykhailo, ed. *Lysty Mykhaila Drahomanova do redaktoriv rosiis'koho sotsiial'no-revoliutsiinoho vydania "Vpered" (1876–1878)*. Lemberg: Drukarnia I. Aikhel'bergera, 1910.

Pchilka, Olena. *Opovidannia z avtobiohrafiieiu*. Kharkiv: Rukh, 1930.

Perrin, Olivier, ed. *Alexandre Choulguine (1889–1960)*. Paris: Académie internationale libre des sciences et de lettres, 1961.

Pikhno, D. I. *Vliianie nekotorykh ekonomicheskikh uslovii na sel'skoe khoziaistvo*. Kiev: Tipografiia T-va I. N. Kushnerev, 1901.

———. *V osade: Politicheskiia stat'i*. Kiev: Tipografiia T-va I. N. Kushnerev, 1905.

———. *Raskrepochshenie krest'ianskoi zemli*. Kiev: Tipografiia T-va I. N. Kushnerev, 1908.

———. *Predstavitel'stvo Zapadnoi Rusi v Gosudarstvennom sovete*. Kiev: Tipografiia T-va I. N. Kushnerev, 1909.

Piskun, Valentyna, ed. *Oleksandr Shul'hyn v ukraïns'komu derzhavotvorenni ta mizhnarodnii politytsi*. Kyiv: Instytut ukraïns'koï arkheohrafiï ta dzhereloznavstva im. M. S. Hrushevs'koho, 2016.

Ptashkina, Nelli. *Dnevnik 1918–1920*. Paris: Russkoe knigoizdatel'stvo Ia. Povolotskago i Ko, 1922.

Romanovich-Slavatinskii, A. V. "Moia zhizn' i akademicheskaia deiatel'nost' 1832–1882 gg." *Vestnik Evropy* 5 (1903): 181–205.

Rusova, Sofiia. "Moï spomyny rr. 1861–1879." *Za sto lit* 2 (1928): 135–75.

———. "Moï spomyny 1879–1915." *Za sto lit* 3 (1928): 147–205.

Sapir, Boris, ed. *"Vpered!" 1873–1877: Materialy iz arkhiva Valeriana Nikolaevicha Smirnova*. Dordrecht: Reidel, 1970.

Sbornik kluba russkikh natsionalistov. 5 vols. Kiev: Tipografiia T-va I. N. Kushnerev, 1909–1913.

Shchegolev, S. N. *Ukrainskoe dvizhenie, kak sovremennyi etap iuzhnorusskago separatizma*. Kiev: Tipografiia T-va I. N. Kushnerev, 1912.

Shcherbyna, Volodymyr. "Pamiaty Iakova Shul'hyna." *Zapysky Ukraïns'koho Naukovoho Tovarystva v Kyïvi* 10 (1912): 5–13.

Shelukhyn, Serhii. "Ukraïnstvo 80-kh rokiv i moï znosyny z Iv. Frankom." *Literaturno-naukovyi visnyk*, no. 7–8 (1926): 260–81.

Shevchenko, Taras. *Haidamaky. Poema*. 1841. Reprint, Saint Petersburg: Drukarnia P. A. Kulisha, 1861.

Shulgin, Basil [V. V.]. "How I Was Hoodwinked by the Bolsheviks." *Slavonic Review* 6 (1927): 505–19.

Shul'gin, Ia. N. "Razvitie krepostnogo prava v Malorossii XVII–XVIII vv." *Severnyi vestnik*, no. 6 (1887): 50–64.

———. "Ocherk kolievshchiny po neizdannym i izdannym dokumentam 1768 i blizhaishikh gg." *Kievskaia starina*, no. 2 (1890): 185–220; no. 3 (1890): 381–418; no. 4 (1890): 22–52; no. 5 (1890): 268–306; no. 6 (1890): 409–26; no. 7 (1890): 1–21; no. 8 (1890): 192–223.

Shul'gin, V. Ia. *O sostoianii zhenshchin v Rossii do Petra Velikago*. Kiev: Tipografiia I. Val'nera, 1850.

———. *Istoriia universiteta Sv. Vladimira*. Saint Petersburg: Tipografiia Riumina i Komp., 1860.

———. *Iugozapadnyi krai v poslednee dvadtsatipiatiletie*. Kiev: Universitetskaia tipografiia, 1864.

———. "Iugo-zapadnyi krai pod upravleniem D. G. Bibikova (1838–1853)." *Drevniaia i novaia Rossiia*, no. 5 (1879): 5–32; no. 6 (1879): 89–131.

Shul'gin, V. V. *Vybornoe zemstvo v iugo-zapadnom krae*. Kiev: Tipografiia T-va I. N. Kushnerev, 1909.

———. *Nedavnie dni*. Kharkov: Tipografiia "Mirnyi Trud," 1910.

———. *Prikliuchenia kniazia Voronetskago. V strane svobod*. Kiev: Tipografiia T-va I. N. Kushnerev, 1914.

———. *Monarkhisty. Stat'i V. V. Shul'gina i A*. Ekaterinodar: Izdatel'stvo "Rossiia," 1918.

———. *Narodopravstvo. Stat'i V. V. Shul'gina i A–"*. Rostov-na-Donu: Voskhod, 1918.

———. *1920 g.: Ocherki*. Sofia: Rossiisko-bolgarskoe knigoizdatel'stvo, 1921.

———. *Dni*. Belgrade: Knigoizdatel'stvo M. A. Suvorin i Ko. "Novoe Vremia," 1925.

———. *Tri stolitsy: Puteshestvie v krasnuiu Rossiiu*. Berlin: Knigoizdatel'stvo "Mednyi vsadnik," 1927.

———. *"Chto nam v nikh ne nravitsia . . .": Ob Antisemizisme v Rossii*. Paris: Russia minor, 1929.

———. *Anshluss i my!* Belgrade: Izdanie N. Z. Rybinskago, 1938.

———. *Ukrainstvuiushchie i my!* Belgrade: Izdanie N. Z. Rybinskago, 1939.

———. *The Years: Memoirs of a Member of the Russian Duma, 1906–1917*. Translated by Tanya Davis. New York: Hippocrene, 1984.

———. *Poslednii ochevidets: Memuary, ocherki, sny*. Edited by N. N. Lisovoi. Moscow: OLMA-Press, 2002.

——. *Teni, kotorye prokhodiat.* Edited by R. G. Krasiukov. Saint Petersburg: Nestor-Istoriia, 2012.

——. *Rossiia, Ukraina, Evropa: Izbrannye raboty.* Edited by A. V. Repnikov. Moscow: Sodruzhestvo "Posev," 2015.

——. *1919 god.* Edited by A. A. Chemakin. 2 vols. Moscow: Kuchkovo pole, 2018.

——. *1921 god.* Edited by A. A. Chemakin. Moscow: Kuchkovo pole, 2018.

——. *"Belye mysli": Publitsistika 1917–1920 gg.* Edited by A. A. Chemakin. Moscow: Kuchkovo pole, 2020.

Shul'gina, E. G. *Konspekt moikh politicheskikh perezhivanii (1903–1922).* Edited by A. A. Chemakin. Moscow: Fond Sviaz' Epokh, 2019.

Shul'gina, M. K., ed. *"Kievlianin" pod redaktsiei Vitaliia Iakovlevicha Shul'gina (1864–1878).* Kiev: Universitetskaia tipografiia I. I. Zavadskago, 1880.

Shul'hyn, Iakiv. *Nacherk koliïvshchyni na pidstavi vydanykh i nevydanykh dokumentiv 1768 i blyzshykh rokiv.* Lemberg: Rus'ka istorychna biblioteka, 1898.

Shul'hyn, Oleksander. *Polityka (derzhavne budivnytstvo Ukraïny i mizhnarodni spravy): Statti, dokumenty, promovy.* Kyiv: Drukar', 1918.

——. *Derzhavnist' chy haidamachchyna? (Zbirnyk statei ta dokumentiv).* Paris: Mech, 1931.

——. *Bez terytoriï: Ideolohiia ta chyn Uriadu U.N.R. na chuzhyni.* Paris: Mech, 1934.

——. "Uryvky iz spohadiv." In *Zbirnyk na poshanu Oleksandra Shul'hyna (1889–1960),* edited by Volodymyr Ianiv, 199–308. Paris, 1969 (=*Zapysky Naukovoho Tovarystva im. Shevchenka* 186).

Shul'hyna-Ishchuk, Nadiia. *Zadachnyk do systematychnoho kursu arytmetyky.* 2 vols. Kiev: Vydannia tovarystva shkil'noï osvity, 1917–1918.

——. "Do storinok istoriï ukraïns'koho shkil'nytstva (spohad)." In *125 rokiv Kyïvs'koï ukraïns'koï akademichnoï tradytsiï 1861–1986,* edited by Marko D. Antonovych, 555–64. New York, 1993.

Sikorskii, I. A. *Russkie i ukraintsy (Glava iz etnologicheskago katekhizisa).* Kiev: Tipografiia "S. V. Kul'zhenko," 1913.

Skoropads'kyi, Pavlo. *Spohady (kinets' 1917–hruden' 1918).* Edited by Iaroslav Pelens'kyi. Kyiv: Instytut ukraïns'koï arkheohrafiï ta dzhereloznavstva im. M. S. Hrushevs'koho NAN Ukraïny, 1995.

Smal'-Stots'kyi, Roman, ed. *Arkhiv Mykhaila Drahomanova. Tom 1: Lystuvannia Kyïvs'koï staroï hromady z M. Drahomanovym (1870–1895 rr.).* Warsaw: Ukraïns'kyi naukovyi instytut, 1937.

Starozhil [S. G. Iaron]. *Kiev v vos'midesiatykh godakh.* Kiev: Tipografiia "Petr Barskii v Kieve," 1910.

Staryts'ka-Cherniakhivs'ka, Liudmyla. *Vybrani tvory: Dramatychni tvory, proza, poeziia, memuary.* Kyiv: Naukova dumka, 2000.

Stempowski, Jerzy. *W dolinie Dniestru. Pisma o Ukrainie.* 1941. Reprint, Warsaw: Towarzystwo "Wież," 2014.

Storozhenko, A. V. *Proiskhozhdenie i sushchnost' ukrainofil'stva.* Kiev: Tipografiia "S. V. Kul'zhenko," 1912.

Strutyns'ka-Sadovs'ka, L. "Ukraïns'ki hromady u vyshchykh zhinochykh peterburz'kykh shkolakh (1912-1917)." In *Z mynuloho. Zbirnyk,* 2:110–22. Warsaw: Ukraïns'kyi naukovyi instytut, 1939.

Trudy podgotovitel'noi po natsional'nym delam kommissii. Malorusskii otdel. Sbornik statei po malorusskomu voprosu. Odessa: Russkaia kul'tura, 1919.

Vernadskii, V. I. *Dnevniki 1917–1921.* Edited by M. Iu. Sorokina. 2 vols. Kyiv: Naukova dumka, 1994–1997.

Vitalii Iakovlevich Shul'gin: Nekrolog i rechi, proiznesennyia nad grobom. Kiev: Universitetskaia tipografiia I. I. Zavadskago, 1879.

Vitte, S. Iu. *Iz arkhiva S. Iu. Vitte: Vospominaniia.* Edited by B. V. Anan'ich. 2 vols. Saint Petersburg: D. Bulanin, 2003.

Vydumki "Kievlianina" i pol'skikh gazet o malorusskom patriotizme. Kiev: Kievskii telegraf, 1874.

Vynnychenko, Volodymyr. *Vidrodzhennia natsiï.* 3 vols. Kyiv: Vydavnytstvo Dzvin, 1920.

Xydias, Jean. *L'intervention française en Russie 1918–1919: Souvenirs d'un témoin.* Paris: Les Éditions de France, 1927.

Zaslavskii, D. I. *Rytsar' monarkhii Shul'gin.* Leningrad: Knizhnie novinki, 1927.

Secondary Literature

Abramson, Henry. *A Prayer for the Government: Ukrainians and Jews in Revolutionary Times, 1917–1920.* Cambridge, MA: Harvard University Press, 1999.

Adams, Bruce. "The Extraordinary Career of Vasilii Shul'gin." *Revolutionary Russia* 5, no. 2 (1992): 193–220.

Akyndzhy, Emre. "Hromads'ko-politychna ta dyplomatychna diial'nist' Oleksandra Shul'hyna (1889–1960)." PhD diss., Pereiaslav-Khmel'nyts'kyi derzhavnyi pedahohichnyi universytet imeni Hryhoriia Skovorody, 2015.

Amacher, Korine, Frithjof Benjamin Schenk, Anthony J. Heywood, and Adele Lindenmeyr, eds. *Personal Trajectories in Russia's Great War and Revolution, 1914–22: Biographical Itineraries, Individual Experiences, Autobiographical Reflections.* Bloomington, IN: Slavica, 2021.

Anderson, Benedict. *Imagined Communities: Reflections on the Origin and Spread of Nationalism.* 1983. Rev. ed. London: Verso, 2006.

Andreyev, Catherine, and Ivan Savický. *Russia Abroad: Prague and the Russian Diaspora, 1918–1938.* New Haven, CT: Yale University Press, 2004.

Andriewsky, Olga. "The Politics of National Identity: The Ukrainian Question in Russia, 1904–1912." PhD diss., Harvard University, 1991.

———. "The Russian-Ukrainian Discourse and the Failure of the 'Little Russian Solution.'" In *Culture, Nation, and Identity: The Ukrainian-Russian Encounter, 1600–1945,* edited by Andreas Kappeler, Zenon E. Kohut, Frank E. Sysyn, and Mark von Hagen, 182–214. Toronto: Canadian Institute of Ukrainian Studies, 2003.

———. "The Making of the Generation of 1917: Towards a Collective Biography." *Journal of Ukrainian Studies* 29, no. 1–2 (2004): 19–37.

Ascher, Abraham. *The Revolution of 1905.* 2 vols. Stanford, CA: Stanford University Press, 1988–1992.

———. *P. A. Stolypin: The Search for Stability in Late Imperial Russia.* Stanford, CA: Stanford University Press, 2001.

Aust, Martin, and Frithjof Benjamin Schenk, eds. *Imperial Subjects: Autobiographische Praxis in den Vielvölkerreichen der Romanovs, Habsburger und Osmanen im 19. und frühen 20. Jahrhundert.* Cologne: Böhlau, 2015.

Baár, Monika. *Historians and Nationalism: East-Central Europe in the Nineteenth Century.* Oxford: Oxford University Press, 2010.

Babkov, D. I. "Politicheskaia publitsistika V. V. Shul'gina v period grazhdanskoi voiny i emigratsii." *Voprosy istorii,* no. 3 (2008): 92–106.

——. *Gosudarstvennye i natsional'nye problemy v mirovozzrenii V. V. Shul'gina v 1917–1939 godakh.* Moscow: ROSSPEN, 2012.

Baker, Mark R. *Peasants, Power, and Place: Revolution in the Villages of Kharkiv Province, 1914–1921.* Cambridge, MA: Harvard University Press, 2016.

Bankowski, Monika. "'Kleinrussischer Separatist' oder 'russischer Nihilist'? M. P. Drahomanov und die Anfänge der ukrainischen Emigration in der Schweiz." In *Asyl und Aufenthalt: Die Schweiz als Zuflucht und Wirkungsstätte von Slaven im 19. und 20. Jahrhundert,* edited by Monika Bankowski, Peter Brang, Carsten Goehrke, and Werner G. Zimmermann, 107–38. Basel: Helbing & Lichtenhahn, 1994.

Barkey, Karen, and Mark von Hagen, eds. *After Empire: Multiethnic Societies and Nation-Building; The Soviet Union and the Russian, Ottoman, and Habsburg Empires.* Boulder, CO: Westview, 1997.

Basenko, Ivan. "The 'German Intrigue' as an Element of the Anti-Ukrainian Campaign: A Case Study of Kyiv's Russian Language Press, 1914–18." *East/West: Journal of Ukrainian Studies* 5, no. 2 (2018): 149–73.

Baumann, Fabian. "The Debate on Ukrainian Identities in the Duma and the Russian Press, 1905–1914." MPhil thesis, University of Oxford, 2014.

——. "Dragged into the Whirlwind: The Shul'gin Family, Kievlianin, and Kiev's Russian Nationalist Movement in 1917." In *Personal Trajectories in Russia's Great War and Revolution, 1914–22,* edited by Korine Amacher, Frithjof Benjamin Schenk, Anthony J. Heywood, and Adele Lindenmeyr, 73–92. Bloomington, IN: Slavica, 2021.

——. "Einseitiger Einheitswunsch—Putins neueste Geschichtslektion." *Religion und Gesellschaft in Ost und West,* no. 9 (2021): 3–5.

——. "Nationality as Choice of Path: Iakov Shul'gin, Dmitrii Pikhno, and the Russian-Ukrainian Crossroads." *Kritika: Explorations in Russian and Eurasian History* 23, no. 4 (2022): 743–71.

——. "Vid spivpratsi Do konfrontatsiï: Mykhailo Drahomanov, rodyna Shul'ginykh i rozbrat u seredovyshchi kyïvs'koï intelihentsiï." *Spadshchyna: Literaturne dzhereloznavstvo, tekstolohiia* 16 (forthcoming).

Beauvois, Daniel. *The Noble, the Serf and the Revizor: The Polish Nobility between Tsarist Imperialism and the Ukrainian Masses (1831–1863).* Chur, Switzerland: Harwood Academic, 1991.

——. *La bataille de la terre en Ukraine 1863–1914: Les Polonais et les conflits socio-ethniques.* Lille: Presses universitaires, 1993.

Berger, Stefan, and Alexei Miller, eds. *Nationalizing Empires.* Budapest: Central European University Press, 2015.

Betlii, Olena. "Kiev—gorod problemnykh identichnostei." In *Goroda imperii v gody Velikoi voiny i revoliutsii: Sbornik statei,* edited by Alexei Miller and Dmitrii Chernyi, 272–317. Moscow: Nestor-Istoriia, 2017.

Bezzub, Iurii, Ninel' Klymenko, and Ol'ga Dudar. "Genderni ustanovky ta praktyky v rodyni B. Hrinchenka za ego-dokumentamy." *Ukraïns'kyi istorychnyi zhurnal*, no. 3 (2022): 119–33.

Bilenky, Serhiy. *Romantic Nationalism in Eastern Europe: Russian, Polish, and Ukrainian Political Imaginations.* Stanford, CA: Stanford University Press, 2012.

———. *Imperial Urbanism in the Borderlands: Kyiv 1800–1905.* Toronto: University of Toronto Press, 2018.

Bödeker, Hans Erich. "Biographie: Annäherungen an den gegenwärtigen Forschungs- und Diskussionsstand." In *Biographie schreiben*, edited by Hans Erich Bödeker, 9–63. Göttingen: Wallstein Verlag, 2003.

Boeck, Brian J. "What's in a Name? Semantic Separation and the Rise of the Ukrainian National Name." *Harvard Ukrainian Studies* 27, no. 1/4 (2004–2005): 33–65.

Bohachevsky-Chomiak, Martha. *Feminists despite Themselves: Women in Ukrainian Community Life, 1884–1939.* Edmonton: Canadian Institute of Ukrainian Studies, 1988.

Boiko, Olena. *Narysy zhyttia Kyieva. 1919 rik: Polityka i povsiakdennist'.* Kyiv: Instytut istoriï Ukraïny NAN Ukraïny, 2015.

Bojanowska, Edyta M. *Nikolai Gogol: Between Ukrainian and Russian Nationalism.* Cambridge, MA: Harvard University Press, 2007.

Bondarenko, D. Ia. "Vremennoe pravitel'stvo i problema avtonomii Ukrainy (iiul'-oktiabr' 1917 g.)." *Otechestvennaia istoriia*, no. 1 (2006): 54–64.

Bortnevski, Viktor. "White Intelligence and Counter-intelligence during the Russian Civil War." *Carl Beck Papers in Russian & East European Studies* 1108 (1995).

Bourdieu, Pierre. "L'illusion biographique." *Actes de la recherche en sciences sociales*, no. 62–63 (1986): 69–72.

———. "À propos de la famille comme catégorie réalisée." *Actes de la recherche en sciences sociales*, no. 100 (1993): 32–36.

Brown, Kate. *A Biography of No Place: From Ethnic Borderland to Soviet Heartland.* Cambridge, MA: Harvard University Press, 2004.

Brubaker, Rogers. *Nationalism Reframed: Nationhood and the National Question in the New Europe.* Cambridge: Cambridge University Press, 1996.

———. *Ethnicity without Groups.* Cambridge, MA: Harvard University Press, 2004.

———. *Grounds for Difference.* Cambridge, MA: Harvard University Press, 2015.

Brubaker, Rogers, Margit Feischmidt, Jon Fox, and Liana Grancea. *Nationalist Politics and Everyday Ethnicity in a Transylvanian Town.* Princeton, NJ: Princeton University Press, 2006.

Bruski, Jan Jacek. *Petlurowcy: Centrum Państwowe Ukraińskiej Republiki Ludowej na wychodźstwie (1919–1924).* Cracow: Arcana, 2000.

Buchen, Tim, and Malte Rolf, eds. *Eliten im Vielvölkerreich: Imperiale Biographien in Russland und Österreich-Ungarn (1850–1918).* Berlin: De Gruyter Oldenbourg, 2015.

Budnitskii, Oleg. *Russian Jews between the Reds and the Whites, 1917–1920.* Philadelphia: University of Pennsylvania Press, 2012.

Bushkovitch, Paul. "What Is Russia? Russian National Identity and the State, 1500–1917." In *Culture, Nation, and Identity: The Ukrainian-Russian Encounter, 1600–1945*, edited by Andreas Kappeler, Zenon E. Kohut, Frank E.

Sysyn, and Mark von Hagen, 144–61. Toronto: Canadian Institute of Ukrainian Studies, 2003.

Chatterjee, Partha. "The Nationalist Solution of the Women's Question." In *Recasting Women: Essays in Indian Colonial History*, edited by Kumkum Sangari and Sudesh Vaid, 233–53. New Brunswick, NJ: Rutgers University Press, 1990.

Chemakin, A. A. "Russkie natsionalisty i elektoral'naia bor'ba v Kieve v usloviiakh revoliutsii i grazhdanskoi voiny (1917–1919)." *Rossiiskaia istoriia*, no. 5 (2019): 132–58.

——. "Iuzhno-Russkii soiuz molodezhi: kievskie gimnazisty-monarkhisty v gody revoliutsii i grazhdanskoi voiny." *Voprosy istorii*, no. 12 (4) (2021): 15–30.

Chernev, Borislav. *Twilight of Empire: The Brest-Litovsk Conference and the Remaking of East-Central Europe, 1917–1918*. Toronto: University of Toronto Press, 2017.

Chlebowczyk, Józef. "Some Issues of National Assimilation and Linguistic-Ethnic Borderland (in the Area of Former Austro-Hungarian Monarchy)." *Acta Poloniae Historica* 108 (2013): 149–95.

Chopard, Thomas. "Identifier, légitimer, stigmatiser: Les matériaux de la délégation ukrainienne à la Conférence de la Paix de Paris (1918–1920)." *Matériaux pour l'histoire de notre temps* 113–114, no. 1–2 (2014): 180–85.

——. *Le martyre de Kiev: 1919. L'Ukraine en révolution entre terreur soviétique, nationalisme et antisémitisme*. Paris: Vendémiaire, 2015.

Clark, Christopher. *The Sleepwalkers: How Europe Went to War in 1914*. London: Allen Lane, 2012.

Cohen, Deborah. *Family Secrets: Shame and Privacy in Modern Britain*. New York: Oxford University Press, 2013.

Cohen, Gary B. *The Politics of Ethnic Survival: Germans in Prague, 1861–1914*. 2nd ed. West Lafayette, IN: Purdue University Press, 2006.

——. "Nationalist Politics and the Dynamics of State and Civil Society in the Habsburg Monarchy, 1867–1914." *Central European History* 40, no. 2 (2007): 241–78.

Coleman, Heather. "History, Faith, and Regional Identity in Nineteenth-Century Kyiv: Father Petro Lebedyntsev as Priest and Scholar." In *The Future of the Past: New Perspectives on Ukrainian History*, edited by Serhii Plokhy, 333–62. Cambridge, MA: Harvard University Press, 2016.

Dahlmann, Dittmar. "Krieg, Bürgerkrieg, Gewalt: Die Wahrnehmung des Ersten Weltkriegs und des Bürgerkriegs in der russischen Emigration und in der Sowjetunion in der Zwischenkriegszeit." In *Der verlorene Frieden: Politik und Kriegskultur nach 1918*, edited by Jost Dülffer and Gerd Krumeich, 91–100. Essen: Klartext-Verlag, 2002.

Danylenko, Andrii. "The 'Doubling of Hallelujah' for the 'Bastard Tongue': The Ukrainian Language Question in Russian Ukraine, 1905–1916." In *The Battle for Ukrainian: A Comparative Perspective*, edited by Michael S. Flier and Andrea Graziosi, 63–95. Cambridge, MA: Harvard Ukrainian Research Institute, 2017.

Davies, Norman. *Heart of Europe: The Past in Poland's Present*. New ed. Oxford: Oxford University Press, 2001.

Depkat, Volker. "Autobiographie und die soziale Konstruktion von Wirklich-keit." *Geschichte und Gesellschaft* 29, no. 3 (2003): 441–76.

Dolbilov, M. D. *Russkii krai, chuzhaia vera: Etnokonfessional'naia politika imperii v Litve i Belorussii pri Aleksandre II.* Moscow: Novoe literaturnoe obozrenie, 2010.

Dolbilov, M. D., and A. I. Miller, eds. *Zapadnye okrainy Rossiiskoi imperii.* Moscow: Novoe literaturnoe obozrenie, 2006.

Dornik, Wolfram, Georgiy Kasianov, Hannes Leidinger, and Peter Lieb, eds. *Die Ukraine zwischen Selbstbestimmung und Fremdherrschaft, 1917–1922.* Graz: Leykam, 2011.

Edelman, Robert. *Gentry Politics on the Eve of the Russian Revolution: The Nationalist Party, 1907–1917.* New Brunswick, NJ: Rutgers University Press, 1980.

Eklof, Ben, John Bushnell, and Larissa Zakharova, eds. *Russia's Great Reforms, 1855–1881.* Bloomington: Indiana University Press, 1994.

Eklof, Ben, and Tatiana Saburova. *A Generation of Revolutionaries: Nikolai Charushin and Russian Populism from the Great Reforms to Perestroika.* Bloomington: Indiana University Press, 2017.

Ely, Christopher. *Underground Petersburg: Radical Populism, Urban Space, and the Tactics of Subversion in Reform-Era Russia.* DeKalb: Northern Illinois University Press, 2016.

Engel, Barbara Alpern. *Mothers and Daughters: Women of the Intelligentsia in Nineteenth-Century Russia.* Cambridge: Cambridge University Press, 1983.

——. *Women, Gender and Political Choice in the Revolutionary Movement of the 1870s.* Jerusalem: Marjorie Mayrock Center for Soviet and East European Research, 1988.

——. *Breaking the Ties That Bound: The Politics of Marital Strife in Late Imperial Russia.* Ithaca, NY: Cornell University Press, 2011.

Engelstein, Laura. *The Keys to Happiness: Sex and the Search for Modernity in Fin-de-Siècle Russia.* Ithaca, NY: Cornell University Press, 1992.

Erlacher, Trevor. *Ukrainian Nationalism in the Age of Extremes: An Intellectual Biography of Dmytro Dontsov.* Cambridge, MA: Harvard Ukrainian Research Institute, 2021.

Fedevych, Klimentii K., and Klimentii I. Fedevych. *Za viru, tsaria i kobzaria: Malorosiis'ki monarkhisty i ukraïns'kyi natsional'nyi rukh (1905–1917 roky).* Kyiv: Krytyka, 2017.

Fedyshyn, Oleh S. *Germany's Drive to the East and the Ukrainian Revolution, 1917–1918.* New Brunswick, NJ: Rutgers University Press, 1971.

Fieschi, Pascal. "L'intervention française à Odessa (décembre 1918–mars 1919) vue à travers l'action du 'Consul de France,' Emile Henno." *Cahiers slaves* 14 (2016): 161–72.

Figes, Orlando. *A People's Tragedy: The Russian Revolution 1891–1924.* London: Jonathan Cape, 1996.

Fleishman, Lazar'. *V tiskakh provokatsii: Operatsiia "Trest" i russkaia zarubezhnaia pechat'.* Moscow: Novoe literaturnoe obozrenie, 2003.

Flier, Michael S., and Andrea Graziosi, eds. *The Battle for Ukrainian: A Comparative Perspective.* Cambridge, MA: Harvard Ukrainian Research Institute, 2017.

Fowler, Mayhill C. "'A Theatrical Mecca': The Stages of Kyiv in 1907." In *Modernism in Kyiv: Jubilant Experimentation*, edited by Irena R. Makaryk, 26–50. Toronto: University of Toronto Press, 2010.

Garboś, Marcel Radosław. "Revolution and the Defence of Civilization: Polish Visions of Nationhood, Property and Territory in Right-Bank Ukraine (1917–22)." *Slavonic and East European Review* 96, no. 3 (2018): 469–506.

Gellner, Ernest. *Nations and Nationalism*. 1983. Reprint, Malden, MA: Blackwell, 2006.

Gilbert, George. *The Radical Right in Late Imperial Russia: Dreams of a True Fatherland?* London: Routledge, 2016.

Gilley, Christopher. *The "Change of Signposts" in the Ukrainian Emigration: A Contribution to the History of Sovietophilism in the 1920s*. Stuttgart: ibidem-Verlag, 2009.

——. "Beyond Petliura: The Ukrainian National Movement and the 1919 Pogroms." *East European Jewish Affairs* 47, no. 1 (2017): 45–61.

——. "Untangling the Ukrainian Revolution." *Studies in Ethnicity and Nationalism* 17, no. 3 (2017): 326–38.

Glassheim, Eagle. *Noble Nationalists: The Transformation of the Bohemian Aristocracy*. Cambridge, MA: Harvard University Press, 2005.

Glushkov, A. V. "Gazeta 'Kievlianin' i progressivnye natsionalisty, 1915–1917 gody." *Vestnik permskogo universiteta* 18, no. 1 (2012): 271–77.

Golczewski, Frank. *Deutsche und Ukrainer 1914–1939*. Paderborn: Schöningh, 2010.

Gousseff, Catherine. *L'exil russe: La fabrique du réfugié apatride (1920–1939)*. Paris: CNRS Ed., 2008.

Grimsted Kennedy, Patricia. "Archeography in the Service of Imperial Policy: The Foundation of the Kiev Archeographic Commission and the Kiev Central Archive of Early Record Books." *Harvard Ukrainian Studies* 17, no. 1–2 (1993): 27–44.

——. "The Postwar Fate of the Petliura Library and the Records of the Ukrainian National Republic." *Harvard Ukrainian Studies* 21, no. 3–4 (1997): 393–461.

Guthier, Steven L. "The Popular Base of Ukrainian Nationalism in 1917." *Slavic Review* 38, no. 1 (1979): 30–47.

Haimson, Leopold H. "The Problem of Social Identities in Early Twentieth Century Russia." *Slavic Review* 47, no. 1 (1988): 1–20.

Hamm, Michael F. "Liberal Politics in Wartime Russia: An Analysis of the Progressive Bloc." *Slavic Review* 33, no. 3 (1977): 453–68.

——. *Kiev: A Portrait, 1800–1917*. Princeton, NJ: Princeton University Press, 1993.

Hanebrink, Paul A. *A Specter Haunting Europe: The Myth of Judeo-Bolshevism*. Cambridge, MA: Belknap Press of Harvard University Press, 2018.

Harders, Levke. "Legitimizing Biography: Critical Approaches to Biographical Research." *Bulletin of the German Historical Institute*, no. 55 (2014): 49–56.

Hasegawa, Tsuyoshi. *The February Revolution, Petrograd, 1917: The End of the Tsarist Regime and the Birth of Dual Power*. Rev. ed. Leiden: Brill, 2017.

Hausmann, Guido. "Das Territorium der Ukraine: Stepan Rudnyc'kyjs Beitrag zur Geschichte räumlich-territorialen Denkens über die Ukraine." In *Die Ukraine: Prozesse der Nationsbildung*, edited by Andreas Kappeler, 145–58. Cologne: Böhlau, 2011.

Hedin, M. S. "Hromads'ka, pedahohichna ta naukova diial'nist' istoryka Ia. M. Shul'hina." PhD diss., Kyïvs'kyi natsional'nyi universytet im. Tarasa Shevchenka, 2008.

Hellbeck, Jochen, and Klaus Heller, eds. *Autobiographical Practices in Russia— Autobiographische Praktiken in Russland*. Göttingen: V&R unipress, 2004.

Hillis, Faith. "Between Empire and Nation: Urban Politics, Community, and Violence in Kiev, 1863–1907." PhD diss., Yale University, 2009.

——. "Ukrainophile Activism and Imperial Governance in Russia's Southwestern Borderlands." *Kritika: Explorations in Russian and Eurasian History* 13, no. 2 (2012): 301–26.

——. *Children of Rus': Right-Bank Ukraine and the Invention of a Russian Nation*. Ithaca, NY: Cornell University Press, 2013.

——. "Making and Breaking the Russian Empire: The Case of Kiev's Shul'gin Family." In *Eliten im Vielvölkerreich: Imperiale Biographien in Russland und Österreich-Ungarn (1850–1918)*, edited by Tim Buchen and Malte Rolf, 179–98. Berlin: De Gruyter Oldenbourg, 2015.

Himka, John-Paul. "Young Radicals and Independent Statehood: The Idea of a Ukrainian Nation-State, 1890–1895." *Slavic Review* 41, no. 2 (1982): 219–35.

——. *Galician Villagers and the Ukrainian National Movement in the Nineteenth Century*. Basingstoke, UK: Macmillan, 1988.

——. "The National and the Social in the Ukrainian Revolution: The Historiographical Agenda." *Archiv für Sozialgeschichte* 34 (1994): 95–110.

Hobsbawm, Eric J. *Nations and Nationalism since 1780: Programme, Myth, Reality*. Cambridge: Cambridge University Press, 1990.

Holquist, Peter. *Making War, Forging Revolution: Russia's Continuum of Crisis, 1914– 1921*. Cambridge, MA: Harvard University Press, 2002.

Horodnia, N. D. "Oleksandr Shul'hin (1889–1960) iak predstavnyk novoï heneratsiï ukraïns'koï natsional'noï elity pershoï polovyny XX stolittia." *Visnyk Kyïvs'koho natsional'noho universytetu imeni Tarasa Shevchenka*, no. 80–81 (2005): 10–13.

Hosking, Geoffrey A. *The Russian Constitutional Experiment: Government and Duma, 1907–1914*. Cambridge: Cambridge University Press, 1973.

——. *Russia: People and Empire, 1552–1917*. Cambridge, MA: Harvard University Press, 1997.

Hroch, Miroslav. *Social Preconditions of National Revival in Europe: A Comparative Analysis of the Social Composition of Patriotic Groups among the Smaller European Nations*. Cambridge: Cambridge University Press, 1985.

——. *Das Europa der Nationen: Die moderne Nationsbildung im europäischen Vergleich*. Göttingen: Vandenhoeck & Ruprecht, 2005.

Hrytsak, Iaroslav. "Do henezy ideï politychnoï samostiinosti Ukraïny." *Ukraïna: Kul'turna spadshchyna, natsional'na svidomist', derzhavnist'* 1 (1992): 119–43.

——. *Narys istoriï Ukraïny: Formuvannia modernoï ukraïns'koï natsiï XIX–XX stolit-tia.* Kyiv: Heneza, 1996.

——. *Ivan Franko and His Community.* Edmonton: Canadian Institute of Ukrainian Studies, 2018.

Hunczak, Taras H., ed. *The Ukraine, 1917–1921: A Study in Revolution.* Cambridge, MA: Harvard Ukrainian Research Institute, 1977.

Hyrych, Ihor. "Ukraïns'ka mova v zhytti diiachiv natsional'no-vyzvol'noho rukhu Naddniprianshchyny XIX–poch. XX st." *Kyïvs'ka starovyna,* no. 2 (2012): 51–67.

——. *Ukraïns'kyi Kyïv.* Kyiv: Penmen, 2017.

Ilchuk, Yuliya. *Nikolai Gogol: Performing Hybrid Identity.* Toronto: University of Toronto Press, 2021.

Ishchuk-Pazuniak, Natalia. "Iakiv Shul'hyn." In *125 rokiv Kyïvs'koï ukraïns'koï akademichnoï tradytsiï 1861–1986,* edited by Marko D. Antonovych, 195–218. New York, 1993.

Johnston, Robert H. *New Mecca, New Babylon: Paris and the Russian Exiles, 1920–1945.* Montreal: McGill-Queen's University Press, 1988.

Judson, Pieter M. *Guardians of the Nation: Activists on the Language Frontiers of Imperial Austria.* Cambridge, MA: Harvard University Press, 2006.

——. *The Habsburg Empire: A New History.* Cambridge, MA: Belknap Press of Harvard University Press, 2016.

Jureit, Ulrike. "Generation, Generationalität, Generationenforschung." *Docupedia Zeitgeschichte,* 2010. http://docupedia.de/zg/jureit_generation_v1_de_2010.

Kal'chenko, T. V. *Kievskii klub russkikh natsionalistov: Istoricheskaia entsiklopediia.* Kiev: Kievskie vedomosti, 2008.

Kappeler, Andreas. *Russland als Vielvölkerreich: Entstehung, Geschichte, Zerfall.* Munich: C. H. Beck, 1992.

——. *Der schwierige Weg zur Nation: Beiträge zur neueren Geschichte der Ukraine.* Cologne: Böhlau, 2003.

——. "Mazepintsy, Malorossy, Khokhly: Ukrainians in the Ethnic Hierarchy of the Russian Empire." In *Culture, Nation, and Identity: The Ukrainian-Russian Encounter, 1600–1945,* edited by Andreas Kappeler, Zenon E. Kohut, Frank E. Sysyn, and Mark von Hagen, 162–81. Toronto: Canadian Institute of Ukrainian Studies, 2003.

——. "Ukrainische und russische Nation: Ein asymmetrisches Verhältnis." In *Die Ukraine: Prozesse der Nationsbildung,* edited by Andreas Kappeler, 191–201. Cologne: Böhlau, 2011.

——. *Russland und die Ukraine: Verflochtene Biographien und Geschichten.* Vienna: Böhlau, 2012.

Kas'ianov, G. V., and A. I. Miller. *Rossiia–Ukraina: Kak pishetsia istoriia.* Moscow: Rossiiskii gosudarstvennyi gumanitarnyi universitet, 2011.

Kasianov, Georgiy, and Philipp Ther, eds. *A Laboratory of Transnational History: Ukraine and Recent Ukrainian Historiography.* Budapest: Central European University Press, 2009.

Kas'ianov, Heorhii. *Ukraïns'ka intelihentsiia na rubezhi XIX–XX stolit': Sotsial'no-politychnyi portret.* Kyiv: Lybid', 1993.

Kelly, Catriona. *Children's World: Growing Up in Russia, 1890–1991*. New Haven, CT: Yale University Press, 2007.

Kenez, Peter. *Civil War in South Russia, 1918: The First Year of the Volunteer Army*. Berkeley: University of California Press, 1971.

———. *Civil War in South Russia, 1919–1920: The Defeat of the Whites*. Berkeley: University of California Press, 1977.

Khiterer, Victoria. "Vasilii Shul'gin and the Jewish Question: An Assessment of Shul'gin's Anti-Semitism." *On the Jewish Street* 1, no. 2 (2011): 137-63.

———. *Jewish City or Inferno of Russian Israel? A History of the Jews in Kiev before February 1917*. Boston: Academic Studies, 2016.

Khmil', I. V. *Na shliakhu vidrodzhennia ukraïns'koï derzhavnosti (Ukraïns'kyi natsional'nyi konhres-z'ïzd 6–8 kvitnia 1917 r.)*. Kyiv: Instytut istoriï Ukraïny NAN, 1994.

Kieniewicz, Stefan. *Powstanie styczniowe*. Warsaw: Państwowe Wydawnyctwo Naukowe, 1972.

King, Jeremy. "The Nationalization of East Central Europe: Ethnicism, Ethnicity, and Beyond." In *Staging the Past: The Politics of Commemoration in Habsburg Central Europe, 1848 to the Present*, edited by Maria Bucur and Nancy M. Wingfield, 112-52. West Lafayette, IN: Purdue University Press, 2001.

———. *Budweisers into Czechs and Germans: A Local History of Bohemian Politics, 1848–1948*. Princeton, NJ: Princeton University Press, 2002.

Klid, Bohdan. "Volodymyr Antonovych: Ukrainian Populist Historiography and the Cultural Politics of Nation Building." In *Historiography of Imperial Russia: The Profession and Writing of History in a Multinational State*, edited by Thomas Sanders, 373-93. Armonk, NY: M. E. Sharpe, 1999.

Klier, John D. "Kievlianin and the Jews: A Decade of Disillusionment, 1864–1873." *Harvard Ukrainian Studies* 5, no. 1 (1981): 81-101.

———. *Russians, Jews, and the Pogroms of 1881–1882*. Cambridge: Cambridge University Press, 2011.

Kohut, Zenon E. *Russian Centralism and Ukrainian Autonomy: Imperial Absorption of the Hetmanate, 1760s–1830s*. Cambridge, MA: Harvard Ukrainian Research Institute, 1988.

Kolerov, M. A. "Russkaia Mysl' (1921-1927). Rospis' soderzhania." *Issledovaniia po istorii russkoi mysli* 1 (1997): 287-317.

Korros, Alexandra. *A Reluctant Parliament: Stolypin, Nationalism, and the Politics of the Russian Imperial State Council, 1906–1911*. Lanham, MD: Rowman & Littlefield, 2002.

Kosyk, Wolodymyr. *La politique de la France à l'égard de l'Ukraine, mars 1917—février 1918*. Paris: Publications de la Sorbonne, 1981.

Kotenko, A. L. "Etnohrafichno-statystychna ekspeditsiia P. Chubyns'koho v pivdenno-zakhidnyi krai." *Ukraïns'kyi istorychnyi zhurnal*, no. 3 (2014): 128-51.

Kotenko, A. L., O. V. Martyniuk, and A. I. Miller. "Maloross." In *"Poniatiia o Rossii": K istoricheskoi semantike imperskogo perioda*, edited by A. I. Miller, D. A. Sdvizhkov, and I. Shirle, 2:392-443. Moscow: Novoe literaturnoe obozrenie, 2012.

Kotsiubinskii, D. A. *Russkii natsionalizm v nachale XX stoletiia: Rozhdenie i gibel' ideologii Vserossiiskogo natsional'nogo soiuza*. Moscow: ROSSPEN, 2001.

Krasiukov, R. G. "Kievliane Mogilevskie—vnebrachnye deti Dmitriia Ivanovicha Pikhno (1853–1913)." *Izvestiia russkogo genealogicheskogo obshchestva* 18 (2006): 46–50.

Křen, Jan. *Die Konfliktgemeinschaft: Tschechen und Deutsche 1780–1918*. Munich: R. Oldenbourg Verlag, 1996.

Kucher, Katharina, and Alexa von Winning. "Privates Leben und öffentliche Interessen: Adlige Familie und Kindheit in Russlands langem 19. Jahrhundert." *Jahrbücher für Geschichte Osteuropas* 63, no. 2 (2015): 233–55.

Kuzmany, Börries. "'Perekhresna istoriia' zakonu pro natsional'no-personal'nu avtonomiiu UNR: Peretikannia ideï vid avstro-marksystiv cherez ievreis'kyi Bund do revoliutsiinoï Ukraïny." In *Revoliutsiia, derzhavnist', natsiia: Ukraïna na shliakhu samostverdzhennia (1917–1921 rr.)*, edited by V. F. Verstiuk, 261–67. Kyiv: Instytut istoriï Ukraïny NAN Ukraïny, 2017.

Leontovych, Olena. *Shul'hyny: Bat'ky, dity, onuky*. Ternopil': Navchal'na knyha—Bohdan, 2012.

Lepore, Jill. "Historians Who Love Too Much: Reflections on Microhistory and Biography." *Journal of American History* 88, no. 1 (2001): 129–44.

Lesyk, L. V. "Do pytannia evoliutsiï mis'koho samovriaduvannia na prykladi mista Nizhyna." *Literatura ta kul'tura Polissia: Zbirnyk naukovykh prats'* 70 (2012): 56–62.

Levinets', R. P. "Zhyttievyi shliakh ta naukovo-hromads'ka diial'nist' V. Ia. Shul'hina." PhD diss., Kyïvs'kyi natsional'nyi universytet im. Tarasa Shevchenka, 2004.

Liber, George. "Ukrainian Nationalism and the 1918 Law on National-Personal Autonomy." *Nationalities Papers* 15, no. 1 (1987): 22–42.

Lieven, Dominic. *Russia's Rulers under the Old Regime*. New Haven, CT: Yale University Press, 1989.

——. *Empire: The Russian Empire and Its Rivals*. New Haven, CT: Yale University Press, 2001.

——. "Empires and Their Core Territories on the Eve of 1914: A Comment." In *Nationalizing Empires*, edited by Stefan Berger and Alexei Miller, 647–60. Budapest: Central European University Press, 2015.

——. *Towards the Flame: Empire, War and the End of Tsarist Russia*. London: Allen Lane, 2015.

Lincoln, W. Bruce. *The Great Reforms: Autocracy, Bureaucracy, and the Politics of Change in Imperial Russia*. DeKalb: Northern Illinois University Press, 1990.

Liubchenko, V. B. "Kyïvs'ki Shul'hiny: Natsional'no rozdilena rodyna v istoriï Ukraïny." *Ukraïns'ka biohrafistyka: Zbirnyk naukovych prats'* 2 (1999): 153–62.

Lohr, Eric. *Nationalizing the Russian Empire: The Campaign against Enemy Aliens during World War I*. Cambridge, MA: Harvard University Press, 2003.

——. "The Russian Press and the 'Internal Peace' at the Beginning of World War I." In *A Call to Arms: Propaganda, Public Opinion, and Newspapers in the*

Great War, edited by Troy R. E. Paddock, 91–113. Westport, CT: Praeger, 2004.

——. "War Nationalism." In *The Empire and Nationalism at War*, edited by Eric Lohr, Vera Tolz, Alexander Semyonov, and Mark von Hagen, 91–107. Bloomington, IN: Slavica, 2014.

Loukianov, Mikhail. "Conservatives and 'Renewed Russia,' 1907–1914." *Slavic Review* 61, no. 4 (2002): 762–86.

——. "The First World War and the Polarization of the Russian Right, July 1914–February 1917." *Slavic Review* 75, no. 4 (2016): 872–95.

Löwe, Heinz-Dietrich. *Antisemitismus und reaktionäre Utopie: Russischer Konservatismus im Kampf gegen den Wandel von Staat und Gesellschaft, 1890–1917.* Hamburg: Hoffmann & Campe, 1978.

Luk'ianov, M. N. "'Rossiia—dlia russkikh' ili 'Rossiia—dlia russkikh poddannykh'? Konservatory i natsional'nyi vopros nakanune pervoi mirovoi voiny." *Otechestvennaia istoriia*, no. 2 (2006): 36–46.

MacMillan, Margaret. *Peacemakers: The Paris Conference of 1919 and Its Attempt to End War.* London: John Murray, 2001.

Magocsi, Paul R. *The Roots of Ukrainian Nationalism: Galicia as Ukraine's Piedmont.* Toronto: University of Toronto Press, 2002.

——. *A History of Ukraine: The Land and Its Peoples.* 2nd ed. Toronto: University of Toronto Press, 2010.

Makarov, V. G., A. V. Repnikov, and V. S. Khristoforov. "Vasilii Vital'evich Shul'gin: Shtrikhi k portretu." In *Tiuremnaia odisseia Vasiliia Shul'gina: Materialy sledstvennogo dela i dela zakliuchennogo*, edited by V. G. Makarov, A. V. Repnikov, and V. S. Khristoforov, 5–132. Moscow: Russkii put', 2010.

Malečková, Jitka. "The Importance of Being National." In *Czech Feminisms: Perspectives on Gender in East Central Europe*, edited by Iveta Jusová and Jiřina Šiklová, 46–59. Bloomington: Indiana University Press, 2016.

Manchester, Laurie. *Holy Fathers, Secular Sons: Clergy, Intelligentsia, and the Modern Self in Revolutionary Russia.* DeKalb: Northern Illinois University Press, 2008.

Mannheim, Karl. "Das Problem der Generationen," 1928. In *Wissenssoziologie*, 509–65. Berlin: Luchterhand, 1970.

Manning, Roberta T. *The Crisis of the Old Order in Russia: Gentry and Government.* Princeton, NJ: Princeton University Press, 1982.

Martyniuk, Ol'ha. "Rosiis'kyi natsionalizm iak sotsial'no-politychnyi fenomen u vybornomu protsesi pravoberezhnoï Ukraïny (1906–1912 rr.)." PhD diss., Kyïvs'kyi politekhnichnyi instytut im. Ihoria Sikors'koho, 2016.

Mashkevich, Stefan. *Dva dnia iz istorii Kieva: 30–31 avgusta 1919.* Kyiv: Varto, 2010.

——. *Kiev 1917–1920. Vol 1: Proshchanie s imperiei (mart 1917–ianvar' 1918).* Kharkiv: Folio, 2019.

Matich, Ol'ga. *Zapiski russkoi amerikanki: Semeinye khroniki i sluchainye vstrechi.* Moscow: Novoe literaturnoe obozrenie, 2017.

Maxwell, Alexander. *Choosing Slovakia: Slavic Hungary, the Czechoslovak Language, and Accidental Nationalism.* London: Tauris Academic Studies, 2009.

——. "Nationalism as Classification: Suggestions for Reformulating Nationalism Research." *Nationalities Papers* 46, no. 4 (2017): 539–55.

McClintock, Anne. "Family Feuds: Gender, Nationalism and the Family." *Feminist Review*, no. 44 (1993): 61–80.

McReynolds, Louise. *The News under Russia's Old Regime: The Development of a Mass-Circulation Press*. Princeton, NJ: Princeton University Press, 1991.

Medvedev, V. G. "Agrarnoe zakonodatel'stvo generala A. I. Denikina." *Gosudarstvo i pravo*, no. 8 (2015): 86–94.

Meir, Natan M. *Kiev, Jewish Metropolis: A History, 1859–1914*. Bloomington: Indiana University Press, 2010.

Melentyeva, Mariya. "Liberals and the Ukrainian Question in Imperial Russia, 1905-1917." *Revolutionary Russia* 33, no. 2 (2020): 151–71.

Miiakovskii, V. V. "'Kievskaia Gromada' (Iz istorii ukrainskogo obshchestvennogo dvizheniia 60-kh g.g.)." *Letopis' revoliutsii*, no. 4 (1924): 127–50.

Miller, Alexei. *The Ukrainian Question: The Russian Empire and Nationalism in the Nineteenth Century*. Budapest: Central European University Press, 2003.

——. "Ukrainophilia." *Russian Studies in History* 44, no. 2 (2005): 30–43.

——. *The Romanov Empire and Nationalism: Essays in the Methodology of Historical Research*. Budapest: Central European University Press, 2008.

——. "The Role of the First World War in the Competition between Ukrainian and All-Russian Nationalism." In *The Empire and Nationalism at War*, edited by Eric Lohr, Vera Tolz, Alexander Semyonov, and Mark von Hagen, 73–89. Bloomington, IN: Slavica, 2014.

——. "The Collapse of the Romanov Empire." In *The Oxford Handbook of the Ends of Empire*, edited by Thomas Martin and Andrew S. Thompson, 179–94. Oxford: Oxford University Press, 2018.

Miller, Alexei, and Mikhail Dolbilov. "'The Damned Polish Question': The Romanov Empire and the Polish Uprisings of 1830–1831 and 1863–1864." In *Comparing Empires: Encounters and Transfers in the Long Nineteenth Century*, edited by Jörn Leonhard and Ulrike von Hirschhausen, 425–52. Göttingen: Vandenhoeck & Ruprecht, 2011.

Milow, Caroline. *Die ukrainische Frage 1917–1923 im Spannungsfeld der europäischen Diplomatie*. Wiesbaden: Harrassowitz, 2002.

Mintz, Matityahu. "The Secretariat of Internationality Affairs (Sekretariiat Mizhnatsional'nykh Sprav) of the Ukrainian General Secretariat (1917–1918)." *Harvard Ukrainian Studies* 6, no. 1 (1982): 25–42.

Mogilner, Marina. *Homo Imperii: A History of Physical Anthropology in Russia*. Lincoln: University of Nebraska Press, 2013.

Morrissey, Susan K. *Heralds of Revolution: Russian Students and the Mythologies of Radicalism*. New York: Oxford University Press, 1998.

Moser, Michael. "Osnova and the Origins of the Valuev Directive." *East/West: Journal of Ukrainian Studies* 4, no. 2 (2017): 39–95.

——. "Geschichte und Gegenwart des Russischen in der Ukraine: Ein Überblick." *Die Welt der Slaven* 67, no. 2 (2022): 393–423.

Motyl, Alexander J. *The Turn to the Right: The Ideological Origins and Development of Ukrainian Nationalism, 1919–1929*. Boulder, CO: East European Monographs, 1980. Distributed by Columbia University Press.

Narizhnyi, Symon. *Ukraïns'ka emigratsiia: Kul'turna pratsia ukraïns'koï emigratsii mizh dvoma svitovymy viinamy*. Prague: Knihtisk, 1942.

Neumann, Matthias. "Mobilizing Children: Youth and the Patriotic War Culture in Kiev during World War I." In *Russia's Home Front in War and Revolution, 1914–22. Book 2: The Experience of War and Revolution*, edited by Sarah Badcock, Adele Lindenmeyr, Christopher Read, and Aaron B. Retish, 273–300. Bloomington, IN: Slavica, 2016.

Onishchenko, O. V. "Zhinky v Ukraïns'kii Tsentral'nii Radi." *Literatura ta kul'tura Polissia: Zbirnyk naukovykh prats'* 85 (2016): 81–90.

Paikova, Ie. V. "Volodymyr Naumenko (1852–1919)." *Ukraïns'kyi istorychnyi zhurnal*, no. 6 (1998): 90–102.

Paliienko, Maryna. *"Kievskaia starina" u hromads'komu ta naukovomu zhytti Ukraïny (kinets' XIX–pochatok XX st.)*. 3 vols. Kyiv: Tempora, 2005.

Peltonen, Matti. "Clues, Margins, and Monads: The Micro-Macro Link in Historical Research." *History and Theory* 40, no. 3 (2001): 347–59.

Petrovsky-Shtern, Yohanan. *The Anti-imperial Choice: The Making of the Ukrainian Jew*. New Haven, CT: Yale University Press, 2009.

Pickering Antonova, Katherine. *An Ordinary Marriage: The World of a Gentry Family in Provincial Russia*. New York: Oxford University Press, 2013.

Planert, Ute. "Vater Staat und Mutter Germania: Zur Politisierung des weiblichen Geschlechts im 19. und 20. Jahrhundert." In *Nation, Politik und Geschlecht: Frauenbewegungen und Nationalismus in der Moderne*, edited by Ute Planert, 15–65. Frankfurt am Main: Campus, 2000.

Plokhy, Serhii. *Unmaking Imperial Russia: Mykhailo Hrushevsky and the Writing of Ukrainian History*. Toronto: University of Toronto Press, 2005.

———. *The Cossack Myth: History and Nationhood in the Age of Empires*. Cambridge: Cambridge University Press, 2012.

Polovynchak, Iuliia. *Hazeta "Kievlianin" i ukraïnstvo: Dosvid natsional'noï samoidentyfikatsiï*. Kyiv: Natsional'na biblioteka Ukraïny im. V. I. Vernads'koho, 2008.

Pravilova, Ekaterina. *A Public Empire: Property and the Quest for the Common Good in Imperial Russia*. Princeton, NJ: Princeton University Press, 2014.

Procyk, Anna. *Russian Nationalism and Ukraine: The Nationality Policy of the Volunteer Army during the Civil War*. Toronto: Canadian Institute of Ukrainian Studies, 1995.

Prymak, Thomas M. *Mykola Kostomarov: A Biography*. Toronto: University of Toronto Press, 1996.

Puchenkov, A. S. *Ukraina i Krym v 1918–nachale 1919 goda: Ocherki politicheskoi istorii*. Moscow: Nestor-Istoriia, 2013.

———. *Natsional'naia politika generala Denikina (vesna 1918–vesna 1920 g.)*. 2nd ed. Moscow: Nauchno-politicheskaia kniga, 2016.

Raeff, Marc. *Russia Abroad: A Cultural History of the Russian Emigration, 1919–1939*. Oxford: Oxford University Press, 1990.

Randolph, John. "'That Historical Family': The Bakunin Archive and the Intimate Theater of History in Imperial Russia, 1780–1925." *Russian Review* 63, no. 4 (2004): 574–93.

———. *The House in the Garden: The Bakunin Family and the Romance of Russian Idealism*. Ithaca, NY: Cornell University Press, 2007.

Rawson, Don C. *Russian Rightists and the Revolution of 1905*. Cambridge: Cambridge University Press, 1995.

Remy, Johannes. "National Aspect of Student Movements in St. Vladimir's University of Kiev 1855–1863." *Skhid-Zakhid: Istoryko-Kul'turolohichnyi Zbirnyk* 7 (2005): 248–73.

———. *Brothers or Enemies: The Ukrainian National Movement and Russia, from the 1840s to the 1870s*. Toronto: University of Toronto Press, 2016.

Renner, Andreas. *Russischer Nationalismus und Öffentlichkeit im Zarenreich 1855–1875*. Cologne: Böhlau, 2000.

Repnikov, A. V. "Vasilii Vital'evich Shul'gin." *Voprosy istorii*, no. 5 (2010): 25–40.

Reshetar, John. *The Ukrainian Revolution, 1917–1920: A Study in Nationalism*. Princeton, NJ: Princeton University Press, 1952.

Reynolds, K. D. *Aristocratic Women and Political Society in Victorian Britain*. Oxford: Clarendon, 1998.

Riabinin-Skliarevs'kyi, Oleksandr. "Z revoliutsiinoho ukraïns'koho rukhu 1870-kh rokiv: Odes'ka hromada 1870-kh rokiv." *Ukraïna. Naukovyi dvokhmisiachnyk ukraïnoznavstva* 19, no. 5 (1926): 117–37.

———. "Kyïvs'ka Hromada 1870-kh r.r." *Ukraina. Naukovyi dvokhmisiachnyk ukraïnoznavstva* 21, no. 1–2 (1927): 144–62.

———. "Z revoliutsiinoho ukraïns'koho rukhu 1870-kh rr. v dobu tymchasovykh heneral-hubernatoriv." *Za sto lit*, no. 1 (1927): 154–65.

Rodkiewicz, Witold. *Russian Nationality Policy in the Western Provinces of the Empire (1863–1905)*. Lublin: Scientific Society of Lublin, 1998.

Rogger, Hans. *Jewish Policies and Right-Wing Politics in Imperial Russia*. Berkeley: University of California Press, 1986.

Rohde, Martin. *Nationale Wissenschaft zwischen zwei Imperien: Die Ševčenko-Gesellschaft der Wissenschaften, 1892–1918*. Göttingen: V&R unipress, 2022.

Rudnytsky, Ivan L. *Essays in Modern Ukrainian History*. Edmonton: Canadian Institute of Ukrainian Studies, 1987.

Ruthchild, Rochelle Goldberg. *Equality and Revolution: Women's Rights in the Russian Empire, 1905–1917*. Pittsburgh: University of Pittsburgh Press, 2010.

Rybas, S. Iu. *Vasilii Shul'gin: Sud'ba russkogo natsionalista*. Moscow: Molodaia gvardiia, 2014.

Safronova, Iu. A. "Vovlechenie v politicheskoe: Revoliutsionnoe narodnichestvo 1870-kh godov kak soobshchestvo chitatelei." *Vestnik permskogo universiteta* 41, no. 2 (2018): 65–74.

Sanborn, Joshua A. *Imperial Apocalypse: The Great War and the Destruction of the Russian Empire*. Oxford: Oxford University Press, 2014.

San'kova, S. M. *Russkaia partiia v Rossii: Obrazovanie i deiatel'nost' Vserossiiskogo natsional'nogo soiuza (1908–1917)*. Orel: S. V. Zenina, 2006.

Saunders, David. *The Ukrainian Impact on Russian Culture 1750–1850*. Edmonton: Canadian Institute of Ukrainian Studies, 1985.

———. "Russia's Ukrainian Policy (1847–1905): A Demographic Approach." *European History Quarterly* 25, no. 2 (1995): 181–208.

Savchenko, Fedir. *Zaborona ukraïnstva 1876 r.* 1928. Reprint, Munich: Wilhelm Fink Verlag, 1970.

Schenk, Frithjof Benjamin. *Russlands Fahrt in die Moderne: Mobilität und sozialer Raum im Eisenbahnzeitalter.* Stuttgart: F. Steiner, 2014.

Schlögel, Karl, ed. *Der grosse Exodus: Die russische Emigration und ihre Zentren 1917 bis 1941.* Munich: C. H. Beck, 1994.

Schmid, Ulrich. *Ichentwürfe: Russische Autobiographien zwischen Avvakum und Gercen.* Zurich: Pano Verlag, 2000.

Sdvižkov, Denis. *Das Zeitalter der Intelligenz: Zur vergleichenden Geschichte der Gebildeten in Europa bis zum Ersten Weltkrieg.* Göttingen: Vandenhoeck & Ruprecht, 2006.

Sereda, Ostap. "Mizh ukraïnofil'stvom i panslavizmon: Do istoriï zmin natsional'noï identychnosti halyts'ko-rus'kykh diiachiv u 60-kh rokakh XIX st. (sproba polibiohrafichnoho doslidzhennia)." *Journal of Ukrainian Studies* 35–36 (2010–2011): 103–19.

Shandra, V. S. *Heneral-hubernatorstva v Ukraïni: XIX—pochatok XX st.* Kyiv: Natsional'na akademiia nauk Ukraïny, 2005.

Shandra, Valentyna. "Kyiv's Intellectual Environment on the Eve of the Valuev Directive." *East/West: Journal of Ukrainian Studies* 4, no. 2 (2017): 97–112.

Shanin, Teodor. *Revolution as a Moment of Truth: Russia, 1905–07.* London: Macmillan, 1986.

Shevchenko, S. I. *Shul'hyny: Inhul's'ka storinka.* Kirovohrad: Imeks-LTD, 2012.

Shevelov, George Y. *The Ukrainian Language in the First Half of the Twentieth Century (1900–1941): Its State and Status.* Cambridge, MA: Harvard Ukrainian Research Institute, 1989.

Shkandrij, Myroslav. *Ukrainian Nationalism: Politics, Ideology, and Literature, 1929–1956.* New Haven, CT: Yale University Press, 2015.

Shklovskii, Viktor. *O teorii prozy.* Moscow: Izdatel'stvo "Federatsiia," 1929.

Simonenko, R. G. "National'no-kul'turnaia avtonomiia na Ukraine v 1917–1918 godakh." *Voprosy istorii*, no. 1 (1997): 50–63.

Skinner, Barbara. "Borderlands of Faith: Reconsidering the Origins of a Ukrainian Tragedy." *Slavic Review* 64, no. 1 (2005): 88–116.

Slezkine, Yuri. *The Jewish Century.* Princeton, NJ: Princeton University Press, 2004.

Smith, Alison K. *For the Common Good and Their Own Well-Being: Social Estates in Imperial Russia.* New York: Oxford University Press, 2015.

Smith, Sidonie, and Julia Watson. *Reading Autobiography: A Guide for Interpreting Life Narratives.* 2nd ed. Minneapolis: University of Minnesota Press, 2010.

Snyder, Timothy. *The Reconstruction of Nations: Poland, Ukraine, Lithuania, Belarus, 1569–1999.* New Haven, CT: Yale University Press, 2003.

———. *The Red Prince: The Secret Lives of a Habsburg Archduke.* New York: Basic Books, 2008.

Soldatenko, V. F. *Ukraïna v revoliutsiinu dobu: Istorychni ese-khroniky.* 4 vols. Kyiv: Svitohliad, 2008–2010.

Soroka, Mykola. "On the Other Side: The Russian-Ukrainian Encounter in Displacement, 1920–1939." *Nationalities Papers* 37, no. 3 (2009): 327–48.

Stadniuk, Tetiana. "Oleksander Iakovych Shul'hyn i ukraïns'ke derzhavotvorennia." *Etnichna istoriia narodiv Ievropy*, no. 7 (2000): 40–45.

Staliūnas, Darius. *Making Russians: Meaning and Practice of Russification in Lithuania and Belarus after 1863.* Amsterdam: Rodopi, 2007.

Staliūnas, Darius, and Yoko Aoshima. *The Tsar, the Empire, and the Nation: Dilemmas of Nationalization in Russia's Western Borderlands, 1905–1915.* Budapest: Central European University Press, 2021.

Stites, Richard. *The Women's Liberation Movement in Russia: Feminism, Nihilism, and Bolshevism, 1860–1930.* Princeton, NJ: Princeton University Press, 1978.

Stockdale, Melissa K. *Mobilizing the Russian Nation: Patriotism and Citizenship in the First World War.* Cambridge: Cambridge University Press, 2016.

Stoff, Laurie S. *Russia's Sisters of Mercy and the Great War: More Than Binding Men's Wounds.* Lawrence: University Press of Kansas, 2015.

Struve, Kai. *Bauern und Nation in Galizien: Über Zugehörigkeit und soziale Emanzipation im 19. Jahrhundert.* Göttingen: Vandenhoeck & Ruprecht, 2005.

Subtelny, Orest. *Ukraine: A History.* Toronto: University of Toronto Press, 1988.

Sunderland, Willard. *The Baron's Cloak: A History of the Russian Empire in War and Revolution.* Ithaca, NY: Cornell University Press, 2014.

Svitlenko, S. I. *Narodnytstvo v Ukraïni 60–80-kh rokiv XIX stolittia: Teoretychni problemy dzhereloznavstva ta istorii.* Dnipropetrovs'k: Navchal'na Knyha, 1999.

Tan, Graham. "Village Social Organisation and Peasant Action: Right-Bank Ukraine during the Revolution 1917–1923." PhD diss., School of Slavonic and East European Studies, 1999.

Tesemnikov, Vladimir A. "Belgrad: Die russische Emigration in Jugoslawien." In *Der grosse Exodus: Die russische Emigration und ihre Zentren 1917 bis 1941,* edited by Karl Schlögel. Munich: C. H. Beck, 1994, 86–111.

Teslia, A. A. *"Istinno russkie liudi": Istoriia russkogo natsionalizma.* Moscow: RIPOL klassik, 2019.

Ther, Philipp. "'Imperial Nationalism' as Challenge for the Study of Nationalism." In *Nationalizing Empires,* edited by Stefan Berger and Alexei Miller, 573–91. Budapest: Central European University Press, 2015.

Tobilevich, O. N., ed. *Russkie govory na Ukraine.* Kyiv: Naukova dumka, 1982.

Tol'ts, Vera. "Diskursy o rase: Imperskaia Rossiia i 'Zapad' v sravnenii." In *"Poniatiia o Rossii": K istoricheskoi semantike imperskogo perioda,* edited by A. I. Miller, D. A. Sdvizhkov, and I. Shirle, 2:145–93. Moscow: Novoe literaturnoe obozrenie, 2012.

Tolz, Vera. *Russia: Inventing the Nation.* London: Arnold, 2001.

———. "Constructing Race, Ethnicity, and Nationhood in Imperial Russia: Issues and Misconceptions." In *Ideologies of Race: Imperial Russia and the Soviet Union in Global Context,* edited by David Rainbow, 29–58. Montreal: McGill-Queen's University Press, 2019.

Troshchyns'kyi, V. P. *Mizhvoienna ukraïns'ka emihratsiia v Ievropi iak istorychne i sotsial'no-politychne iavyshche.* Kyiv: Intel, 1994.

Turton, Katy. *Family Networks and the Russian Revolutionary Movement, 1870–1940*. London: Palgrave Macmillan, 2018.

Veidlinger, Jeffrey. *In the Midst of Civilized Europe: The Pogroms of 1918–1921 and the Onset of the Holocaust*. New York: Metropolitan Books, 2021.

Velychenko, Stephen. "Identities, Loyalties and Service in Imperial Russia: Who Administered the Borderlands?" *Russian Review* 54, no. 2 (1995): 188–208.

———. *State Building in Revolutionary Ukraine: A Comparative Study of Governments and Bureaucrats, 1917–1922*. Toronto: University of Toronto Press, 2011.

Venturi, Franco. *Roots of Revolution: A History of the Populist and Socialist Movements in Nineteenth Century Russia*. London: Weidenfeld & Nicolson, 1964.

Verhoeven, Claudia. *The Odd Man Karakozov: Imperial Russia, Modernity, and the Birth of Terrorism*. Ithaca, NY: Cornell University Press, 2009.

Verstiuk, V. F., O. D. Boiko, V. I. Holovchenko, and H. H. Iefimenko. *Narysy istoriï ukraïns'koï revoliutsiï 1917–1921 rokiv*. 2 vols. Kyiv: Naukova dumka, 2011–2012.

von Hagen, Mark. "The Great War and the Mobilization of Ethnicity in the Russian Empire." In *Post-Soviet Political Order: Conflict and State Building*, edited by Barnett Rubin and Jack Snyder, 34–57. London: Routledge, 1998.

———. *War in a European Borderland: Occupations and Occupation Plans in Galicia and Ukraine, 1914–1918*. Seattle: University of Washington Press, 2007.

von Winning, Alexa. *Intimate Empire: The Mansurov Family in Russia and the Orthodox East, 1855–1936*. Oxford: Oxford University Press, 2022.

Vulpius, Ricarda. *Nationalisierung der Religion: Russifizierungspolitik und ukrainische Nationsbildung 1860–1920*. Wiesbaden: Harrassowitz, 2005.

———. *Die Geburt des Russländischen Imperiums: Herrschaftskonzepte und -praktiken im 18. Jahrhundert*. Cologne: Böhlau, 2020.

Wcislo, Francis W. *Tales of Imperial Russia: The Life and Times of Sergei Witte, 1849–1915*. Oxford: Oxford University Press, 2011.

Weber, Eugen. *Peasants into Frenchmen: The Modernization of Rural France, 1870–1914*. Stanford, CA: Stanford University Press, 1976.

Weeks, Theodore R. *Nation and State in Late Imperial Russia: Nationalism and Russification on the Western Frontier, 1863–1914*. DeKalb: Northern Illinois University Press, 1996.

Weinberg, Robert. *Blood Libel in Late Imperial Russia: The Ritual Murder Trial of Mendel Beilis*. Bloomington: Indiana University Press, 2014.

Weintraub, Jeff. "The Theory and Politics of the Public/Private Distinction." In *Public and Private in Thought and Practice: Perspectives on a Grand Dichotomy*, edited by Jeff Weintraub, 1–42. Chicago: University of Chicago Press, 1997.

Wendland, Anna Veronika. *Die Russophilen in Galizien: Ukrainische Konservative zwischen Österreich und Russland, 1848–1915*. Vienna: Verlag der Österreichischen Akademie der Wissenschaften, 2001.

———. "Ukraine transnational: Transnationalität, Kulturtransfer, Verflechtungsgeschichte." In *Die Ukraine: Prozesse der Nationsbildung*, edited by Andreas Kappeler, 51–66. Cologne: Böhlau, 2011.

Werner, Michael, and Bénédicte Zimmermann. "Penser l'histoire croisée: Entre empirie et réflexivité." *Annales. Histoire, Sciences Sociales* 58, no. 1 (2003): 7–36.

Wirtschafter, Elise Kimerling. *Social Identity in Imperial Russia*. DeKalb: Northern Illinois University Press, 1997.

Worobec, Christine. "Conceptual Observations on the Russian and Ukrainian Peasantries." In *Culture, Nation, and Identity: The Ukrainian-Russian Encounter, 1600–1945*, edited by Andreas Kappeler, Zenon E. Kohut, Frank E. Sysyn, and Mark von Hagen, 256–76. Toronto: Canadian Institute of Ukrainian Studies, 2003.

Wortman, Richard. *Scenarios of Power: Myth and Ceremony in Russian Monarchy*. 2 vols. Princeton, NJ: Princeton University Press, 1995–2000.

Yekelchyk, Serhy. "The Body and National Myth: Motifs from the Ukrainian National Revival in the Nineteenth Century." *Australian Slavonic and East European Studies* 7, no. 2 (1993): 31–59.

———. "The Nation's Clothes: Constructing a Ukrainian High Culture in the Russian Empire, 1860–1900." *Jahrbücher für Geschichte Osteuropas* 49, no. 2 (2001): 230–39.

———. *Ukraine: Birth of a Modern Nation*. New York: Oxford University Press, 2007.

———. "Bands of Nation Builders? Insurgency and Ideology in the Ukrainian Civil War." In *Empires at War: 1911–1923*, edited by Robert Gerwarth and John Horne, 107–25. Oxford: Oxford University Press, 2012.

Zahra, Tara. *Kidnapped Souls: National Indifference and the Battle for Children in the Bohemian Lands, 1900–1948*. Ithaca, NY: Cornell University Press, 2009.

———. "Imagined Noncommunities: National Indifference as a Category of Analysis." *Slavic Review* 69, no. 1 (2010): 93–119.

Zaionchkovskii, P. A. *Kirillo-Mefodievskoe obshchestvo (1846–1847)*. Moscow: Izdatel'stvo Moskovskogo Universiteta, 1959.

Zavorotna, Nadia. *Scholars in Exile: The Ukrainian Intellectual World in Interwar Czechoslovakia*. Toronto: University of Toronto Press, 2020.

Zettelbauer, Heidrun. *"Die Liebe sei Euer Heldentum": Geschlecht und Nation in völkischen Vereinen der Habsburgermonarchie*. Frankfurt am Main: Campus, 2005.

Zhytets'kyi, Ihnat. "'Kievskaia starina' sorok rokiv tomu." *Za sto lit* 3 (1928): 126–46.

———. "Kyïvs'ka Hromada za 60-kh rokiv." *Ukraïna. Naukovyi dvokhmisiachnyk ukraïnoznavstva* 26, no. 1 (1928): 91–125.

Zweynert, Joachim. *Eine Geschichte des ökonomischen Denkens in Russland: 1805–1905*. Marburg: Metropolis-Verlag, 2002.

Index

Women usually appear under their married name, with other names in brackets, if relevant.
Page numbers in italics refer to illustrations.

Agatovka (estate), 110, 112, 138
agriculture. *See* landownership
Aksakov, Ivan, 28
Aksakov, Sergei, 75
Alekseev, Mikhail, 185
Alexander II (tsar), 23, 41, 51, 53, 108
Alexander III (tsar), 98, 106, 119, 194
Algirdas (grand duke), 62
All-Russian National Union. *See*
  Nationalist Party
Andriewsky, Olga, 86
Annenkov, Nikolai, 27–28
Anne (tsaritsa), 69
antisemitism: antirevolutionary, 116, 122,
  179, 191–92, 224–25; economic, 30, 50,
  108–11; in *Kievlianin*, 30, 108, 116–18,
  158; popular, 118; racial, 146–47, 225;
  among Ukrainophiles, 50
Antonovich, Platon, 41, 60
Antonovych, Dmytro, 89
Antonovych, Varvara (Mikhel'), 23
Antonovych, Volodymyr, *24*, 29, 47,
  85; as activist during youth, 23–27;
  cooperation with *Kievlianin*, 33; as
  family man, 73, 79–80, 88–89; as
  historian, 34, 61–63, 65–67, 69, 199,
  253n66; and imperial state, 41–42, 56,
  60, 81, 256n129; memory of, 136, 211;
  political views of, 43, 51; as teacher, 34,
  37, 77; as Ukrainophile leader, 36, 60;
  views on mixed families, 75
Antsiferov, Nikolai, 92
assimilation, 6–7, 30, 88, 108, 233
Austria. *See* Habsburg Monarchy
autobiography, 12–13, 205–6, 209–19,
  221–29
autocracy, 29, 101, 118–20, 144–45, 157,
  159–61, 225. *See also* monarchism
Azbuka (secret agency), 185–86, 189, 194

Bagalei, Dmitrii, 252n61
Bakunin, Mikhail, 52
Balashev, Petr, 155
Baranovs'kyi, Khrystofor, 165
Beilis, Mendel, 146–47, 231
Beilis affair, 146–47, 217
Berenshtam, Vil'iam, 35, 38
Bibikov, Dmitrii, 19, 29
Bilenky, Serhiy, 8
Bilimovich, Aleksandr, 100, 137, 142,
  193, 220
Bilimovich, Alla (Shul'gina), 42, 105, 137,
  154, 261n12, 282n195
Bilimovich, Tat'iana, 220
biography as genre, 8–12
Black Hundreds, 119–20, 144, 181, 223
Bobrinskii, Aleksei, 129
Bobrinskii, Georgii, 162
Bobrinskii, Vladimir, 155
Bogdanov, Sergei, 143
Bolsheviks: as government in Petrograd,
  172–74; as seen by nationalists,
  174, 178, 182–84, 188, 191–92, 196,
  224–25; in Ukraine, 165, 173, 181–82,
  189–91, 197, 200–204
Breshkovskaia, Ekaterina, 52
Brest-Litovsk, treaty of, 173,
  182, 197
Brodskii, Lazar', 105, 262n37
Brubaker, Rogers, 9, 11, 142
Bulgakov, Mikhail, 1, 58, 176
Bulgaria, 153–54, 197–98
Bulygin, Aleksandr, 115
Bunge, Nikolai, 36, 54–55, 58, 100–101,
  103, 105–6
Burtsev, Vladimir, 208

Catherine II (tsaritsa), 69
Catholic Church, 29, 61, 66

censorship, 49, 61, 81; abolition of, 64–65, 84, 171; of *Kievlianin*, 160, 264n80; Soviet, 223; of Ukrainophile publications, 63–64, 68–70, 75
census, 40, 107, 199, 237n7
Central Powers, 153, 172–73, 197–98
Central Rada, 163–74, 176, 178, 203, 214. *See also* Ukrainian People's Republic
Chaplinskii, Georgii, 146
Cheberiak, Vera, 146
Cheka, 190–91, 194–95, 218, 220, 227
Chepurnyi, Okhrim, 118
Chernyshevskii, Nikolai, 34
Chigirin, 99, 102
Chkheidze, Nikolai, 160
choice of nationality, 4, 10, 26, 47, 106, 148, 231
Chubyn'skyi, Pavlo, 23, 35–37, 41–42, 44
Chykalenko family, 77, 79–80
Chykalenko, Ievhen, 73, 75, 211; in 1917, 169; as family man, 80, 87–88; as Ukrainophile activist, 65, 77, 84–85, 94–95
Chykalenko, Levko, 87, 91–92
civil war, 173–74, 182–96, 200–204, 214–16, 218–20, 222
Clemenceau, Georges, 200
Cohen, Deborah, 140
Cohen, Gary, 83
Conan Doyle, Arthur, 121
Constantinople, 195, 220–21
Constituent Assembly, 163, 180–81, 186
Constitutional-Democratic Party. *See* Kadets
constitutionalism, 83, 115, 136, 165
Cooper, Frederick, 11
Cossacks, 20, 66–67, 91, 133, 171; as national myth, 51, 61–62, 73–75, 82, 174, 176; noble families and, 17, 37–38, 71
Council of United Societal Organizations, 164–65
Crimea, 171, 194–95, 222
culturalism, 49, 59–60, 85, 91, 96
Cyrillo-Methodians, 21–22, 25, 51
Czech nationalism, 83, 87, 167
Czechoslovakia, 167, 172, 201, 208
Czernin, Otto, 198

Danilevich, Vasilii, 252n61
Darwin, Charles, 34
Debogorii-Mokrievich, Vladimir, 51
Demchenko, Vsevolod, 132, 143, 155

Demidov, Igor', 185
Denikin, Anton, 187–89, 192–93, 196, 200, 204
Dickens, Charles, 75
Directory. *See* Ukrainian People's Republic
Dragomirov, Abram, 194
Dragomirov, Mikhail, 63
Drahomanova, Liudmyla, 73
Drahomanov family, 73, 78
Drahomanov, Mykhail, 47, 79; cooperation with *Kievlianin*, 32–33; in exile, 50, 54, 58–61; and imperial state, 41–42, 53, 245n70; influence of ideas, 49, 91, 100, 163–64; memory of, 211; polemic with *Kievlianin*, 39–42, 44; political views of, 35, 38–39, 43; as teacher, 33–35, 37
domestic life, 4, 11, 137–41, 249n3; and Ukrainophile activism, 49, 70, 73–75, 78–82, 96, 215
Dondukov-Korsakov, Aleksandr, 35, 41, 43
Dontsov, Dmytro, 197, 206
Doroshenko, Dmytro, 86, 196–97, 213–14
Dovnar-Zapol'skii, 252n61
Dubrovin, Aleksandr, 119, 144
Duchiński, Franciszek, 259n183
Duma. *See* State Duma
Durnovo, Ivan, 58

education: by home-schooling, 73–75; role in nationalization, 32, 43, 86–87, 167; in state schools, 82–83, 89; in Sunday schools, 23, 32; for women, 22, 71, 90; for workers, 37, 100
Efimenko, Aleksandra, 253n65
elections: All-Russian Constituent Assembly, 180–81; Kiev City Duma, 180–81; State Duma, 84, 124–26, 128–29, 132, 146; Ukrainian Constituent Assembly, 181–82; zemstvo, 132
electoral curiae. *See* Russification: of electoral politics
Elisavetgrad, 55, 71–72, 87, 230
émigrés. *See* Russian emigration, Ukrainian emigration
Ems Ukaz, 8, 41, 168; amendments of, 75; effects of, 45, 48–49, 83, 95–96, 233; lifting of, 64–65

Entente, 172, 176, 184–85, 188–89, 197–201, 214–15

Erenburg, Il'ia, 192

ethnography, 19–20, 25, 35–36, 42, 44, 46, 90–9

Evdokha (servant), 112

family: as ideological model, 144–45, 177, 211–12; as intimate community, 137–41, 215; as political vehicle, 4, 11, 78, 137, 141–44, 149, 215, 234–35

fatherhood, 75–76, 89, 102, 145, 248n132, 261n12

fascism, 2, 195–96, 206, 207, 225, 227, 284n9

February revolution. *See* revolution of 1917

federalism: during revolution, 163–64, 170–74, 187, 197–98, 208; among Ukrainophiles, 21, 25, 38–39, 51, 84, 92, 94–96

feminism, 4, 143, 235

Ferdinand (king), 197

Florinskii, Timofei, 64, 129, 190

Fourier, Charles, 34

France, 161, 172, 185, 187–89, 198–202, 207, 209–11

Franko, Ivan, 38, 251n30

Galagan, Mykola, 78, 86

Galicia, 5, 49, 238n12, 249n139; as center of Ukrainian nationalism, 63–64, 83, 95, 103; civil war army of, 188, 190; interwar, 206–7; Ukrainian press in, 41, 54, 68–69, 78, 81; and UNR, 198, 200–201; during World War I, 154–55, 162, 165

Gellner, Ernest, 238n13, 285n21

General Secretariat (Central Rada), 165–67, 169–73

General Ukrainian Organization, 77, 79

generations, 43–44, 85–89, 135, 142, 166–69, 212

Geneva, 50, 59, 201, 214

German nationalism, 83

Germany, 33, 41–42, 211; as occupying power, 159, 172–76, 182–85, 187, 196–97; and Ukrainian nationalism, 165–66, 178, 188, 196, 200, 214, 278n12; as war enemy, 151, 153, 157, 225

Gogol', Nikolai, 39–40, 74–75, 136, 211

Goremykin, Ivan, 157, 272n29

Gradovskii, Grigorii, 123

Great Britain, 140, 161, 172, 185, 199–200

Great Reforms, 23, 101

Great Russians: and Central Rada, 169–71; according to Kostomarov, 25; as official category, 40, 170–71; according to Pogodin, 62; as seen by Ukrainian nationalists, 6, 68–69, 71, 91, 174, 212–13

Greek Catholic Church. *See* Uniate Church

Gringmut, Vladimir, 119, *129*

Grishin-Almazov, Aleksei, 188–89

Guchkov, Aleksandr, 161

Gurko, Vladimir, *129*

Habsburg Monarchy, 9, 46, 153, 167, 173, 197; and Ukrainian nationalism, 133–34, 158, 162, 178, 278n121. *See also* Galicia

Haidamaks, 43, 66–68, 73

Henno, Emile, 185, 188

Hetmanate (1918), 1–2, 174–76, 184, 186–88, 196–98

Hillis, Faith, 8, 267n129

historiography: émigré, 211–14; liberal, 22; on nationalism, 9–11; on nineteenth-century Ukraine, 7–8; on Shul'gin/Shul'hyn family, 13; Ukrainophile, 61–63, 65–70

Hlibov, Leonid, 73–74

Hobsbawm, Eric, 73

Homer, 73

Hrinchenko, Borys, 85

Hroch, Miroslav, 7, 20, 42, 260n200

Hromada. *See* Kiev Hromada, Odessa Hromada

Hromada (journal), 50, 59–60

Hromads'ka dumka (newspaper), 84

Hrushevs'kyi family, 240n37

Hrushevs'kyi, Mykhailo, 1, 65, 80, 173, *183*; as Central Rada president, 163–64, 169; as historian, 63, 67, 69–70, 199, 204, 259n184; on Iakov Shul'gin, 58; memory of, 211; as political activist, 85, 133, 158

Hrushevs'kyi, Oleksandr, 252n61

Hugo, Victor, 50

Iakhnenko family, 99

Iaroslav (grand prince), 20

identity, 11

Iefremov, Serhii, 165, 167
Imperial Academy of Sciences, 64–65
Imperial Geographical Society. *See* Kiev
 Geographical Society
imperial state: collapse of, 159–62, 203,
 221–25; and nationalist movements,
 4–5, 7, 27, 203; and peasants, 46, 109;
 as seen by Ukrainophiles, 68–69
independence of Ukraine, 92, 95, 164,
 173–74, 199–200, 208, 233
intelligentsia, 36–39, 42–44, 102,
 203, 206; critique of, 160, 216, 224;
 emergence of, 18; Ukrainian, 72–73,
 78–79, 166
Ishchuk, Roman, 273–74n54
Iushchinskii, Andrei, 146
Iuzefovich, Boris, 249n138
Iuzefovich, Mikhail, 28–29, 32, 36,
 41–45, 138, 249n138

Jassy conference, 187
Jews: and 1905 revolution, 115–16, 122;
 and Bolsheviks, 191–92, 194, 196, 224;
 and Central Rada, 169–71; economic
 role, 16, 108–11; and Haidamak
 uprisings, 66–67; as seen by Russian
 nationalists, 30, 146–47, 158, 224–25;
 as seen by Ukrainian nationalists, 50,
 71; during World War I, 152, 156

Kadets, 84, 124, 135, 155–57, 184–85,
 187, 217
Kamanin, Ivan, 34
Kamiński, Wacław, 221
Kareev, Nikolai, 90
Karpenko-Karyi, Ivan, 72, 87–88
Kartavtsov, Evgenii, 107
Kashovka (estate), 110
Katkov, Mikhail, 26–27, 32
Kenez, Peter, 195
Kerenskii, Aleksandr, 160
Khliboroby party, 197
khlopomany, 23–27, 29–32, 51–52
Khrystiuk, Pavlo, 165, 213, 274n61
Khrushchev, Nikita, 227
Kiev: in 1830s, 19; 1905 revolution in,
 89, 115–18, 122; 1917 revolution
 in, 163–66, 172, 176–84; civil war
 in, 150, 173–74, 184–85, 190–94; as
 conservative stronghold, 125, 129–32,
 142–43, 182; Darnitsa neighborhood,
 191; Demievka neighborhood, 37, 100,
 122; growth and modernization of,

107–8; Luk'ianovka neighborhood,
 146, 182; Novoe stroenie
 neighborhood, 22–23, 79–81;
 present-day, 230; Soviet, 226–27;
 Ukrainophile spaces in, 79–81, *80*
Kievan Rus', 62–63, 112
Kiev Archaeographic Commission, 19,
 21, 28, 44
Kiev City Duma, 106–7, 115–16, 122,
 180, 182
Kiev Club of Russian Nationalists,
 129–35, 142–43, 146–47, 180, 190,
 267n129
Kiev First Gymnasium, 16, 58, 179
Kiev Geographical Society, 35–36, 39–45
Kiev Hromada: clandestine activities
 of, 48, 51–52, 77–79, 81–82, 100;
 foundation of, 23; political views of
 members, 38–39, 50–51, 59, 124–25;
 scholarship of, 35–36, 59, 61, 77, 85
Kievlianin (newspaper): and censorship,
 160, 264n80; editorial office of,
 23, 81, 105, 137, 177–78, 184; as
 enterprise, 109–11, 141–43, 271n209;
 establishment of, 28; expansion and
 success of, 98–99, 105; and February
 revolution, 176–77; on Jews, 30,
 115–16, 146–47, 191–92; and Kiev
 Geographical Society, 39–41; on Poles,
 29–30, 152, 158–59; as political force,
 117–18, 124, 156–57, 177–81, 190–94;
 repressions against, 181; as source, 12;
 on Ukrainian nationalism, 30–33, 64,
 102–3, 133–35, 152, 169, 178, 192; on
 World War I, 151–54, 184
Kiev Literacy Society, 81, 103
Kievskaia mysl' (newspaper), 271
Kievskaia starina (journal), 60–66, 70–71,
 77, 80–81, 85
Kievskii telegraf (newspaper), 39–41
Kiev University: economists at,
 101–2, 105–7; establishment of,
 19; at mid-century, 22, 27; student
 protests at, 19, 26, 34–35, 114, 121;
 Ukrainophiles at, 33–37
Kiev Workers' Soviet, 165
King, Jeremy, 231
Kistiakivs'kyi, Oleksandr, 23, 33, 37; on
 Antonovych, 60; on Iakov Shul'gin, 45;
 memory of, 211; on Pikhno, 101–2,
 138, 261n12; on Ukrainophilism, 59
Kizevetter, Aleksandr, 216
Klichko, Vitalii, 230

Kliuchevskii, Vasilii, 204
Koliivshchyna, 65–70
Komarov, Mykhailo (Komar), 88
Konys'kyi, Oleksandr, 77, 79–80, 85
Kornilov, Lavr, 181
Korzon, Tadeusz, 68
Kosach family, 77, 79–80
Kosach, Petro, 73, 85
Kotliarevs'kyi, Ivan, 73, 188, 211
Kostomarov, Nikolai, 21, 25, 44, 47,
  61, 199
Krestovskaia, Mariia, 139
Krushevan, Pavel, *128*
Kruty, battle of, 1, 174, 214, 277n106
Kulish, Panteleimon, 21, 25
kul'turnytstvo, see culturalism
Kurgany (estate), 110–12, 137, 155, 193,
  195, 215–16, 221

landownership, 99, 107–13, 129, 131–32,
  148, 193
language. *See* Russian language,
  Ukrainian language
Lavrov, Petr, 35, 43, 51–52
Lazarevskii, Aleksandr, 60
Lazarevskii, Vladimir, 287n77
League of Nations, 201–2
Lebedintsev, Feofan, 60–61
Lebedintsev, Petr, 60
left-bank Ukraine: 16–17, 23, 62, 69,
  242–43n18
Lemberg, 63, 70, 85
Leontovich, Ivan, 257n151
Leontovich, Konstantin, 82
Leontovich, Marusia (Ustimovich), 82
Leontovych, Volodymyr, 257n151
liberalism, 34–35, 100–101, 106, 118,
  134–35, 149
Lidval', Fedor, *128*
Linnichenko, Ivan, 252n61
literature, 19–21, 40, 66, 73–75, 77,
  121, 136
Lithuanian Grand Duchy, 62, 67, 253n64
Little Russians: according to Kostomarov,
  23; according to Maksimovich, 20–21;
  as official category, 40, 61, 68, 188–90,
  199; according to Pogodin, 62; as
  political self-description, 5–6, 8, 42, 46,
  134–36, 188–90, 232–33
Lotots'kyi, Oleksander, 91–92
Luchitskii, Ivan, 124–25, 129
L'vov, Georgii, 161, 178
Lypyns'kyi, Viacheslav, 197

Lysenko family, 73, 77, 80, 88
Lysenko, Mykola, 73, 79, 81; as composer,
  36, 39, 136; death of, 85, 95; and
  Ukrainian Club, 83, 129

Maklakov, Vasilii, 188, 200, 224, 226
Maksimovich, Mikhail, 19–21, 28, 36, 44,
  46, 246n91
Mal'ovanyi, Volodymyr, 51
Margolin, Arnol'd, 198, 200, 202
Markov, Nikolai, 129
Martos, Borys, 165, 167
Martynyuk, Olha, 126, 267n129
Marxism, 34, 83, 106, 114, 135;
  Austro-Marxism, 170; and Ukrainian
  nationalism, 88–90, 164
Marx, Karl, 34, 88–90, 192
Masaryk, Tomáš, 172
Matich, Olga, 261n12
Mazepa, Ivan, 133
Mazepists, 133–34, 178
McClintock, Anne
Meir, Natan, 116
memoirs. *See* autobiography
Mensheviks, 160, 165
Mickiewicz, Mieczyław, 169–70
microhistory, 12
Mikhail (grand duke), 161
Mikhnovs'kyi, Mykola, 260n199
Miliukov, Pavel, 159–61, 177
Miller, Alexei, 7–8
Mill, John Stuart, 34
mixed marriages, 75
Mogilevskaia, Elena (Merkulova),
  269n164
Mogilevskaia, Lina (Shul'gina), 42, *140*,
  190, 222–23; in emigration, 220,
  282n195; as landowner, 111, 221; as
  newspaper manager, 142–43, 177;
  private scandals of, 105, 137–41,
  261n22
Mogilevskii, Aleksandr, 105
Mogilevskii, Aleksandr (jr.), 105
Mogilevskii, Filipp, 105, 142, 155, 195,
  269n164
Mogilevskii, Ivan, 105
monarchism, 126–27, 143–44, 148; in
  interwar emigration, 206, 223–25;
  mobilization for, 117–20, 123; in
  revolution and civil war, 160–61, 179,
  186. *See also* autocracy
Moscow, 40, 71, 115, 119, 185–86,
  226–27

Moskovskiia vedomosti (newspaper), 32
motherhood, 4, 11, 72–77, 145, 218–19, 228, 235
music, 36, 39, 41
Mussolini, Benito, 196, 284n9

Nansen, Fridtjof, 202
narodniki, 37, 43, 51–53, 106, 109. *See also* socialism
national indifference, 9–10, 82–83, 87–88, 112, 204, 219, 233–34
nationalism: and 1917 revolution, 203; democratic component of, 149; and gender, 4, 11, 75–77, 143, 179–80, 217–19, 234–35; as political choice, 4, 10, 47, 148, 179, 231; transformed by crisis, 119–21, 153, 202. *See also* Russian nationalism, Ukrainian nationalism
Nationalist Party, 130–31, 136, 143–44, 147–48, 155–56, 220
National Labor Alliance of the New Generation, 227
national-personal autonomy, 169–71
nation as cognitive category, 9
Naumenko, Vera (Shul'gina), 45, 54, 79–80, 255n109
Naumenko, Volodymyr, 54, 102, 255n109, 280n165; and 1917 revolution, 167–69, 174; as family man, 79, 88; and imperial state, 56, 81, 96; and Kiev Hromada, 45, 79–81; as *Kievskaia Starina* editor, 61, 63–65, 78, 85; memory of, 211; murder of, 190; political views of, 84–85, 197; youth of, 34, 37–38;
New Economic Policy, 226–27
Nezhin, 17–18
Nezhyvyi, Semen, 67
Nicholas I (tsar), 20
Nicholas II (tsar), 115, 124, 127, 144, 157, 161
Nikolai Mikhailovich (grand duke), 160
Nikolai Nikolaevich (grand duke), 153
Novitskii, Vasilii, 55–56, 58, 81
Novoe stroenie (Kiev neighborhood), 22–23, 79–81

Obshchee delo (newspaper), 208
October Manifesto, 115, 117, 122
October revolution. *See* Bolsheviks, revolution of 1917

Octobrist Party, 129–31, 133, 146–47, 146
Odinets, Dmitrii, 171
Odessa, 105, 162; in 1870s, 50–53, 64; in 1905, 114; civil war in, 186–89, 194–95, 198, 215, 218
Odessa Hromada, 51–52
Orthodox Church, 6, 66–67, 82, 105, 125–26, 162
Osnova (journal), 25–26, 28
Ottoman Empire, 153, 197

Pale of Settlement, 30, 108, 152
pan-Slavism, 21, 38–39
Pares, Bernard, 129
Paris, 50, 52, 91, 188; interwar emigration in, 205, 207–9, 215, 219, 221; peace conference, 198–201
Paustovskii, Konstantin, 58, 251n41
Pchilka, Olena (Ol'ha Kosach), 73
peasants: and electoral politics, 125–26; exoticization of, 238n18; as historical protagonists, 67; imitation of lifestyle, 23–24, 51–52; as *Kievlianin* readers, 117–18; and revolution, 166, 193; as seen by nationalists, 5, 43, 46, 71–72, 109, 111–12; self-image of, 10, 234; and serfdom, 19, 21, 25, 69; as soldiers, 154; and Ukrainian press, 85
Peter I (tsar), 22, 69
Petliura, Symon, 86, 89, 162; as general secretary, 164–65, 167; as leader of Directory, 2, 188, 190, 201–2
Petrograd. *See* Saint Petersburg
Petropavlovskaia Borshchagovka, 2
physical anthropology, 90–91
Pichon, Stephen, 200
Picton Bagge, John, 172
Pikhno, Dmitrii, 81, 98–99, *101*, 121, *127*, *139*, 231; antisemitic views of, 108, 114–16, 147, 224; and constitutional politics, 124, 127–32, 136; death of, 145; as economist, 106–9; as entrepreneur, 142–43, 262n37; as family man, 137–39, 144–45, 177; and Iakov Shul'gin, 56, 100, 102, 106, 148; as landowner, 109–12, 221; memory of, 216–17, 223; national choice of, 106, 148; as newspaper editor, 102–5, 116–18; political views of, 113–17, 132, 144, 149, 159, 181; private scandals of, 45, 261n12, 261n22; social mobility of,

105–6, 233; on Ukrainian nationalism, 103; youth and education of, 99–102

Pikhno, Dmitrii (jr.), 105, 110, 137, 145, 195, 220

Pikhno, Mariia (Merkulova), 137, 141, 145

Pikhno, Pavel, 105, 110, 137, 142, 195

Pikhno-Shul'gina, Mariia (Popova), 27, 42, 45, 102–3, *104*, 110, 137

Pikhno, Vasilii, 111

Pirogov, Nikolai, 23

Pisarev, Dmitrii, 34

Platon of Chigirin (bishop), 124

Plehve, Viacheslav von, 54, 58

Pobedonostsev, Konstantin, 103, 105

Pogodin, Mikhail, 62

pogroms: 17th-century, 66–67; in 1905, 116–17, 122–23, 223; in 1917, 170, 274–75n69; during civil war, 188, 191–92, 194–95; late imperial, 108

Poland: autonomy of, 152, 158–59; Kingdom of, 115, 151; partitions of, 19, 66; second republic of, 200–202, 205, 207, 214, 221

Poles: and 1831 uprising, 19; and 1863 uprising, 26; and 1905 revolution, 115; and Central Rada, 169–71; cultural work under partitions, 59; nobility, 16, 23, 26, 109–11, 125–26, 131; as seen by Russian nationalists, 29–30; as seen by Ukrainophiles, 62, 67–68; during World War I, 151–52

Poliakov, Solomon, 224

police, 52, 54–58, 71, 81–82, 95, 134, 256n129. *See also* Cheka

Polish-Lithuanian Commonwealth, 26, 66

Polish nationalism, 5, 46, 98, 171

Popova, Liubov' (Tkachenko, Pikhno), 137, 154–55, 187, 221, 269n165

populism. *See narodniki*

Porsh, Mykola, 89

praca organiczna, 59. *See also* culturalism

Prague, 83, 205, 208, 216, 219, 221

private life. *See* domestic life

Procyk, Anna, 195

Progressive Bloc, 156–60, 202

Prosvita Society, 81, 83, 133–34

Protsenko, Vasilii, 129

Provisional Government, 161–65, 176, 178–80, 185, 200

Proudhon, Pierre-Joseph, 34

Purishkevich, Vladimir, 129

Putin, Vladimir, 2–3, 231

race, 90–91, 113, 146–47, 153–54, 259n183–84

Rada (newspaper), 84–85

Rada (parliament). *See* Central Rada

radicalism. *See narodniki*, Marxism, socialism

railways, 103, 108, 113, 117, 161, 201

Red'ka (peasant), 118

Reitlinger, Ol'ga, 118

Remy, Johannes, 8

Renner, Karl, 170

Revolutionary Ukrainian Party, 83, 86, 88–89, 115, 167, 211

revolutionary underground, 51–52, 77

revolution of 1905, 83–85, 88–89, 114–23, 216, 223

revolution of 1917, 160–72, 176–84, 209, 212–14, 217–18, 223–25

Riabtsov, Evgenii, 182

Riga, treaty of, 202, 221

right-bank Ukraine, 8, 126, 132, 202; as seen by Russian nationalists, 28–29; as seen by Ukrainophiles, 62; socioethnic composition of, 16, 19, 68, 107–11, 120

right-wing parties, 119–20

Rodyna Club. *See* Ukrainian Club in Kiev

Rodzianko, Mikhail, 160–61

Romania, 167, 194–95, 201

Rossiia (newspaper), 186–88

Rostropovich, Mstislav, 228

Rousseau, Jean-Jacques, 214–15

Rudanovskaia, Sofiia, 137

Rudnyts'kyi, Stepan, 199

Rudykovs'kyi, Ostap, 20–21

Rusov, Aleksandr, 38

Rusova, Sofiia (Lindfors), 38

Russian Assembly, 119

Russian emigration, 50, 205, 220–22, 226–27, 229

Russian Empire. *See* imperial state

Russian invasion of Ukraine (2022), 2, 231

Russian language: as language of high culture, 88, 90, 212; in public sphere, 82–83, 120; relationship with Ukrainian, 6; among Ukrainophiles, 38, 72, 76, 93

Russian Monarchist Party, 119

Russian nationalism, 5–7; ideology of, 119–21; and mass politics, 136, 144, 148, 180–82, 223; mobilization of, 118–20; and Ukraine, 5–6, 135–36; during World War I, 158–59

Russian Social Democratic Workers' Party, 89–90, 126, 136, 163. *See also* Bolsheviks, Mensheviks, Ukrainian Social Democratic Workers' Party

Russian-Ukrainian rivalry, 5–8, 10, 42; attempt to negotiate, 33, 36, 232–33; in emigration, 208–9, 229; in Galicia, 238n12, 249n139; ideological differences, 88, 120, 233; for intelligentsia loyalties, 88, 171, 178; periodization of, 232; and public opinion, 133–36

Russification: of electoral politics, 126, 130–32; resistance against, 211; of rural economy, 26, 30, 106–7, 109–11, 221; of self, 18, 102, 106, 148

Russkaia mysl' (journal), 221, 288n81

Russkoe bogatstvo (journal), 59

Rus' Society, 178–80

Russo-Japanese War, 83, 99, 113–14, 123, 157, 216, 223

Sadovs'kyi, Valentyn, 165, 167

Saint Petersburg (Petrograd): 1917 revolution in, 160–65, 177, 212–13; as administrative capital, 54, 56, 63–64, 103, 117; imperial politics in, 84, 106, 127, 130–31, 142–43, 155; as Ukrainian nationalist hub, 25, 90–94

Saint Petersburg University, 90–92

Sankt Peterburgskiia vedomosti (newspaper), 32

Savenko, Anatolii, 132, 146–47, 152–54, 268n155, 270n182; anti-Ukrainian campaign of, 133–36; in civil war, 186, 189, 192–93, 280n165; and Kiev Club, 129; and *Kievlianin*, 142–43; and Progressive Bloc, 155–57

Sazonov, Sergei, 200

scandals, 99, 137–41, 224

schools. *See* education

Scott, Walter, 75

Sedlaczek, Eduard, 48

serfdom. *See* peasants

Shchegolev, Sergei, 129, 134, 190

Sheptyts'kyi family, 240n37

Shcherbina, Aleksandra (Shul'gina), 54, 248n134

Shcherbina, Vladimir, 34, 79

Shevchenko, Taras, 21, 25, 53, 66; as national symbol, 61, 73, 95, 120–21, 136, 211

Shevchenko Scientific Society, 70

Shklovskii, Viktor, 248n132

Shteingel', Fedor, 124

Shul'ga, Ignatii, 242n4

Shul'gina, Ekaterina (Gradovskaia), *122*, 159, 189, 194–95, 203; antisemitic views of, 158; in emigration, 205, 215–16, 219–20; as family woman, 187, 218–19; and February revolution, 176; as journalist, 142, 153–54, 177–78; as landowner, 110–12, 155; as memoirist, 12, 206, 215–19, 228; as political activist, 130, 143, 151, 179–81, 184–85, 235; political socialization of, 121, 123; private scandals of, 105, 137, 141; on Ukrainian nationalism, 184, 219

Shul'gina, Iuliia (Devel'), 17–18, 27

Shul'gina, Mariia (Rudykovskaia), 20, 27

Shul'gina, Mariia (Sedel'nikova), 220, 227

Shul'gina, Nadezhda, 248n134

Shul'gin, Dmitrii, 112, 218, 282n195

Shul'gin, Iakov, 3, *57*, *101*, 231, 233–34; antisemitic views of, 50; arrest and exile, 52–54; break with Vitalii Shul'gin, 44–45, 102; death of, 58, 85; and Dmitrii Pikhno, 56, 100, 102, 106, 148; as family man, 70–73, 75, 79–80, 164; as historian, 61, 65–70; and imperial state, 54–59, 69, 82, 95, 106; memory of, 211–12, 226, 251n41; national choice of, 37, 47; and political radicalism, 35, 50–52, 89; travels abroad, 41–42, 49–50; youth and education of, 33–37

Shul'gin, Iakov (Iakiv Shul'ha), 17–18, 27, 231

Shul'gin, Nikolai, 18, 27

Shul'gin, Vasilid, 2–3, 112, 179, 185–87, 215–16, 218

Shul'gin, Vasilii, 2, 42, 81, 99, 116, *122*, 202–3; antisemitic views of, 146–47, 158–59, 191–92, 224–25, 271n206; birth of, 45, 102, 138, 261n12; clandestine activities of, 184–85; and constitutional politics, 124–32, 151, 155–60, 180–82, 266n114; in emigration, 205, 219–21, 227; and fascism, 195–96; and February revolution, 160–62, 176–78, 223; as landowner, 110–12; as memoirist, 12, 206, 221–29, 240n39; memory of, 13, 215, 217, 230–31, 241n42; as newspaper editor, 142–43, 279n152; political socialization of, 121–23; political views of, 132, 149, 186; private scandals of, 105, 137, 141, 145, 221; as soldier, 154–55; and Soviet Union, 226–28, 289n113, 289–90n4; on split in the family, 1, 226, 289n104; on Ukrainian nationalism, 134, 136, 158, 171, 186, 225–26; as White ideologue, 187–96, 222–23

Shul'gin, Veniamin, 112, 176, 185, 195, 218, 220, 282n194

Shul'gin, Vitalii, 3, *31*, 81, 98, 109, 231; academic career of, 20–22; childhood of, 18; death of, 42, 137–38; and Kiev Geographical Society, 36, 40, 44–45; memory of, 190, 212, 215; as newspaper editor, 27–33, 98; political views of, 28–30, 43, 46, 106; as teacher, 102; and Ukrainophiles, 30–33, 36, 40–42, 44, 46

Shul'hyna, Lidiia (Bublyk), 92, 162, 285n17

Shul'hyna, Liubov (Ustymovych), 3, 49, 70, *74*, 205, 273n54; as educator and activist, 73–80, 162–63, 167, 235; rural roots of, 71–72, 76, 82;

Shul'hyna, Nadiia (Ishchuk), 71, *74*, 89–90, 205, 274n54, 284n1; as Ukrainian activist, 86, 162–63, 167

Shul'hyn, Mykola, 71, 162, 167, 205, 284n1

Shul'hyn, Oleksander: 1–2, *74*, 81, *93*, 181, *210*, 232; as Central Rada politician, 151, 163–67, 169–74; childhood of, 71–76; as diplomat, 196–202; in emigration, 206–9, 214–15; and February revolution, 163, 212–13; foreign policy of, 171–76, 207, 214–15; Marxist sympathies of, 89–90; as memoirist, 12, 56, 71, 86–87, 90, 111, 206, 209–15, 229; memory of, 13, 97, 230, 289n104; political views of, 94, 174, 202–3; on Russians, 174, 184, 212–13; on split in the family, 1, 100, 215, 226; youth and education of, 90–94, 96, 162

Shul'hyn, Volodymyr, 71, 73, 167, *168*; death of, 1–3, 174, 214; memory of, 214, 230

Siberia, 52–54

Sienkiewicz, Henryk, 121

Sikorskii, Ivan, 113, 130, 146, 153

Skoropadskii, Pavel, 174–76, 184, 186–87, 196–98, 201–2, 206, 280n165

Smakovskaia (Gradovskaia), Sofiia, 142

Smakovskii, Konstantin, 142, 177

SMERSH, 227

Smolens'kyi, Leonid, 50, 88

Social Democrats. *See* Bolsheviks, Mensheviks, Russian Social Democratic Workers' Party, Ukrainian Social Democratic Workers' Party

socialism: and Duma politics, 126; repression against, 53; and Ukrainian nationalism, 35, 37–38, 43, 51–53, 88–90, 164–66

Socialist-Federalists. *See* Ukrainian Party of Socialist-Federalists

Socialist Revolutionary Party, 126, 163. *See also* Ukrainian Party of Socialist Revolutionaries

Society of Ukrainian Progressives (TUP), 84–85, 163

Sokhvyne (estate), 71–72, 82

Solzhenitsyn, Aleksandr, 227–28

South Russians. *See* Little Russians

Southwest region. *See* right-bank Ukraine

Soviet of Workers' and Soldiers' Deputies, 163

Soviet Union, 206–7, 214, 223, 226–29

Special Council on Defense, 157

Special Council (Volunteer Army), 187

Spencer, Herbert, 34

Stańczycy, 59

Staryts'ka-Cherniakhivs'ka, Liudmyla, 86

Staryts'kyi family, 77, 80

Staryts'kyi, Mykhailo, 35, 39, 73, 85

Stasiuk, Mykola, 165, 167

State Council, 106, 127, 130–32, 134, 148

State Duma, 83, 115, 148, 217; and February revolution, 159–61, 177; and World War I, 152, 154–57; nationality issues in, 131–32, 133, 136; political culture of, 126–29; Ukrainian delegates in, 84. *See also* elections: State Duma

state service, 18, 48, 76, 82, 94–96, 154

Stebnyts'kyi, Petro, 169

Stempowski, Jerzy, 10

Stepanov, Vasilii, 185

Steshenko, Ivan, 78, 165, 167, 169

Stolypin, Petr, 126–27, 129–33, 144, 149, 163, 193, 217

Storozhenko family, 240n37
Struve, Petr, 135, 221
Stürmer, Boris, 159–60
St. Vladimir University. See Kiev
    University
Switzerland, 42, 50
Sydorenko, Hryhorii, 198, 283n215
Symyrenko family, 99
Symyrenko, Vasyl', 65

Tabouis, Georges, 172, 210
Tartakivs'ka, Lidiia, *168*
theater, 41, 75, 77, 81–82, 103
Tolstoi, Aleksei, 75
Tolstoi, Lev, 37, 71, 94, 109
Totleben, Eduard von, 53
Trehubov, Ielisei, 79
Troitskii narodnyi dom, 81
Trudoviks, 124, 126
Turgenev, Ivan, 75
Tsvitkovs'kyi, Iurii, 35

Ukraïna (journal), 85
Ukrainian Club in Kiev, 83, 129, 134, 163,
    268n155
Ukrainian Democratic-Radical Party,
    84, 164
Ukrainian emigration, 50, 205–6,
    214–15, 229
Ukrainian Free University, 208, 285n17,
    285n19
Ukrainian language: and bureaucracy,
    166; dictionary of, 34, 36, 77, 85,
    256n28; in high culture, 39, 95;
    ideological significance of, 72–73, 79,
    92–93, 120; as literary language, 25, 38,
    64, 73–75; and motherhood, 75–77;
    in press, 63, 84–85, 156; relationship
    with Russian, 6; repression against,
    26–27, 41, 96, 162; among Russian
    nationalists, 100, 112; in schooling,
    32, 73, 133–34; standardization of,
    72, 85; in theater, 75, 77, 81, 103;
    Ukrainophiles' knowledge of, 37–38,
    72, 92–94, 96
Ukrainian Military Organization, 207
Ukrainian National Congress, 163–64
Ukrainian nationalism, 5–7; ideology of,
    120; as seen by Russian nationalists,
    133–36, 178, 188–89, 196, 225–26;
    territorial claims of, 62, 198–200;
    and war experience, 165–66; as
    seen in Western Europe, 198–201;

before World War I, 94–95. *See also*
    Ukrainophiles
Ukrainian Party of Socialist-Federalists,
    164–65, 174, 181, 274n61
Ukrainian Party of Socialist
    Revolutionaries, 164–65, 181–82,
    188, 206
Ukrainian People's Republic (UNR):
    defense of, 1–2, 173–74, 234; Directory
    of, 187, 192, 198, 201, 283n220;
    establishment of, 171–73; in exile,
    202, 207, 209, 214–15; minority policy
    of, 170–71; at Paris peace conference,
    198–201
Ukrainian Scientific Society in Kiev,
    85, 133
Ukrainian Social Democratic Workers'
    Party, 83–84, 89, 115, 164–65, 166,
    181–82, 206
Ukrainian Socialist Soviet Republic, 172,
    201–2, 232, 285n14
Ukrainization: of army, 166, 234; of
    citizenship, 186; protest against,
    181–82, 186; of schools, 167, 169,
    180n165; of self, 37–38, 47, 206,
    208–9, 231–32
Ukraïnka, Lesia (Larysa Kosach), 73,
    86, 95
Ukrainophiles: accused of separatism,
    26–27, 31–32, 39–41; cautiousness of,
    48–49, 60, 68–69, 233; domestic spaces
    of, 75–83; introduction of term, 6,
    21; and *narodniki*, 51–53; nonpolitical
    activism of, 59–60; scholarship of,
    34–37, 42, 60–63, 199
Ukraïns'kyi student (journal), 91
Uniate Church, 66, 162
Union of Russian Men, 119
Union of the Russian People, 119, 125,
    143, 219
Universals (Central Rada), 165, 171, 173
Ustimovich, Liubov', *175*
Ustimovich, Nikolai, 71, 211,
    254–55n100
Ustimovich, Nikolai (jr.), 82, 174–76, *175*,
    197, 277n111
Ustymovych, Iefrosyniia, 71, 76, 211–12
Ustrialov, Nikolai, 253n64

Valuev Circular, 26–27, 33, 41
Valuev, Petr, 26–27, 255n100
Vasylenko, Mykola, 197
Vernadskii, Vladimir, 194, 197

Verne, Jules, 75, 121
violence
Vienna, 37, 41, 49–50
Vitalii of Pochaev (monk), 125–26
Vladimir, 227–28
Volhynia, 110–12, 119, 121, 125–26, 129, 132, 221. *See also* Kurgany (estate), right-bank Ukraine
Volunteer Army, 185–97, 220, 222
Voronyi, Mykola, 69
Vovk, Fedir, 35, 52, 89, 91, 94, 199, 259n183
Vpered! (journal), 35
Vrangel', Petr, 195, 220
Vynnychenko, Volodymyr, 86, 88–89, 164–67, 173, 187, 213

Warsaw Positivists, 59, 68
Wasilewski, Wincenty, *24*
Western zemstvo crisis, 130–32
West Ukrainian People's Republic, 200–201
Whites (civil war), 150–51, 185–96, 200–204, 219–23

Wilhelm II (emperor), 153
Witte, Sergei, 64, 103, 105, 113–17, 138
women as nationalist activists, 4, 73–77, 143, 167, 179–80, 217–18, 234–35
World War I, 150–57, 162–63, 176, 198, 202, 225
World War II, 215, 227

Xydias, Jean, 200

youth. *See* generations
Yugoslavia, 220–21, 227

Zalivanshchina (estate), 110
Zaslavskii, David, 13, 223
zemstvos, 107, 125, 130–32, 155–56, 267n132
Zheliabov, Andrei, 51
Zhmerinka, 52–53
Zhytets'kyi, Pavlo, 33, 35, 79, 88
Ziber, Nikolai, 34–35, 37–38
Zil'berfarb, Moshe, 170

Printed in the USA
CPSIA information can be obtained
at www.ICGtesting.com
LVHW040053240823
756070LV00002B/286